RUSSIA'S
CAPITALIST
REVOLUTION

WHY MARKET REFORM

SUCCEEDED AND

DEMOCRACY FAILED

ANDERS ÅSLUND

RUSSIA'S
CAPITALIST
REVOLUTION

WHY MARKET REFORM
SUCCEEDED AND
DEMOCRACY FAILED

PETERSON INSTITUTE FOR INTERNATIONAL ECONOMICS
Washington, DC
October 2007

Anders Åslund, known to repeatedly challenge conventional wisdom on "transition economies," is a leading specialist on postcommunist economic transformation with more than 30 years of experience in the field. He boldly predicted the fall of the Soviet Union in his *Gorbachev's Struggle for Economic Reform* (1989). In *How Russia Became a Market Economy* (1995) he firmly stated that the only choice Russia had was market reform. In his new book, *Russia's Capitalist Revolution*, he explains why Russia's market reform succeeded and democracy building failed.

Dr Åslund joined the Peterson Institute for International Economics as senior fellow in January 2006. He has worked as an economic adviser to the Russian government (1991–94), to the Ukrainian government, and to the president of the Kyrgyz Republic.

Before joining the Peterson Institute he was the director of the Russian and Eurasian Program at the Carnegie Endowment for International Peace. He was founding director of the Stockholm Institute of Transition Economics and professor at the Stockholm School of Economics (1989–94). He earned his doctorate from the University of Oxford.

PETER G. PETERSON INSTITUTE FOR INTERNATIONAL ECONOMICS
1750 Massachusetts Avenue, NW
Washington, DC 20036-1903
(202) 328-9000   FAX: (202) 659-3225
www.petersoninstitute.org

C. Fred Bergsten, *Director*
Edward Tureen, *Director of Publications, Marketing, and Web Development*

Printing by Kirby Lithographic Company, Inc.
Typesetting by BMWW
Cover photos: Getty Images

Printed in the United States of America
10 09 08   5 4 3 2 1

Library of Congress Cataloging-in-Publication Data

Åslund, Anders, 1952–
  Russia's capitalist revolution :
    why market reform succeeded and
    democracy failed? / Anders Åslund.
      p. cm.
  Includes bibliographical references and index.
    ISBN-13: 978-0-88132-409-9 (alk. paper)
  1. Russia (Federation)—Economic conditions—1991–   2. Capitalism—Russia (Federation) I. Title.

  HC340.12.A844 2007
  330.947—dc22   2007034725

For
Anna, Carl, and Marianna

Contents

Preface

Russia has surged among the world's high-growth countries with an average annual expansion of 6.7 percent for the last nine years. Less than 10 years after its financial crisis and debt defaults, it has accumulated the world's third largest holdings of foreign exchange. Its macroeconomic stability is impressive. At the same time, Russia has reverted in the last few years to political authoritarianism. Hence its metamorphosis poses serious challenges to social science analysis as well as to the contemporary world. Why has market reform succeeded while democracy has failed, at least for the time being? Where are both going?

To sort out these questions, Senior Fellow Anders Åslund has written this comprehensive study of Russia's economic and political transformation from 1985, when Mikhail Gorbachev launched his reforms, until the present. It is the first analysis of both political and economic development in Russia from 1985 until now.

The book argues that Russia's marketization succeeded because a critical mass of reform was undertaken early on in a brief window of opportunity. In particular, prices and imports were liberalized and large-scale privatization launched. These radical and early steps irreversibly implanted a market economy.

However, Åslund emphasizes two adverse preconditions of the Russian transformation that was launched in 1991. First, Gorbachev's gradual reforms had constructed a rent-seeking machine that generated larger rents as a share of GDP than the world has ever seen. Politically, it was extremely difficult to defeat these successful rent seekers. The best cure would have been early parliamentary elections after the democratic breakthrough in August 1991.

Second, Russia's transformation is best understood as a revolution and revolutions have a characteristic dynamic. At the height of the revolution in August 1991, most institutions were suspended and a window of opportunity opened that lasted briefly until April 1992. Only early radical reforms that were launched, or at least initiated, in this short period were successful, unlike gradual reforms.

Unfortunately, the Russian market economy did not become effective until 1998, when the reforms became complete. For the first couple of years, Russia's monetary policy was lax, and the inflationary ruble zone persisted with a dozen central banks issuing currency without coordination. The budget deficit remained excessive. The gradualism of these measures caused serious social harm.

The reason why democracy failed was that a minimum was done early on. In 1991, Boris Yeltsin decided to postpone political reform as less urgent. In addition, neither he nor anybody else had a clear idea about how to build democracy. Without idea and action, democracy could only fail. Too late, Yeltsin dissolved the predemocratic and unrepresentative parliament. The late dissolution led to serious bloodshed, harming Russia's budding democracy. Yeltsin's 1993 constitution contained excessive presidential powers, which his successor Vladimir Putin exploited to restore authoritarianism.

The central argument of this book is that Russia's current economic success is the result of a critical mass of economic reforms undertaken in the 1990s: deregulation, privatization and eventually financial stabilization. From a historical perspective, it is impressive that Russia built a dynamic market economy in only seven years. The Russian financial crash of 1998 delivered the catharsis Russia unfortunately needed to adopt responsible fiscal policies. Vladimir Putin is not the generator of Russia's current economic success but its beneficiary and custodian. He has also greatly benefited from high international oil prices.

At present, Russia has ended up with an unusual combination of a reasonably free market economy and increasingly authoritarian politics reminiscent of the tsarist period. The concluding argument of the book is that such a situation is not likely to hold. Russia is too wealthy, educated, pluralist, and open to be so authoritarian. In the not too distant future, a new democratization is likely to arise.

The short-term concern is that a small group of KGB officers from St. Petersburg has seized control of the state and its corporations. They let inefficient state mastodons purchase successful private companies and often these renationalizations are not voluntary. However worrisome these tendencies are, the economic results are likely to be so harmful even in the short term that the Russian leadership, with its focus on economic growth, will be deterred and correct the damage it is causing.

The Peter G. Peterson Institute for International Economics is a private, nonprofit institution for the study and discussion of international economic policy. Its purpose is to analyze important issues in that area and to develop and communicate practical new approaches for dealing with them. The Institute is completely nonpartisan.

The Institute is funded by a highly diversified group of philanthropic foundations, private corporations, and interested individuals. About 30 percent of the Institute's resources in our latest fiscal year were provided by contributors outside the United States, including about 12 percent from Japan. The Victor Pinchuk Foundation provided generous support for this particular study.

The Institute's Board of Directors bears overall responsibilities for the Institute and gives general guidance and approval to its research program, including the identification of topics that are likely to become important over the medium run (one to three years) and that should be addressed by the Institute. The director, working closely with the staff and outside Advisory Committee, is responsible for the development of particular projects and makes the final decision to publish an individual study.

The Institute hopes that its studies and other activities will contribute to building a stronger foundation for international economic policy around the world. We invite readers of these publications to let us know how they think we can best accomplish this objective.

C. FRED BERGSTEN
Director
October 2007

Acknowledgments

Russia has been my passion and labor of love since I learned Russian 35 years ago. Throughout the years I was lucky to be surrounded by wonderful friends and colleagues. They inspired and supported my intellectual quest, and out of our collaboration and discussions this book was born.

The intellectually fertile environment of the team at the Peter G. Peterson Institute for International Economics, artfully coached by its Director C. Fred Bergsten, has allowed me to work with joy and inspiration. My colleagues challenged me to produce a book our Institute could call its own. It was extremely helpful for me to present my rough ideas at a seminar at the Institute. I am grateful to Fred Bergsten, Martin Baily, William Cline, Kim Elliott, Morris Goldstein, Gary Hufbauer, Jacob Kirkegaard, Nicholas Lardy, Michael Mussa, Marcus Noland, Arvind Subramanian, Ted Truman, and John Williamson, who lent their time and formidable talents to comment and improve on ideas and draft chapters. Keith Crane, Julija Remeikaite, and my wife, Anna, read the whole manuscript and offered invaluable comments. Julija Remeikaite offered me eminent research assistance of impeccable quality. Ivan Yuryk assisted with the chronology. Madona Devasahayam, Marla Banov, and Ed Tureen expediently published this book.

A testing seminar on the thesis of this book chaired by Michael McFaul at Stanford University was truly useful, and it offered valuable comments.

My extraordinarily knowledgeable colleagues at the CERES at Georgetown University, Angela Stent, Marjorie Balzer, and Harley Balzer, are a steady source of inspiration while my inquisitive graduate students never fail to challenge me with their intelligent questions.

I think with special gratitude of Eva Lundin and the late Adolf Lundin, Victor Pinchuk, as well as Hans and Märit Rausing, who provided me with valuable intellectual input and generous financial support for my research and travels.

I have been privileged to receive sharp and precise insights from many conversations with Carl Bildt, Stanley Fischer, James A. Harmon, Simon Johnson, George Soros, Lawrence Summers, and James Wolfensohn.

This book includes lessons from my quarter of a century long journey in the field of Russian and East European Studies. Professor Wlodzimierz Brus inspired me immensely intellectually when I started this voyage with a doctorate at the University of Oxford. Andrzej Kozlowski and other Oxford friends have been important sources of thoughtful insights for me ever since.

I am grateful to Ambassador Torsten Örn for offering me out of many young Swedish diplomats the chance to work at the Swedish Embassy in Moscow, just as stagnation was about to turn into perestroika. Together with my dear friend and colleague Mats Staffansson, I traveled extensively in the Soviet Union. During those years I learned a lot from eminent scholars Leonid Abalkin, Abel Aganbegyan, Anatoly Miliukov, Nikolai Petrakov, Nikolai Shmelev, Ruben Yevstigneev, and Gennady Zoteev, who shared their insights into Soviet realities of the Gorbachev period. Geoffrey and Kathy Murrell's home offered a pleasant and intellectual meeting spot.

The Stockholm School of Economics and the Stockholm Institute of East European Economics provided a good base for observing the Russian drama that unfolded next door during the years 1989–94. I remember fondly conversations with Göran Ennerfelt, Ardo Hansson, Grigori Khanin, Sten Luthman, Örjan Sjöberg, Michael Sohlman, Eva Sundquist, and Michael Wyzan.

It was a great honor and excitement to work for legendary reformers Yegor Gaidar, Boris Fedorov, and Anatoly Chubais as an economic advisor to the Russian government in 1991–94. I enjoyed my partnership with such strong strategic thinkers as Jeffrey Sachs and David Lipton. When the Russian radical economic reforms were launched, I was laboring side by side with Sergei Aleksashenko, Petr Aven, Maxim Boycko, Aleksandr Dynkin, Sergei Glaziev, Andrei Illarionov, Vladimir Mau, Alexei Mozhin, Aleksandr Shokhin, Aleksei Ulyukaev, Dmitri Vasiliev, Sergei Vasiliev, and the wise man of Russian reforms, Yevgeny Yasin. They made those years truly unforgettable. I am also grateful to my Western colleagues for their friendship and cooperation: Andrew Berg, Lars Bergström, Peter Boone, Elizabeth Brainerd, Marek Dąbrowski, Bozidar Delic, Jacques Delpla, Brigitte Granville, Jonathan Hay, Georg Kjällgren, Richard Layard, Torun Litzén, Judith Shapiro, Andrei Shleifer, Andrew Warner, Jochen Wermuth, and Charles Wyplosz.

In 1994 Morton Abramowitz and Stephen Sestanovich welcomed me to the Carnegie Endowment for International Peace in Washington, DC, where I spent 11 fruitful years. I learned a lot from them as I did from my excellent colleagues Mikhail Dmitriev, Thomas Graham, David Kramer, Andrew Kuchins, Masha Lipman, Tatyana Maleva, Michael McFaul, Martha Olcott, Nikolai Petrov, Lilia Shevtsova, Dmitri Trenin, and Ksenia Yudaeva, while the Carnegie Moscow Center allowed me to continue spending substantial time in Russia. During my visits to Moscow, Swedish Ambassadors Örjan Berner and Sven Hirdman kindly offered me hospitality and advice.

Since moving to Washington, I have breathed with delight its intellectually dense atmosphere. I always benefit from stimulating conversations with Leon Aron, Keith Crane, Clifford Gaddy, Nancy Lee, Johannes Linn, Mark Medish, Branko Milanovic, John Odling-Smee, Andrei Piontkovsky, Boris Pleskovic, Marcelo Selowsky, Vito Tanzi, and Poul Thomsen.

I treasure every opportunity to talk to and learn from outstanding journalists Catherine Belton, Lynn Berry, Celeste Bohlen, Pilar Bonet, Rose Brady, Patrick Cockburn, Alan Cullison, Michael Dobbs, Steven Erlanger, Chrystia Freeland, Michael Gordon, Fred Hiatt, Jim Hoagland, David Hoffman, Andrew Jack, Robert Kaiser, Bill Keller, Andrei Kolesnikov, Yuliya Latynina, John Lloyd, Arkady Ostrovsky, John Parker, Quentin Peel, Paul Quinn-Judge, Sabrina Tavernise, Robert Siegel, Sven-Ivan Sundquist, John Thornhill, Martin Walker, and Martin Wolf.

I want to express my special gratitude to Viktor Chernomyrdin, Irina Karelina, Irina Khakamada, Aleksandr Livshits, Boris Nemtsov, Yevgeny Saburov, Valentina Vedeneeva, Inna Voennaya, Grigori Yavlinsky, Mikhail Zadoronov, and the late Arkady Volsky for helping me understand Russia through their captivating details about Russian life, which often puzzles foreign scholars.

Gifted and knowledgeable businessmen recognized early on Russia's great economic prospects, and they enlightened me about how Russia really works. I would like to especially thank Aivaras Abromavicius, Martin Andersson, Al Breach, Per Brilioth, Peter Elam Håkansson, Christopher Granville, Ian and Lukas Lundin, Michael Marrese, Seppo Remes, Nathaniel Rothschild, Charles Ryan, and Glen Waller. I have learned a lot from many Russian businessmen whose names I omit out of discretion.

Most of all I dedicate this book to my wife, Anna, and our children, Carl and Marianna. They surrounded me with love and support, turning every day into a fresh and exciting adventure. I greatly appreciate their tolerance as they endured all the stages of this book's preparation with admirable patience.

ANDERS ÅSLUND
Washington, DC
October 2007

Abbreviations

ABM	Anti-Ballistic Missile Treaty
CC	Central Committee
CBR	Central Bank of Russia
CFE	Treaty on Conventional Armed Forces in Europe
CIS	Commonwealth of Independent States
Comecon	Council of Mutual Economic Assistance
CPSU	Communist Party of the Soviet Union
EBRD	European Bank for Reconstruction and Development
ECE	Economic Commission for Europe (UN)
FAPSI	Federal Agency for Government Communication and Information Services
FSB	Federal Security Service
G-7	Group of seven largest industrialized democracies
GATT	General Agreement on Tariffs and Trade
GDR	German Democratic Republic
GKChP	State Committee for the State of Emergency
Goskomstat	State Committee on Statistics
Gosplan	State Planning Committee
IFI	International financial institution
IMF	International Monetary Fund
INF	Intermediate-Range Nuclear Forces Treaty
IPO	Initial public offering
KGB	Committee for State Security
LDPR	Liberal Democratic Party of Russia
NATO	North Atlantic Treaty Organization
NKVD	People's Commissariat for Internal Affairs
OECD	Organization for Economic Cooperation and Development

OSCE	Organization for Security and Cooperation in Europe
SALT	Strategic Arms Limitation Talks Treaty
SDI	Strategic Defense Initiative
SPS	Union of Right Forces
START	Treaty on the Reduction and Limitation of Strategic Offensive Arms
SVR	Foreign Intelligence Service
UNDP	United Nations Development Program
USAID	United States Agency for International Development
USSR	Union of Soviet Socialist Republics
VAT	Value-added tax
WTO	World Trade Organization

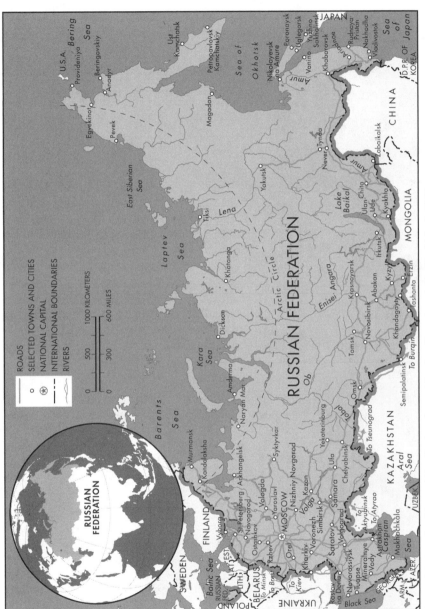

Source: Printing, Graphics and Map Design, General Services Department, The World Bank, 2007.

Introduction

Russia has just completed its Capitalist Revolution, which brought down the system created by the Great Russian Socialist Revolution of 1917. The collapse of the Soviet Union, the end of communist dictatorship, and the termination of the Soviet command economy concluded the 20th century. This book takes stock of these great events and explains Russia's Capitalist Revolution.

Today, the result is evident: Russia has adopted a market economy, but it has reverted to authoritarianism. The main question of this book is: Why did market reform succeed while the building of democracy failed?

Revolutions develop along a distinct trajectory and have many similarities, even if each has its peculiarities. In a revolution, the old institutions temporarily cease to function. For a short time, this hiatus offers political leaders much greater opportunities than in ordinary times. The drawback is that the tools of government are rudimentary.

To understand the dynamics of Russia's new revolution, we need to look at the whole period of the revolution and examine both economic and political developments. Therefore this book gives equal emphasis to Russia's economic and political transformation. Foreign policy is discussed only as far as it affected Russia's internal transformation.

Russia's revolutionary surge started on March 11, 1985, when Mikhail Gorbachev was elected general secretary of the Communist Party of the Soviet Union (CPSU). Appalled by the petrification of the Soviet Union, he instantly started a broad and energetic attempt to reform communism, but as Leszek Kołakowski once told us students at a seminar at the University of Oxford: "Communism with a human face is like a baked snowball."

It is more difficult to say when the revolution was over. Currently, Russia is undoubtedly experiencing postrevolutionary stabilization. The year 2007 appears a suitable end date, because President Vladimir Putin's second term is about to finish, and he has successfully built an authoritarian system.

When institutions are suspended, political leaders become all the more important. During its two decades of transformation, Russia has had only three political leaders, Presidents Mikhail Gorbachev, Boris Yeltsin, and Vladimir Putin. Each of their insights and beliefs has had great impact on Russia's course.

This book is academic but nontechnical, designed to be accessible to a wide range of readers. It focuses on policymaking—how and why key policies were made. At the time of its writing, this is the only book covering the whole period of the Russian revolution that discusses both politics and economics. I hope that it will bring about a better understanding not only of what happened in Russia's Capitalist Revolution but also of what the actual alternatives were.

Definitions of Democracy and Market Economy

To avoid confusion, the terms democracy and market economy need to be defined. Juan Linz (1978, 5) defines democracy with a suitable degree of detail:

> Legal freedom to formulate and advocate political alternatives with the concomitant rights to free association, free speech, and other basic freedoms of person; free and nonviolent competition among leaders with periodic validation of their claim to rule; inclusion of all effective political offices in the democratic process; and provision for the participation of all members of the political community, whatever their political preferences.

The definition of a market economy has attracted less scholarly interest, because most people take it for granted. Legally, the United States and the European Union define market economies as opposed to state-trading countries in their antidumping legislation.

The US Customs Code defines a "nonmarket economy country" as "any foreign country that the administering authority determines does not operate on market principle of cost or pricing structures so that sales of merchandise in such a country do not reflect the fair value of the merchandise."[1] In making that assessment, the US Department of Commerce considers six criteria: (1) currency convertibility; (2) free bargaining for wages; (3) "the extent to which joint ventures or other investments by firms of other foreign countries are permitted in the foreign country"; (4) "the extent of government ownership"; (5) "the extent of government control over the allocation of resources and over the price and output decisions of

---

1. United States Code [19 U.S.C. 1677(18)], available at the US Government Printing Office website, www.access.gpo.gov (accessed August 9, 2007).

enterprises"; and (6) other appropriate factors. Since 2004, the United States has assessed that Russia fulfills these criteria.

For our purposes, however, this definition is too slanted toward trade considerations. A market economy is best understood as the opposite of a socialist economy, as János Kornai (1992, 360–79) outlined it. First, the economic actors must be independent from the state and act freely without state commands. Second, private ownership of enterprises should dominate, and property rights need to be reasonably safe. Third, prices and trade should be predominantly free, and fourth, state subsidies must be limited. A fifth criterion could be that transactions are largely monetized. Price stability, however, is not a condition. None of these criteria is absolute, because all states distort their economies somewhat.

Theses of This Book

To offer the reader an overview of the conclusions of this book, I present a brief summary of the main arguments here.

Gorbachev's Gradual Reforms Built a Rent-Seeking Machine

Massive rent seeking characterized the collapse of the Soviet system and the early postcommunist period. Unwittingly, Gorbachev built this rent-seeking machine with his gradual reforms because the state enterprise managers, who dominated late Soviet politics, accepted only such reforms. The best way to become truly wealthy in 1990 was to purchase oil from a state enterprise at the official price of $1 a ton and sell it abroad for $100 a ton and finance the transaction with cheap state credits.

Limited decentralization of foreign trade rights started in 1986. The May 1988 Law on Cooperatives allowed state enterprise managers to set up private trading companies as well as unregulated private banks. The Law on State Enterprises, which came into force in January 1988, made the state enterprise managers the true masters of state enterprises. Oil prices stayed regulated far below the market level until 1993. State interest rates were minimal until 1993, and credit emission was ample, guaranteeing high inflation.

The reformers were aware of this boondoggle, but they did not have the necessary power to break it early on. They failed to gain control over the Central Bank of Russia in November 1991. Nor could they persuade Yeltsin to liberalize energy prices in January 1992.

Until August 1991, the state enterprise managers appeared progressive because they favored market reform and political liberalization. After August 1991, however, they were the main opponents of radical market reform because they wanted the transition period to be long and distorted to generate maximum rents, and they objected to further political reforms, which would have checked their power.

Multiple Causes Overdetermined the Soviet Collapse

By 1991, the collapse of the Soviet Union, its political system, and its economic system was certain for many reasons. The Soviet economic system was moribund, and perestroika (literally: restructuring) moved the USSR from stagnation to fatal crisis. The patently irresponsible fiscal policy from 1986 onward made hyperinflation virtually inevitable. This unfortunate policy was not caused by political pressures but by the leaders' ignorance, induced by ideological blinkers. The gradual reforms drove a wedge between control rights and cash rights and bred a machine of rent seeking. The Soviet finances collapsed in 1991 because the constituent republics stopped delivering revenues to the union treasury, and 16 central banks competed in issuing ruble credits, which sent inflation skyrocketing. All these factors rendered the financial and monetary disasters terminal in late 1990. Each of these economic problems was sufficient to terminate the Soviet Union, and together they guaranteed its demise.

National tensions sufficed to break the Soviet Union up. They were bound to erupt when repression eased because the Soviet Union lacked legitimacy in the eyes of several of its constituent nationalities. The countries and territories that had been incorporated into the Soviet Union during World War II through the Molotov-Ribbentrop Pact—the three Baltic countries (Estonia, Latvia, and Lithuania), Moldova, and Western Ukraine—had never accepted Soviet occupation. They aspired to nothing less than national independence. Georgia and Armenia had similar aspirations. Gorbachev did not comprehend nationalism, and he allowed only limited use of force, which was not enough to hold the Soviet Union together.

The final blow was that Russia democratized more than the Soviet Union through its parliamentary elections in March 1990 and presidential election in June 1991, which rendered Russia more legitimate than the Soviet Union. When Ukraine voted for independence on December 1, 1991, the Soviet Union could not be saved. The multiple Soviet collapse was a revolution that could not be stopped in its midst.

Why Did the Soviet Union not Pursue Chinese Reforms?

The natural starting point for comparison is China in 1978 and the Soviet Union in 1985, when Deng Xiaoping and Gorbachev, respectively, initiated their reforms. Virtually all preconditions were very different. China was in a political and economic shock after the Cultural Revolution, while the Soviet Union was absolutely stable after two decades of Brezhnevism.

The Chinese bureaucracy accepted change, but the Soviet party apparatus resisted it tooth and nail. Gorbachev was always forced to compromises that seriously distorted his reforms, but Deng had evidently more power.

The Chinese peasants started working hard at the first signs of reforms, while the Soviet workers knew better than to believe that reforms would last, because they had seen too many reversals.

Both Deng and Gorbachev experimented pragmatically, but in the Soviet Union the interests of state enterprise managers were dominant. They bred a rent-seeking machine, which caused the breakdown of the Soviet Union and its economic system.

After having experimented for two to three years without any economic success whatsoever, Gorbachev realized that no economic reform was possible if he did not check the party elite through political liberalization. China, on the contrary, recorded early economic successes, which continued.

The economic structures could hardly have been more different in these two countries. The Soviet Union was overindustrialized, while three-quarters of the Chinese worked in agriculture. Soviet enterprises were predominantly large-scale and mechanized, whereas Chinese production was small-scale and manual. Chinese agriculture could easily be reformed through the introduction of quasi-property rights for peasants, which was impossible in the Soviet Union. Soviet industry was too big and distorted to be omitted, but it was also too powerful to be reformed.

From 1986 onward, the Soviet budget deficit exceeded 6 percent of GDP, and the country was heading toward hyperinflation, while China escaped macroeconomic destabilization, because the memory of hyperinflation in the 1940s and its cure were still in living memory. In the end, the Soviet Union collapsed, but China did not.

The situation in China and the Soviet Union differed in almost every political and economic regard. The problem was not that Gorbachev did not follow the Chinese lead but rather that he followed it too closely under very different preconditions.

How to Pursue Policymaking in the Midst of a Revolution

The critical insight from Russia's postcommunist transformation is that it was a revolutionary process with a characteristic radicalization. At the height of the revolution, from August 1991 to April 1992, most state institutions were suspended, and so were most social forces. This suspension offered policymakers a unique window of opportunity. During a short period of five months, truly radical measures were possible, but time was very scarce and state capacity minimal. The policymakers had to hasten to carry out key measures, which had to be sufficiently simple to be implemented in the chaos of revolution. Mistakes were inevitable, but the biggest mistake was to wait, because to wait meant to fail.

Adequate policymaking in a revolution requires six steps. First come ideas, which must be clear, simple, and relevant. Second, the ideas need to be translated into a set of policy actions. Third, the political leader takes the lead and makes an authoritative policy declaration. Fourth, the leader appoints a group of policymakers who can execute the reforms. Fifth, parliamentary support is necessary for substantial legislative work. Sixth, key policies must be implemented within this brief window of opportunity—"extraordinary politics," as Leszek Balcerowicz (1994) called it. International organizations can assist with advice and financing, but timeliness is crucial.

Why Did Market Reform Succeed?

Market reform succeeded in Russia because a critical mass of market reforms was implemented in the brief window of opportunity in the winter of 1991–92. The Yegor Gaidar team had a clear idea of how to build a market economy. President Boris Yeltsin supported this idea and presented it with a set of policy actions to the Russian parliament on October 28, 1991. The parliament approved of his program in a nearly unanimous vote. Yeltsin appointed a government of outsiders, young academic economists, who knew better than anybody else what to do. In January 1992 the reform government unleashed a sufficient mass of radical reform measures to render them irreversible, although they were insufficient for an early return to economic growth.

Until 1998, the economic results were poor because of lasting high inflation, inherited communist distortions, and too gradual reforms. Russia maintained a vast budget deficit averaging 9 percent of GDP from 1993 to 1998. Monetary policy was beyond the control of the reformers and very loose until the end of 1993. The inflationary ruble zone persisted until September 1993. The reformers failed to persuade Yeltsin to liberalize energy prices in early 1992. As a consequence, rent seeking prevailed, and high inflation persisted until 1996. The financial crash of August 1998 functioned as a catharsis that eliminated barter and the excessive budget deficit, cleansing Russia's market economy. Yet, the initial package of radical reforms was sufficient to ensure that the market economy survived.

Why Did Democracy Fail?

Democracy failed because of the absence of any clear idea of how to build it. Therefore, little was done in real life. The brief window of opportunity when a democracy could have been built was missed. Yeltsin should have dissolved the old, unrepresentative parliament within half a year after the aborted August 1991 coup, which delivered Russia's democratic breakthrough. He should have held an early founding election to stabilize Russia's democracy and disbanded the KGB. Instead, a major conflict evolved between president and parliament, and since the parliament did not really represent anything, it had no reason to compromise. Two years too late, Yeltsin dissolved the parliament, but it was recalcitrant and Yeltsin's administration inept, which caused serious bloodshed. The bloodletting stained Russia's nascent democracy.

A new constitution was adopted in a referendum in December 1993. It was democratic but suffered from numerous shortcomings. Presidential executive powers were excessive and not transparent. Powers between the federal and regional governments were not clearly divided. The Constitutional Court was weak. The parliamentary elections were not fully proportional, which left political parties feeble. The upper chamber, the Federation Council, became appointed and thus unrepresentative. Great, unregulated state powers and the weak rule of law prompted vast business funding of politics. President Vladimir Putin wanted to build an authoritarian state, and with these building blocks he could easily do so in the apolitical mood of postrevolutionary stabilization.

Early and Radical Reform Worked Best

A large number of early and radical reforms were effective, successful in achieving their objectives, and irreversible. Yeltsin disbanded the Soviet Union one week after the overwhelming Ukrainian vote for independence had doomed the Soviet Union, securing its peaceful dissolution. The price deregulation and liberalization of imports in January 1992 were accepted, worked, and were not reversed. Gaidar's drastic cut in military procurement in January 1992 defeated the military-industrial complex with surprising ease. Small-scale privatization was done fast and was not controversial. However, voucher privatization was controversial, but it transferred most enterprises to the private sector, and minimum renationalization has ensued. These reforms were successful because they were undertaken or at least initiated within the short window of opportunity. They also changed the paradigm, which made them credible and consistent.

By contrast, four gradual reforms were miserable failures. First, the early, loose monetary policy boosted inflation and harmed output. Second, the gradual dissolution of the ruble zone caused hyperinflation in 10 of its 12 constituent states in 1993. Third, the gradual hike in energy prices created one of the largest sources of rents the world has ever seen. Fourth, democratization was the most gradual and least successful reform.

The obvious conclusion is that under revolutionary circumstances little but radical reform is likely to succeed, and the earlier and simpler the better. The focus must be on principles and speed, not on details.

The Essence of Privatization Is Legitimate Property Rights

Private enterprise is nearly always better than public enterprise. Public enterprises breed corruption, monopolies, and subsidies, and if they dominate a country, neither democracy nor market economy can be maintained. Privatization has to be sufficiently fast to render the private sector dominant before the revolutionary moment is lost. At the same time, property rights must become legitimate to bar reversal. Enterprises are often bought and sold, which renders the original form of privatization increasingly irrelevant, while the extent and acceptance of privatization are vital. State revenues from privatization are immaterial, because successfully privatized companies soon pay more in annual taxes than what a perfect auction of them would have reaped.

The conclusion is that privatization has to be simple and undertaken in whatever way is politically acceptable, has to be done fast, and has to generate respect for the resulting property rights. That means Russia's combination of insider and voucher privatization was close to ideal. Any sale of big enterprises to outsiders was controversial, and such privatizations have been particularly exposed to renationalization. Considering that the remaining state enterprises easily instigate renationalization within that industry, state enterprises are like cancer that may cause metastasis. Hence, almost any privatization was better than no privatization.

Market Economy, and Renewed Democratization?

Russia has established a market economy with largely free prices and trade and predominant private ownership. It is an open economy. The business environment might not be great but is world average, and property rights are somewhat stronger (World Bank and International Finance Corporation 2006). The government is focused on maintaining macroeconomic stability and a high growth rate of 6.7 percent a year. In spite of some renationalization of big corporations, this market economic system is firmly set and does not appear threatened.

Politically, Putin's eight-year rule has been characterized by a systematic political deinstitutionalization and centralization of authoritarian power in his own hands. However, this is not a Soviet restoration. Ideology is conspicuously absent. Instead, Putin's authoritarian rule is reminiscent of long-past tsarism. Russia is simply too wealthy, educated, open, and economically pluralist to be so authoritarian. Either the market economy or the authoritarian rule will have to give in a not-too-distant future, and the market economic system appears much stronger than the still mild authoritarianism. Russia is likely to move toward a new wave of democratization.

The Structure of This Book

The structure of this book is chronological-thematic. It consists of seven chronological chapters and one concluding chapter with overall analysis. The first seven chapters may be seen as acts in a great revolutionary drama. Within each period, the main themes are analyzed.

Chapter 1, which covers the period 1985–87, presents perestroika, the great awakening. Gorbachev started perestroika because he believed in the Soviet system and wanted to breathe new life into it. Chapter 2 discusses the collapse of the Soviet Union. This period, 1988–91, saw a duel between Gorbachev, the moderate revolutionary, and Yeltsin, the revolutionary hero. Chapter 3 describes the revolution during 1991–93. Yeltsin oversaw the dissolution of the Soviet Union and a radical economic reform, but he did little to build a democracy.

Chapter 4, which covers the period 1994–95, is devoted to the rise and fall of the state enterprise managers, who were the initial victors of rent seeking and insider privatization. Chapter 5 deals with the period 1996–98, when the so-called oligarchs were dominant. The period ended with the dramatic financial crash of August 1998. Postrevolutionary stabilization followed the crash, as is discussed in chapter 6, which covers 1999–2003. Vladimir Putin became president in 2000, and he started centralizing power. In his second term, 2004–07, covered in chapter 7, Putin instigated more recentralization and built authoritarian rule. Chapter 8 offers major conclusions.

1

Perestroika—The Great Awakening: 1985–87

For that they all perish!
— Popular toast about the Soviet leaders in the 1980s

We can no longer live like this!
— Mikhail Gorbachev to Eduard A. Shevardnadze in 1984

In November 1984, I was driving from Helsinki, Finland, to Moscow. No border in the world marked a greater divide than that between Finland and the Union of Soviet Socialist Republics. In Finland, all was modern and wealthy. When you crossed the border into the USSR you stepped 70 years backward into history and poverty. The Soviet frontier regions looked as if nothing had changed since World War II. Only decay and grayness had proceeded.

Police supervision along the road was extraordinary, as this was one of the few Soviet roads open to foreigners, who were kept from seeing anything but a few carefully selected and cleansed show places, such as Moscow and Leningrad. We had to apply for a visa for every road we traveled. The number of crossroads was small, but a police station guarded each of them. Every time we reached a crossing, the police called the next checkpoint to report that we had been there. Once, we took a break on the road. Within ten minutes, a police car approached us, and we were commanded to drive again. Didn't we know that we were not allowed to stop? Many police officers halted us seemingly just for the sake of it. Their demeanor revealed that they ruled the land. Even so, soon after passing the border we were hailed down by some men in the dark. Presuming they were policemen, we halted, but at the last minute we realized they were robbers and sped away.

This was the "highway" that connected the two biggest cities of the Soviet empire, Moscow and Leningrad. Yet it had only two lanes and was marred by potholes. Traffic was minimal, because the Soviet Union never developed mass car ownership, and travel was severely restricted. From time to time, a sign informed us "telephone 30 km," because ordinary villages had no phones.

One little village followed after the other, with their quaint Russian wooden cottages. They were almost indistinguishable and would have been romantic had they not been so dilapidated and unpainted. Ice clung to the windows. One village was tellingly called *Chernaya gryaz*—"Black Dirt." In each village, a stooping babushka carried a heavy yoke with two buckets of water, because there was no tap water or sewage. Admittedly, they had electricity, and television spread the regime's imbecile propaganda of success amidst this disheartening poverty. I sent a sympathetic thought to Alexander Radishchev, the Russian 18th century dissident who was exiled to Siberia for seven years by Catherine the Great because of his miserable observations in his 1790 book, *Journey from St. Petersburg to Moscow*.

The biggest secret, hidden from both the Russian population and the West, was that the Soviet Union was a Third World country, successfully parading as a superpower, which it was in one single regard, namely military might. The Soviet foreign policy specialist Aleksandr Bovin coined the somewhat exaggerated but apt phrase "Upper Volta with nuclear arms."

In 1983, Zbigniew Brzezinski observed, "The Soviet Union is a world power of a new type in that it is one-dimensional . . . the Soviet Union is a global power only in the military dimension" (Brzezinski 1983, 12). Tellingly, the militaristic Russian nationalist Aleksandr Prokhanov agreed: "One could say that until the Soviet Union achieved military-strategic parity with the West, the USSR had no other national goal than that of survival and defence."[1] Once, on the train from Moscow to Warsaw, a Russian woman from the provinces told me how fantastic Moscow was: You could even buy oranges there!

Soviet society was standing still, but in 1985 change erupted that led to a revolution. This chapter first discusses why Gorbachev's economic reforms, perestroika (literally: restructuring), began. The explanation lay in the contradicting demands of the arms race with the United States, and a stagnant economy. A new generation of leaders emerged. Although impressive in many ways, the severe limitation of the Brezhnev system had made them quite parochial. The new general secretary of the Communist Party of the Soviet Union (CPSU), Mikhail Gorbachev launched economic

---

1. *Detente*, nos. 9–10, 1987, 26.

reform on a broad front, but as this chapter shows, his many efforts led to minimal improvements.

As a reaction to the failures of his initial economic reform, Gorbachev tried to open up the public debate through glasnost (openness), and he allowed public criticism against the old system to escalate. Gorbachev also launched an active foreign policy called "new thinking" to reduce high military costs, which was one of the greatest successes of his early reform efforts. A frequent criticism of Gorbachev is that he should have opted for the same kinds of economic reforms that the Chinese had done, but the problem was rather that he tried similar reforms while the results were far worse because of completely different preconditions.

Why Perestroika Started

No place was as petrified as the Soviet Union in the early 1980s. Leonid Brezhnev, who ruled as general secretary of the CPSU from 1964 to 1982, abhorred change. He ended the circulation of staff, leaving everybody in the same post for years. Officials did little, because no initiative was appreciated by the rulers. They just grew older. By the early 1980s, the Soviet leadership was an inert gerontocracy ridiculed by all. The average age of the ruling Politburo members had risen above 70, while the average life expectancy for men was 63 (Brown 1996). The Soviet Union was ruled by dying people. Throughout the state and party administration, high office holders never retired but occupied their posts until they died, impeding all promotions. By 1985, many ministers and regional first party secretaries had held the same job for two decades.

The main political events were ornate funerals on the Red Square accompanied by Frederic Chopin's "Funeral March." In a quick sequence, the music played ever more frequently: Brezhnev died in November 1982, his successor Yuri Andropov in February 1984, and his successor Konstantin Chernenko in March 1985, not to mention other Politburo members. Sarcastically, Russians joked about "Five Years of Fancy Funerals" (*Pyatiletka Pyshnykh Pokhoron*).

The inertia was mind-boggling, and the public perception was that nothing could change. The carefully censored official data indicated that the economy and welfare were growing moderately but steadily. The only apparent concern was that the Soviet Union was locked in a nuclear arms race with the United States, which cost the country an ever larger share of economic output.

By its own standards, the Soviet regime did well in domestic politics. The Communist Party was the only game in town, and the domestic political scene was exceedingly calm and stable. The Soviet Union was a secret police state with ample means of repression, thousands of political prisoners, and complete censorship, but it did not need to apply much force, because people saw no hope for change. By and large, state terror had ended with Joseph Stalin's death in 1953, and an implicit social contract developed. As long as people did not express any political views in public or have contact with foreigners, they had jobs and could live in peace in their tiny apartments.

Political dissidents, human rights activists, and nationalists of many stripes persisted, but they posed no systemic threat to the regime. Tens of thousands of Jews and dissidents were allowed to emigrate to the West. The authorities tolerated some nascent popular movements for the defense of the cultural, historical, and environmental heritage. One of the most vibrant cultural movements centered on "village prose," which gathered Russian nationalists cherishing traditional rural life (Parthé 1992).

But the pacification of the population gave rise to social problems such as demoralization, alienation, and apathy, breeding a widespread sense of social, cultural, and ecological decay. This demoralization aggravated a staggering alcoholism, which reduced male life expectancy from the early 1970s. Characteristically, the Brezhnev regime responded with no concrete measures other than the suppression of the publication of these unfortunate statistics (Davis and Feshbach 1980). A popular anecdote described how different Soviet leaders reacted when their train stopped on the track. Stalin ordered the instant execution of the engineer, whereas Brezhnev just told his staff to draw the curtains and shake the train so that it felt like moving.

Brezhnev's Soviet Union was most successful in foreign policy. It caught up with the United States in the nuclear arms race, and the two superpowers sparred with one another across the world. As late as the 1980s, many Westerners foresaw a coming Soviet supremacy. The Soviet Union had 30,000 nuclear warheads and 5 million men under arms. It had deployed potent intermediary SS-20 nuclear missiles in Eastern Europe. The North Atlantic Treaty Organization (NATO) was trying to catch up by deploying American Pershing missiles to defend Europe from that threat, but this prompted massive peace demonstrations in Western Europe.

Already in control of Eastern Europe, the Soviet Union expanded its grasp to faraway places such as Ethiopia, Angola, and Mozambique. In December 1979, the Soviet Union invaded Afghanistan with a limited number of troops, but it overreached. The Soviet armed forces became bogged down in a deleterious and unwinnable war.

The popular attraction of Marxism-Leninism as an ideology, however, had ceased. The Soviet Union could no longer appeal to the world with its values, but these insights were barely known to the Soviet leaders because of the tight censorship. The flourishing of reform communism during the Prague spring of 1968 was the last time serious intellectuals believed that communism could be reformed and assume a human face. The impending death of communism became evident with the spontaneous eruption of the independent Solidarity trade union in Poland in August

Figure 1.1 Soviet economic growth rate, 1961–85
(average annual growth in percent, comparable prices)

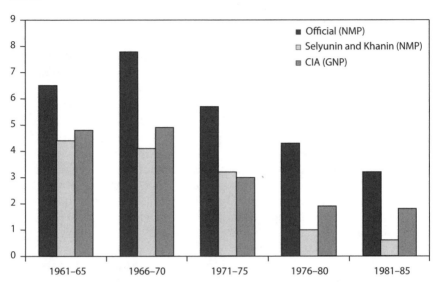

percent

Legend:
- Official (NMP)
- Selyunin and Khanin (NMP)
- CIA (GNP)

NMP = net material product
GNP = gross national product

Sources: Goskomstat SSSR (1986, 38; 1990, 9); Selyunin and Khanin (1987, 194–95); CIA (1990, 64).

1980. In reality, it was a democratic national front, which was so strong that it persisted for 16 months until Poland's president, General Wojciech Jaruzelski, declared martial law in December 1981.

The Soviet Union's crucial contradiction was that its economic growth was insufficient to guarantee the country's future military might. Officially, the Soviet economic growth rate was 3.2 percent a year in the first half of the 1980s, which corresponded to the annual increase in arms expenditure. The Western mainstream analysis concurred. The baseline projection of a major American study published in 1983, *The Soviet Economy: Toward the Year 2000*, which involved the greatest names in the American study of Soviet economics, forecast a Soviet GNP growth at 3.2 percent a year for the last two decades of the 20th century (Bergson and Levine 1983). Its greatest worry was that the growth of per capita consumption could fall below 1 percent a year, which could arouse a "crisis scenario" (p. 21).

But reality was worse. The two iconoclastic economists Vasili Selyunin and Grigori Khanin (1987) calculated that in the first half of the 1980s Soviet real growth was merely 0.6 percent a year—that is, stagnation (figure 1.1). Prime Minister Nikolai I. Ryzhkov (1992, 42) shared this perception: "The situation in the country was straightforward frightening. The last years of 'Brezhnevshchina' left us with a heavy inheritance. . . . In 1982, the real incomes of the population did not grow—for the first time after the war!"

In reality, the Soviet Union appears to have entered complete economic stagnation by 1979. The country was still a superpower, but the military expenditures rose at the cost of everything else. The US Central Intelligence Agency (CIA) assessment was that Soviet military expenditures increased steadily by 3 percent a year, and the CIA gradually raised its estimate of the military share of Soviet GNP to 15–17 percent in 1987. But as the CIA overestimated Soviet GNP, a share close to 25 percent of GNP was more likely (Åslund 1990, Bergson 1997, Berkowitz et al. 1993). US defense expenditures, by contrast, stopped at 6 percent of GDP during President Ronald Reagan's rapid arms buildup.

Not all Western Sovietologists agreed with the mainstream. Brzezinski (1983) realized that the Soviet Union was a Third World country, which was obvious to all foreigners who lived there. In 1976, the US administration formed a Team B that challenged the conventional wisdom of the CIA. It argued that the Soviet economy was smaller and the defense burden greater (Pipes 2003, 132–43).

One of its members was Richard Pipes, the outstanding historian of Russia. After a stint in Reagan's White House, he published a forceful article in *Foreign Affairs* in 1984, which argued that the "communist societies, the Soviet Union included . . . are in the throes of a serious systemic crisis which sooner or later will require action of a decisive kind. . . ." Both the political and economic crisis "arise from a growing discrepancy between the responsibilities assumed by the communist elites at home and abroad, and the human and material resources with which to carry them out" (Pipes 1984, 49). "A crisis of such dimensions, camouflaged by massive disinformation and saber-rattling, fits very well the concept of a 'revolutionary situation' as defined by Lenin. The term meant to him a condition of stalemate between the ruling elite of a country and its population: the former could no longer rule, and the latter would no longer let themselves be ruled in the old way" (pp. 50–51). Pipes noticed the "universal disillusionment with political violence in the Soviet Union" and precluded the risk of restoration of Stalinism.

Pipes concluded that the country was likely to reform: "A Soviet Union that will turn its energies inward will of necessity become less militaristic and expansionist." Furthermore, "the greater the pressures on the Soviet regime to deal with genuine crises at home instead of artificially created crises abroad, the greater its dependence on its citizens, and the greater in consequence the ability of these citizens to deflect their governments from foreign adventures" (Pipes 1984, 60). Richard Pipes' foresight was close to perfect, and his analysis shows that Russia was no enigma. On this advice, Reagan embraced the Strategic Defense Initiative (SDI), known as "star wars," a high-tech defense against nuclear missiles that would numb the Soviet nuclear force.

The high-tech arms race was escalating, and personal computers were spreading across the world, but the Soviet Union resisted them because of technological conservatism, trade protectionism, and, most of all, a fear of free information flows. For the same reason, photocopiers were strictly forbidden in the Soviet Union. Excluded from the mounting information technology revolution, Soviet society became ever more backward.

The new guard in the Communist Party, and their outstanding leader Mikhail Gorbachev, saw this new reality. As second secretary of the CPSU, Gorbachev made a great programmatic speech in December 1984. Focusing on the critical nexus of the arms race, insufficient economic growth, and technological backwardness, Gorbachev (1987a, 86) formulated his goal to modernize and reinforce the Soviet economy to catch up with the United States in the arms race: "Only an efficient, highly developed economy can reinforce [our] country's position on the international stage and allow it to enter the [next] millennium with dignity as a great and flourishing power."

Soon after he had become general secretary of the CPSU in March 1985, he elaborated further on this theme:

> The necessity of an acceleration of the social-economic development is also dictated by serious external circumstances. The country has been forced to devote considerable means to defense . . . facing the aggressive policy and threat of imperialism, it is necessary to strengthen the defense power of the Motherland persistently and not allow military superiority over us. (Gorbachev 1985, 5)

By 1987, Gorbachev had abandoned the military theme, apparently having become aware of how serious the Soviet backwardness was. As a consequence, he focused on growth, efficiency, quality, and innovation, with the industrialized West as his unstated standard.

> The economic growth rates fell to a level that was actually approaching economic stagnation. We started evidently falling behind in one way after the other. The gap in efficiency of production, quality of products and scientific-technical progress began to widen in relation to the most developed countries, and not to our benefit. (Pravda, June 26, 1987)

An underlying reason for the course of Soviet development was the fortunes of the country's oil and natural gas production (Gaidar 2006). In the 1970s, the Soviet Union had developed huge new findings of oil and natural gas in Western Siberia, which were accessed through monumental new pipelines to Europe. In 1973, the first oil crisis struck. Energy prices skyrocketed and stayed high until 1981, granting the Soviet Union enormous windfall profits. The Soviet leaders directed this wealth primarily to military expenditures. Because of this apparent abundance of money, they did nothing to improve the economic system in the 1970s. In the late

1980s, oil and natural gas production approached a peak with the available Soviet technology, and prices had fallen. To the Soviet public, the financial impact of the energy markets on the country's economy was not known, because international financial transactions were deeply guarded state secrets. Yet, the state finances were no longer tenable. Something had to give.

Mikhail Gorbachev and the Outstanding Provincials

In his essay *Will the Soviet Union Survive until 1984?* dissident Andrei Amalrik argued that the negative selection of leaders that was so striking under Brezhnev would cause the Soviet Union's collapse. To a considerable extent he turned out to be right, though the quality of the new leaders was surprisingly impressive.[2]

In 1980, the all-powerful CPSU Politburo was profoundly divided. The old Brezhnev loyalists were content with the situation and wanted no change whatsoever. Some of them were conspicuously corrupt, others simply conservative. Their adversaries were a mixed bunch. Their only common denominator was that they thought the Soviet Union could do better. Therefore, they desired change. These ambitious and restless men were initially led by Yuri Andropov and later by Mikhail Gorbachev.

By the time Brezhnev finally died in November 1982, he had been incapacitated by illness for much of the time since 1974. The background of his successor as general secretary, Andropov, was rather frightful. As ambassador to Hungary, he had overseen the bloody Soviet invasion of Hungary in 1956. For 15 years, he had chaired the feared Committee on State Security (KGB) when its techniques of repression had been perfected. He wanted to revitalize the Soviet economy through stricter discipline, and he aroused expectations of change.

Andropov started a febrile search for more dynamic cadres. He appointed whomever he could find to the higher ranks of the party to energize the country, drawing on an array of ambitious and frustrated provincial officials. Foremost among them was Gorbachev, who had already been a secretary of the Central Committee since 1978 and a full member of the Politburo since 1980, but Gorbachev had spent 23 long years rising in the party organization in his desolate home region of Stavropol in southern Russia.

Another Andropov favorite was Ryzhkov, who became Central Committee secretary for economic affairs in November 1982. He had spent 25 years in an engineering career largely in one company in his hometown of Sverdlovsk (today Yekaterinburg) in the Urals until he advanced to be-

---

2. This section draws primarily on Åslund (1991) and Brown (1996).

come deputy minister of heavy machine-building in 1975 and then deputy chairman of the State Planning Committee (Gosplan).

A third Andropov appointee was Yegor K. Ligachev, whom Andropov made Central Committee secretary for personnel in December 1983. Ligachev came from Tomsk in Siberia, where he had been regional first party secretary for 18 years, bitterly regretting that he was not promoted to a senior party job in Moscow (Ligachev 1993, 50).

Andropov sacked corrupt, lazy, alcoholic, and overaged officials and replaced them with accomplished middle-aged men. He issued a decree on "the strengthening of socialist work discipline" and arrested some top officials for corruption. Conspicuous raids were undertaken against Moscow bath houses, where officials frolicked during working hours. Economists from the Soviet Academy of Sciences were discreetly asked about the country's economic problems. Minor economic "experiments" were attempted adjusting managers' incentives and the wage system. In spite of some new vibrancy, little was accomplished, because after a few months in office Andropov became fatally ill.

Andropov was succeeded as general secretary by Konstantin Chernenko, who had been Brezhnev's closest collaborator. He was a humble man who had much to be humble about. He had never been particularly dynamic, and he was seriously ill from the beginning. Literally nothing was done. Ligachev (1993, 34, 36) called Chernenko a "virtuoso apparatchik," inclined to "office work and papers, and [with] scant knowledge of real life." The Andropov triumvirate of Gorbachev, Ryzhkov, and Ligachev survived. Gorbachev replaced Chernenko as second secretary and chaired the important Central Committee Secretariat, which prepared all matters for the Politburo, and he even presided in the Politburo during Chernenko's long illness.

When Chernenko died after just 13 months in office, Gorbachev was elected general secretary the next day, on March 11, 1985. All top party officials who wanted change supported Gorbachev and they advanced swiftly. Ryzhkov became prime minister, and Ligachev replaced Gorbachev as second secretary. These three men formed a new ruling triumvirate. Personnel changes were quick and deep. Soon the entire aging leadership had been replaced by men mostly in their mid-50s, and these new managers pursued a similar revitalization of the whole Soviet administration. One of the first Gorbachev appointees was the first party secretary of Georgia, Eduard A. Shevardnadze, who became minister of foreign affairs in July 1985. The first party secretary of the Sverdlovsk region, Boris N. Yeltsin, was promoted to first party secretary of Moscow in December 1985.

These five new leaders—Gorbachev, Ryzhkov, Ligachev, Shevardnadze, and Yeltsin—had much in common. For better or worse, they were outstanding provincials. At a time of cynicism, corruption, and passivity, they were earnest and ambitious. They wanted to improve their country. None of them had benefited from a privileged background. They were all self-made men who had made their careers thanks to intelligence and hard work. Their rise bore witness to the openness of Soviet society, where such able men could enter the best schools and make high-flying party careers, as long as they accepted being obedient communists.

These men were the best and the brightest of the Brezhnev administration, but they also shared its weaknesses. Each of them had spent almost his entire life in his home region, apart from one or two spells of a few years in Moscow. As a result, they were quite ignorant about their own country. None of them spoke any foreign language, and they had only been abroad for several weeks as part of some circumscribed party delegation. They were excluded from the international policy debate and knew little about international economics or politics. Everything was presented to them through the rose-tinted glasses of Soviet propaganda.

To make their careers in the Soviet hierarchy, they were compelled to act as servile sycophants and compromise with the unacceptable. Few elites have been more poorly trained for major changes. In his memoirs, Ryzhkov (1992, 37) candidly reveals his own inadequate training, when Andropov offered him the job of Central Committee secretary: "I am a producer and not a party functionary. I toiled for 25 years at a factory, and three years in the Ministry of Heavy Machine-Building . . . then Gosplan. . . . I have no experience whatsoever of party work."

The economic and international ignorance reflected in the memoirs of both Ryzhkov and Ligachev is moving. In the midst of economic collapse in 1991, Ligachev (1993, 64) saw all the supply problems as being caused by political demonstrations that pulled people away from the potato harvest: "If everyone had cooperated in bringing in the harvest, they would have been torn away from all those senseless demonstrations and returned to real life. . . . In Western countries, when the weather is poor, the army helps farmers with the potato harvest." The parochialism of these able men must not be underrated.

The pretendents were frustrated at having waited so long for promotion. In his memoirs, Yeltsin (1990) details how at every turn he was promoted neither early enough nor high enough. Ligachev concurred:

> During the entire Brezhnev period, for the seventeen years that I had worked as first secretary of the Tomsk Province Party Committee, I had not managed to speak a single time at the Central Committee plenums. In the early years I regularly signed up on the speakers' list, but in time my hopes waned. . . . [W]hen Andropov became General Secretary, I, like many other provincial Party secretaries, was impatient for change, uncomfortably aware that the country was headed for social and economic disaster. (Ligachev 1993, 16)

One man in the new leadership, however, was very different and far more qualified: Aleksandr N. Yakovlev. He was the ultimate Moscow insider. From 1952 to 1972 he worked in the International Department of the Central Committee apparatus. He learned English and attended Columbia

University in New York in 1959. In 1972, he published an article, "On Anti-Historicism," frontally attacking Russian nationalism, labeling it "patriarchal mentality, nationalism, and chauvinism." Not surprisingly, this brave act led to his ouster, but as a senior party official he was exiled to Canada as ambassador for 11 years, where Gorbachev detected him during a visit in 1983.

Ligachev (1993, 94, 108), who was seen as the toughest apparatchik and Yakovlev's foremost rival, called Yakovlev "one of the most experienced apparatchiks in the Central Committee. . . . [He has] the gift of persuasion and follows the thread of conversation with precise logic." While the calculating Yakovlev replaced newspaper editors, "we had no idea what a powerful and dangerous weapon the media could be in glasnost and pluralism. Alexander Yakovlev, who had spent many years in the West, naturally had a much better understanding of this than the other members of the Politburo . . ." (p. 105). Not by chance, Yakovlev, who was both an apparatchik and intellectual of world class, became the chief ideologist of perestroika.

All the new leaders realized that the Soviet Union was in bad shape and had to improve in many ways, but, with the possible exception of Yakovlev, they presumed that all solutions had to be socialist. The shock they were to face was that Soviet socialism was no solution but a dead end: Soviet communism could not be reformed, only destroyed. But if they had understood that, they would never have reached their high posts and might never have started to reform communism.

In due time, they would part company. By 1990, Ligachev and Ryzhkov had reverted to Brezhnevian conservatism, whereas Yeltsin and Yakovlev marched on to a liberal market economy and democracy. Only Gorbachev preserved his belief that Soviet communism could be reformed.

Early Perestroika: Cautious Economic Reforms to Boost Growth

In 1985, the new Soviet leaders were united in their desire to revitalize the Soviet economy and society.[3] Gorbachev and Shevardnadze reported that they met in the southern resort of Pitsunda in December 1984 and agreed: "We can't go on living like this" (Brown 1996, 81).

Against these "young" radicals aged 54 to 62 stood the Brezhnevian septuagenarians, who favored total passivity in economic policy and firm repression in domestic politics. After the Soviet invasion of Czechoslovakia in 1968, theirs had been a conservative, do-nothing government. Few of them were guided by any ideological conviction. In hindsight, they were

---

3. This section draws on Åslund (1991).

more prescient than it seemed at the time, thinking that a major change would be dangerous.

Economic policy dominated the early stage of perestroika. As Gorbachev and his allies came to power, a new five-year plan for 1986–90 was being prepared, and they tried to make their imprint on this important policy document.

Three Different Programs of Perestroika

The incoming Soviet leaders were unified in their desire for rapid change, but they had very different ideas about what to do. Although they all favored common sense, their perception of common sense varied greatly, constrained as they were by ideological blinkers and parochialism.

A first group led by Ligachev advocated socialist morality, wanting little but the reinforcement of communist discipline. A second group led by Ryzhkov opted for technocratic improvements within the Soviet system. The most daring program advocated a socialist market economy, as was already in place in Hungary and Poland, with elements of private enterprise. This approach had no full-fledged advocate in the Politburo, but Gorbachev lent it partial support.

Ligachev (1989, 95) was not too unhappy: "We have no crises or unemployment, poor or homeless, no exploitation of the working masses. We are not suppressing other nations. In our country, the national repression has been liquidated." Ligachev (1985, 92) used terms such as "norms of socialist morals." He wanted in "every conceivable way to confirm the authority of honest and conscientious labor." He was a puritan who saw consumerism as the main evil, and he called for "vigilance in the struggle with bourgeois influences alien to our ideology and morals" (Ligachev 1985, 85–86). As early as June 1985, Gorbachev and Ligachev publicly expressed widely differing views. Slyly, Ligachev diffused Gorbachev's terms by altering them slightly. In his memoirs, however, Ligachev (1993, 97) alleged that they started parting company only in 1987.

Ryzhkov (1992) was a soft-spoken man with technocratic perspectives. I once sat diagonally across the table from him at a dinner in the Kremlin, and I was struck by his gentle manner. Ryzhkov (1992, 171) reported that at the beginning of perestroika: "I and my protagonists wanted only one thing: to stop the decline, to use all means and measures to move the economy forward." He aspired to improve organization and incentives and to decentralize management from the center to large regional units, while reducing the role of the party. One of his main preoccupations was the Law on State Enterprises, which would "precisely determine the rights and duties of enterprises and their place in the economic system" (p. 165). He favored a market economy for developed countries, but not for the Soviet Union. Its prices had to be regulated, while their regulation should improve. He advocated greater tolerance and pragmatism: "Where power lies in the hands of *one* ideology, there is no place for different thoughts" (p. 84), but even so he insisted on the rule of the CPSU. It is easy to feel sympathy for Ryzhkov and his apparent honesty, but his astounding lack of economic insight made him lead the Soviet economy into its abyss (Yasin 2002, 118–21).

Yakovlev was the most radical member of the Politburo, but as a political scientist and historian he did not focus on the economy but democracy. When asked whether a full plan for reforms existed in 1985, he answered: "There was an understanding of what had to be rejected—authoritarianism and the command-administrative system. There was an urgent need for democracy, but we had to find out by what means and in what forms" (Yakovlev 1991, 33–34). Yakovlev gathered true democrats who desired a normal market economy with free prices and trade as well as predominant private ownership. But it took some time before they dared to utter such words, and no economist of market economic inclinations was a major economic policymaker until 1991. The leading economic reformers in the early perestroika were academic economists of Gorbachev's generation, primarily Academicians Abel Aganbegyan and Leonid Abalkin.

Initially, Gorbachev advocated the most radical reform program. Until November 1987, he was never outflanked by radicals, but he was an ideal compromiser who acted as a catch-all. True, he made the most radical statements first, but he also agreed to many measures that did not pertain to the radical agenda. Gorbachev revealed his reform agenda in his major ideological speech on December 10, 1984, three months before his elevation to general secretary of the CPSU. He referred to all three alternative reform programs and used most of his later famous slogans. He called moderately for the "acceleration of social-economic progress," "a deep transformation of the economy and the whole system of social relations," and "perestroika of economic management." But he also called for "revolutionary decisions," "competition" (without the compulsory attribute "socialist"), "self-management," "self-government," "glasnost" (openness), and even "democratization." Wisely, he avoided being specific (Gorbachev 1987a, 75–108).

At the 27th Party Congress of the CPSU in February 1986, Gorbachev for the first time called for "a radical economic reform." He had a clear idea of the direction of his political and economic strategy, but he also cleverly appealed to a broad coalition of all those who wanted any kind of change. Therefore, his reform attempts were never consistent. In July 1986, he stunned everybody by stating: "I would equate the word perestroika with revolution."[4] If only he had known how right he was.

Gorbachev was elected general secretary against strong resistance from the old Brezhnevites, who constituted half the Politburo, and his own coalition for change was riddled with divisions. Even so, he started out

---

4. *Pravda,* August 2, 1986.

fast and hard. His early reform efforts amounted to an attempt to carry out all three reform programs with great energy, however contradictory they may have been. As none of the reform measures brought about any positive change, the literature tends to ignore them. Yet they were important because they set the course. The policymaking activity was impressive, and this wild trial-and-error period taught the new Soviet leaders how difficult the situation was.

Futile Technocratic Attempts at Accelerated Economic Growth

The new leaders all agreed on many technocratic improvements of the Soviet economic system, derived from Ryzhkov's program. They included higher growth targets, change of investment policy, and improved wage policy and quality control. Waste and misallocation were so widespread that they reckoned improvement would be easy.

One of Gorbachev's early slogans was "acceleration" of economic growth, which he wanted to boost from about 3 percent a year to at least 4 percent (Gorbachev 1987a, 214). However, if the real growth was close to stagnation, as Selyunin and Khanin (1987) argued, 4 percent was a distant target. Another early focus was investment policy. Gorbachev sent back the draft 12th Five-Year Plan for 1986–90 three times, demanding higher growth and investment targets. Although the new leaders talked about the need for a higher standard of living, they preferred to raise the accumulation in national income substantially from 25 percent in 1985 to 27.6 percent in 1990 (Faltsman 1987, 12), glossing over the conflict between increasing investment and consumption, and unpublished defense expenditures were also supposed to rise.

The late Brezhnev administration had concentrated on major "complex" programs, such as the Food Program (1982) and the Energy Program (1982), which set policies and directed investment to these industries. The early perestroika reinforced this focus on branch planning. Several new programs were adopted, a Consumer Goods and Services Program (1985), Chemicals Program (1985), and Machine-Building Program (1986), which led to huge, inefficient overinvestment. Soviet managers had strong incentives to start new investment projects to attract state funds, but not to complete them, because then their funds were cut. Many investment projects lasted for a decade or two. The number of investment projects ought to be cut, the managers' incentives preserved the long-lasting construction projects (*dolgostroii*).

The new leaders emphasized the importance of the "human factor." They ended the gerontocracy through sweeping personnel changes, but the old Soviet remuneration system impeded any positive impact from this well-intended housecleaning. For three decades, income differentials had continually shrunk, and the rewards for qualifications had declined so that unqualified blue-collar workers were paid more than engineers and physicians. The new rulers wanted to raise the salaries of the intelligentsia to stimulate people to enhance their qualifications as well as relate wages to final results of work, but a command economy possessed no relevant measure of final results.

The quality of Soviet output was miserable and declining. The Brezhnev regime had preferred carrots to sticks, and bureaucracy to markets, offering bonuses to producers who improved quality. But producers judged the quality themselves, naturally always sufficiently satisfied to receive their bonuses. Only military quality control was independent of producers. In late 1986, the Soviet authorities decided to create an independent inspection for state quality control (*gospriemka*), with highly qualified inspectors of great integrity and high pay. The new quality controllers did act severely, but their impact disrupted output volumes dramatically.[5] This decline in production, and related bonuses, was more than the system could tolerate. Although *gospriemka* was the main economic theme in Soviet media from November 1986 until March 1987, this fierce campaign fizzled within a couple of months.

Disciplinary Campaigns Against Alcohol and Private Incomes

Most damaging in the early perestroika were two old-style disciplinary campaigns, one against alcohol and another against private or "unearned" incomes. Both were throwbacks to Stalinist attitudes spearheaded by Gorbachev and Ligachev, while technocratic reformers, such as Ryzhkov, opposed them from the beginning.

Gorbachev unleashed the anti-alcohol campaign in May 1985.[6] Alcoholism was Russia's greatest social concern, and Russian women welcomed this campaign, but the philosophy of this campaign was entirely administrative—to reduce the production of alcohol and make it difficult to buy. It was not sustainable and was probably a cause of the later drop in life expectancy. The number of shops and licensed restaurants selling alcohol was reduced to less than half. Astoundingly, the number of licensed restaurants in Moscow, a city of 10 million people, was slashed to 87. Public sales of alcohol fell by more than half from 1984 to 1987, and production was cut by half. Prices were hiked, although not all that much, and enormous lines for alcohol arose. Vodka lines were easily identified because they were populated by men, whereas other queues were the preserve of women. This was a full-fledged disciplinary campaign of Stalinist

---

5. The substandard civilian machine-building sector experienced a drop in output of 7.9 percent in January 1987. *Ekonomicheskaya gazeta*, no. 8, 1987.

6. This section draws on White (1996) and Åslund (1991, 78–80, 158–63).

vintage, staged with impressive stamina, though punishments were limited to fines and dismissals.

When visiting Soviet ministries before the campaign, I was usually offered cognac from 10 a.m. A visiting foreigner was a good excuse to begin drinking. Initially, the anti-alcohol campaign had a tremendous positive impact, as alcohol-related diseases, crimes, and accidents plummeted. The death rate and infant mortality declined, and life expectancy for men rose by two years. You would no longer see unconscious, dead-drunk men lying in the streets. In the short term, the social impact was impressive. Women were happy, but men were furious.

The economic impact, by contrast, was disastrous. In 1984, alcohol sales had accounted for 17 percent of total retail sales. The halving of these sales left a big hole in total supplies, which boosted all shortages. Almost 90 percent of alcohol sales went to turnover taxes, so tax revenues plummeted. Mainly because of the anti-alcohol campaign, the Soviet budget deficit in 1986 more than doubled to 6 percent of GDP, never to be reined in again. But the Soviet leaders did not even consider the fiscal effects.

The initial positive social results were not sustainable. The shortage of alcohol bred a large underground economy with ballooning organized crime thriving on moonlighting, poisonous liquor, and black market trade. Alcohol poisoning became a mass killer. The initial improvements were set to turn into equally great deteriorations. Perhaps more than any other single measure, the anti-alcohol campaign hastened the economic collapse of the Soviet Union.

Having learned nothing and forgotten nothing, like the Bourbons, the CPSU in the summer of 1986 launched another vicious neo-Stalinist campaign targeting private incomes. The official target was "unearned incomes," which were never defined. The diffuseness of the target suited the control agencies, which could act at will, deciding whom to persecute. Fortunately, punishments were limited to confiscation and fines. In practice, this campaign was directed against small private earnings, primarily production sold through the collective farm markets.

Outrageously, this campaign concentrated on poor pensioners, who badly needed this income for their subsistence. It was replete with quotas for the planned number of culprits in each region. The media had already gained considerable freedom, and the public criticism of this campaign was devastating. An article titled "The Criminal Tomato" by Igor Gamayunov in *Literaturnaya gazeta* (August 12, 1987) reported how a local "commission for the struggle against negative phenomena" had ordered convicted hoodlums to carry out the lawless destruction of hundreds of greenhouses for tomatoes in the Volgograd region.

The direct effect of the campaign against "unearned incomes" was that private food supplies shrank and prices on the relatively free *kolkhoz* markets rose manifold. The campaign encouraged police to indulge in lawless racketeering against marginal private entrepreneurs. It contradicted early talk about the establishment of a rule of law, and it ran counter to Gorbachev's whole policy, whereas Ligachev praised it in every speech from the summer of 1986, lamenting "speculators." This campaign embodied Ligachev's urge for police activism and socialist morality, underlining the limitation of Gorbachev's power. It faded away in the second half of 1987.

Everything was wrong with these two neo-Stalinist campaigns. They were voluntaristic initiatives by two Politburo members who acted without prior analysis. Both campaigns were economically harmful, aggravating shortages. The anti-alcohol campaign seriously undermined the budget, whereas the campaign against unearned incomes reduced supply by scaring people away from private enterprise and fostering lawlessness by the authorities. To the Soviet public, these two campaigns were the dominant economic policies from 1985 to 1987, which badly undermined public confidence in Gorbachev, who was responsible for these government-made disasters.

Attempts to Improve the Economic System

The changes in economic policy and the disciplinary campaigns were launched swiftly and with great determination, but attempts at systemic reform were much more tentative. A dominant complaint was that enterprises had no "masters," and managers' incentives were flawed. Several experiments aiming at improving enterprise management were under way, and they led to the landmark Law on State Enterprises in 1997.

The main goal of the enterprise experiments was to make enterprises more independent through decentralization, to enhance managers' power at the expense of branch ministries, and to improve managers' incentives. The most radical experiments involved self-management with elected managers and work councils. In the 1960s, the experiments preceding economic reform undertaken by then-Premier Alexei Kosygin had engendered impressive results. They had been more radical than the reform itself, and had aroused a conservative reaction (Nove 1969, 1977).

Now the contrary was happening. The initial experiments were cautious and embraced by a reasonably broad political consensus, but their economic results were deplorable. Some of the more radical experiments, such as self-financing and profit sharing in small units, had an initial positive economic impact, but they were effectively resisted by branch ministries whose powers they reduced. As a result, they inspired radical criticism that called for more far-reaching changes, breeding a radical momentum in the public debate.

The pedagogic value of the experiments was considerable, promoting economic analysis and showing that limited changes were not enough. The experiments exposed the intrinsic shortcomings of the command economy. Enterprise management could not be improved in isolation; arbitrarily set prices distorted all incentives; shortages of supplies emasculated attempts at cutting costs; no incentives could raise quality within the flawed system; the isolation from foreign markets nullified any interest in exports; and without any relevant objective function for enterprises, no remuneration system made sense. A political snowball effect was under way.

The technical complexity of many experiments necessitated economic analysis, which promoted economists within enterprises and in the national debate. Chief economists started replacing chief engineers as deputy directors at enterprises. A reformist vanguard was formed in the Central Committee apparatus, among academic economists and journalists. Managers made their careers on economic experiments and commissions for experiments established networks among reformers. But resistance was also consolidating in industrial ministries, Gosplan, Gossnab (the State Committee for Material and Technical Supplies), Goskomtsen (the State Price Committee), and the Ministry of Finance. The struggle between reformers and bureaucrats intensified.

The Emergence of Private Enterprise

Communism abhorred private enterprise.[7] The nationalization of the means of production was a fundamental tenet of communism, yet many problems in the Soviet economy could not possibly be solved within the public sector. Numerous goods and services were scarce, of substandard quality, or missing altogether. The black market filled the worst holes, but organized crime was not an acceptable solution. According to an official estimate, one-third of the demand for consumer services was satisfied by the public sector, another third by the unregistered private sector, and the remaining one-third was left unsatisfied. Private individuals could supply what was missing, but only if they were allowed.

Stalin had been determined to abolish private enterprise, chasing even artists into cooperatives, but minor remnants survived. The Soviet constitution of 1977 spelled out as permissible "individual labor activity in the sphere of handicrafts, agriculture, and consumer services for the population, as well as other types of activity, based exclusively on the personal labor of citizens and members of their families" (*Konstitutsiya* 1977, 9). In November 1986, 97,000 registered private entrepreneurs persisted, mostly odd arts and handicrafts. The most substantial private activity was 35 million private household plots, which accounted for 25 to 30 percent of all Soviet agricultural production. For many poor people, notably millions of old people without state pensions, these plots provided their subsistence. Some of the produce was sold on rather free collective farm markets. Surprisingly, 41 percent of the total housing area was private, essentially all the poor village housing and dachas. Besides, there were many cooperatives,

---

7. This section draws on Åslund (1991, 154–58).

but only some of them were real cooperatives, notably cooperative housing, while cooperative farms or shops functioned like public enterprises.

The black market was very limited. Otherwise, shortages would not have been so cumbersome and prices on the black market so outrageous. A major study based on interviews with Soviet émigrés in the late 1970s estimated that 10 to 12 percent of total personal incomes, or 3 to 4 percent of GDP in the urban European part of the Soviet Union, originated from private activity, whether legal or illegal (Ofer and Vinokur 1992, 100). Even so, many Soviets were upset about black marketeering because marketeers were filthy rich in a country that was otherwise gray and egalitarian.

On November 19, 1986, the Law on Individual Labor Activity was adopted and it came into force in May 1987.[8] It legalized acceptable forms of individual labor activity. Economically, it was of minor significance, because the conditions offered were not very attractive. In 1989, only 300,000 people were registered as working in individual labor activity (Goskomstat SSSR 1990, 47).

Ideologically, however, this law was important and it contained several interesting innovations. One was that "other kinds of handicrafts are allowed, if their occupation is not forbidden in legislation." The Soviet standard until then had been that everything that was not explicitly allowed was prohibited. Surprisingly, planning and pricing were not even mentioned. This law initiated private enterprise, which was soon to rise with the support of six subsequent decrees on various kinds of independent cooperatives and individual farming adopted from October 1986 to October 1987. Each broke more ground for private enterprise, and the new cooperatives and individual labor were backed up by an impressive media campaign from the end of 1986.

Failure of Economic Reforms Breeds Radicalization

These many reform efforts were uncoordinated, lacking both theoretical and empirical basis. The top politicians made one impromptu decision after the other. After two years of intensive economic reform efforts, the conclusions were obvious. Small changes no longer contributed to economic improvements, but significant systemic changes were blocked or distorted by the all-powerful bureaucracy. A comprehensive reform was required, and it had to be market-oriented.

Gorbachev mastered these insights. In June 1987, he organized a Central Committee plenary meeting on economic reform to take the reforms further. Exasperated, he exclaimed, "we shall not succeed with the tasks of perestroika, if we do not firmly pursue democratization."[9] He con-

---

8. *Pravda,* November 21, 1986.

9. *Pravda,* June 26, 1987.

cluded that the Soviet Union must proceed with more radical economic reform. He outlined a reform program that he summarized in five points:

1. the extension of enterprise independence with self-financing;

2. perestroika of centralized economic management;

3. a cardinal reform of planning, price formation, and the credit system as well as the introduction of wholesale trade;

4. a new organizational structure; and

5. transition from centralized command management to self-management.

All these ideas were incorporated in the Law on State Enterprises, which also comprised a general program for economic reform (chapter 2).

Glasnost: Shattering All Illusions

Today it is difficult to imagine how stereotypical and controlled the Soviet media were. Each evening, the TV news started with a review of the meetings of the top officials that day. Bizarrely, the news showed a blast furnace from a steel mill every evening, and in the summer, interested viewers could follow the harvest. Brezhnev mumbled out his long speeches, seemingly unaware of what he was reading. Once during a major speech, he read the same page twice. The people were fed a steady diet of supposed success stories. No bad news such as crime was allowed, although in their daily life people saw a gray, drab, stagnant world. Kremlinologists developed methodologies on how to interpret the communist liturgy and read between the lines. Soon after his election as general secretary of the CPSU, Gorbachev made these techniques superfluous. In 1985 it was difficult to find any information in Soviet media, but by 1989 media freedom was nearly complete, and the problem was to find out what was true.

In his December 1984 speech, Gorbachev introduced glasnost, which was his elastic code word for greater public openness. Like most of Gorbachev's key expressions, glasnost had no ideological connotation and its meaning was diffuse. It meant openness rather than freedom of speech. In May 1985, Gorbachev caused a first great shock, which marked the beginning of glasnost. During a visit to Leningrad, he mingled with a huge crowd and spoke without script in front of television cameras, a far cry from the traditional Soviet leaders' isolation from the people with strict, formal meetings and prepared speeches. Russians were stunned to see a leader who could walk and talk. The extraordinary Soviet censorship started to falter. In one step after the other, the many ideological taboos were broken.

Quaintly, most great revelations were published in the traditional thick, monthly literary journals, notably the liberal *Novy mir*. In many Russian homes, you still notice literary journals from the years 1986 to 1989. Those were the great years of glasnost. People learned things they had never expected to hear. Several Soviet friends told me that they would save these journals forever to remember that once their country had actually been so free.[10]

On April 26, 1986, one of the large nuclear reactors in Chernobyl, slightly north of Ukraine's capital Kiev, melted down, and substantial radiation was released into the atmosphere. Although glasnost was well under way, the Soviet authorities kept absolutely quiet, and the news was released by the Swedish authorities. As a Swedish diplomat working in Moscow, I asked a cabdriver a week after the accident if he knew about it and he did not. "They never tell us anything!" he exclaimed. That day, *Pravda* published a small notice on its second page that some accident had occurred at the Chernobyl nuclear power station, but only the elite accustomed to reading between the lines understood the gravity of these words. Skillfully, Gorbachev utilized this stunning underreporting by the old establishment to force greater public openness after Chernobyl.

In June 1987, the literary journal *Novy mir* published an article by the liberal economist Nikolai Shmelev called "Advances and Debts." It was a breathtaking attack on the Soviet economic system, debunking most Soviet economic taboos. Shmelev started his onslaught:

> The state of our economy does not satisfy anybody. Its two central, inbuilt defects, the producer's monopoly under the conditions of shortage and the enterprises' disinterest in scientific-technical progress, are probably clear to everybody. (Shmelev 1987, 142)

The economy bred pervasive shortages, was highly inefficient compared with Western economies, produced awful quality, and was unable to accept innovations. He also complained about *dolgostroii*, the long-lasting investment projects, expensive overinvestment, extraordinary hoarding of inputs, and all kinds of waste. All these problems of the Soviet economy were well known, but they had typically been presented as special cases, whereas Shmelev made clear they were innate to the Soviet economic system: "From the very beginning this whole system was characterized by economic romanticism, tightly linked to economic illiteracy." He dismissed central planning as anarchic: "Today we have a shortage [economy], unbalanced on virtually all accounts and in many ways unmanageable, and to be completely honest, an economy which almost does not yield to planning" (p. 144).

The Soviet system bred the very demoralization and alienation it was supposed to have abolished:

---

10. At the time of this writing in the summer of 2007, these statements seem to harbor even more foresight than they did at the time.

Apathy and indifference have become mass phenomena as well as theft, disrespect of honest work and simultaneously an aggressive jealousy of those who earn a lot, even if they earn honestly. Signs have appeared of an almost physical degradation of a substantial part of the population because of drunkenness and idleness. (Shmelev 1987, 145)

Shmelev famously exclaimed: "Let us lose our ideological virginity." The main hindrance was "the worry that we let out the evil spirit of capitalism" (pp. 146–47). His key idea was that markets had to be balanced and that Russia must move from the seller's market to the buyer's market. But even Shmelev cited Lenin to defend his position. Although he obviously favored a market economy, his actual proposals were merely incremental steps. Perhaps most daringly, he advocated the acceptance of joint stock companies as a means to absorb the population's excess savings, and he thought enterprises should focus on profit and their physical plan targets be abolished. He also suggested that bad enterprises should be closed, workers disciplined through dismissal, and frictional unemployment be deemed acceptable.

This article reflected the contradiction between urgency and hesitation that would be so characteristic of the Russian reforms. On the one hand, Shmelev (1987, 142) warned of partial reforms as in 1953 and 1965 because "half-measures are often worse than passivity." On the other hand, he considered it unrealistic to expect rapid changes, as reforms would require years, perhaps generations.

For a month, Shmelev's article dominated conversation in Moscow. It became such an issue that Gorbachev expressed his public support, in effect allowing full-fledged attacks on central planning.[11] After the publication of this article, profound criticism of the socialist economic system and pure market economic thinking were permitted.

In its following issue, *Novy mir* published a letter with the title, "You Cannot Be a Little Pregnant." The letter was written under the pseudonym "L. Popkova" (1987) by Larisa Piyasheva, a neoliberal researcher specializing on Germany at an institute of the Academy of Sciences. She argued that it was not enough to adopt some capitalist features; a consistent capitalist system was needed.

Similar articles criticizing all aspects of Soviet society appeared one after the other, mostly written by liberal stars within the old intellectual establishment. At the height of glasnost, one anecdote reported on a man who phoned a friend:

"Have you read the article on the first page of *Pravda* today?"

"No, what does it say?"

"Sorry, I dare not tell you on the phone."

Nothing seemed too tragic to be expressed. Criticism of the Soviet system suited Gorbachev well, but after the flood gates had been opened its

---

11. *Pravda,* June 22, 1987.

flows could not be contained, and the truths that were finally made public were truly shocking. Although all Soviet people know about many disasters, few knew all of them, and the bombardment of all these old truths was overwhelming.

The collectivization of agriculture in the 1930s, and the killings of millions in the process, could not be justified. In Ukraine as well as Kazakhstan, about a quarter of the population had been killed in an artificial famine imposed by secret police troops in connection with collectivization (Conquest 1986). The terror of 1937, which had killed about one million of the old Communist Party elite, was unforgivable. The three small Baltic nations had never wanted to join the Soviet Union, and their occupation was concluded in the infamous Molotov-Ribbentrop Pact with Nazi Germany in August 1939. According to *Encyclopaedia Britannica*, World War II population losses in the Baltic states amounted to 25 percent in Estonia, 30 percent in Latvia, and 15 percent in Lithuania, much of these coming from Soviet deportations. How could that ever become legitimate?

As the openness increased, previously suppressed acts and statements of brutality by Lenin, Gorbachev's remaining great hero, were made public. Lenin had indeed indulged in arbitrary terror and established the Gulag, the Soviet prison camp system. The Communist Party apologized for its repression of its own members in the 1930s but not much more.

Gorbachev's ultimate problem was that he was defending a regime and a history that nobody could defend. Until the end, he insisted that socialism and Lenin were good, which made no sense. He had no plausible narrative about Soviet history, and his only defense was obfuscation.

Even so, Gorbachev and his closest collaborator Yakovlev were the driving forces behind glasnost. In May–June 1989, virtually all communist taboos were broken and in practice the freedom of public expression was established. The revolutionizing event was the first session of the USSR Congress of People's Deputies. Its proceedings were directly broadcast on television and published in full in the main newspapers. Almost half the population watched these broadcasts as the most exciting soccer match. Everything could be said and it was said. The radicals might have dominated, but they encountered full-fledged resistance from Stalinists. The Soviet public's perception of their country changed forever.

New Thinking on Foreign Policy

One of Gorbachev's early slogans was "a new thinking in foreign policy." It was even more unclear than his other slogans—perestroika and glasnost—which was his intention. The 27th Party Congress in February 1986 adopted Gorbachev's "concept of a contradictory but interconnected, interdependent and, essentially, integral world" (Gorbachev 1987b, 139).

His new foreign policy was verbose and full of platitudes, but it had several clear purposes. One was to diminish the cost of Soviet foreign policy. Most of all, Gorbachev wanted to impede the nuclear arms race with the United States because the USSR could no longer afford it. As Ligachev (1993, 329) put it:

> After April 1985 we faced the task of curtailing military spending. Without this, large-scale social programs could not have been implanted: the economy could not breathe normally with a military budget that comprised 18 percent of the national income.

Another aim was to end the war in Afghanistan, which was very unpopular, had cost many lives, and had brought about a serious social problem, as many war veterans came back as drug addicts and hardened criminals.

Gorbachev's foreign policy had domestic goals as well. He had little leeway in domestic politics, and like so many heads of state he used his foreign policy skills to enhance his authority domestically. By de-ideologizing foreign policy and trying to open his country to the outside world, Gorbachev undermined the grasp of sterile Marxism-Leninism in the Soviet Union.

In addition, as in all of Gorbachev's policies, he sought the unexpected and the unknown. Later on, he was to launch the concept of "the common European house," but he never managed to endow it with substance. Gorbachev just loved foreign policy. It offered him breathing space, delight, and unanticipated luck. While leading a Soviet delegation to Canada in the summer of 1983, he met Yakovlev. During his first high-profile trip to England in December 1984, Prime Minister Margaret Thatcher surprisingly and memorably declared: "I like Mr. Gorbachev. We can do business together" (Brown 1996, 77). He acquired the unique knack of letting his limousine halt unannounced to mingle with crowds during his foreign travel. He was soon mobbed like a rock star, being the greatest political celebrity in the world. In 1987, *Time* magazine named him the man of the year.

When Gorbachev came to power, Soviet foreign policy was in a deep freeze and the Cold War was at its last height. The country had been extremely closed all along, but Soviet relations with the West had been badly aggravated by three recent events. The first was the Soviet invasion of Afghanistan in December 1979, which appeared to be a Soviet attempt to widen its sphere of influence in the world. As a consequence, the United States boycotted the Olympic games in Moscow in 1980, and the Soviet Union retaliated by boycotting the Olympic games in Los Angeles in 1984.

The second event was the big Soviet-American dispute over intermediary nuclear forces. In 1977, the Soviet Union started installing new intermediary nuclear missiles (SS-20) in Eastern Europe, which enabled it to reach targets in Western Europe, North Africa, the Middle East, and a good part of Asia within a quarter of an hour (Goldblat 2002, 84). The West was particularly worried about the absence of a warning period. A Soviet surprise attack on Western Europe had become much more possible. In December 1979, NATO responded by preparing to deploy its own intermediary nuclear missiles (Pershing II) and the ground-launched Tomahawk cruise missiles in Germany and other European NATO members. A large left-wing peace movement in Europe protested against the plans to deploy Western missiles but not against the Soviet SS-20s, which were already in place. Despite this public outcry, in 1984, the United States began to put its intermediary nuclear missiles in West Germany, Italy, and the United Kingdom.

The third big event was the formation of the independent trade union Solidarity in Poland in August 1980. It was curtailed after only 16 months through the imposition of martial law by Poland's president, General Wojciech Jaruzelski, as demanded by the Soviet leadership. The Soviet view was that Solidarity was a Western subversive action.

Against this backdrop, the United States reinforced its long-lasting embargo on exports of technology to the Soviet bloc and opposed the building of the Urengoy-Uzhgorod natural gas pipeline from the newly developed gas fields in Western Siberia to Europe, primarily Germany. In spite of a US embargo against deliveries to the pipeline construction, the Europeans went ahead, which caused a major rift between America and Western Europe. The United States argued that European gas imports would strengthen the Soviets by increasing their hard currency earnings (thus financing the Soviet military effort) and weaken the allies by making them dangerously dependent on the Soviets. Despite severe US opposition, the pipeline was completed in 1983, and France, Austria, West Germany, and Italy received natural gas through it. The Kremlin was determined to show that Reagan's attempts to block construction of the pipeline through economic sanctions had been a failure, and they won. The US pipeline embargo, which created a political storm on both sides of the Atlantic, was eased at the end of 1982 (Jentleson 1986).

Arguably, in the early 1980s the relationship between the Soviet Union and the West was worse than at any time after the Cuban missile crisis in 1962. The last US-Soviet summit had taken place in 1979, when Leonid Brezhnev met Jimmy Carter in Vienna. They signed the Strategic Arms Limitation Talks Treaty (SALT II), which was supposed to limit the number of strategic offensive weapons systems, but it was never ratified and thus did not come into force. Neither Andropov nor Chernenko even contemplated a Soviet-American summit during their brief spells in power.

In the United States, Reagan was elected president in 1980 on an aggressive anti-Soviet platform, advocating extensive American nuclear armament and the SDI. In 1983, Reagan famously called the Soviet Union "the evil empire." The mutual confidence between the Soviet Union and the United States was close to zero, and accidents such as the 1983 Soviet shooting down of a South Korean passenger airplane that had inadvertently entered Soviet air space further aggravated these miserable relations. The danger of a nuclear war caused by misunderstanding had hardly ever been greater.

Resolutely, Gorbachev decided to change all this. His first opportunity was at the funeral of his predecessor Chernenko in March 1985. He saw an unprecedented number of foreign leaders, giving preference to Westerners. From the outset, Gorbachev traveled the world. His most important aim was to develop good relations with Reagan. A first summit between them took place on neutral ground in Geneva in November 1985, and they forged good personal relations. Gorbachev and Reagan issued a joint statement that "a nuclear war cannot be won and must never be fought."

From that time, Reagan-Gorbachev summits became regular events and quite a craze. The two leaders got along extremely well, and their aims were complementary. Reagan had pursued a tough arms buildup in order to win the arms race, and he took Gorbachev's desire for arms control as a sign of victory. Gorbachev, on the other hand, wanted to reduce the Soviet military's material demands, which an arms control agreement would give him.

The most important summit between Gorbachev and Reagan took place in Reykjavik, Iceland, on October 11–12, 1986. Gorbachev surprised everybody by proposing the elimination of all nuclear arms by 2000, and Reagan concurred. To the immense relief of Reagan's aides, the leaders did not conclude any agreement, but the ice was broken. The question was no longer whether the Soviet Union and the United States would make an agreement on nuclear arms control but the details.

Gorbachev's goal was to impose restraints on the American SDI, while Reagan was reluctant to compromise. He proposed reducing offensive capabilities by eliminating intermediary nuclear forces, while jointly building up a defensive system sharing the SDI technologies. Reagan's aim was to convince the Soviet Union of the mutual advantages of sharing the benefits of strategic defenses. Defense would dominate over offense, rendering nuclear weapons obsolete. But Gorbachev did not take the idea of shared SDI seriously, regarding it as an offensive technology. The Soviet leaders saw SDI as a means to force the Soviet Union to greater military expenditures, which was exactly what Gorbachev wanted to avoid (Matlock 2004).

The Reykjavik meeting fell apart over the issue of whether the Anti-Ballistic Missile Treaty (ABM) signed by the United States and the Soviet Union in 1972 permitted research, development, and testing of high-technology space-based defensive systems (as the United States argued) and over Gorbachev's attempt to confine the SDI program to "laboratory" research. Still, Reykjavik was one of the most remarkable summits ever held between US and Soviet leaders. US Ambassador to Moscow Jack

Matlock (2004, 250) called Reykjavik a "psychological turning point." At the same time he concluded that "it was good that the meeting did not reach the understanding on arms reduction that Gorbachev had proposed and to which Reagan had come close to agreeing . . . because the agreements would not have worked" (p. 249).

The progress achieved in Reykjavik led to the signing of the bilateral Intermediate-Range Nuclear Forces (INF) Treaty between the United States and the Soviet Union in Washington on December 8, 1987. Matlock (2004, 271) calls the INF Treaty "the most significant step the United States and Soviet Union had ever taken to reverse the direction of the arms race." It provided for the complete elimination by the United States and the Soviet Union of intermediate-range missiles (ranges of 500 to 5,500 kilometers). The agreed reductions were asymmetrical: the destruction of 1,836 missiles on the Soviet side, but only 859 missiles on the US side (Goldblat 2002, 86). Both nations were allowed to inspect each other's military installations to ensure compliance. This breakthrough became possible after the INF agreement had been decoupled from the SDI; the Soviet Union initially had insisted on them being negotiated as a package. Another Soviet concession was that the treaty was confined to US and Soviet armaments only, ignoring British and French nuclear forces. The INF Treaty left both countries with large nuclear arsenals, but many weapons were destroyed and it was a precedent for further arms reductions.

Gorbachev's other big foreign policy task was to withdraw from Afghanistan. The Soviet Union did not need to agree with anybody, just withdraw. Gorbachev and Shevardnadze understood that this had to be done. As early as October 17, 1985, they received initial approval from the Politburo. In an attempt to secure an orderly retreat and the maintenance of a pro-Soviet government in Kabul, Gorbachev opted for an international agreement, the Geneva accord, on ending of the Soviet intervention in Afghanistan. It was signed on April 14, 1988 by Afghanistan, Pakistan, the United States, and the Soviet Union. The withdrawal of Soviet troops started in May 1988, and the last Soviet soldier departed in February 1989 (Brown 1996). A sad chapter of unprovoked and foolhardy expansionism had been closed.

Within three years, Gorbachev had achieved his three main foreign policy objectives. He had concluded a major arms control agreement with the United States that made it possible to reduce Soviet defense expenditures after 1988. The Soviet Union had ended its meaningless war in Afghanistan without any future commitments. And Gorbachev had greatly improved relations between the Soviet Union and the West. In addition, he was universally seen as the greatest international star in the world. The phrase "Gorbomania" was coined for good reasons. Arguably, Gorbachev's first three years of foreign policy were his greatest success in any sphere. He knew what he wanted and he achieved it.

Why Gorbachev's Attempt at Chinese Reforms Failed

A huge literature has criticized the Soviet and later the Russian leadership for not having copied the Chinese economic reforms. Common complaints are that Russia did not experiment enough, had too fixed an idea of a Western market economy, did not start with agricultural reform, and privatized too fast.[12]

Let us compare the actual situations. The natural starting point for comparison is China in 1978 and the Soviet Union in 1985, when Deng Xiaoping and Gorbachev, respectively, initiated their reforms.[13] The differences in preconditions were substantial. They concerned politics, macroeconomics, and economic structure.

A fundamental difference between China and the Soviet Union was that China had just gone through the Cultural Revolution, which had terrorized the party bureaucrats, while the Soviet Union had indulged in two decades of Brezhnevism, which accommodated bureaucrats in every regard. In China, the apparatchiks were still on the defensive, which made it possible for Deng Xiaoping to impose reforms from above. In the Soviet Union, by contrast, the bureaucrats were supreme and accepted no undesirable changes.

In April 1985, one month after his accession to power, Gorbachev issued a decree on a minor agricultural reform. I paid a visit to Gennady Kulik, an old-style apparatchik and then head of the foreign relations department of the Soviet Ministry of Agriculture. When I asked what Gorbachev's decree really meant, he replied: "Not a thing! Why should I care about a decree signed by the general secretary of the Communist Party?!" I thought this was an old-timer on his way out, but Kulik went on to become minister of agriculture and deputy prime minister, so he was no fool but an accomplished bureaucratic player.

The decree implied some minor decentralization, which would have reduced the power of the Ministry of Agriculture, which thus refused to implement the decree. The agricultural bureaucracy knew it was unbeatable. Wisely, Gorbachev abandoned all attempts to reform agriculture until he reformed the ministry itself, but that did not help because the result was only bureaucratic chaos. In contrast to this overbearing agricultural bureaucracy, in China the initial reforms, which focused on agriculture, could introduce quasi property rights for those who worked the land.

Another Soviet political peculiarity was that the general secretary had very limited power within the Politburo. Gorbachev never managed to achieve a majority in the Politburo for his own cause. After he had defeated the old Brezhnevites, his own appointees, Ligachev and Yeltsin, turned against him from opposing sides. Toward the end, he became a hostage of

---

12. Goldman (1996, 2003); Nolan (1995); Stiglitz (1999a, 2002).

13. I elaborated on this topic in Åslund (1989).

communist stalwarts. Gorbachev's strengths were compromise and manipulation, but his weak power, lack of firm principles, and the absence of consensus were disastrous for the consistency of the policy pursued.

It was not true that the Soviet leaders did not experiment. They experimented in the 1920s, 1950s, 1960s, and 1980s, and undertook far more experiments than the Chinese. The Soviet leaders were guided by pragmatism and common sense, exactly as the Chinese advocates of reform, but pragmatism was a major problem for the Soviets. Gradually realizing that much of Marxism-Leninism was bunk, the Soviet leaders were left empty-handed intellectually. They had no theory and no analytical framework. They were a crowd of the blind, being led by almost equally blind Soviet academicians who had not been allowed to travel abroad or study any of the foreign (capitalist) theories of the last few decades.[14] They were not even permitted to see real Soviet statistics. The early perestroika bears witness to the danger of economic experimentation without any theory.

To the Soviet people, the economic reforms in the 1920s, 1950s, and 1960s were dispiriting experiences. They knew that pioneers would be likely punished some day regardless of what the top politicians said today, so they were understandably reluctant to stick their necks out. Too many heads had been chopped off. Consequently, their response to Gorbachev's initial reform attempts was muted. The Chinese, by contrast, responded to reforms with an enthusiasm similar to that of the Soviet peoples in the 1920s, and they achieved early impressive results.

The Cultural Revolution had left China in serious economic and social discomfort, which rendered major changes necessary. In the Soviet Union of 1985, by contrast, there was no sense of crisis, but an overwhelming sense of constancy. Most Western analysts thought little would happen for decades (Bergson and Levine 1983). Few but Gorbachev and his allies could imagine that change was possible. At the time of Gorbachev's elevation to general secretary of the CPSU in March 1985, I asked several people in Moscow what had been the most important event that week. The dominant answer was that the cucumbers had arrived at the kolkhoz markets, so their price had fallen by half. No ordinary Soviet citizen could imagine that a new party leader could alter anything in their stagnant country.

Economically, the structural differences between the Soviet Union and China were large and significant (Sachs and Woo 1994). In the Soviet Union, industry accounted for about half of GDP in 1985, while three quarters of the Chinese worked in agriculture. And the early Gorbachev reforms caused no economic improvements, only aggravated shortages in 1978. Thus, in China, it was possible to omit industry in the early stages

---

14. When I met Abel Aganbegyan, the foremost Soviet reform economist, for the first time in 1988, he told me upfront that he had been prohibited from traveling to the West for ten years. Unlike most of the old academicians, Aganbegyan spoke English and he went on to become a true supporter of a free market economy.

of reform, while that was impossible in the Soviet Union. Because Soviet industry was so dominant and powerful, it could be neither circumvented nor simply nudged along. The only viable options were frontal attack or compromises benefiting the captains of industry. Naturally, the old communist establishment preferred the latter option. With its limited state industry, China could bear the resulting costs, whereas in the Soviet Union those costs were overwhelming.

Another structural disparity was that Soviet enterprises were predominantly large-scale and mechanized, while China was dominated by manual labor. Any reform in the Soviet Union had to touch upon large enterprises. Even Soviet agriculture aimed at economies of scale, and a normal collective farm had some 5,000 hectares and matching equipment, because small firms and farms were perceived as backward in the Soviet Union.

While China's defense expenditures were high by international standards, those of the Soviet Union were outlandish. The Soviet Union had to try to reduce its defense outlays from about one-quarter of GDP to perhaps one-twentieth. This required both arms control agreements with the United States and withdrawal from Afghanistan, two major problems that absorbed much of the leaders' time. China had no corresponding concerns.

Macroeconomic policy varied greatly between the Soviet Union and China. Gorbachev allowed the previously small budget deficit to rise to 6 percent of GDP in 1986, and it only grew. By ignoring this deficit, Gorbachev guaranteed a future macroeconomic crisis with high inflation. Nobody who was anybody in the Soviet Union had a clue about macroeconomics. Not even the top Soviet academicians knew that a budget deficit could be damaging or that it needed to be financed. "Macroeconomics" was about as negative a word as "capitalism." Among the many senior officials Gorbachev appointed, none was younger than he, and no nonparty heretics were permitted, and of course no foreigners. China had not fallen as deep into the enforced economic ignorance of communism as the Soviet Union, presumably because its period of communist rule had been much shorter.

Unlike China, the Soviet Union was also hit by a major external shock. In China, the memory of hyperinflation in the 1940s was vivid, and macroeconomic conservativism prevailed. The Soviet Union had benefited from very high international oil prices throughout the 1970s, which had precluded reforms. In the 1980s, oil prices fell, reaching their lowest level in 1986, when Gorbachev launched perestroika, and they were to stay low for years. Together with the large budget deficit, the low oil prices undermined the Soviet Union's international finances, which drove the need for more radical reforms (Gaidar 2006). China was less dependent on commodity prices.

In the end, the situations in China and the Soviet Union differed in almost every political and economic regard. The problem was not that Gorbachev did not follow the Chinese lead but rather that he followed it too closely under very different circumstances. Both countries experimented, but the Soviet Union suffered more from the lack of economic theory. The Chinese were sufficiently aware of public finances to avoid any financial crisis, while the Soviet leaders were profoundly ignorant and brought their country to the verge of the abyss of hyperinflation. In China, central power was sufficient, which was not the case in the Soviet Union. The Chinese experienced a profound sense of crisis after the Cultural Revolution, while the dominant Soviet view after the Brezhnev period was that change was not only wrong but impossible. The Soviet bureaucracy was strong and adamantly opposed to reform, while the Chinese bureaucracy was relatively smaller and softened by the Cultural Revolution. The Soviet people had seen too many reforms to react positively, whereas the Chinese embraced reform enthusiastically. The large-scale and overindustrialized Soviet Union could not avoid reforming large industrial companies, while those companies were marginal in China and could be omitted from reform. When international oil prices fell, the Soviet Union had little choice but to reform. As a consequence of these preconditions, Soviet communism proved unreformable, while the predicament of Chinese communism goes beyond this study.

An Untenable Mix of Changes

The sudden burst of activity in the Soviet Union over 1985–87 broke two decades of petrification. The reform started from the top, which was the only possibility, with a sweeping change of leaders. Gorbachev and his colleagues concentrated on three major policies during their first three years in power: economic perestroika, new thinking in foreign policy, and glasnost, with remarkably different outcomes.

From the outset, the Gorbachev team's top priority was to revitalize the economy. Eclectically, they tried all kinds of measures with great energy, but they invariably failed. No positive impetus was added to economic growth. Shortages were greatly aggravated because tax revenues declined with the anti-alcohol campaign, and a larger share of GDP was diverted to inefficient investment. Meanwhile the campaign against "unearned incomes" reduced private food supplies. Perestroika fell miserably short of its main goal to boost economic growth. Official growth lingered at 2–3 percent a year, which probably meant actual stagnation.

Gorbachev took everybody by storm with his new thinking on foreign policy and his success in containing the arms race through arms control agreements with the United States. The Politburo also decided that the Soviet Union had to leave Afghanistan. Rather than increasing the resources available for Soviet armaments, Gorbachev cleverly reduced the need for more armaments. Soviet relations with the West swung from a low to an all-time high. Quite unexpectedly, his foreign policy stood out as a resounding success in the early perestroika.

Glasnost took off later than the other policies and much more gradually. It came into its own in 1987 and freedom of speech was attained in 1989. Gorbachev unleashed glasnost in order to undermine hard-line communist opposition to his reforms, but glasnost turned into an unguided missile. It condemned not only dogmatism and bureaucracy, but the very foundation of the Soviet state and especially its ruthless policies against various nationalities. Rather than strengthening the Soviet state, glasnost eventually suggested that it was not viable.

2

The Collapse: 1988–91

After two years of attempts at radical economic reform Mikhail Gorbachev concluded that little could change in the Soviet Union without profound political reform. He wanted to move toward democracy, but he was always ambiguous whether he wanted a full-fledged democracy as we understand it in the West. His purpose was to undermine the orthodox party apparatus, but he was unclear about whether to transform or demolish the party. Naturally, if he had said openly what he intended to do, he would have been ousted in short order, but what is not said is not clear.

For two and a half years, Gorbachev had been the most radical among the Soviet leaders. In November 1987, however, he was outflanked by one of his appointees, Boris Yeltsin. By ousting Yeltsin, Gorbachev made him the popular alternative to himself, and a long duel between them ensued. Eventually, Yeltsin won because he was a true revolutionary who radicalized at pace with public opinion and he was prepared to face the judgment of the voters. His ultimate victory was to be elected president of Russia in June 1991.

The period between 1988 and 1991 was extremely intense. The stage was set by the divide between three top leaders, Gorbachev, Yeltsin, and Yegor Ligachev. Gorbachev's dominant endeavor was democratization, but he faced one unexpected event after the other. National revivals surged and disputes erupted. When central planning evaporated, massive rent seeking evolved. The reformers composed a foray of reform plans in 1989–90, but in the end no plan was adopted. In 1989, the outer Soviet empire in Eastern Europe collapsed with Gorbachev's consent. In parallel, a multifaceted and profound economic collapse took place. Hapless, Gorbachev was left on a political middle ground that was rapidly disappearing, while Yeltsin rose as the master of the democratic revolution. In late 1991, the Soviet Union collapsed, an implosion that was overdetermined by multiple causes.

Elite Division: Yeltsin, Ligachev, and Gorbachev Part Company

Gorbachev appointed Yeltsin the first party secretary of Moscow in December 1985.[1] Yeltsin had spent a brief spell as Central Committee secretary and before that had been first party secretary of the Sverdlovsk region in the Urals for nine years. The Moscow party leadership was a big job, usually lending its holder a full membership in the Politburo, although Yeltsin to his chagrin was only a candidate (or alternate) Politburo member.

Living in Moscow at the time, we could feel a fresh wind after Yeltsin had come in. He broke with the privileges of the *nomenklatura*, the Soviet ruling class, taking the metro and visiting ordinary shops. Soon, complaints arose that Yeltsin had sacked so many city officials for sloppy work and corruption that the city's reserve of personnel was exhausted. Somewhat amateurishly, he set up booths in the streets to supply goods to the population, but they worked poorly because price controls and the old centralized supply system persisted. Yeltsin became very popular among Muscovites for his vibrant activity and ruthlessness against the old apparatchiks, but it was unclear whether he was a populist or a democrat.

When Gorbachev was on holiday in the summer of 1987, Ligachev chaired the Politburo and clashed with Yeltsin. After a skirmish over *nomenklatura* privileges, Yeltsin wrote to Gorbachev, submitting his resignation as first party secretary of Moscow and as a candidate member of the Politburo. His letter contained no specific political reason, only cryptic complaints about Ligachev's "unsystematic and crude" work (Yeltsin 1990, 4–7). It gives the impression of a severe collision between two strong-headed and ambitious leaders. Yeltsin later protested that Ligachev was dogmatic and authoritarian.

Gorbachev tried to ignore this conflict, but at the Central Committee plenum in October 1987, Yeltsin violated party protocol by ex promptu asking for the floor. This time his speech was political. He complained that "nothing has changed in the style of work of either the secretariat of the central committee or of Comrade Ligachev." He objected to coercion by party bosses, advocating democracy within the Communist Party, including in its highest organs. Yeltsin also criticized undue flattery of Gorbachev. He complained that perestroika had slowed down and that "people's faith began somehow to ebb." Yet, he appealed for the restoration

---

1. Overall sources for this section and the next are Aron (2000), Brown (1996), Ligachev (1993), and Yeltsin (1990).

of Leninist principles and did not abandon communism (Yeltsin 1990, 144–47). Yeltsin sensed the radicalization of the public mood, which soon mounted to a revolutionary wave, and he realized that the reforms were insufficient.

Gorbachev, obviously surprised, summarized Yeltsin's critique and invited other members of the Central Committee to comment. One after the other, the old party hacks savaged Yeltsin in lockstep in an old-style communist onslaught. Even liberal Aleksandr Yakovlev and mild Prime Minister Nikolai Ryzhkov joined the attack. Gorbachev ordered a vote and the Central Committee unanimously condemned Yeltsin's speech as "politically erroneous." A couple of weeks later, he was hospitalized with severe chest pain. While Yeltsin was in the hospital, Gorbachev ordered him to come to the Moscow party committee on November 11, 1987. Pumped with tranquilizers, Yeltsin was forced to run a political gauntlet led by Gorbachev. All the speakers scolded Yeltsin for unimaginable mischief. Yeltsin was shocked and devastated by their virulence. He confessed his guilt in the old party fashion, and the party committee sacked him in great unity (Aron 2000).

In this ugly moment, Gorbachev succumbed to typical old Stalinist persecution. But, to quote Talleyrand, it was worse than a crime, it was a blunder. This was the political turning point for perestroika, marking the split of the liberals from Gorbachev. For the first time, Gorbachev had been outflanked by a top liberal and he would never retrieve his position as a leading radical. Yeltsin, with his strong political instinct, would continue to ride the wave of radicalization.

After this party meeting, however, Gorbachev returned to his usual mild manner. He phoned Yeltsin himself and offered him a position as a junior minister of construction, which Yeltsin accepted, disappearing from the public stage for some time. Two years later, Yeltsin (1990, 2) commented magnanimously:

> In Stalin's time ex-politicians were shot; Khrushchev pensioned them off; in Brezhnev's 'era of stagnation' they were packed off as ambassadors to distant countries. Here, too, Gorbachev's *perestroika* has set a new precedent: a dismissed politician is given the chance of returning to political life.

On March 13, 1988, the hard-line communist newspaper *Sovetskaya Rossiya* published a full-page article by Nina Andreeva, an unknown lecturer in chemistry in Leningrad. Tellingly, the title was "I Cannot Forsake My Principles." *Sovetskaya Rossiya* was an authoritative party newspaper, and this article was obviously approved by the Politburo. Cleverly, Ligachev had let this article be published when both Gorbachev and Yakovlev were going abroad, although he denied that was the case. The liberal intelligentsia was stunned because this was a Stalinist manifesto, repudiating in detail every element of glasnost and perestroika, presenting them as treason against good communism. Was perestroika dead?

Three weeks later came the relief. *Pravda*, the foremost party organ, published an equally large article that repudiated the Andreeva article. Yakovlev was the main author, but it was published without signature, which implied full party authorization. The Nina Andreeva affair was only a hiccup, but it showed how tenuous perestroika, glasnost, and Gorbachev's hold on power were. Glasnost was no longer the privilege of the liberals. They had to contend with vocal hardliners as well. The result of this affair was that its instigators, notably Ligachev, were demoted (Ligachev 1993, 298–311; Brown 1996).

At the turn of 1987, the Gorbachev group in the party leadership had fractured. Yeltsin was about to emerge as the leader of the democrats, whereas Ligachev had become the leader of the hardliners. Yakovlev and Shevardnadze stayed with Gorbachev, but Gorbachev had became a man of the political center that was going to shrink fast, although not quite yet.

Democratization

As early as December 1984, Gorbachev pronounced his desire for "democratization" (*demokratizatsiya*), but, as with everything else he said, it remained a guessing game for years what this oracle meant. To begin with, Gorbachev seems to have desired little but "to breathe new life into existing institutions and to remove the formalism of intra-party life and in the activity of the soviets," as Brown (1996, 155) saw it, which was hardly "democratization" but political liberalization.

Over time, Gorbachev grew more radical, as he realized how difficult it was to revitalize Soviet society and economy. In January 1987, the Central Committee held a plenum, which became the starting point for Russia's democratization, and Gorbachev's speech was a radical departure: "Perestroika itself is possible only through democracy and thanks to democracy. It is the only way to give scope to socialism's most powerful creative force—free labor and free thought in a free country" (Gorbachev 1987c, 317). Gorbachev proposed real elections within the party. The plenum did not make concrete decisions about democratization, but it decided that a rare party conference was to take the issue further.

The 19th Party Conference in June–July 1988 marked a new degree of glasnost. For the first time, Soviet citizens could see Politburo members being attacked on national television. Yeltsin and Ligachev indulged in a public duel, and Ligachev's words—"You are wrong, Boris!"—became a popular saying. Ryzhkov accused Yeltsin of "political nihilism." Gorbachev let radicals and conservatives fight it out, balancing one another, and he towered over the proceedings. The road lay open for the destruction of the CPSU and the democratic transformation of the Soviet Union. Gorbachev's power had reached its peak.

The resolutions of the 19th Party Conference incredibly introduced real elections. The bogus parliament, the Supreme Soviet, which met ceremoniously twice a year for a couple of days to rubber-stamp one or two laws, was to be replaced with a large new USSR Congress of People's Deputies. It would have 2,250 members, of which 1,500 would be elected and 750 selected by political or social organizations, such as the CPSU. Any candidate could be nominated and free elections were supposed to prevail, but no political party other than the CPSU was permitted. The Congress, in turn, would within itself elect a bicameral Supreme Soviet that would be convened as an ordinary legislating parliament for eight months a year.

This solution was pure Gorbachev. It was a compromise that was somehow accepted by everybody but drove developments in the direction he desired. The hardliners thought they could manipulate the elections and maintain their dominance, while reformers saw a big step forward. A major reform required plenty of legislation and the new parliament offered substantial legislative capacity. The problem, however, was that the large Congress of People's Deputies was too cumbersome to work. Nor was it representative, as the elections/appointments were not very democratic, and the Supreme Soviet was even less representative. Gorbachev had built a house of cards that was a transitional solution, and it was unclear how it would evolve.

Gorbachev was equally radical in his treatment of the party. In all but name, he abolished both the Politburo and the Central Committee Secretariat. Although the secretariat persisted formally, it stopped meeting, because Ligachev remained its chair. It was replaced by six Central Committee Commissions, which worked independently of one another. Gorbachev also slashed the size of the Central Committee apparatus, the heart of the party, halving its number of departments. Ligachev (1993, 109–10) commented:

> The commissions were established, and the secretariat's meetings simply ended of their own accord. The Party was deprived of an operating staff for its leaders. This had a deleterious effect on the activity of both the Central Committee and the regional Party committees. Executive discipline decreased sharply, and control weakened. . . . The center seemed to vanish and vertical ties as well.

Gorbachev was destroying the CPSU from the top, but since the party remained his center of power, he was sawing the branch upon which he sat. Reformers advised him to abandon the party altogether. By staying the head of an organization that he had discredited and failed to reform, he undermined his own power. Furthermore, by weakening "democratic centralism," that is, the dictatorship within the party, he gave party hardliners free sway to attack liberals and himself.

The first semi-free parliamentary elections to the Congress of People's Deputies of the USSR were held on March 26, 1989. One-third of the deputies were appointed by social organizations, including 100 top officials by the CPSU, headed by Gorbachev. Other political parties were not permitted, and the possibilities of campaigning were very limited. The elections were reasonably free in the western parts of the USSR, the most nationalist republics, and the big cities. The turnout was Soviet-like at nearly 90 percent, and 87 percent of the candidates elected were members of the CPSU. Yet, by this time party membership did not mean all that much. About one-third of the deputies were reformers. The leading drama in the elections was Yeltsin's election as a deputy for the city of Moscow, winning almost 90 percent of the votes after a magnificent grassroots campaign. Yeltsin had established himself as the democratically elected political leader, whereas Gorbachev was appointed by the CPSU.

Somewhat foolhardily, Gorbachev became chairman of the USSR Congress of People's Deputies. In May-June 1989, the first session of the Congress marked the breakthrough of freedom of speech in Russia, and Gorbachev as its active chairman was scolded by liberals and hardliners alike, which undermined his authority. In addition, its long sessions demanded far too much of his time.

The Brezhnev constitution of 1977 was the first Soviet constitution to mention the CPSU, and its Article 6 enshrined its leading role and thus its monopoly of power. At the USSR Congress of People's Deputies in December 1989, Academician Andrei Sakharov, the saint of the liberal opposition, called for the elimination of Article 6. Gorbachev rebuffed Sakharov and loud deputies jeered him away from the podium. Sakharov shook his head sadly and died a few days later. Gorbachev attended his funeral. The Central Committee made the decisive recommendation to abolish Article 6 in February 1990. Gorbachev caught up with Sakharov's demand, but rather than being the trailblazer, he had become a reluctant accepter always lagging behind the revolution that was about to gain momentum. The public dispute with Sakharov just before his death damaged Gorbachev's reputation.

Finally, Gorbachev decided to "legalize" his own position and become president of the USSR rather than only general secretary of the Communist Party. He had replaced old Andrei Gromyko ("Mr. Nyet") as chairman of the USSR Supreme Soviet in October 1988. In March 1990, the Congress of People's Deputies instituted the new office of president of the USSR. Gorbachev made his perhaps most fatal mistake when he decided not to go for a popular election of himself. The president was to be elected by the USSR Congress of People's Deputies, which had a guaranteed communist majority. Gorbachev was elected, but humiliatingly only 59 percent of the deputies voted for him and 495 of 1,878 votes cast were against him in an uncontested ballot (Aron 2000, 371–72; White 1993, 66). According to the best opinion polls, he still enjoyed the approval of 49 percent of the Russian population in December 1989, but one year later his rating had fallen to 14 percent, never to recover (Brown 1996, 271).

National Revival and Disputes

An age-old concern of Soviet leaders had been the national question. Like the Habsburg Empire, the multinational Russian Empire had been called "a prison of nations." Each Soviet leader had his own pertinent understanding of how to handle this intrinsic problem.

In his Machiavellian style, Stalin made sure to divide territories so that each troublesome nationality faced another problematic nationality in its own territory, having to appeal to Moscow for support. During World War II, he deported 11 large ethnic groups altogether to Siberia and Central Asia, notably the Volga Germans, the Crimean Tartars, the Chechens, and several other people in Northern Caucasus. In addition, he carried out mass deportations and massacres of elites. After the Baltic nations and Western Ukraine were incorporated into the Soviet Union during World War II, large parts of their populations were deported to Siberia or executed.

Brezhnev, by contrast, tried to keep everybody happy in their own corner. He allowed the titular ethnic group in each republic to dominate the local politics as never before, even accepting discrimination against ethnic Russians in all the union republics. Yet, manifestations of national revival were clamped down upon with as much violence as was necessary, and many nationalists were imprisoned.

When Gorbachev became Soviet leader, the share of ethnic Russians had declined to only 53 percent of the Soviet people. French historian Hélène Carrère d'Encausse (1978) argued that the greatest threat to the Soviet Union was that most newly born Soviet children would soon be Muslim. While she rightly focused on the national threat to the Soviet Union, it came from the more developed nations in the western and southern part of the union rather than from the underdeveloped east. Unlike his hardened predecessors, Gorbachev was uniquely naïve about national issues. His 1987 book *Perestroika* illustrates his delusions:

> The Revolution and socialism have done away with national oppression and inequality, and ensured economic, intellectual and cultural progress for all nations and nationalities. . . . If the nationality question had not been solved in principle, the Soviet Union would never have had the social, cultural, economic and defense potential as it has now. Our state would not have survived if the republics had not formed a community based on brotherhood and cooperation, respect and mutual assistance. . . . Socialism, which has helped each nation to spread its wings, has all the conditions for solving nationality problems on the basis of equality and cooperation. (Gorbachev 1987b, 118–19)

Gorbachev repeated old Soviet propaganda, but his actions indicated that he believed this propaganda. He persistently ignored national problems. When they exploded he tried to explain them away as unrelated to nationalism. As a consequence, his reign was shaken by one national conflict worse than the other, and Gorbachev was invariably caught off-guard. He did not understand that if he eased political repression, not only democracy but also national struggles would erupt.

Cautious Brezhnev had selected the first party secretary from the dominant ethnic group in each union republic. In December 1986, however, Gorbachev replaced an old Brezhnev protégé as first secretary of Kazakhstan with a Russian outsider, Gennady Kolbin. Riots broke out in Kazakhstan's capital of Alma-Ata, and Moscow responded with its old repressive tactics, leaving some people dead and many injured. Although Kolbin's appointment was an obvious mistake, he was not replaced until 1989, with a Kazakh, Nursultan Nazarbayev (who remains Kazakhstan's president).

The three Baltic nations, Estonia, Latvia, and Lithuania, had all been independent in the interwar period. Because of the Molotov-Ribbentrop Pact between the Soviet Union and Nazi Germany in August 1939, they were occupied by the Red Army in July 1940 and forcefully incorporated into the Soviet Union. A hopeless guerilla war continued for many years after the end of World War II, and these nations never accepted their occupation, although a large part of the population was deported or executed. Humanely, Gorbachev reacted against the repression in the Baltics and eased it, but the Balts showed him no gratitude, demanding independence instead. In 1988, broad anticommunist national fronts were formed in all three republics. They held huge, peaceful manifestations centered around their traditional song festivals. From 1989, they openly stated their aim of national independence. Baltic nationalism was so strong that it penetrated the republican communist parties. In December 1989, the Lithuanian Communist Party departed from the CPSU. The Estonian Communist Party took the same course in March 1990, and the more hard-line Latvian Communist Party split (Lieven 1993).

In the Baltic countries, Gorbachev demonstrated that he did not understand nationalism. He appreciated the Balts' liberalism, and seemed personally hurt that they still wanted to secede from his country. During repeated visits, Gorbachev was perplexed and infuriated, but most of all sad. Unlike Gorbachev, the Balts knew what they wanted, and they got it. In the first reasonably free republican parliamentary elections in February–March 1990, the popular fronts won landslide victories with more than two-thirds majority in each of the three national parliaments, and they assumed executive power. They declared their independence from the Soviet Union, which responded with an oil embargo on Lithuania. The Balts were ready for an endgame that could only lead to national sovereignty.

In the Caucasus, Orthodox Christian Armenia and Muslim Azerbaijan harbored old animosities. Stalin had left an Armenian exclave, Nagorny Karabakh, in neighboring Azerbaijan in his endeavor to aggravate national conflicts. In February 1988, the regional council of Nagorny Karabakh demanded their territory be transferred to Armenia, their ethnic homeland. Hundreds of thousands of demonstrators gathered in Armenia's capital of Yerevan to support their demand. Azerbaijanis responded with a popular pogrom against Armenians in the industrial Azerbaijani city of Sumgait, in which at least 32 people died. The Kremlin insisted that no borders must be redrawn, which alienated both nations (Brown 1996).

After the Sumgait massacre, the Soviet Union was caught in a hamster's wheel of aggravating national conflicts. The small elite troops, the special forces (*spetsnaz*) of the Ministry of Interior, were sent to quash one national wildfire after another in escalating bloodshed.

Georgia was another ancient Caucasian nation. Although it had belonged to the Russian empire for nearly two centuries, with a brief interruption in 1918–21, it harbored a strong nationalist opposition against the repressive local communist leadership. On April 9, 1989, the Soviet military attacked a peaceful demonstration of thousands of Georgian nationalists in the capital of Tbilisi with poison gas and spades, killing 20 demonstrators and injuring hundreds. This massacre attracted considerable publicity. Gorbachev and his associates denied responsibility, which remained murky. The local hard-line communist leaders were blamed and sacked, but the massacre was probably instigated by conservative communists in Moscow. Nationalists won the relatively free parliamentary elections in the spring of 1990 and assumed executive power (Slider 1997).

In January 1990, a sudden and vicious pogrom of the city's large Armenian community occurred in Azerbaijan's capital of Baku. As usual, Soviet internal troops were flown in. Subsequently, I spoke with a Soviet major in the special forces. He estimated that some 600 to 700 people had been killed in a massive bloodletting during one single night and thought Moscow had provoked it. This was the worst massacre Soviet forces carried out under Gorbachev's leadership, but it received little public attention because the Azerbaijani nationalists might also have been guilty. As a consequence, the Popular Front of Azerbaijan lost out, and strict communist dictatorship prevailed in that republic. In Armenia, on the other hand, the nationalist opposition won the upper hand. After Armenia and Azerbaijan had become independent, full war broke out between them over Nagorny Karabakh in February 1992.

National strife was aggravating ever faster, as law and order broke down. One of the most absurd, and awful, incidents occurred in the Osh region in southern Kyrgyzstan in the summer of 1990. Regional party officials gave a collective farm where ethnic Uzbeks worked to ethnic Kyrgyz. Kyrgyz and Uzbek peasants started slaughtering one another, and before the authorities had gotten the situation under control, some 300 people had been killed.[2] This happened in the fertile but poor and overpopulated Fergana Valley. Worries arose that this region would explode into warfare between the Kyrgyz, Uzbeks, and Tajiks who shared it. Fortunately, that has not happened yet.

---

2. According to conversations with local officials in Osh in 1998.

In short, Gorbachev's nationality policy was nothing but a disaster, because he never recognized nationalism as a force. By the summer of 1990, Moscow had lost control of the three Baltic countries, Armenia, and Georgia. Armenia and Azerbaijan were about to go to war, while Tajikistan, Georgia, and Moldova were on the cusp of civil wars of varying severity. Yet Gorbachev used as little violence as possible, and Dominic Lieven's (2000) judgment holds that no empire has collapsed with so little bloodshed, for which both Gorbachev and Yeltsin should be honored.

The Demise of the Plan and the Rise of Rent Seeking

Gorbachev's economic reforms were eclectic but driven by a strong sense of direction.[3] After all the minor reforms had failed, Gorbachev wanted to proceed with more radical economic reforms, with decentralization within the state system and liberalization on the margin. These ideas pertained to a socialist market economy, although rarely stated, because the reformers avoided an ideological conceptualization to escape the wrath of hard-line communists. They spoke about "marketization" but added the attribute "socialist" and they never talked about a "free market." Eventually, they proposed "de-statization" (*razgosudarstvlenie*), but never privatization (*privatizatsiya*). Soviet reformers frowned upon macroeconomics as wicked capitalism, which explains their near-complete ignorance of this subject. Major Marxist dogmas, such as the necessity of nationalization and the dislike of money and free prices, remained strong.

American capitalism was continuously condemned as cruel and inhuman. Instead, the Gorbachev reformers praised three other capitalist models, the Swedish, German, and Japanese models.[4] They sought a maximal social welfare state, with huge social transfers that required high progressive income taxes. They also focused on two Soviet experiences, Alexei Kosygin's partial reforms of 1965 and Lenin's radical New Economic Policy of the 1920s.

In reality, however, the Soviet reformers did not choose any economic model, but cherry-picked. Soviet economists were surprised by Gorbachev's radicalism and poorly prepared intellectually for real market reform. They had not been allowed to travel abroad or study foreign economic literature, and few knew foreign languages. The top academic

---

3. An overall source to this section is Åslund (1991).

4. In 1988 and 1990, I participated in a Soviet-Swedish roundtable on economic reform in Sweden and Moscow, respectively. It involved senior Soviet reform economists, notably Leonid Abalkin, Abel Aganbegyan, and Anatoly Milyukov, and primarily right-wing Swedish social democratic reformers. The Soviet reformers were earnest about learning about the Swedish experience. They held similar roundtables with Japanese economists.

economists had been used to criticizing shortcomings in their existing system and offering incremental improvements. Foreign advice was not acceptable until 1990. Under these conditions, the Russian reform was bound to be a tortuous process of trial and error.

Reformers tried to undertake all ideologically permissible reforms. They could make headway when their reform proposals found support among state enterprise managers, who had become a key constituency, but the managers accepted only what benefited their material interests. The unintended consequence was that the naïve Soviet reformers contributed to the building of an extraordinary machine of rent seeking.[5]

On the one hand, each reform undermined communist dogmas and helped liberalize both the economy and society. On the other, the reforms contributed to the enrichment of a small elite of state enterprise managers and related operators. These partial reforms actually aggravated economic performance and caused an extraordinary macroeconomic crisis (Boycko 1991; Murphy et al. 1992, 1993). But this policy also drove a wedge between the newly rich and the old party ideologists, dividing the *nomenklatura* (Dobbs 1997). Large-scale rent seeking caused a horrendous economic crisis and facilitated the peaceful collapse of the Soviet Union.

By 1987, Gorbachev's patience had run out. He organized a Central Committee plenum on economic reform in June 1987, which made the most important economic decisions of his reign. The Soviet leadership adopted the principal documents on the reform of the state economy, namely the Law on State Enterprises and Basic Provisions for Fundamental Perestroika of Economic Management. They were complemented with 10 decrees on major functions of the economic system and published as a book (*O korennoi perestroiki* 1987). This first attempt at a comprehensive reform came into force in January 1988. However, the outline of this reform compared poorly in quality, clarity, and consistency with the similar Hungarian socialist market reform of 1968, because many basic principles were muddled by compromise.

The outcome of the reform was very different from what Gorbachev had intended. From 1987 until 1991, he built a hothouse of rent seeking, undoubtedly without realizing that he was doing so (Yasin 2002, 118–21). The economic reforms contributed to this rent seeking by minimizing central oversight over state enterprises without demanding accountability, introducing free-wheeling cooperatives, accepting unregulated banks, and partially liberalizing foreign trade (Åslund 1996). The adverse results of all these partial reforms led to a continuous radicalization of the emerging economic thinking on markets.

---

5. Rents can be defined as "profits in excess of the competitive level" (Brealey and Myers 2000).

Partial Foreign Trade Deregulation

One of Gorbachev's first reforms was a partial liberalization of foreign trade. It started as early as August 1986, long before the domestic market was liberalized. Its primary goal was to break the foreign trade monopoly of the Ministry of Foreign Trade to the benefit of large state enterprises.

By 1988, more than 200 corporations had been granted the right to pursue foreign trade, and by 1990 their number approached 20,000 (Åslund 1991, 141). This liberalization was very popular among the managers of big state corporations, because they obtained an opportunity to make money through arbitrage on the enormous differences between low domestic prices and many-times-higher world prices.

In parallel, up to 3,000 so-called currency coefficients were introduced, as every significant foreign trade good was assigned its own exchange rate. The ratio between these currency coefficients varied from 1 to 20, offering extraordinary opportunities for arbitrage. In late 1990, these coefficients were replaced by a unified commercial exchange rate, but even so the Soviet Union had one official rate, one commercial rate, and one plummeting black market exchange rate, permitting ever greater arbitrage gains.

State Enterprises: Freedom Without Accountability

The Law on State Enterprises changed everything for state enterprises. It did not abolish central planning, but it brought about a stalemate. The state could no longer govern enterprises, but nor could enterprises rely on any market. The Soviet economy was neither here nor there. It was about to fall into a deep chasm between two systems.

An eternal ambition of all bureaucrats is to perfect administration. Several organizational changes were attempted. At the top, the aim was to improve central coordination by introducing superministerial bodies or by merging ministries. The reformers wanted to weaken the industrial ministries. Therefore, the number of union ministries was reduced from 64 in 1979 to 55 in March 1988 to 37 in July 1989. The staff of the ministries was reduced by no less than 46 percent, from 1.6 million in 1986 to 871,000 in 1989 (Goskomstat SSSR 1990, 50).

A traditional Soviet dilemma had been how to link enterprises to ministries. An array of intermediary associations had been tried, but Gorbachev wanted to do away with them to emasculate their "petty tutelage" of enterprises. As a result, each ministry would supervise about a thousand industrial enterprises, which was impossible. Gorbachev responded by calling for a merger of the 37,000 industrial enterprises into several thousand large production associations. The outcome was that the branch ministries, which had virtually owned the state enterprises, could no longer supervise them, so enterprises gained great autonomy. However, no market could evolve amidst huge and rising shortages, and the result was chaos rather than a more market-oriented order.

Workers' self-management was a vital part of the Law on State Enterprises, and by the end of 1987 more than 36,000 managers had been elected in industry and construction. Gorbachev himself had taken a clear stand in favor of workers' self-management as early as December 1984:

> Marx, Engels, and Lenin considered a transition to self-management by workers a practical task for the proletariat from the moment it assumed power. The main content of this idea was to assure an ever larger mass of workers' real, practical participation in management. (Gorbachev 1987a, 82)

Initially, "self-management" transferred the power over enterprises from ministries to local party committees, which organized "elections" through actual appointments, but this aroused such public criticism that the managers won. By 1989, managers could no longer be removed and had effectively become quasi-owners of state enterprises. The dream of workers' democracy, however, never became a reality in the Soviet Union.

On paper, the Law on State Enterprises abolished central planning: "Annual plans are elaborated and confirmed by an enterprise independently on the basis of its five-year plan and concluded economic agreements."[6] Yet, enterprises were admonished to consider control figures, state orders, long-term economic normatives, and quotas, which allowed the central planning authorities to command enterprises as before. This turned out to be one of many Pyrrhic victories of the conservatives, because glasnost allowed an extraordinary public reaction against Gosplan for its failure to implement the reform. By 1990, this central tutelage had collapsed. The enterprise managers were free to do what they wanted.

Both Soviet conservatives and reformers chose pricing as the central battleground for a genuine public debate. Reformers rightly saw price liberalization as critical for the success of market reform, while the conservatives felt confident of political support from the bureaucracy, the public, and communist ideology. Given the prevalence of shortages, price liberalization would mean much higher prices, which was naturally unpopular. To the public, price reform meant higher prices of heavily subsidized meat. As a result, the price reforms adopted in 1987 were partial and contradictory. Prices for enterprises could be raised but not prices of consumer staples. Prices of the most important products remained centrally fixed, but more prices could be set independently. The idea was to reduce state subsidies and bring prices closer to world market prices. In reality the opposite happened because of aggravated macroeconomic imbalances, the plummeting exchange rate, and the prohibition against any significant adjustment of consumer prices. Enterprises could alter their production mix to products with higher margins, which led to aggravated economic

---

6. *Pravda*, July 1, 1987.

performance, hidden inflation, and shortages. Why produce more if you could raise prices instead?

Gradually, finances and money became relevant to enterprises, but here the ministries held sway in the formal economy. They refused to standardize taxes, and corporate profit tax rates varied by enterprise from 0 to 90 percent (Shmelev 1988, 166). Nor were these tax rates stable, but adjusted by the ministries at will. Well-managed enterprises were penalized, while loss makers benefited.

After a couple of years, the managers assumed supreme control over "their" state enterprises and were not accountable to anybody. They possessed the cash-flow rights but not the control rights, which meant that they could tap money from the enterprise but not sell it. Through its very failure, the Law on State Enterprises demonstrated the need for a fundamental reform of the very economic system.

Cooperatives: The First Real Private Enterprises

In 1986, the Law on Individual Labor Activity legalized a multitude of microenterprises designed for craftsmen. In May 1988, the revolutionary Law on Cooperatives was enacted. Its contents were amazingly liberal, representing the real breakthrough for private enterprise in the Soviet Union.

The Law on Cooperatives was the first legal act with consistent market economic thinking. Any three adults could open a cooperative, and they were allowed to hire as many people as they wanted. These cooperatives were truly self-managing, self-financing, and profit-oriented. They operated freely on the market without plans, centralized supplies, or price regulation. The law explicitly permitted cooperatives to engage in any kind of activity not forbidden by law. They could even set up banks and pursue foreign trade. The only formal requirement was to register their statutes with the local authorities, who were compelled to decide within one month whether to approve them. Unlike individual labor, the cooperatives benefited from very low tax rates, even if tax practices were unstable.

This was a complete victory for the reformers. Gorbachev declared unequivocally: "We need highly efficient and technically well-equipped cooperatives that are capable of providing goods and services of the highest quality and competing with domestic and foreign enterprises."[7] Reformist Academician Leonid Abalkin argued that cooperatives would saturate the market demand for goods and services of high quality, mobilize additional labor, and stimulate state production to become less bureaucratic.[8]

Soon, stunning cooperatives emerged that looked like modern Western companies. In Moscow, one of the first new cooperatives was a wonderful

---

7. *Pravda*, March 24, 1988.

8. *Voprosy ekonomiki*, no. 11, 1987, 142.

Russian restaurant on Kropotkinskaya Street. Unlike Soviet restaurants, it was cozy, had excellent service, and served the best of Russian food, but its prices were Western. Because of their economic freedom, these new enterprises offered better services and products of higher quality, and their economic efficiency was invariably impressive. The government promoted cooperatives as a success in a propaganda campaign.

Regardless of excellent economic results, a massive popular reaction against the first cooperatives and private enterprises surfaced as early as the summer of 1987. Most upsetting to this still-socialist society was the sudden emergence of large, unconcealed private earnings. On March 21, 1987, a harbinger was a headline in the popular broadsheet *Komsomolskaya pravda*: "They Will Become Millionaires!" The few bold entrepreneurs who skimmed the market did very well. Another concern was high cooperative prices, which were probably three to four times higher than state prices because of massive shortages. The very idea of free pricing was as incomprehensible as it was indecent to many Soviet citizens. Naturally, complaints about economic crime and immorality emerged. Competition and taxes were minimal and regulations vague. Nobody knew how long this bonanza would last. The whole setup appeared designed to make a few people rich, but Abalkin explained that these cushy conditions had been established "deliberately to enliven and develop that sphere."[9]

The new cooperatives were real capitalist enterprises, running counter to all the principles of the socialist economy. Repercussions were multiple. They made enterprise money real money. A black market for the "wooden" account rubles for transactions between enterprises developed, valuing them at one-third of ordinary cash rubles in early 1990.

As state enterprise managers were becoming increasingly independent of the ministries, they wanted to channel the fortunes in their state corporations to themselves. Managers established private cooperatives on a mass scale and attached them to "their" state enterprises to transfer dead enterprise money into their own pockets. They sold attractive goods at low state prices to their private cooperatives, which accumulated the profit. Soon, they passed on the profit to offshore companies to keep it safe abroad. This management theft mechanism was fully established by mid-1988. From that moment, it was only a matter of time before the economic system would collapse (Yasin 2002, 118; Solnick 1998). Not only the state enterprise managers but also most of the later oligarchs started their businesses as cooperatives in 1988. Legalized theft from state enterprises through cooperatives and foreign trade was the name of the game.

Other forms of nonstate ownership emerged as well. The Law on State Enterprises allowed various forms of self-management, blurring the distinction between cooperatives, self-managed units of state enterprises, and leaseholds. At the end of 1987, joint stock companies with private owner-

9. Soviet Television, Foreign Broadcast Information Service, April 1, 1988, 55.

ship were also formed without any support from new legislation. Thousands of enterprise managers "leased" their state enterprises, which became a means of gradual spontaneous privatization.

Complete polarization prevailed in the debate over ownership. Reformers made cooperatives the centerpiece of their attack on the command economy, with ample support from state enterprise managers, whose strong material interest explains the political success of cooperatives. Another reason was that the Law on Cooperatives was so lucid and categorical that it was difficult to roll back. The hardliners understood the danger and mounted a determined struggle, but they lost.

The Rise of an Unregulated Banking Sector

Peculiarly, the Law on Cooperatives even allowed the formation of commercial banks as cooperatives. Soon cooperative banks mushroomed without any regulation. At the time of the collapse of the Soviet Union, Russia already had 1,360 registered commercial banks (Johnson 2000).

Throughout the world, banks are the most regulated companies, but not so in the late Soviet Union. People were allowed to set up banks with minimal knowledge and tiny capital. These banks became means of activating dead enterprise money and many banks were attached to state enterprises. The old state banks joined the spoils by multiplying through splits.

In 1990, inflation started to rise, but the government refused to increase state interest rates from the low single digits. As a consequence, private commercial banks gained huge inflationary profits. They extracted vast state credits at minimal nominal interest rates, effectively usurping the mounting inflation tax.

Eventually, the Soviet Central Bank, Gosbank, tried to regulate the new commercial banks, but in 1990 it encountered competition from the newly formed Central Bank of Russia. These two central banks started competing for bank registration by driving down both taxation and reserve requirements for banks, leaving the banks the most deregulated companies in the Soviet Union. They also competed in the issue of credit. Any serious budding future capitalist established his own commercial bank. With such a banking sector, hyperinflation could hardly be avoided.

A Perfect Rent-Generating Machine

A perfect rent-generating machine had been constructed. The liberalization of foreign trade allowed state enterprises to carry out arbitrage between low domestic prices of raw materials and high world market prices and between greatly varied exchange rates. The Law on State Enterprises permitted enterprises to keep the remaining profits, which had previously been confiscated by the state at the end of a year. The new cooperatives made it possible for enterprise managers to transfer the profits of their state enterprises to their private companies. The new commercial banks provided them with cheap state credits to finance their business.

One example illustrates how outrageous the distortions and rent seeking were. In 1990, a pack of Marlboro cigarettes cost $1 or 30 rubles in the street, which was also the black market exchange rate on the dollar. Incidentally, the official Soviet wholesale price of one ton of crude oil was exactly 30 rubles. However, the wholesale price was set in bank money, and one could purchase three bank rubles for one cash ruble at that time. Therefore, with the right contacts, a Soviet operator could purchase three tons of crude oil, worth $300 on the world market, for $1 or one pack of Marlboro. Little wonder that oil trading became the main source of early fortunes. Similarly, Yegor Gaidar (1999, 122) noted that at the end of 1991, someone with an official export quota for oil could pay as little as one ruble for one dollar, when the free exchange rate was 170 rubles per dollar.

Ironically, this rent-seeking machine had been formed by earnest reformers who wanted to establish a market economy, but they believed in gradual reforms. They sought support from state enterprise managers against dogmatic communists, but the businesspeople only accepted reforms from which they could benefit personally. These practices are often blamed on Yeltsin and his economic reformers, but Gorbachev and Ryzhkov established them between 1987 and 1990.

A Parade of Reform Programs

The evident failure of the Gorbachev reforms of 1987–88 passed a severe judgment on partial and gradual reforms. A broad understanding evolved that economic reforms had to be more radical and comprehensive. For one year, from October 1989 to October 1990, Moscow was enamored with an intense discussion of economic reform programs.[10] None of these programs was implemented, but they had great intellectual and ideological impact because they introduced normal market economic thinking in Russia.

In early 1990, a young economist, Yegor Gaidar, published his annual economic policy review in the journal *Kommunist*. Gaidar stood out because he was almost the only Russian economist who wrote about the Soviet economy as a Western economist reviewing the macroeconomic situation. His judgment on economic policy in 1989 was severe: "The traditional administrative management system is no longer able to serve the economy, but conditions for the effective functioning of a market economy have not been created. A strange situation with an absence of economic management has emerged" (Gaidar 1990, 23).

---

10. This section draws on Åslund (1991, 206–12).

After the 19th Party Conference the CPSU apparatus lost most influence over economic policy. The Council of Ministers and its subordinated Gosplan took over. In July 1989, a Reform Commission was established under the Council of Ministers. It was headed by a leading reform economist, Leonid Abalkin, who also became deputy prime minister. In 1990, a new center of economic policymaking emerged around the president's office. In January 1990, Nikolai Petrakov, a leading reform economist, became Gorbachev's personal economic advisor, and in March 1990, when Gorbachev became president, he appointed a Presidential Council, which included Academician Stanislav Shatalin, another prominent reform economist.

The first comprehensive Soviet reform program—the Abalkin Program—was presented by the Reform Commission in October 1989. It was stunningly radical, opting for a full-fledged market economy and breaking a whole range of communist taboos. "From our own experience, we have been able to convince ourselves that there is no worthy alternative to the market mechanism for coordinating actions and interests of economic subjects." Moreover, the market had to have "free prices and economic competition to function efficiently." The Abalkin program also made advances on ownership, but it stopped short of private ownership.[11]

In parallel, Gosplan worked out an alternative, more conservative program that was presented by Prime Minister Ryzhkov in December 1989.[12] No marketization would be undertaken for three years, and the Ryzhkov program took exception to private ownership and denationalization.

In early 1990, three young economists connected with Abalkin's Reform Commission—Grigori Yavlinsky, Mikhail Zadornov, and Aleksei Mikhailov—presented their sensational "400-day program," which was inspired by the radical market reform that had just been launched in Poland. It advocated rapid and massive privatization and full marketization within 400 days to stabilize the economy. Its authors argued: "The time for gradual transformation has been missed and the inefficacy of partial reforms has been proved by the experiences of Hungary, Yugoslavia, Poland, and China."[13] Reflecting the swift political radicalization and the aggravation of the economic crisis, both Abalkin and Ryzhkov spoke approvingly of this purely capitalist program, whereas Gorbachev talked more vaguely about the need for the "radicalization of economic reform," "a full-blooded market," and "a land reform."[14]

But in March 1990, the CPSU suffered a severe blow in republican parliamentary elections. Many Soviet leaders realized that they had nothing

---

11. *Ekonomicheskaya gazeta*, no. 43, 1989.

12. *Izvestiya*, December 14, 1989.

13. *Delovoi mir*, July 31, 1990.

14. *Pravda*, March 28, 1990.

to gain from radicalization. In May 1990, Ryzhkov presented a second government reform program, which was merely a concretization of his December 1989 program. Foolhardily, this document detailed the planned increases of retail prices, unleashing a massive run on the already nearly empty shops and extraordinary hoarding, which lasted until the government announced that it would postpone the price hikes.

In June 1990, the Russian Congress of People's Deputies under Yeltsin's leadership embraced the 400-day program, which had been renamed the 500-day program. Gorbachev stunned the public by meeting Yeltsin in July 1990, seemingly giving in to Yeltsin. They agreed to form a joint working group, which would prepare a new "concept of a union treaty" and "the transition to a market economy." The economic reform debate had reached its crescendo. Gorbachev and Yeltsin sent off their top economists to a dacha outside Moscow for the month of August to write such a program. Gorbachev selected his two most liberal economists: Shatalin, who became chairman, and Petrakov. Yeltsin sent a brash band of young and radical economists, including Yavlinsky, Zadornov, and Boris Fedorov. A third group of participants was made up of outstanding economists from the Academy of Sciences. A leading liberal economist from Abalkin's Reform Commission, Yevgeny Yasin, was also included. These were the best and brightest of Russia's economists, though still no foreign input was permitted. Abalkin, however, refused to participate. He had parted company with the radical reformers. Ryzhkov was even more hostile.

The popular expectations were enormous, and the Shatalin group did not disappoint. After three weeks of perpetual work it published two books, which became a sensation. One contained the actual program and was called "Transition to the Market: Conception of a Program" (*Perekhod* 1990a). The second volume contained 21 draft legal acts (*Perekhod* 1990b). The Shatalin program advocated a rapid financial stabilization and transition to a market economy as well as large-scale privatization and a broad delegation of powers to the union republics. It contained a concrete schedule for such a transition in the course of 500 days. The word socialism was not even used. The Shatalin or 500-day program stands out as the breakthrough for nonsocialist economic thinking in the USSR. The liberal gauntlet was cast.

The government felt the heat. Without much attention, Ryzhkov and Abalkin sat with the government's top economists at another dacha outside Moscow and worked on their own program, which was ready a few days after the Shatalin program. Its tellingly bureaucratic title was "The Government Program for the Formation of Structures and Mechanisms of a Regulated Market Economy" (*Pravitel'stvennaya* 1990).

These two alternative reform programs were presented to the USSR Supreme Soviet in September 1990, and the general expectation was that Gorbachev would adopt the Shatalin program. Instead Gorbachev organized a political circus, an art in which he was far superior to Yeltsin. First, he criticized the government program because of its absence of a credible financial stabilization plan. Next, he favored a compromise between the two programs, although both sides stated that their approaches were irreconcilable. Then, he asked the highly respected liberal Academician Abel Aganbegyan to produce a synthesis. Obediently, Aganbegyan did so, but his synthesis coincided largely with the Shatalin program. Now, Gorbachev turned critical, complaining that the Aganbegyan program contained "controversial clauses." In the end, the Supreme Soviet did not adopt any program. In all likelihood, Gorbachev engaged in the 500-day program only to kill it. He waited because it was too popular and Yeltsin had embraced it, but by October 1990 he might have felt that his obfuscation had done the trick and deflated its popularity.

By October 1990, Moscow's political mood had changed, as hard-line communists went on the offensive. The reform discussion ceased. The popular sentiment was that the Soviet Union had seen too many reform programs (ten), but that nothing was done. The Soviet Union was sailing into a devastating economic crisis without a strategy. Actual economic policy became a mixture of desperate measures within the framework of the old Soviet system.

Gorbachev's politicking in September 1990 was irresponsible in the extreme. This was his last opportunity to salvage his country from hyperinflation, and he intentionally missed the moment to adopt a comprehensive program of market reform for his political intrigues. By October 1990, a consensus had evolved among serious Russian economists that hyperinflation was inevitable and that the Soviet Union was bound to collapse. The thoughtful liberal insider Yevgeny Yasin (2002, 166) reckons that Gorbachev's departure from power was set in motion by his rejection of the 500-day program. "At this moment, he gave in to the group of conservative party colleagues," who would instigate the coup in August 1991.

Gorbachev had destroyed the CPSU as a policymaking machine, and nobody ever figured out what he wanted the Presidential Council to do, so it never did anything. The Council of Ministers stopped at routine management. The Soviet Union was left without serious policymaking and thus without policy. The lonely and increasingly desperate Gorbachev devoted his time to long and empty televised speeches and to foreign policy. Not only Shatalin and Petrakov, but even Abalkin and Ryzhkov, abandoned the rudderless sinking ship within the next three months. So did Yakovlev and Shevardnadze. State administration was taken over by the conservative lower rungs of the CPSU.

Effectively, Gorbachev's presidency was over and he could as well have resigned. The only questions left were how and when the collapse would occur. At that very time, Gorbachev was awarded the Nobel Peace Prize.

Collapse of the Outer Empire

Gorbachev spent much of his time on foreign policy, especially preoccupied with summit diplomacy with the US presidents.[15] After the Intermediate-Range Nuclear Forces (INF) Treaty between the United States and the Soviet Union was concluded in 1987, Soviet military expenditures had been capped. Other agreements were less vital for the Soviet Union. To a considerable extent, they aimed at keeping the Soviet military-industrial complex at bay.

Gorbachev signed several important international agreements, notably the agreement on the reunification of Germany and the Treaty on Conventional Armed Forces in Europe, but they laid him open to accusations of giving away too much to the West. He seemed primarily interested in reconfirming the superpower status of the Soviet Union and his own position as world leader. He toyed with the idea of a "common European house," but he never imbued this concept with real substance. His prolonged love fest with the West seemed increasingly like a celebration of himself.

The main development in foreign policy in the last years of the Soviet Union was the collapse of the outer empire, the Soviet bloc in Eastern Europe—East Germany, Poland, Czechoslovakia, Hungary, Bulgaria, and Romania.[16] After the Soviet invasion of Czechoslovakia in 1968, the Soviet Union officially declared its commitment to the defense of socialism in any part of the socialist bloc. This policy was named the Brezhnev doctrine. It meant that no country that had come under Soviet dominance could become free again. The Soviet withdrawal from Afghanistan was the first harbinger of the end of the Brezhnev doctrine.

On December 7, 1988, Gorbachev made a dramatic speech to the United Nations in New York. In nonideological language, he clarified that the Brezhnev doctrine was over and that the socialist countries could choose for themselves:

> For us, the necessity of the principle of freedom and choice is clear. Denying that right of peoples, no matter what the pretext for doing so, no matter what words are used to conceal it, means infringing even that unstable balance that it has been possible to achieve. Freedom of choice is a universal principle and there should be no exception. (Gorbachev 1988)

With the bad luck that became Gorbachev's hallmark during his last years in power, a severe earthquake shook Armenia and killed some 50,000 people at about the same time that Gorbachev made his earth-shaking speech at the United Nations. He had to rush back to the Soviet Union the next day, unable to elaborate on his great speech. The Armen-

---

15. The excellent memoirs of his foreign policy aide Anatoly Chernyaev (2000) are a general source to this section.

16. The best source on the liberation of Eastern Europe is Ash (1990). See also Åslund (2002).

ian earthquake exposed the dysfuntion of the Soviet system. New apartment buildings collapsed like houses of cards because the builders had stolen cement and replaced it with sand. Rescue operations were bungled in every conceivable way. What Gorbachev had designed to be his greatest moment of international glory became a national humiliation.

The Eastern Europeans needed no explanation of Gorbachev's speech. They understood it was meant for them. Soviet rule in the region had never been legitimate, and none of these countries had chosen communism or alliance with the Soviet Union. Stalin had imposed Soviet power and the Iron Curtain upon them at the end of World War II. They had revolted repeatedly, but one at a time—East Germany in 1953, Hungary in 1956, Czechoslovakia in 1968, and Poland in 1956, 1970, 1976, and 1980. Soviet forces had quashed the popular uprisings in the first three countries, whereas the Polish communist government had done so itself. After the failure to reform Soviet socialism to adorn it with a human face in Czechoslovakia in 1968, communism had lost the little appeal it had. After 16 months of Solidarity in Poland in 1980–81, it was only a matter of time before communism in Eastern Europe would collapse.

When Gorbachev came to power in 1985, Poland and Hungary had already introduced market socialism, and their authoritarianism was mild. East Germany, Czechoslovakia, and Bulgaria, by contrast, were strict Soviet dictatorships with gerontocratic leaders. Politically, Romania was more independent from the Soviet Union, yet it was the most atrocious dictatorship, nicknamed "socialism in one family." Gorbachev showed little interest in the region and even contempt for the dogmatic Eastern European leaders. He saw them as little as protocol allowed.

Arguably, Gorbachev never had a clear policy on Eastern Europe. He was against the use of military force, and as early as 1986 he reassured the Eastern European leaders that the Soviet Union would not use armed invasions against them again (though they were hardly convinced). Gorbachev wanted good all-European relations to build his nebulous "common European house," to which the Iron Curtain and the division of Germany were serious impediments. The costs of the large Soviet garrison in East Germany seemed excessive to him. Yet he did not want to rock the boat. Until 1989, little happened in Eastern Europe, and the received wisdom was that nothing could change there without Moscow's consent.

Gorbachev's UN speech in December 1988 sounded the signal the Eastern Europeans had been waiting for: a convincing commitment that the Soviet Union would not use military force against them. Their response was swift but not what Gorbachev had expected. Within one year, the Soviet outer empire had been liquidated.

Poland and Hungary were the front-runners in reform. Gorbachev's UN speech informed their liberal communist leaders that they had better democratize to maintain authority and power. These two countries competed over democratic reforms. The Polish communist leaders convened a roundtable with the opposition and agreed to hold partially democratic parliamentary elections on June 4, 1989. That day the outer Soviet empire broke. Sixty-five percent of the seats were reserved for the communists and their allies, but Solidarity won all the free seats in a landslide victory. The Communist Party's authority was finished. Its allies started defecting to Solidarity, and by September, Solidarity was able to form a coalition government, which soon launched a radical market economic reform. Poland had carried out a peaceful transition to democracy.

The Hungarian government organized a roundtable with the opposition in the summer of 1989 that led to full democratization with free parliamentary elections in March 1990, when the communists were thoroughly defeated.

The most contentious country was East Germany. Under Erich Honecker, its regime was most dogmatic, and Gorbachev did not even try to hide his disdain for Honecker. At the 40th anniversary of the German Democratic Republic in October 1989, Gorbachev stated publicly that "life punishes those who come late." He made clear that the Soviet Union would not defend Honecker's regime. One month later not only Honecker but the whole state was gone. East Germany's political destabilization started when Hungary opened its border to Austria on September 11. Thousands of young East Germans fled through that border to West Germany, where they were welcomed as citizens. The East Germans who remained behind reacted with democratic demonstrations, which culminated on November 9, when large numbers of demonstrators, chanting "Gorby! Gorby!," stormed the hated Berlin Wall and made their way to the West. The feared East German security police were not ordered to shoot because of the restraint imposed by Gorbachev.

The East German state had no legitimacy. In parliamentary elections in March 1990, the rightwing Christian Democratic Union won, and in October 1990 East Germany acceded to the Federal Republic of Germany. The two Germanys, the Soviet Union, the United States, France, and the United Kingdom engaged in intense negotiations for almost a year on the reunification of Germany, which Gorbachev accepted with remarkable ease. Gorbachev even conceded to East Germany joining the European Union and the North Atlantic Treaty Organization (NATO).

West Germany contributed some financing, which was extremely limited, only 12 billion deutsche marks in grant financing for the transfer of Soviet troops out of East Germany plus 3 billion deutsche marks in an interest-free loan, a total of less than $12 billion (Zelikow and Rice 1995, 351–52).[17] This paltry sum may be compared with the $80 billion that West Germany poured into East Germany every year since 1990 (World Bank 2002). Even so, Gorbachev had to bargain hard for this pittance.

---

17. At the time, 1 deutsche mark was equal to $0.78.

The large Soviet tank armies in Europe were both redundant and obsolete. The West insisted on a multilateral treaty on Conventional Armed Forces in Europe (CFE), which Gorbachev accepted. It was signed in Paris in November 1990 by the United States, Russia, and 20 other countries. The collapsing Soviet Union committed itself to the withdrawal of Soviet forces from Central and Eastern Europe, which was already under way. This treaty ensured that the Soviet forces in Europe, including European Russia, would be halved and remain so restricted for the foreseeable future. It specified how many troops Russia was allowed to have in various regions. By 1994, more than half a million soldiers, dependents, and civilians had been withdrawn from Germany (Zelikow and Rice 1995, 364–65).

In Bulgaria, Todor Zhivkov, the communist dictator since 1954, was overthrown in an internal coup on November 10, 1989, the day after the fall of the Berlin Wall. The putsch appeared instigated by Moscow, but it began a democratization process that was led by reform communists. A roundtable negotiation in early 1990 led to democratic elections in June 1990, which resulted in a narrow communist victory (Bell 1997).

On November 17, 1989, the so-called Velvet Revolution started in Czechoslovakia. Hundreds of thousands of Czechs took to the streets, and after three weeks the hard-line communist President Gustáv Husák was forced to resign. Parliamentary elections were held in June 1990 and parties arising out of the opposition Civic Forum won.

The last Eastern European satellite to go was Romania. On December 21, 1989, its ruthless dictator Nicolae Ceauşescu ventured to give a speech on the balcony of the party headquarters to tens of thousands of people on a wintry day in Bucharest. Suddenly, the crowd starting booing and stormed the party building. Ceauşescu escaped from the roof by helicopter, and wild shooting broke out in the capital. A few days later, the fugitive dictator was arrested and summarily executed. Democracy ensued, but the brusque regime change favored the communists, who managed to maintain power as in Bulgaria after democratic elections.

A year after Gorbachev had told the Eastern Europeans that they could do what they wanted, they had done so. All of them had opted for full democratization, which was more than Gorbachev desired. They also wanted full market economies, unlike Gorbachev. They immediately turned their backs on the Soviet Union, abandoning the Warsaw Pact and the Council for Mutual Economic Assistance (Comecon), the Soviet bloc trade organization. Both organizations were abolished in short order. Instead, the East European nations applied for membership in the European Union. The only consolation for Gorbachev was that Bulgaria and Romania were led by reform communists, that the Soviet Union had received limited compensation from West Germany for East Germany, and that he was enormously popular in the West.

When he was awarded the Nobel Peace Prize in October 1990, Gorbachev was honored "for his leading role in the peace process which today characterizes important parts of the international community." The West and Eastern Europeans all have reasons to be grateful to Gorbachev. He allowed the peaceful democratization of six countries to the benefit of over 100 million souls.

Fortunately, Soviet hardliners were taken by even greater surprise than Gorbachev by the demise of communism in Eastern Europe and did nothing. In March 1990, Ligachev wrote a letter to the Central Committee: "The Party expects an analysis of the events in Eastern Europe from the Central Committee. The socialist community is falling apart and NATO is growing stronger. The German question is a priority." Ligachev drew the logical conclusions with considerable foresight: "The Party and Motherland are in danger, I would say in great danger. The possible breakup of our federation would be a world shock, an irreparable blow against socialism and the international Communist and workers' movement" (Ligachev 1993, 117).

The collapse of the outer Soviet empire in Eastern Europe reinforced all the anti-Gorbachev constituencies in the Soviet Union. The hardliners cemented their opposition to reform. The 500-day program was rejected at the time of Germany's reunification. Multiple nationalist movements prepared for secession. Liberals started hoping for real democracy and a market economy. As polarization intensified, Gorbachev was left hanging in the disappearing center.

In the midst of these earth-shattering events in the Soviet front yard, Gorbachev focused on arms control. Another arms control treaty—the Treaty on the Reduction and Limitation of Strategic Offensive Arms, subsequently called the START I treaty—was signed in July 1991, followed by the START II treaty concluded in 1993. START I required further deep cuts in both countries' nuclear arsenals, but unlike the INF, it did not call for the elimination of an entire category of armaments. Instead, it contained different ceilings for how many strategic nuclear weapons each side could deploy. By reducing the number of the most threatening ballistic missile warheads and substantially cutting the aggregate missile throw-weight, the START I treaty reduced the risk of nuclear attack and also allowed the superpowers to decrease their military spending significantly (Goldblat 2002, 91).

Economic Collapse

By 1989, the signs of economic crisis amassed, and in 1990 the Soviet economy entered a terminal crisis.[18] The chronic shortages became unbearable and prompted extensive rationing. The only good in surplus was money, and people hoarded whatever they could buy. Every Soviet home was filled with basic durable staples such as sugar, soap, and toilet paper. In

---

18. This section draws on Åslund (1991, 182–202) and Åslund (1995, 47–50).

Table 2.1   USSR budget revenues, expenditures, and balance, 1985–91
(percent of GNP)

	1985	1986	1987	1988	1989	1990	1991
State expenditures	49.7	52.2	52.2	52.5	51.2	51.3	n.a.
State revenues	48.0	46.5	45.9	43.3	42.6	47.2	n.a.
Budget balance	–1.7	–5.7	–6.3	–9.2	–8.6	–4.1	–31[a]

n.a. = not available

a. For Russia, European Bank for Reconstruction and Development (EBRD). Different sources give highly varying numbers.

Sources: Author's calculations from Goskomstat SSSR (1991, 15–16); EBRD (1995, 205); Åslund (1991, 193–94).

1989, coal miners went on strike when the state could not even supply them with soap.

In the early perestroika period, the traditional Soviet budget deficit of 2 to 3 percent of GDP had risen to 6 percent in 1986 (table 2.1). Expenditures on state investment, consumer subsidies, and social expenditures each increased by about 1 percent of GDP. At the same time, revenues declined because of smaller alcohol sales and lower world market prices for oil (resulting in lower foreign trade taxes). These fiscal problems were serious, although reparable, but the government just ignored them.

In the second stage of macroeconomic destabilization, 1988–89, the paramount problem was that annual wage increases more than doubled as a consequence of the Law on State Enterprises (figure 2.1). Managers concentrated on products with large profit margins, which boosted hidden inflation, and they happily passed on their inflationary gains to their workers as wage hikes. With lower tax rates, enterprise tax revenues declined by 3.7 percent of GDP from 1986 to 1989, and foreign trade taxes shrank with lower oil revenues by 1.8 percent of GDP from 1985 to 1989 (Goskomstat SSSR 1990, 612). Meanwhile, consumer subsidies grew by 3.4 percent of GDP from 1985 to 1989, because producer prices rose more than consumer prices, which were more strictly controlled. As a consequence, the budget deficit expanded to 9 percent of GDP in 1988 and 1989. The government was still able to act, drastically halving public investment expenditures from 1988 to 1990. Strangely, public expenditures remained roughly constant as a share of GDP from 1986 to 1990. The financial problems were grave but still manageable.

Toward the end of 1990, however, the Soviet macroeconomic crisis turned wild. One new driver was a populist social policy. The USSR Congress of People's Deputies suddenly decided to raise social benefits by 25 percent, in competition with the Russian legislature, and in 1991 those benefits surged beyond control by 81 percent in Russia (Åslund 1991, 188; Goskomstat 1996, 116). The communists struggled to maintain power and

Figure 2.1   USSR personal incomes, social benefits, and inflation, 1985–90

annual increase in percent

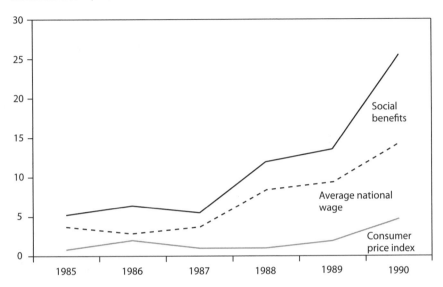

Sources: Goskomstat (1996, 116); UN Economic Commission for Europe (1992, 105, 298); EBRD (1994, 167); Åslund (1991, 188).

hold the Soviet Union together by opting for populism, sacrificing any remnant of fiscal sanity. Like state enterprises, the USSR Congress was allowed much latitude but no responsibility. Wage increases continued to accelerate, and they skyrocketed by 97 percent in 1991 (Goskomstat 1996, 116). The summer of 1990 was the last time when the Soviet economic collapse could have been averted, and when Gorbachev dismissed the 500-day program in October 1990, he sealed the fate of his country.

In 1991, state finances broke down during the final stage of macroeconomic destabilization. The decisive blow came when the union republics that had declared themselves sovereign or independent in 1990 refused to deliver their revenues to the union treasury. They did not honor Soviet legislation, competing with the union in cutting taxes. The statistics for 1991 are sketchy because the Soviet accounts for 1991 were never completed and all crises were galloping. In any case, union revenues collapsed and the budget deficit skyrocketed to 31 percent of GDP, according to the European Bank for Reconstruction and Development (EBRD 1994). By the summer of 1991, the Soviet Union was no longer a financially viable state.

The Soviet government had ceased to pursue economic policy, limiting itself to certain acts of desperation. On January 14, 1991, Minister of Finance Valentin Pavlov replaced Ryzhkov as prime minister. His preoccupation was quick fixes to improve the market balance. He instantly shocked the public by declaring large ruble banknotes null and void, causing panic. At the same time, he partially liberalized producer prices, but not retail prices. In April 1991, the Soviet government at long last raised retail prices. The average consumer price level surged by no less than 70 percent, but that was by no means sufficient to clear the market (Koen and Phillips 1993). A free commercial sector evolved with prices several times higher and it absorbed some excess demand, but it remained marginal. Because prices were not liberalized, shortages continued to aggravate. Even so, by the end of the year the consumer price index had risen by 144 percent in Russia (EBRD 1994, 167).

In 1990, after the union republics had declared themselves independent, they established their own central banks. They started issuing credits in Soviet rubles, which meant that the Soviet Union had no less than 16 mutually independent central banks issuing ruble credits in competition with one another. This monetary competition was a guarantee in itself of the collapse of the Soviet Union. William Nordhaus (1990, 302–03) estimated that in 1989 the general price level had to rise by about 50 percent to eliminate the monetary overhang, and it skyrocketed for the next two years.

The external account was strained as well, but the trade deterioration was strangely limited, according to available Western statistics (figure 2.2). Presumably, the real situation was worse but hidden from Western eyes through transactions outside the area of the Organization for Economic Cooperation and Development (OECD). Soviet exports to the West were tiny at $29 billion in 1990. They were dominated by oil, and they suffered three blows. First, world oil prices fell sharply in 1986 and stayed low. Second, Soviet oil production peaked in 1987–88 and started falling. Third, Soviet production plummeted while Soviet consumption surged, and the government reduced imports of investment goods to boost imports of food to keep popular discontent, and democratic pressures, at bay.

The foreign debt situation was considerably worse. From 1986, international loans were increasingly used to finance the Soviet budget deficit, although most of it was not financed by anything but money emission. The net foreign debt surged from $14.2 billion at the end of 1984 to $56.5 billion at the end of 1991 (figure 2.3). The outside world saw the mounting economic crisis, and the country's creditworthiness declined. As a result, foreign debt service was increasingly short term and became alarming in 1990. Soviet foreign trade enterprises failed on a massive scale to pay on time toward the end of 1989, and by the fall of 1990 the accumulated international arrears amounted to $5 billion (IMF et al. 1991). Soviet foreign debts were not all that large in themselves, but the government's refusal to deal with them until the country had run out of all foreign currency reserves was totally irresponsible.

The foreign trade data and the Soviet national assets do not tally. Something else was going on. Between 1989 and 1991, the Soviet Union used up

Figure 2.2   USSR trade with the West, 1985–91

billions of US dollars

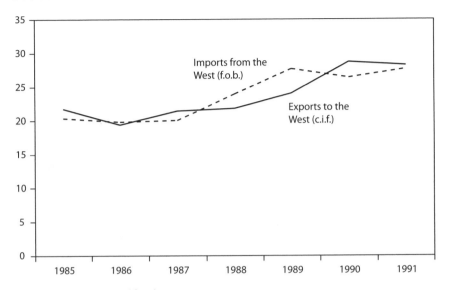

c.i.f. = cost, insurance, and freight
f.o.b. = free on board

Note: The term "West" refers to the countries in Western Europe (including Turkey and Yugoslavia), North America, and Japan.

Source: UN Economic Commission for Europe (1993, 287).

about $15 billion of international currency reserves and hit a ghastly low of $100 million in December 1991. Substantial gold reserves, presumably 1,000 tons, worth $12 billion, were sold. The considerable monetary holdings of the CPSU were transferred to certain private individuals in 1990 and 1991. A reasonable guess is that they were on the order of $20 billion. The Central Committee ordered the transfer of the money through the services of the KGB through the Soviet-owned banks abroad to select individuals. The capital flight from the Soviet Union is usually assessed at about $20 billion in each of the years 1990 and 1991, but all numbers are uncertain. What is clear is that the ailing Soviet state and the CPSU were robbed of tens of billions of dollars in cash, which was taken out of the country if it was not already abroad. The Central Committee treasurer, Nikolai Kruchina, who was in charge of this gigantic money transfer, died after falling from his home window a few days after the August 1991 coup (Klebnikov 2000, 59–66, 76; Gaidar 1999, 117–18). Russia was robbed empty.

Although the exchange rate was not liberalized officially, a partial liberalization occurred and the official exchange rate became increasingly irrelevant. The black market exchange rate was perceived by the public as the

Figure 2.3 USSR foreign debt and debt service in convertible currencies, 1985–91

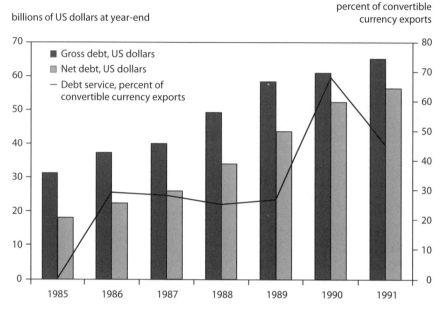

billions of US dollars at year-end

percent of convertible currency exports

- ■ Gross debt, US dollars
- ▨ Net debt, US dollars
- — Debt service, percent of convertible currency exports

Sources: UN Economic Commission for Europe (1993, 289); Christensen (1994, 42).

"real" exchange rate. For years, the standard black market exchange rate had been five rubles to the dollar, but in 1990 it moved from 20 to 30 rubles, that is, it rose six times from the end of 1988 to the end of 1990. In November 1989, the government allowed currency auctions for select state enterprises, and this overvalued official exchange rate moved from 10 rubles to the dollar at the end of 1989 to 25 rubles to the dollar by January 1991. By December 1991, the average Russian salary at the free exchange rate had plummeted to as little as $6 a month, which was a gross humiliation to the Soviet elite. As the ruble lost all value, the public hoarded cash dollars, and a far-reaching dollarization had taken place by 1991.

Officially, output grew slightly in the first five years of perestroika, but in 1990 not even official statistics could claim growth any longer, and in 1991 output approached free fall. The most plausible number is a decline in output of no less than 15 percent (figure 2.4). Because people had to spend ever more time queuing to use their money, it made little sense for them to work to earn more worthless money, and they reduced their real work time. The shortages also harmed production because factories suffered from scarcities of all kinds of inputs.

In the summer of 1990, the Group of Seven (G-7) of the wealthiest democracies in the world requested, with Gorbachev's consent, that four

Figure 2.4   USSR output, 1985–91

annual change in percent

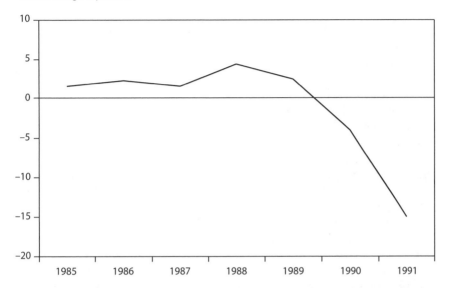

Note: This figure shows the annual growth of official net material product, a communist concept of national income, which excluded "nonmaterial" services.

Source: UN Economic Commission for Europe (1992, 105).

international financial institutions undertake a substantial study of the Soviet economy. At long last, the Soviet Union opened its doors to multiple international economic experts. The international financial institutions—the International Monetary Fund, World Bank, Organization for Economic Cooperation and Development, and the newly founded European Bank for Reconstruction and Development—published a comprehensive report in early 1991 that contained a great deal of previously secret information, and they sensibly recommended a radical economic reform as in Poland (IMF et al. 1991). But no Soviet leader was prepared to listen.

In the second half of 1991, the Soviet Union faced financial ruin. Soviet economic policy had evaporated, and no progress in economic policy occurred during the last one and a half years of Soviet government. An economic collapse was under way.

Political Collapse: Yeltsin at His Peak

In the elections to the USSR Congress of People's Deputies on March 26, 1989, Yeltsin had won in the country's largest constituency, Moscow, with more than five million or nearly 90 percent of the votes, running against a decent party representative.[19] From that moment on, Yeltsin was unstoppable, although he possessed neither organization nor media nor money. He was only a member of parliament, but he did not lose a beat. He was a lonely popular hero, but a giant, who stood up against the Communist Party and all its forces. At each turn, he dealt a new defeat to his nemesis Gorbachev and the communist establishment.

Yeltsin was a clever popular politician who played on many themes. One was liberalism and democracy. Another was radical marketization, as expressed in his wholehearted support for the 500-day program. A third theme was Russian nationalism, and a fourth was, paradoxically, sympathy for other nationalities desiring independence from Russia. He also raised populist demands for higher wages and social benefits.

In July 1989, the liberals in the new Soviet parliament formed what was called the Inter-Regional Group. One of its cochairmen was Yeltsin, who was received with suspicion by the other cochairmen, who were outstanding liberal intellectuals, such as Andrei Sakharov. Subsequently, the Inter-Regional Group would lay the foundation for the broad popular movement called "Democratic Russia," which was formed before the elections to the Russian Congress of People's Deputies in March 1990.

Foreigners often consider the Soviet Union a Russian Empire, but, curiously, Brezhnev's policy of empowering national elites had led to discrimination against Russians in all of the 14 non-Russian union republics. Unlike Russia, all those republics had their own Communist Party and Academy of Sciences, not to mention KGB and Ministry of Interior, while Russia had to make do with Soviet institutions. Aggravated economic hardship also bred Russian nationalism. This nationalism was not aggressive but defensive. It was preached by Russian nationalist writers, such as Vasily Belov and Valentin Rasputin, who praised elementary Russian values, such as goodness and endurance, idealizing the Russian villages (Parthé 1992). These Russian nationalists did not want to rule over foreign nations, but withdraw to a pure Russia, while cutting the expenditures of empire. At the path-breaking first session of the USSR Congress of People's Deputies in 1989, Rasputin proposed that Russia should leave the Soviet Union (Yasin 2002, 118).

Two streams were apparent among the Russian nationalists, and, although opposites, they were often intermingled. The dominant tendency was liberal nationalism, with Yeltsin as the self-evident leader, leaving Gorbachev as the obsolete Soviet leader. After the semi-democratic elections to the USSR Congress of People's Deputies, the natural next step was somewhat more democratic elections to the republican parliaments. No deputies were appointed but political parties were still not permitted.

---

19. This section draws on Dunlop (1993, 16–37), which is an excellent detailed account of these events. Aron (2000) adds tantalizing details of this extraordinary Yeltsin campaign.

The elections to the Russian Congress of People's Deputies occurred on March 4, 1990. Because they were more democratic than the Soviet parliamentary elections held a year earlier, the republican parliaments enjoyed greater legitimacy than the Soviet parliament. This time Yeltsin ran in his hometown of Sverdlovsk, and he won with 84 percent of the vote, cementing his reputation as unbeatable in a democratic election. He became one of the cochairmen of the "Democratic Russia" faction.

The other Russian nationalist stream was hard-line, almost neo-Stalinist. In June 1990, they founded a Russian Communist Party and elected Ivan Polozkov, an outspoken hardliner, their leader. Polozkov defeated Oleg Lobov, one of Yeltsin's close associates from Sverdlovsk, but only with a limited margin. After Polozkov's victory, the Russian Communist Party became the home for hard-line nationalists. Gorbachev was left in the middle between Polozkov's nationalists and Yeltsin's democrats.

The big political prize was the chairmanship of the new Russian Congress of People's Deputies. The two candidates were, logically, hard-line Polozkov and liberal Yeltsin. On May 29, 1990, Yeltsin won with a tiny majority in the third round against a replacement candidate. He proclaimed that Russia must acquire real sovereignty. On June 12, 1990, the newly elected Russian Congress of People's Deputies adopted a declaration of Russian state sovereignty, with 907 votes, only 13 against and 9 abstentions (Yasin 2002, 121). It also declared the supremacy of Russian law over union legislation.

A war of laws between the union and the republics erupted. In Moscow, political legitimacy and initiative moved from the Soviet to the Russian authorities. Yeltsin led sovereign Russia, but he had no real power as yet, and Gorbachev remained Soviet president. Moscow faced dual powers. Yegor Gaidar (1999, 66) has tellingly characterized the situation in August 1991:

> Yeltsin had a large reserve of popular trust, unimaginable responsibilities, and almost no levers of control. After all, up to this very moment the Russian republic, as a government structure, had been purely decorative. Nothing in it was connected to anything else. It had no army, no KGB, no MVD [Ministry of Interior], no control over other regions of the country. . . . It effectively had no central bank. No control over the greater part of industry. No customs service. In fact, nothing at all, except the name—the Russian state.

A parade of sovereignties ensued. All the 15 union republics held parliamentary elections at about the same time, and all declared either outright independence or somewhat vaguer "sovereignty" in 1990, and many subordinate territories declared themselves sovereign as well. Rather than reacting against these declarations, Yeltsin embraced them and preached radical decentralization. In August 1990, during a trip to Kazan, the capital of Tatarstan, the biggest of the Muslim autonomous republics within the Russian Federation, Yeltsin made his famous statement: "Take as much independence as you can" (Dunlop 1993, 62). With these words, he disarmed the explosive nationalist issue in Russia.

Gorbachev did not give up. He was still both Soviet President and general secretary of the CPSU. In July 1990, he convened the 28th Party Congress of the CPSU and won an all-out victory against Ligachev and his ilk, who were ousted from the Central Committee. But so was Yakovlev. Gorbachev had undermined the last vestiges of communist power and seemed free to move as he liked, but he had run out of steam. Elegantly, Yeltsin deprived Gorbachev of the laurels of his victory by dramatically departing along with other leading party reformers from the CPSU, making it look politically obsolete.

When Gorbachev dismissed the 500-day program in October 1990, he departed for a hard-line political desert for half a year. The last remnants of his old team either resigned or were sacked and he undertook multiple erratic institutional changes. Gorbachev dissolved the Presidential Council and sacked its relatively liberal members, including Yakovlev, in November 1990. In December 1990, Minister of Foreign Affairs Shevardnadze resigned in protest against Gorbachev's political turn, with good foresight warning against a hard-line coup. Gorbachev appointed a clowns' gallery of hardliners in their places. Mediocre party apparatchik Gennady Yanaev became vice president and Minister of Finance Valentin Pavlov became prime minister (Brown 1996, 269–79). Gorbachev had dug his own political grave.

The main beneficiary of Gorbachev's departure to the hard-line wilderness was Yeltsin, who attracted most of Russia's liberal intelligentsia and reinforced his position as the country's unquestioned democratic leader. As columnist Flora Lewis wrote: "Mr. Yeltsin is collecting a highly competent team, not so much by attraction as by gathering the bright, innovative people Mr. Gorbachev keeps pushing away."[20]

The old guard was on the offensive, and on January 13, 1991, KGB special forces (*spetsnaz*) stormed the TV tower in Vilnius to suppress the free Lithuanian television station. They killed 14 unarmed Lithuanians, and hundreds were injured. Soon afterward, several Latvian nationalists were killed in the center of Riga. Gorbachev appeared complicit, which was his last straw for many in the Russian liberal intelligentsia. Characteristically, Yeltsin immediately flew to Estonia's capital Tallinn, where he assembled the three Baltic presidents the next day. They issued a common statement in support of the independence of the Baltic states. Yeltsin knew where he stood, and he acted instantly (Aron 2007).

In February and March 1991, both the democrats and hardliners were fully mobilized. In repeated demonstrations in Moscow, the democrats mobilized at least 300,000 and possibly 500,000 people, and the hardliners were not far behind. Large demonstrations were held in other big cities as well. These were the biggest popular demonstrations the Soviet Union ever saw and they remained peaceful. Russia's civil mobilization and ma-

---

20. *International Herald Tribune*, December 13, 1990.

ture political culture took everyone by surprise. In February 1991, Yeltsin was strangely allowed to speak on Soviet television. He utilized his opportunity fully and demanded Gorbachev's resignation (Aron 2000).

Gorbachev made an attempt to return to political relevance by driving a wedge between Yeltsin's moderate Russian nationalism and his support for the independence of the other republics. He launched a referendum on the future of the USSR, which was held in March 1991. He formulated the ambiguous question: "Do you consider necessary the preservation of the Union of Soviet Socialist Republics as a renewed federation of equal sovereign republics, in which the rights and freedom of an individual of any nationality will be fully guaranteed?" (Dunlop 1993, 33). How could anyone answer such a question? Yeltsin could do nothing but accept it, but he cleverly avoided making this referendum a political issue. In Russia, 71 percent of voters answered yes, but the three Baltic states, Georgia, Armenia, and Moldova, boycotted the referendum, which further alienated these republics from the Soviet Union. Gorbachev won the referendum, but this was another Pyrrhic victory, because nobody understood what the question meant and Gorbachev did not gain anything. Once again, he had proved himself too clever by half.

Yeltsin, by contrast, knew what mattered. He wanted to be democratically elected president of Russia. After having become chairman of the Russian parliament, he stubbornly pursued this course, and he managed to persuade the parliament of the need for a popularly elected Russian president. As the towering candidate, he pursued a third outstanding election campaign, this time across Russia. Although the dominant official media and the Soviet administration opposed him, Yeltsin won an outright victory in the first round with 57.3 percent of the votes cast, and participation was high at 75 percent. The runner-up was no Gorbachev man but former Soviet Prime Minister Ryzhkov, who had recast himself as a hard-line communist and received 16.9 percent of the votes (table 2.2). Yeltsin compensated for his continuing lack of real power with the solemnity of his inauguration as Russia's first president.

Gorbachev finally regretted that he had painted himself into a corner with the hardliners. In April 1991, he returned to the idea of a new union treaty and started intense consultations with the presidents of the eight republics that were still interested in a continued union after the Balts, Georgians, Armenians, Moldovans, and soon also the Azerbaijanis had withdrawn. The negotiations took place at Gorbachev's residence, Novoe Ogarevo, outside of Moscow. The last negotiated version was published in August 1991, and it was supposed to be signed in Moscow on August 20, upon Gorbachev's return from a long and badly needed summer holiday in the Crimea.

Now the hardliners felt betrayed by Gorbachev. On August 19, his closest collaborators staged a coup and set up the State Committee for the State of Emergency (GKChP) with eight members. Formally, they were headed

Table 2.2 Results of presidential election, June 12, 1991

Candidate	Percent of votes
Boris Yeltsin	57.3
Nikolai Ryzhkov	16.9
Vladimir Zhirinovsky	7.8
Aman-Geldy Tuleev	6.8
Albert Makashov	3.7
Vadim Bakatin	3.4
Against all	1.9
Voter turnout	*74.7*

Source: Official election results published by the Central Electoral Commission in *Rossiiskaya gazeta*, June 20, 1991.

by Vice President Yanaev. Other leaders were Prime Minister Pavlov, the heads of the KGB, the Ministry of Defense, the Ministry of Interior, the military-industrial complex, a state industry association, and the organization of *kolkhoz* chairmen. The CPSU was well represented though not formally part of the committee.

The timing of the coup was dictated by the planned signing of the union treaty. The GKChP issued a manifesto, "An Appeal to the Soviet People." Its first goal was to stop "the liquidation of the Soviet Union" as well as to hinder the collapse of the state and the seizure of power by the opposition. Another aim was to block market reforms, and a third purpose was to fight crime, "cleansing the streets of criminal elements." Not even the GKChP protested against the political reforms, but favored "truly democratic processes."

The GKChP was reactionary, representing all the losing bodies—the party, state security, and the communist economic system (Dunlop 1993, 194–99). It was a desperate, poorly organized attempt to stop history and reestablish the old regime. It had a flare of tragicomic operetta and failed quickly. The coup makers appeared at one press conference at which Yanaev was dead drunk and his hands were shaking. All the leaders were nervous. They put Gorbachev under house arrest, suspended political activity and most newspapers, and sent some troops into Moscow, but they did not carry out mass arrests or even impose a curfew.

Oddly, the putschists did not arrest Yeltsin, who drove from his dacha outside Moscow to the White House, where the Russian parliament was located, when he heard of the coup. In a dramatic gesture, he wrote an appeal to the citizens of Russia, declaring the GKChP and its coup illegal. Since all media were closed to him, Yeltsin went out of the White House and scaled a T-72 tank to read his appeal himself from the top of the tank

(Aron 2000, 444–45). This was Yeltsin's greatest moment. He exuded unlimited strength and confidence.

The coup went nowhere. Clearly, its organizers had expected that Gorbachev would join them, since he had voluntarily selected and appointed all of them. But he did not. The putschists commanded troops to attack the White House, and three young men died in its defense, but fortunately the coup organizers were not sufficiently determined to use force, and multiple troops, including top generals, refused to fight and defected to Yeltsin. Yeltsin (1994, 60) saw the weakness of the coup from the onset:

> The putschists did not want bloodshed; they wanted to save face with Western governments. And it was this ambiguity in their motive that undid them. They were grossly mistaken in their choice of tactic, and we owe them enormous gratitude for that error.

Tens of thousands of Muscovites came to the White House in support of democracy. By August 21, the coup had collapsed. Gorbachev could return to Moscow, but instead of the triumph he had expected, he was soon to realize that power had moved to Yeltsin and the Soviet Union was over. Yeltsin, by contrast, had a full grasp of the historical importance of this event:

> I believe that history will record that the twentieth century essentially ended on August 19 through 21, 1991. The election of the first freely chosen president of Russia was a national event, but the failure of the August coup and the disappearance of the Soviet Union that resulted was a global event of the greatest importance. (Yeltsin 1994, 41)

At the funeral of the three young defenders of the White House, Yeltsin showed his human side:

> It was our children who rushed to defend the honor of Russia, its freedom, its independence and its democracy. . . . I bow to the mothers and fathers of Dmitri, Volodia, and Ilya, and express my deepest condolences to them and all their relatives. . . . Forgive me, your President, for not being able to defend, to protect your sons. (Quoted in Aron 2000, 465)

As institutions evaporated, the leading political personalities became all the more important. The Soviet endgame was a duel between two men, Mikhail Gorbachev and Boris Yeltsin.

Gorbachev was the initiator of the revolution. He was the dominant policymaker who brought about the collapse of the Soviet Union. His role was supreme and the outcomes depended greatly on his idiosyncrasies. Gorbachev's skills were those of a man who can instigate change from within the system. He was charming and likable. His outstanding political talent was compromise. In all major policy decisions from 1985 until 1990, Gorbachev embraced the winning position.

The drawback of his apt compromising was that he never made a clear-cut choice or formulated a lucid strategy. When facing two contradictory principles, Gorbachev always tried to straddle the center, even when it was impossible. He stuck to a disappearing middle ground, always committed to partial solutions, eventually rendering himself not only unpopular but irrelevant. His nemesis, Yeltsin, delivered perhaps the most telling description of Gorbachev:

> He wanted to combine things that cannot be combined—to marry a hedgehog and a grass snake—communism and a market economy, public-property ownership and private-property ownership, the multiparty system and the Communist Party with its monopoly on power. But these things are incompatible. He wanted to retain some of the old things while introducing new reforms. In his latest mistake, he wanted our country to be a single state. That is impossible; that is unrealistic. But he decided to stick to his illusions and bide his time.[21]

Gorbachev's fundamental shortfall was that he believed in Lenin and communist ideology. He was one of the last people to believe that communism could be reformed, but otherwise, he would no doubt have been ousted early on. He was a natural transitional figure, a moderate launching a revolutionary process to be overtaken by radicals. He saw the shortcomings of the Soviet system, but he wanted to reform the system to make it better, refusing to draw the logical conclusion to abandon communism. As Yeltsin (1994, 17) put it: "Gorbachev had always been an advocate of socialism with a human face."

Although he broke down the old system, he failed to present a plausible alternative, falling into a deep intellectual void. "Even the reformer Gorbachev was more afraid of breaking and destroying the system than anything on earth," wrote Yeltsin (1994, 19). Yegor Gaidar (1999, 46) aptly characterized Gorbachev: "He had let the genie of political liberalization out of the bottle but could neither control it nor stuff it back in. Nor could he decide what he truly wanted. And herein lay Gorbachev's most serious weakness—his inability to make the necessary, if risky, decisions and then follow through with them."

As his political standing deteriorated, Gorbachev's peculiar response was to speak for hours on television with ever less substance. In the last years of his rule, he was nicknamed the chatterbox (*boltun'*). Still, Gorbachev was strongly committed to peaceful solutions and managed to avoid violence to an impressive extent. His greatest accomplishment was to destroy the Soviet Union, but that was never his intention, leaving him with the aura of a tragic hero.

As multiple crises turned catastrophic, political polarization proceeded. A clear choice had to be made, which was Yeltsin's strength. Gorbachev and Yeltsin were the same age and came from similar backgrounds, but their personalities were very different. Yeltsin was no compromiser, and

---

21. " 'We Are Taking Over' " (interview with Yeltsin), *Newsweek*, January 6, 1992, 11–12.

his expulsion from the communist leadership in 1987 caused the personal trauma he needed to rethink his direction. From that moment he radicalized with public opinion.

Few people are as free from their prior beliefs and as unprejudiced as Yeltsin. He was an intuitive politician who faced a situation, felt the people, and drew his conclusion is with ruthless logic. He had all the characteristics of a revolutionary leader. He surged as the phoenix from 1989 to 1991, as the confusion and crisis grew worse. When others wavered or were afraid, Yeltsin was calm, secure, and evidently happy. When he mounted a tank outside the White House on August 19, 1991, he reached his summit.

An Overdetermined Collapse

The collapse of the Soviet Union was one of the great dramas of the 20th century. Was it inevitable? My answer is not only yes, but that it was overdetermined by several causes, because the collapse was multiple: an empire, an economic system, and a political system collapsed. It was a revolutionary process in which the existing state institutions were gradually undermined and then collapsed.

The Soviet economic system was moribund, and its shortfalls were well known, but this petrified system could have persisted until the next oil boom in the same way as lonely North Korea and Cuba vegetate today. Perestroika brought about the acute economic crisis that moved the USSR from stagnation to fatal crisis. The economic problems that resulted can be divided into three categories.

First, financial policy was patently irresponsible from 1986, with an unsustainably large and rising budget deficit recklessly financed with the emission of money. Gorbachev and Ryzhkov bear the prime responsibility for the exploding budget deficit, which Gorbachev (1990) impressively accepted: "[S]erious errors really occurred. And the very worst among them—that we allowed such a situation in the financial system. . . . For that I reckon that we are responsible. . . ." Gorbachev (1990) defended himself by stating that when his old friend Yuri Andropov was general secretary in 1983, "he did not allow us [Gorbachev, Ryzhkov, and V. I. Dolgickh] to approach the budget and data on military expenditures. But I was at that time Politburo member and chaired the meetings of the CC Secretariat." This statement clarified not only how restricted access to key information was, but also how ignorant Gorbachev and Ryzhkov were, which is obvious from their memoirs (Gorbachev 1995, Ryzhkov 1992). Macroeconomic destabilization, economic ignorance, and inability to use relevant expertise made a catastrophe inevitable.

Second, the gradual reforms separated control rights from cash rights and bred a machine of rent seeking. Incentives were distorted, and accountability disappeared altogether. Managers were preoccupied with tunneling state wealth out of public enterprises to private offshore havens. By 1990 this rent seeking made economic collapse inevitable.

Third, the partial national and democratic empowerment of the Soviet peoples bred populism, because nations and their peoples were allowed to demand more economic benefits, but they were not permitted actual power. The Soviet finances collapsed in 1991 because the republics stopped delivering revenues to the union treasury, and much of the inflation was caused by the competitive issue of ruble credits by 16 central banks. This rendered the financial and monetary disasters terminal in late 1990.

Each of these three economic problems was in itself sufficient to terminate the Soviet Union, and together they guaranteed its demise.

The downfall of the Soviet empire consisted of three steps. The outer empire, Eastern-Central Europe, had been occupied after World War II. All these nations were kept in the Soviet sphere through the threat of armed invasion and they waited for their freedom. Gorbachev was both wise and humane in accepting their aspirations, and no decolonization has been more peaceful than the liberation of Eastern-Central Europe.

The second wave of decolonization involved the countries that had been incorporated into the Soviet Union during World War II through the Molotov-Ribbentrop Pact: the three Baltic countries (Estonia, Latvia, and Lithuania), Moldova, and Western Ukraine. None of these territories had ever accepted Soviet occupation, and despite severe repression they waited for nothing less than national independence. Georgia and Armenia slid out of the empire in the same fashion. Gorbachev did not comprehend nationalism, but he allowed only limited use of force, which was not sufficient to hold the Soviet Union together.

The only question is why Russia itself wanted to become independent of the USSR. Gorbachev supporters accused Yeltsin of playing the Russian card and destroying the Soviet Union for his desire to gain power, but that is not very plausible. Yeltsin himself (1994, 35) described the situation after he had been elected Russian president in June 1991:

> Gorbachev represented the Union, the empire, the old power, and I represented Russia, an independent republic, a new and as yet nonexistent country. . . . Even the very word *Soviet* was no longer possible to pronounce. . . . The Soviet Union could not exist without the image of the empire. The image of the empire could not exist without the image of force. The USSR ended the moment the first hammer pounded the Berlin Wall.

This is the language of a great intuitive politician. Yeltsin felt that "Soviet" was politically impossible. So did Polozkov, the hard-line Russian communist, as both right and left voted for Russia's sovereignty. Yeltsin, the revolutionary, felt what he had to do. Linz and Stepan (1992) have offered the most plausible explanation. Russia enjoyed greater legitimacy than the Soviet Union because Russia held more democratic elections than the Soviet Union did. Therefore, the Soviet Union could not be held together. Yeltsin grasped this, while Gorbachev did not.

Political scientists have raised the most doubts about the necessity of the collapse of the Soviet political system, but the fundamental political explanation is that the Soviet political transformation was a revolutionary process (Aron 2000, Mau and Starodubrovskaya 2001, McFaul 2001). You cannot stop a revolution in its midst. As revolutionary momentum evolves, radicalization proceeds, and only those who radicalize at pace survive politically. This was Yeltsin's prime talent. To demand consistency or moderation from a politician in a revolutionary situation is to call for political suicide.

Another characteristic of a revolution is the temporary collapse of the state. Inadvertently, Gorbachev contributed to the demise of governance, because he absurdly believed that socialism/communism/Leninism was superior and he wanted to reform it. By tinkering with the system, he created a revolutionary situation. Yeltsin's superiority was electoral and Russia's revolution was democratic. Hence, Yeltsin stood in competitive popular elections against the establishment in 1989, 1990, and 1991, and he won them all with big majorities in the first round. McFaul (2001, 6) emphasized the logic of transition once a revolution is under way:

> First, a split within the ancien régime occurs between soft-liners and hard-liners. Soft-liners believe that some degree of reform is necessary, whereas hard-liners oppose any reform at all. When the soft-liners gain the upper hand, they initiate a policy of political liberalization, which in turn allows for new societal actors to organize and mobilize. These forces . . . also split into two camps—moderates and radicals.

Yeltsin understood this process and radicalized, whereas Gorbachev stayed moderate, ending up on the disappearing middle ground.

Bunce (1999) presented an original argument about Soviet institutions, suggesting that their very structure brought about the downfall of the system. Her thinking continued on Andrei Amalrik's (1980) famous essay, *Will the Soviet Union Survive until 1984?* Bunce's proposition was that the Soviet system was so distorted and petrified that it could not meet new challenges for long. The Soviet system could not reform, only stay the same or collapse. The problem with this line of explanation is that the timing of the collapse does not follow. In 1919, Ludwig von Mises (1920/1972) made quite a similar argument about the Soviet system not being viable because a market could not function without private property rights. In the end, he proved right, but only after 70 years.

3

Revolution: 1991–93

When Mikhail Gorbachev returned to Moscow from his house arrest in the Crimea on August 22, 1991, he expected to be greeted as a hero. He did not realize that the hero who had defeated the coup was none other than Boris Yeltsin.[1] Gorbachev's position looked dubious, because the putschists had expected that he would join them, and Gorbachev had appointed them all. At his first press conference after the coup on August 22, 1991, in Moscow, Gorbachev made a fatal gaffe. Although the coup had shown that communism needed to be finished off, he declared like a latter-day Don Quixote: "I am convinced that socialism is correct" (Dunlop 1993, 259). He would "fight to the end for the renewal of the party" (Aron 2000, 458).

From that moment, Gorbachev was history, although he formally remained president of the USSR until December 1991. The popular view was that the party was over. As Aron (2000, 459) observed: "The political 'centre' . . . disappeared. This was a revolution, and in revolutions there is no centre."

Also the Soviet Union was over. The aborted August coup was Russia's revolution. The new ruler of Russia was its popularly elected president, Boris Yeltsin. He believed in an open and free society without any official ideology or ruling party. The values he emphasized were democracy, a multiparty system, the defense of human rights, a market economy, private property, and free travel. The dominant slogan was to build "a normal society." The eternal Russian ambition to be original was gone. Yeltsin recognized how great a task he was facing, and he was morally prepared. Gaidar (1999, 64) characterized him "like a warrior-knight in a fairy tale

---

1. This chapter draws heavily on Åslund (1995), which is the source when no other reference is indicated.

who had crushed the foe and burst into the enchanted castle only to find, instead of his long-suffering and beautiful princess, nothing but darkness, neglect, and piles of garbage. And now he was the one who had to deal with it all."

Yeltsin thought strategically and moved radically on three issues. First, he had to secure his power. Second, he needed to dissolve the Soviet Union. Third, the rampant economic crisis cried for instant deregulation and financial stabilization. Nobody can do everything at the same time, so Yeltsin postponed political reform. Surprisingly, Russia succeeded in undertaking mass privatization in the midst of this turmoil. The initial attempt at financial stabilization failed, but the foundation for later success was laid.

Although Russia was the major international topic of interest in the West at this time, the West did next to nothing for Russia. Yeltsin's attempt at a capitalist revolution ended in political calamity. In the fall of 1993, the parliament rose up in armed revolt against him, and Yeltsin was forced to call in special forces to quell the uprising. He stayed in power, but the revolution was finished.

Yeltsin's Assumption of Power

After the August 1991 coup, the USSR ceased to function as a political entity. The three Baltic republics—Estonia, Latvia, and Lithuania—claimed their independence. Yeltsin recognized them on August 24. Georgia, Armenia, Moldova, and Azerbaijan were well on their way toward national independence. The other republics were more hesitant, with Ukraine being pivotal. Yeltsin realized that he had to dissolve the Soviet Union before he could proceed with other policies. Nor could the rampant economic crisis wait. Soviet shops were empty in spite of galloping inflation. Output was in free fall and worries about impending mass starvation were great. Something had to be done very fast, but few knew what to do.

At the time, the Russian political system seemed the least urgent problem. Russia had just democratically elected a president; the parliament had also been popularly elected even if its election had not been fully democratic; the Soviet Russian Constitution of 1978 could be amended to serve a democracy. Nor was it obvious what a political reform should look like. Yeltsin concluded that his extraordinary popularity and authority enabled him to put off political reform, but he made one exception: He wanted a new constitution.

Yeltsin undertook one major political act. On August 23, he signed a decree that "suspended" the activity of the CPSU during the investigation of the party's "anti-constitutional activity" during the coup. The party was prohibited in several steps, with some decisions made by Yeltsin, others by Gorbachev. On August 24, Gorbachev resigned as general secretary of the

CPSU and dissolved its Central Committee (Remnick 1994, 495). The Russian authorities sealed off the Central Committee headquarters in the center of Moscow. After the dissolution of the CPSU, Gorbachev as president of the USSR confiscated the extensive CPSU property, while the Communist Party won its right to survival through a lengthy court appeal (Aron 2000, 468). Yeltsin transferred the CPSU property in Russia to the presidential administration, which became financially autonomous within the state. Three of the leading putschists committed apparent suicides. Gorbachev arrested the others, but they were soon let out, and nothing really happened to them. Several of them could relaunch their political careers. Yeltsin harbored no vindictiveness.

In the immediate aftermath of the coup, a crowd had torn down the monument of the reviled founder of the Soviet secret police, Feliks Dzerzhinsky, outside Lubyanka, the KGB headquarters. But Moscow soon turned quiet and little happened. Everybody waited for Yeltsin's next move, and the public was upset when he went to Sochi at the Black Sea for a long vacation instead of consolidating his victory (Aron 2000). Yeltsin (1994, 106) noted in his memoirs: "Everything depended on my taking a position of brutal consistency."

September–October 1991 was a strange time. Formally, both Yeltsin and Gorbachev claimed sovereignty over Russia, but nobody took Gorbachev seriously. To his credit, he accepted the situation. Gorbachev managed foreign affairs and worked on a new union treaty, while Yeltsin ruled Russia. Everybody just waited for what Yeltsin would decide.

Yeltsin minimized political reform and opted for a provisional political solution. He demanded the right to rule by decree for one year from November 1, 1991. The still-obedient Russian parliament granted him far-reaching powers to change government structures, appoint all ministers, and adopt a large number of decisions on economic reform by decree (Shevtsova 1999). Yeltsin's official explanation was that the economic crisis was so serious that it demanded a temporary solution.

Popular sentiment against the party and bureaucracy was severe. This was possibly the one and only opportunity to break down the secret police that had plagued the Soviet Union. Yeltsin did act against the KGB, but he split it rather than abolished it. In October 1991, he divided the Russian republican branch of the KGB into five agencies. The Ministry of Security was the repressive heart of the old KGB, which guarded domestic security. Gradually, its range expanded, and in 1995, it was renamed the Federal Security Service (FSB). Other agencies arising from the KGB were the Foreign Intelligence Service (SVR), the Federal Agency for Government Communication and Information Services (FAPSI), which handled eavesdropping and electronic interception, the Federal Border Guard Service (FSP), and the Federal Tax Service, which treated taxpayers like organized criminals (Remington 2006, 235). The KGB was humiliated and weakened, but it was not broken.

Dissolution of the Soviet Union

Yeltsin understood that the Soviet Union was over, but he had to dissolve the union in a way that was politically acceptable to the Russians. In his memoirs, Yeltsin (1994, 115) presented the union dissolution as a positive choice: "I was convinced that Russia needed to rid itself of its imperial mission."

The decisive moment was December 1, 1991, when Ukraine held a referendum on its independence, which won overwhelming support of 90 percent. Simultaneously, Ukraine's communist leader Leonid Kravchuk was elected Ukraine's president with a large majority, and he stated unequivocally that Ukraine would be independent. Ukraine was seen as the keystone in the arch, without which the Soviet Union was not viable.

Yeltsin acted instantly. In complete secrecy, he organized a meeting one week later with Kravchuk and the reformist speaker of the Belarusian parliament, Stanislav Shushkevich. They met with only a handful of aides at a desolate Belarusian hunting lodge (Belovezhskaya Pushcha). Together these three heads of state agreed to dissolve the Soviet Union. As Yeltsin (1994, 113) saw it: "In signing this agreement, Russia was choosing a different path, a path of internal development rather than an imperial one." He insisted that this was "a lawful alteration of the existing order," because it "was a revision of the Union Treaty among [the] three major republics of that Union."

As a replacement for the USSR, they set up the loose Commonwealth of Independent States (CIS), which appeared most inspired by the British Commonwealth. Soviet President Gorbachev was not invited to the meeting and was kept in the dark. His continuing attempts to form a looser version of the Soviet Union, a "Union of Sovereign States," had been jeopardized. The CIS agreement meant that the Soviet Union was finished. Yeltsin emphasized that the CIS would be a minimal organization: "There will be no coordinating organs. . . . If there is coordination, it will be between the heads of state of commonwealth members. They will have some kind of a working group to resolve certain questions, and that's it."[2]

Yeltsin's next delicate task was to persuade the Soviet military to accept the dissolution of the Soviet Union. On December 11, 1991, Yeltsin stormed into our conference room in the White House in Moscow like a bull, beaming with manic self-confidence, energy, and happiness. I never saw a stronger man in my life. First Deputy Prime Minister Gennady Burbulis told me that they had come from the Ministry of Defense. Yeltsin had given a speech to the Soviet general staff and convinced them to join Russia. Yeltsin had salvaged the peaceful dissolution of the union. The previous day, Gorbachev had tried to convince the same generals to stand up for the Soviet Union, but he failed. Possibly dissuaded by the failure of the

---

2. "'We Are Taking Over'" (interview with Yeltsin), *Newsweek*, January 6, 1992, 13.

August coup, the Soviet/Russian military stayed calm. Earlier Yeltsin had won the loyalty of several senior generals who defected to him during the coup (Dunlop 1993, 248).[3]

Some Russian democrats were taken aback by Yeltsin's abrupt abolition of the Soviet Union and abandoned him, but a protest in Moscow that evening gathered only a few thousand demonstrators. Instead, most of the Soviet republics that had been left out of the Belarusian meeting wanted to join the CIS. Yeltsin quickly accommodated them, and on December 21, a meeting for all the republican heads of states was held in Alma-Ata, then the capital of Kazakhstan. The CIS was expanded to include 11 republics. Only Georgia and the already independent Baltic states stayed outside. The treaty of 1922 on the formation of the Soviet Union was formally abrogated, leaving the remaining Soviet institutions and Soviet President Gorbachev without legal foundation.

All the many Soviet institutions had to be reconsidered. Yeltsin moved swiftly. About 80 superfluous Soviet industrial ministries and state committees were disbanded, and their assets were taken over by the newly independent states. Russia took control of the Soviet State Bank as of January 1, 1992 (Aron 2000, 473–74). Essential Soviet institutions were merged with their Russian counterparts and subordinated to Russian ministers. One new CIS authority of note was established, a single joint command for the strategic forces, to avoid nuclear proliferation. Only one important Soviet institution survived, the Soviet ruble, which would cause considerable harm.

Yeltsin decided that Russia would not make any claims on territories of other former Soviet republics, although many such claims could be justified, because Stalin had altered most of the republican borders. In 1954, Khrushchev had grandly presented the Crimea to Ukraine on the tercentenary of its union with Russia. No fewer than 25 million ethnic Russian lived in other Soviet republics. Large Kazakh territories were traditionally Russian and inhabited by ethnic Russians. Furthermore, the new state borders were neither demarcated nor watched. By consistently respecting the existing borders, Yeltsin left a valuable, peaceful legacy.

On Christmas Day 1991, Gorbachev and Yeltsin met for a whole day in the Kremlin, settling Gorbachev's resignation as USSR president. Although no love was lost between them, both behaved like gentlemen. Yeltsin granted Gorbachev quite comfortable conditions for the rest of his life, while Gorbachev transferred the nuclear briefcase and other ultimate state secrets to Yeltsin, who moved his office to the Kremlin.

In 1992, some talked about the possibility of a subsequent breakup of the Russian Federation, but that was never very likely. To begin with, Russia's population is 80 percent ethnically Russian, and Russian is the all-

---

3. Yeltsin went on to give us, a group of Western economists, an excellent presentation of his radical economic reform plans for forty minutes without any notes.

dominant language. Only about 17 percent of Russia's population lives in territories considered ethnic minority regions, and in many of them the majority of the population is not of that ethnic group. The Muslim population is usually assessed at 10 percent. Chechnya, with a large and compact Chechen population on the border of Russia, is quite an exception (Remington 2006).

Attempt at Radical Market Reform

Another major task Yeltsin focused on was building a market economy. In September and October 1991, Moscow saw an unusual development. Five different competing economic policy teams were created.[4] Each of them aspired to form Yeltsin's next government. They sat at different dachas outside Moscow where they elaborated on their economic programs. Yeltsin took his time and listened to their proposals.

After two months, he made his decision. On October 28, 1991, Yeltsin made his greatest speech ever to the Russian Congress of People's Deputies:

> I appeal to you at one of the most critical moments in Russia's history. Right now it will be decided what kind of country Russia will be in the coming years and decades. . . . I turn to you with determination to stand unconditionally on the road of profound reforms with support from the whole population. . . . The time has come to act decisively, firmly, without hesitation. . . . The period of moving with small steps is over. . . . A big reformist breakthrough is necessary. (Yeltsin 1991)

Yeltsin declared that the two central economic tasks were to establish economic freedom and financial stabilization:

> We have a unique opportunity to stabilize the economy within several months and to start the process of recovery. We have defended political freedom. Now we have to give the people economic [freedom], remove all barriers to the freedom of enterprises and entrepreneurship, offer the people possibilities to work and receive as much as they earn, after having relieved them of bureaucratic pressures. (Yeltsin 1991)

Yeltsin emphasized the need for an instant liberalization of prices, macroeconomic stabilization, and privatization, providing a reasonable amount of detail. The Russian parliament, which had elected Yeltsin its chairman only on the third vote in May 1990, received Yeltsin's speech with rousing applause. Cleverly, Yeltsin put his programmatic speech for radical economic reform to a vote, and the deputies voted 876 to 16 in

---

4. They were headed, respectively, by Grigori Yavlinsky (liberal but supported the maintenance of the Soviet Union), Yegor Gaidar (consistent market liberal and for Russia's independence), Yevgeny Saburov (liberal but cautious), Yuri Skokov (illiberal), and Oleg Lobov (illiberal). I talked to the first three camps during two visits to Moscow in September 1991.

favor (Aron 2000, 491). Yeltsin had received a nearly unanimous parliamentary mandate.

Yeltsin contemplated his choice of economic reform strategy. A major problem with prior Soviet and Russian reforms was inconsistency: "Russia's trouble was never a shortage or an abundance of reformers. The trouble was an inability to adhere to a consistent policy. . . . Not a single reform effort in Russia has ever been completed. . . . The goal I have set before the government is to make reform irreversible" (Yeltsin 1994, 145–47). Yeltsin acknowledged the depth of the economic crisis, and by the fall of 1991, "the rationing of virtually everything had reached its limit. The shelves in the stores were absolutely bare" (p. 150).

Russia was in a rampant economic crisis with nearly complete shortages and an actual state bankruptcy. Yeltsin reckoned that a radical economic reform had to be introduced as soon as practically possible. He and his chief reformer Yegor Gaidar wanted to launch the radical economic reform as one package. In his reform speech, Yeltsin had warned that it would be in mid-December 1991, but the other union republics protested that they were not ready. Although Yeltsin had declared: "We have no possibility to coordinate the terms of the reforms with the conclusion of all-embracing inter-republican agreements," as a good will gesture to the other republics, he delayed Russia's reform launch until January 2, 1992 (Yeltsin 1991).

Gaidar (1999, 114) justified his choice of early price deregulation: "There *were* no reserves to ease the hardships that would be caused by setting the economic mechanism in motion. Putting off liberalization of the economy until slow structural reforms could be enacted was impossible. Two or three more months of such passivity and we would have economic and political catastrophe, total collapse, and a civil war."

After the ten reform programs that had been presented between October 1989 and October 1990, Russians were tired of programs and called for action. Gaidar opposed formulating another detailed reform program. He wanted to present his program through deeds, although he wrote articles and made many public appearances to clarify his policies. A list of 70 planned legal acts was approved through a government decree in November 1991.

As it turned out, not formulating a formal reform program was a serious mistake (Yasin 2002, 167–68). First, neither ordinary Russians nor the elite quite understood what a market economy was. They preferred cherry-picking and did not understand the need for a consistent system. The reformers badly needed a pedagogic and lucid reform program to teach the population their policy. Second, all governments need a program as a tool for coordination, especially at a time of profound change. An official program would have been especially useful in the revolutionary chaos. Third, the reformers had not thought all their ideas through or agreed on them. The elaboration of a reform program would have improved their own consistency. Finally, the old Soviet civil service remained in place, and it was deeply hostile to reform. A reform program would have dictated the direction of government policy to them.

Russia appeared set to repeat the radical economic reforms of Poland in 1990 and Czechoslovakia in 1991, with a concentration of major reform measures in a "big bang" in January 1992. Yet, Yeltsin (1991) did not quite speak of a big bang, but suggested vaguely: "The reform goes along a number of directions simultaneously, all-embracing and dynamically." In the early fall of 1991, Gaidar (1993) did not envision full liberalization and stabilization until Russia had introduced its own national currency, which he reckoned could be done only after nine months. The Gaidar team's initial working document proposed a gradual stabilization and liberalization program to be implemented in the course of one year, not too different from the 500-day program (Dąbrowski 1993a).

As the macroeconomic crisis deepened in late 1991, the reformers turned more radical and opted for a more concentrated big bang. Both Yeltsin and Gaidar used the term "shock therapy," although their actual approach to reform was somewhat partial. The reforms came to lack the desired concentration and comprehension, but that was difficult to avoid in the post-Soviet chaos.

A New Type of Reform Government

Yeltsin's next step was to form a new government, which was equally daring and innovative. He decided to put the government in the hands of Russia's best economists: "When forming the government, we discard the priority of political considerations to the benefit of professionals" (Yeltsin 1991). "It was high time to bring in an economist with his own original concept, possibly with his own team of people. Determined action was long overdue in the economy, not just in politics" (Yeltsin 1994, 124).

His reform speech was largely drafted by Gaidar, arguably the best and most erudite Russian economist. He had set up his own Institute of Economic Policy in Moscow, where he had gathered the cream of Russia's young economists, with a sister institute in St. Petersburg. Gaidar had the best team of economists ready to take over the Russian government, and Yeltsin moved quickly, making this team his new government. However, Yeltsin considered it impossible to have a 35-year-old nonpolitician confirmed as head of the government by the Russian parliament (Yeltsin 1994, 125). Over November 6–8, 1991, Gaidar became deputy prime minister as well as minister of finance and economy. Yeltsin made himself prime minister, and his chief political aide Gennady Burbulis became first deputy prime minister. A row of young reformists aged 35 to 40 took over major portfolios in the government. Anatoly Chubais, who became minister of privatization, was to be the most prominent.

Gaidar's new ministers were professional economists with doctoral degrees who knew English and had studied mainstream Western economics, although largely on their own in the Soviet Union. They were the most intelligent and well-educated children of the foremost intellectual *nomenklatura*. The Soviet Union had cut itself off from the world so completely that none of them had earned a degree abroad. One of the young reformers, Sergei Vasiliev (1999, 86), characterized their group like this: "A group of professional economists, the Gaidar team, had some understanding of the situation and proposed a more or less adequate approach to handling the economic challenges at hand. No other group of economists was able to come up with a comprehensive programme." Their dilemma was that they were highly elitist and distant from the population. They undermined their credibility by proudly calling themselves a kamikaze government.

When forming the new government, Yeltsin restructured it completely. The old Soviet government had a dozen deputy prime ministers and almost 100 ministers, but Yeltsin's new Western-style government had only three deputy prime ministers and 23 ministers. All the many industrial ministries were abolished. The State Planning Committee (Gosplan) was renamed the Ministry of Economy and deprived of most of its old functions. The Ministry of Finance became the dominant ministry, as in a normal capitalist government. The main innovation was a State Property Committee, which was a ministry of privatization. Over time, several branch ministries returned. The number of ministers would steadily increase, as did the number of deputy prime ministers, but the new type of government persisted.

A big question was what to do with the tens of thousands of apparatchiks, predominantly in their 50s and 60s because of the Soviet gerontocracy. Several Eastern European countries had launched lustration of officials, dismissing senior party officials and secret police informers. Three lines of thought dominated Yeltsin's thinking. First, Stalin had made purge a dirty word from which Yeltsin (1994, 127) distanced himself:

> In seventy years, we have grown tired of dividing people into "clean" and "unclean." . . . To break everything, to destroy everything in the Bolshevik manner was not part of my plans at all. While bringing into the government completely new, young and bold people, I still considered it possible to use in government work-experienced executives. . . .

Second, immediately after the Russian revolution in February 1917, the provisional government headed by Prince G. E. Lvov had decided to dissolve the tsarist civil service, which had caused chaos in the whole country (Pipes 1990, 298–300). Yeltsin (1994, 129) was acutely aware of this historical precedent and wanted to avoid it at any price: "It would have been disastrous to destroy the government administration of such an enormous state. Where it was possible to put in experienced 'old' staff, we did. And sometimes we made mistakes."

The third reason for Yeltsin's reluctance to purge the old administration was that he originated from it. He was proud of his achievements as a party official (Yeltsin 1990), and a large group of his old comrades from Sverdlovsk joined him in the Kremlin. Yeltsin also harbored a strange and exaggerated affection for state enterprise managers, which would lead him into jeopardy time and again in the years ahead (Yeltsin 1994, 168–73).

Yeltsin made this conscious and premeditated choice himself, and its consequences were fundamental. The old *nomenklatura* survived, and no real discontinuity occurred, especially at the regional level, where democratization was limited. His most serious omission was not to dissolve the KGB, which was to reemerge as the dominant state power a decade later. Presumably, Yeltsin felt that he needed the old security police after the coup, and the armed uprising in October 1993 reinforced his resolve. Several top KGB officers were to become Yeltsin's drinking partners, and they drew out all of his worst traits, as documented by his chief bodyguard Aleksandr Korzhakov (1997) in his mean-spirited memoirs.

Yeltsin's private life complicated his policies and particularly his personnel decisions. Like most old party apparatchiks, he was a heavy drinker. When he drank, he wanted privacy and liked the company of big, heavy, middle-aged men such as himself. These men tended to be enterprise managers, KGB officers, and old apparatchiks. A *banya* (sauna) company developed, which included Yeltsin's chief bodyguard Korzhakov, and his later appointees, FSB Chairman Mikhail Barsukov, First Deputy Prime Minister Oleg Soskovets, Minister of Defense Pavel Grachev, Kremlin Property Manager Pavel Borodin, and Yeltsin's tennis trainer Shamil Tarpishchev. These men were reactionaries and several were serious criminals who fought the reformers during the day and drank with Yeltsin at night. The *banya* team intentionally made Yeltsin as drunk as possible, to promote their policy line. The reformers had no access to this company, and their drinking habits were no match either. For long periods, Yeltsin disappeared from the public eye, and the suspicion was that he devoted himself to heavy drinking in this bad company. He was a Janus-faced man because he pursued a Janus life (Shevtsova 1999).

Yeltsin was remarkably tolerant. He allowed full press freedom and accepted untold criticism of himself. The Soviet Union had persistently discriminated by ethnicity, favoring Russians and the dominant ethnicity in each union republic. Jews in particular had suffered discrimination. Yeltsin ignored ethnicity and opened the floodgates to all ethnic minorities. His government always had several Jewish ministers. Yeltsin was also keen on promoting young people, appointing many ministers and two prime ministers in their 30s. Being strong himself, he was not afraid of highly educated people or strong personalities. He appointed the occasional woman minister, but only in this regard did he not advance much from Gorbachev's time.

Yeltsin was also tolerant of foreigners. He invited the International Monetary Fund (IMF) and the World Bank, which obtained extensive access from the beginning. He accepted that a sizable group of foreign economic advisors assisted his government. Professor Jeffrey Sachs of Harvard University was the most prominent advisor. I was his partner in this endeavor. I remember the exhilarating feeling when, in early December 1991, I received my own office in the old Central Committee headquarters at the Old Square, which had been taken over by the reform government. In the old days, this building was hermetically closed to foreigners.[5] In the corridors, rows of safes were standing, because the new liberal government was to be open. The safes were to be sold to the new commercial banks. Our work was hectic and highly productive because the reformers knew how to use experts.

Launch of Market Reform

The all-dominant problems were massive shortages and high inflation, leading to demonetization and dollarization. Half a liter of vodka or a pack of Marlboro were more useful currencies than ruble bills. Output was still in free fall.

Yet some gained from the high inflation, which is the most regressive of taxes. A small rent-seeking elite of state enterprise managers and their companions benefited from subsidies and subsidized credits paid by the state, but society paid the inflation tax that financed their fortunes. The destabilizing subsidies were often extracted through bribery, and since such contracts were not legal and thus could not be secured in court, the many commercial banks that thrived on the high inflation became a gangster killing field. Bringing down inflation was vital for the well-being of society, but it was resisted by a commercial elite that was as powerful as it was criminal.

Every possible macroeconomic problem was present. Fifteen central banks issued ruble credits without control or coordination. Both the Central Bank of Russia and the Ministry of Finance were weak and rudimentary. The payment system was a relic of the prior nonmonetary world. Money was not unified, because different shops existed for people with special coupons, and rationing was extensive. Nor was the exchange rate unified. According to the most credible estimates, the Soviet budget deficit in 1991 was about 31 percent of GDP (EBRD 1994). Public expenditures skyrocketed beyond control. Since prices remained regulated, price subsidies surged with rising costs. Russia also suffered from a huge monetary

---

5. I had that office for 16 months. Then we were transferred to the premises of the Ministry of Finance, which was quite a reasonable decision.

overhang, because people were compelled to hold much more money than they desired.

As if to add insult to injury, Russia was hit by several severe external shocks. The USSR effectively defaulted and lost all access to international financing, which sent the exchange rate plummeting. In 1991, the trade system of the nations of the Council for Mutual Economic Assistance fell apart. In 1992, trade with other former Soviet republics plummeted as the Soviet trade system collapsed.

The question was where to start. A popular idea among Russian economists was currency reform, because Lenin had done so in the 1920s (Kazmin and Tsimailo 1991). He had introduced a new parallel currency that had been convertible, while the old ruble had been inflated away. However, the objections against a currency reform were manifold. No preparations had been made, and Gaidar (1993) estimated that a currency reform would require nine months of preparations. Soviet Prime Minister Valentin Pavlov had just carried out a limited and highly unsuccessful currency reform in January 1991, so why repeat an unpopular failure? A currency reform would only eliminate the surplus stock of money, while the imbalance between the flows of incomes and expenditures would remain (Gaidar 1990). The unfortunate consequence of this decision, however, was that the harmful ruble zone lasted until the fall of 1993. A currency reform would have terminated it earlier.

Since currency reform was not a realistic option, the monetary overhang and the imbalance between supply and demand could be eliminated only through price rises. The Russian reformers believed that a swift, comprehensive deregulation of prices had to start the transition to a market economy. On December 3, 1991, Yeltsin signed a decree on "the transition to free (market) prices and tariffs, formed under the influence of supply and demand" on producer goods, consumer goods, services, and labor.[6] This price deregulation was truly far-reaching, involving 80 percent of producer prices and 90 percent of consumer prices. Among producer prices, energy, some commodities, and transportation were excluded, but most of these prices were hiked fivefold. A basket of essential consumer staples, such as milk and bread, was initially excluded as well to ensure that nobody would starve, but these prices were liberalized from March to May 1992 (Koen and Phillips 1993).

The year 1992 started as intended with a big bang. Gaidar led the charge with intelligence and determination. His two main policies were radical price liberalization and the balancing of the consolidated state budget. The long-awaited price liberalization took place as announced on January 2, 1992. It was preceded by tremendous fear. People lived as under Damocles' sword. They thought that the sky was the limit for un-

---

6. "Decree of the President of the Russian Federation on Measures to Liberalize Prices," *Ekonomicheskaya gazeta*, special issue, December 1991.

regulated prices, because the huge monetary overhang made the existing free prices extremely high. The authorities were worried about a possible explosion of popular anger and brought in extra police on the day of price liberalization. But no public protest was reported, although prices rose instantly by about 250 percent, far more than the 100 percent the government had expected. Gradually, shortages diminished. One after the other, goods that had not been seen for years reappeared in shops, and many perishable products that had never survived the Soviet distribution system, such as bananas and kiwi fruit, suddenly surfaced. Yet shortages disappeared more slowly than had been the case in Poland, because many local regulations persisted, such as ceilings on profit margins.

A serious concern was domestic trade. Most Russian reformers doubted that it could be liberalized rapidly, but the absence of trade liberalization preserved shortages. Their slow elimination enabled Gaidar to convince Yeltsin to sign a truly radical presidential decree on freedom of trade on January 29, 1992, that stated: "Enterprises, regardless of their form of ownership, and citizens are granted the right to engage in trade . . . without special permission. Enterprises and private citizens may sell things . . . in any place of their convenience."[7]

The purpose was to free retail trade completely so that it could develop from the bottom up. Poland's reformer Leszek Balcerowicz had done the same there in January 1990. The popular reaction was as extraordinary in Russia as it had been in Poland. All kinds of people took to the streets, not to protest but to sell. Suddenly, everything was available, but soon a political reaction arose. Well-to-do Muscovites objected to the disorder and dirt of street bazaars, and the quality of what was being sold was often dubious. The official trade system naturally opposed this stiff competition. Municipal authorities complained about not receiving any revenue from the untaxed street trade, and racketeers were upset over not being able to charge street traders their horrendous protection fees. The popular understanding of the benefits of rational allocation through free trade was limited. After three months, Moscow Mayor Yuri Luzhkov prohibited street trade and the mayors of other big cities followed suit. The otherwise passive police made the pursuit of street traders a priority task. Protection rackets secured their hold over retail trade.

The reformers wanted to liberalize foreign trade, unify the exchange rate, adjust it to the market, and make the ruble convertible, but their endeavors were impeded by the communists' complete depletion of Russia's currency reserves, and the subsequent extremely low exchange rate of the ruble. Still, the reformers succeeded in a near-complete deregulation of imports for the first half of 1992. It was not controversial because

---

7. "Decree of the President of the Russian Federation on the Freedom of Trade," *Rossiiskaya gazeta*, February 1, 1992.

everybody wanted to end shortages, and the extremely low exchange rate allowed any decent Russian product to be sold.

Given that the prices of oil and natural gas, Russia's main exports, were regulated far below world market prices, export licenses and quotas had to be maintained. The commodity exporters insisted on these regulations, which made them millionaires daily. The government could do little but introduce a complex system of surrender requirements for exporters to tax exporters somewhat and make sure that they repatriated some earnings. Yet from July 1992 the exchange rate was essentially unified and allowed to float. Two big problems remained. One was export control for commodity exports, and the other was the lingering state trade within the CIS (Michalopoulos and Drebentsov 1997).

Gaidar's second great task after price liberalization was to balance the consolidated state budget. He focused on a few major cuts, while trying to maintain a high level of revenues. First, the price liberalization instantly eliminated large price subsidies. Gaidar's second big strike was against military procurement, which he initially slashed by 85 percent, which eventually became 70 percent. For the rest, he tried to keep state subsidies and public investment low.

Gaidar accepted the common view that a major tax reform had to wait. Still, the old sales tax, which differed for every good, had to go. Gaidar replaced it with a value-added tax (VAT), which he unwisely put as high as 28 percent. His assumption was that the parliament would bargain for a lower VAT and agree on something like 20 percent, but the unpredictable parliament just voted it through. This excessive rate had to be slashed to 20 percent after a year. The payroll or social security tax stayed at 38 percent of the wage fund. Corporate profit taxes had come down to 32 percent and personal income taxes stayed at 12 percent for most people, with a maximum of 30 percent for the wealthy, who somehow escaped income taxes anyway (IMF 1993). The tax burden remained high because of Gaidar's fear that collection would founder.

The union treasury was starved in 1991, but only because the republics had revolted against the union. The old tax collection system continued to function amazingly well, because taxes were still collected from big state enterprises by state banks. State enterprises were even forced to pay their taxes in advance each month through automatic deductions, granting the state a positive Tanzi-Olivera effect (that is, the Treasury gained revenues from the inflation tax). Amazingly, Gaidar succeeded in turning a budget deficit of 31 percent of GDP in 1991 to a slight budget surplus on cash basis of 0.9 percent in the first quarter of 1992.

The price liberalization and fiscal tightening put the Central Bank of Russia under extraordinary pressure. The monetary overhang was eliminated, and the real money supply (M2) shrank by two-thirds, from 77 percent to 25 percent of GDP (RECEP 1993, 116). On November 22, 1991, the reformers suffered their first serious defeat in the parliament when the government's request for control over the Central Bank was rejected. Instead, Ruslan Khasbulatov, the speaker of the parliament, supervised the Central Bank, and he turned against radical market reform at this time.

Khasbulatov nominated Georgy Matiukhin, a professor of economics, as chairman of the Central Bank in August 1991. Khasbulatov's support for Matiukhin made the reformers suspicious of him, but he belonged to neither camp and felt closer to Gaidar (Matiukhin 1993). He ended up in a hopeless intermediary position, honestly trying to pursue a moderately strict monetary policy. On one hand, he tried to push for positive real interest rates as fast as possible. On the other, he allowed the money supply to increase substantially. As a result, the money supply (M2) expanded by as much as an average of 11 percent a month from January to May 1992. After spiking at 245 percent in January 1992, monthly inflation declined to 12 percent in May 1992 (figure 3.1).This initial attempt at financial stabilization started unraveling in April 1992, when the parliament started a serious onslaught on the reform government, and it fell apart altogether in June.

The precipitous fall in output continued, but it appeared to moderate. In 1991, industrial production had plummeted by 14.7 percent, and the decline had accelerated during the year, but the slump was somewhat less, at 13.5 percent, during the first half of 1992 (RECEP 1993, 116). Although this was a substantial decline, it was expected. Eastern Europe had experienced similar contractions, and since the Soviet economy was far more distorted, its output drop had to be bigger (Winiecki 1991, Kornai 1994).

The reform government had succeeded in making a breakthrough for the establishment of a market economy, but it was not even close to halting inflation or reviving the economy. One of Gaidar's advisors, Sergei Vasiliev (1999, 86), reflected:

> In the period following the Soviet Union's collapse, all the major social groups were, in effect, paralysed. Actions taken by the government, consequently, were of tremendous significance. . . . The reform government failed to make good use of that short period when it had virtual freedom to do what it deemed necessary. The reformers claimed that there was no significant resistance to reform, but in practice they constantly made compromises with the conservatives. . . . Still, thanks to the institutional vacuum, many transformations were quite smooth. The first phase of the reform was more successful than the reformers had expected, but that period did not last long. As early as spring 1992, the government came under strong pressure from various lobbies. The agrarian lobby was the most effective, and by summer of 1992 it had actually wiped out the success of stabilization in the early months of reform.

Parliamentary Revolt Against the President

In the fall of 1991, Yeltsin was Russia's unquestioned political leader. Even the communists in the parliament supported him. He left political reform

100

Figure 3.1 Monthly inflation and monetary expansion, 1992–94

percent

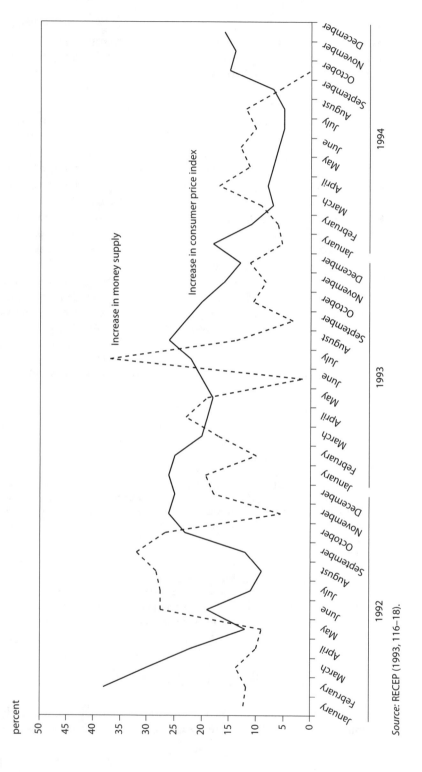

Source: RECEP (1993, 116–18).

for later, a major mistake and arguably the greatest of his career. Unfortunately, he would not change this decision until September 1993, when it was too late, as Yeltsin recognized in his memoirs:

> Maybe I was in fact mistaken in choosing an attack on the economic front as the chief direction, leaving government reorganization to perpetual compromises and political games. I did not disperse the Congress. . . . Out of inertia, I continued to perceive the Supreme Soviet as a legislative body that was developing the legal basis for reform. I did not note that the very *Congress* was being co-opted. The deputies suddenly realized their omnipotence, and an endless bargaining process ensued . . . but the painful measures proposed by Gaidar, as I saw it, required calm—not new social upheavals. Meanwhile, without political backup, Gaidar's reforms were left hanging in midair. (Yeltsin 1994, 127)

Russia's political foundations were much shakier than Yeltsin realized, because according to the old Brezhnev constitution the parliament was sovereign. The constitution could be amended instantaneously through a vote by two-thirds of the deputies. Yeltsin favored a new constitution, but provisionally he had the old one altered in a democratic manner. This solution had two serious shortfalls. First, a qualified majority could change the constitution at any time in any manner. Second, the Brezhnev constitution did not provide for any division of power: the Congress of People's Deputies was sovereign, as had been the case in Europe until the 18th century when Montesquieu's (1748/1977) ideas of division of power spread. Constitutions with sovereign parliaments tended to be dysfunctional and lead to violent resolutions, such as the partition of Poland in 1772, the royal coup in Sweden the same year, or the civil war in England in the mid-17th century.

The Russian Congress of People's Deputies had been elected in March 1990 before full democratization. It was poorly structured, with the deputies floating between changing factions. In the spring of 1992, roughly one-third of the deputies identified themselves as communists, and one-third were democrats supporting Yeltsin. The final third were so fluid that they were called the "marsh" (*boloto*). Soon the marsh was for sale, leading to substantial parliamentary corruption, and it floated in the direction of the state enterprise lobby. Many deputies were accidental, because they formed a second echelon of politicians after the first echelon had been elected to the USSR Congress of People's Deputies in March 1989. They did not represent their voters, or even maintain contact with their constituencies, so they were neither responsible nor accountable.

The Congress styled itself comically like an operetta. In February 1992, I visited Speaker Khasbulatov's chief of staff in the White House, which the Congress had taken over. The White House is huge and has many entrances. At the first entrance, I was met by a fierce-looking group of armed men dressed in White Guard uniforms from the Civil War. At the second entrance, an equally intimidating horde of uniformed and armed Cossacks told me off. Finally, I found the right entrance, where Khasbulatov's staff met me. They were dressed in the gray suits or black leather jackets characteristic of the old Central Committee, where they had all worked before. I made sure to remember the right entrance for my later visits.

Russia needed a constitutional order with a stable division of power as well as a founding parliamentary election, which could have led to the creation of real political parties as well as a democratic majority (McFaul 2001). Yeltsin was supreme from August until November 1991, and he could have asked the Russian Congress of People's Deputies to dissolve itself, and it would have obediently accepted. Yeltsin's failure to do so was a major sin of omission that might well have been the most important reason for the subsequent failure of democracy in Russia.

However, Yeltsin alone was not at fault. He had wanted a new constitution but did not manage to hammer out an agreement before the political consensus fell apart. Hardly anybody surrounding him had a good understanding of democracy building. Nor was any relevant advice from foreign political scientists apparent. Most prominent Western political scientists denounced the radical market reforms that Yeltsin realized were necessary, and their preoccupation was increased social benefits rather than democracy building.[8]

Many considered the old Soviet constitution legitimate, just because it was a constitution, although it was unrelated to democracy. The transitologists who dominated Western comparative politics regarded negotiated solutions as preferable (Karl and Schmitter 1991). At this time, many economists went to Moscow to tell Yeltsin and Gaidar in no uncertain terms how to carry out the economic reforms.[9] Some political scientists met with them as well, but they appear not to have pushed any clear policy advice.[10] Many books put forth policy advice on how to undertake the economic transition to capitalism,[11] but I am unaware of any normative book that proposed how to build a democracy. Thus, mainstream Western political scientists were neither right nor helpful.[12] If they played any role it would have contributed to Yeltsin's failure to dissolve parliament in the fall of 1991.

Ironically, Yeltsin himself had promoted the two men who were to lead the opposition against him. After Yeltsin had been elected Russian president in June 1991, he supported the candidacy of his first deputy, Khasbulatov, as speaker. Ethnically, Khasbulatov was a Chechen, and he was a

---

8. A case in point is Przeworski (1991), the dominant political science book on transition at the time.

9. I know, because I did, but so did many others.

10. I owe this point to Michael McFaul.

11. See Allison and Yavlinsky (1991), Åslund (1992), Blanchard et al. (1991), Kornai (1990), Peck and Richardson (1991), and World Bank (1991).

12. Naturally, there are exceptions, but the best publications appeared much later, notably Diamond (1995), Bunce (1999), and McFaul (2001).

respected professor of international economics at the Plekhanov Academy, Moscow's prime business school. Unfortunately he knew virtually nothing about economics, as was so often the case with Soviet professors of political economy.[13] As chairman of the parliament, however, Khasbulatov showed extraordinary skills, manipulating the majority at will and persuading it to make the most unexpected decisions. Before the presidential elections in 1991, Yeltsin had coopted a reformist communist general, Alexander Rutskoi, to gain votes from moderate communists and made Rutskoi his vice presidential candidate. Rutskoi's main attractions were his good looks and that he was a general (Yeltsin 1994).

Yeltsin did not get much of a honeymoon after the August coup—only three months, of which he rested for two months. Vice President Rutskoi made his first attack on the new government on November 18, 12 days after its appointment, insinuating that its ministers were toddlers. Four days later, Khasbulatov incited the parliament to refuse to give the reformers control over the Central Bank, which made monetary stabilization impossible. Khasbulatov and Rutskoi became the opposition leaders, clearly disappointed to have been left out of the government, and their opposition would grow ever greater until the storming of the Russian parliament in October 1993.

Yeltsin's appointment of a government of young, outstanding economists was brave, and the economic reforms required them. But many were upset about these appointments. The Russian parliamentarians saw themselves as victorious revolutionaries. The parliament had defeated the August coup, and revolutionaries not only know that they are right, they also think that they have the right to everything. They were exceedingly pompous and irresponsible. This was particularly true of Khasbulatov and Rutskoi. The activists in Democratic Russia also felt they had been let down, although they continued to support Yeltsin and his government. And the old *nomenklatura* was, of course, furious all along. Such divisions are associated with any revolution, but they were aggravated because the Russian parliament did not have much of a legislative role, with Yeltsin legislating by decree in 1991–92. Therefore, the new ministers did not have to appear much before parliament and were poorly known by the parliamentarians, who became idle and frustrated.

The powerful state enterprise managers also felt excluded. So did the old reform communist economists, who had no role to play in the economic reforms, which they opposed. The old academicians spoke contemptuously of the ministers as "junior researchers" and opposed shock therapy as "unprofessional," arguing for a larger budget deficit, looser monetary policy, and price regulation, which revealed their complete eco-

---

13. In May 1990, I held a seminar with Khasbulatov at the Stockholm School of Economics. His résumé stated that he was fluent in English, but he spoke none. When a banker asked him what to do about the monetary overhang in the Soviet Union, Khasbulatov responded that it was no problem at all—the more money there was, the more production there would be.

nomic ignorance.[14] Most of them joined the reestablished Communist Party of the Russian Federation.

The revolutionary staff rivalry was aggravated by Russia's immense generational divides. Most who had been hardened by the Great Terror in 1937 and World War II as adults remained Stalinists. Gorbachev and his cohort, by contrast, identified themselves as the "children of the 20th Party Congress" in 1956 who had come of age during Khrushchev's thaw. They were the last believers in socialism and its possible reform. The next generation, which had matured under Brezhnev, was cynical and passive. Having never been allowed to make careers, they have played a minimal role in Russian politics. Sensibly, Yeltsin boldly reached out to the more idealistic and ambitious post-Brezhnev generation of Gaidar.

At the World Economic Forum in Davos, Switzerland, in January 1992, Academician Oleg Bogomolov complained about the ignorance of the new Russian ministers. One of them, Deputy Prime Minister Aleksandr Shokhin, a young professor of economics, responded that unlike the older generation, his generation had learned English and had read the international economic literature.[15] "We did not only read your books—we wrote them," Shokhin added sarcastically, because many old Soviet academics did not write themselves but exploited younger ghostwriters. The mutual aggression between the older and younger generation of Russian economists was extraordinary, just like the generational divide between feudal fathers and radical sons in Ivan Turgenev's novel *Fathers and Sons* from 1861.

When the old-style critics had no other argument left, they denied that general laws of social science applied to Russia with quotations from the 19th century romantic Russian poet Fedor Tyutchev: "Russia cannot be understood with the mind, or measured by an ordinary yardstick: She has a special status—All you can do is believe in Russia." This was a motto of the Slavophiles. A famous quote by Winston Churchill added to the obfuscation: "Russia is a riddle wrapped in a mystery inside an enigma." But he uttered those words in 1939, when the Soviet Union was as closed as a society can be.

Along these mystic lines, one group of reform communists argued: "Our situation is special. It cannot be described with general rules" (Petrakov et al. 1992). Khasbulatov (1992) concurred: "The economic reforms must not be based on abstract and extremely simplified models, but on decisions derived from real life, on considerations of the real situation in the economy, the population of the country, and the experiences of the whole political and socioeconomic history of Russia." In practice, these

---

14. See Abalkin (1992), Arbatov (1992), Bogomolov (1992, 1993), Fedorenko et al. (1992), Khasbulatov (1992), and Petrakov et al. (1992).

15. I attended that session.

old Slavophile arguments won in politics, but eventually they lost out in economics.

The Gaidar government's political management left much to be desired. The new ministers were Russia's best young economic researchers belonging to the intellectual elite in Moscow and St. Petersburg. Most of them had been members of the CPSU, because that was a requirement for elite membership, but they were no politicians. Yeltsin explicitly stated that he appointed them as professionals, and they were proud of not being politicians. They delegated politics upwards to First Deputy Prime Minister Burbulis and Yeltsin. The liberal Burbulis was the single link between the young reform ministers and Yeltsin, and that was not enough. After several months, they became politicians, but that was too late.

However radical and resolute Yeltsin sounded, he was a politician who hedged his bets, and he was more intuitive than consistent. After appointing his young reform ministers, he kept them at a distance and gave them no direct access to himself. "The ministers would clear all matters requiring my involvement through Burbulis" (Yeltsin 1994, 156). Even Gaidar had minimal access to Yeltsin. The government was housed in the old CC headquarters at the Old Square, while Yeltsin and his presidential administration sat ensconced in splendid isolation in the Kremlin. Although President Yeltsin formally was prime minister, he rarely participated in the weekly cabinet meetings. No radical reform would have occurred without Yeltsin's blessing, but his involvement was insufficient for full-fledged political support. Regardless of Yeltsin having arranged this himself, he became disenchanted:

> Soon it became evident that the Gaidar government, which was rapidly making one decision after another, was in complete isolation. Gaidar and his people never traveled around the country to take the pulse of the nation. From the outset, these ministers perceived the Khasbulatov parliament as an instrument of pressure on them, as a symbol of everything that was reactionary, everything that had to be fought. That was their attitude to Rutskoi, the vice president, as well. . . . [B]y sophisticatedly refusing to "dirty their hands with politics" and leaving all political initiative to their chief, the Gaidar team made a tactical error that cost us all a great deal. (Yeltsin 1994, 158–59)

The first severe confrontation between the reform government and the Russian Congress of People's Deputies took place in April 1992. Khasbulatov had mobilized a majority of the parliament in opposition to Yeltsin. His two key demands were a looser, even more inflationary, fiscal policy, and reduced power of the president. From this time, a new constitution was a permanent topic of discussion, but no common ground was to be found. The Congress wanted to have all power, which Yeltsin opposed.

Yeltsin was a patently poor negotiator. When negotiating with the Congress, he started with concessions, making certain personnel changes before its session and promising to replace three to five ministers with experienced industrialists, but he did not secure anything in return. Characteristically, he did not even talk to Gaidar about this important issue but "passed this list on to Gaidar through Burbulis, since [Yeltsin] considered it premature to meet with the government at this time." Feeling abandoned by Yeltsin and under heavy attack from the congress, Gaidar and his ministers walked out of the Congress and submitted their collective resignation, to Yeltsin's surprise and appreciation. Thanks to their determined action, the government survived. Gaidar grew to be a politician, but the political isolation of the reformers was overwhelming (Yeltsin 1994, 164–67; Murrell 1997, 100–104). As a concession to parliament, Yeltsin (1994, 159–60) dismissed Burbulis as first deputy prime minister in April 1992, which absurdly left the Gaidar government with minimal contact with its boss.

Rather than taking the lead, Yeltsin took a lot of time off in early 1992. He marveled over how wonderful Russia's state enterprise managers were. They were well organized in the Russian Union of Industrialists and Entrepreneurs, which had been founded by the old liberal CPSU apparatchik Arkady Volsky, who was a skillful man for all seasons. Volsky opposed radical market reforms, because his constituency benefited from subsidized credits and foreign trade arbitrage. Now, Yeltsin had forgotten why he had launched radical economic reform and wanted "industrialists" in his government, not understanding that they were the main opponents of his reforms (Yeltsin 1994, 164–73).

After having failed to liberalize energy prices at the beginning of 1992, Gaidar tried to do so repeatedly, but now Yeltsin was dead set against it. At a cabinet meeting in May 1992, Yeltsin sacked Gaidar's minister of energy, Vladimir Lopukhin, for having advocated energy price liberalization, which Gaidar did as well. Yeltsin did so without having informed Gaidar (Yeltsin 1994, 166–67).

In May–June 1992, Yeltsin appointed three heavy industrialists as deputy prime ministers. Most prominent among them was Viktor Chernomyrdin, the last Soviet minister of gas industry and the founder of Gazprom, the state corporation that compounded all the Russian assets of his former ministry. In June 1992, the parliament sacked Matiukhin as chairman of the Central Bank, accusing him of excessively strict monetary policy. In came the last chairman of the Soviet State Bank, Viktor Gerashchenko, although he had been complicit in the August 1991 coup and had carried out the unpopular Pavlov monetary confiscation in January 1991. Yeltsin elevated Gaidar to acting prime minister in June 1992, but these personnel changes meant that the first attempt at radical economic reform was over. For the rest of 1992, Russia slid toward hyperinflation with a minimum of policy.

A consequence of this fierce standoff between the president/government and the legislature was that no reform legislation could be adopted from June 1992 until December 1993. "[D]ecisions made by one branch of government were automatically canceled out by the decisions made by another" (Gaidar 1999, 230). Considering that the transition to a market economy required hundreds of new laws, the reform effort was impeded and distorted. Many concrete decisions concerning privatization or deregulation could be undertaken by decree, but general laws and legal codes had to be negotiated in parliament.

Ambitious Mass Privatization

Political attitudes toward privatization were peculiarly volatile. Nationalization of the means of production was one of the last communist dogmas to fall, but after the 500-day program had made privatization acceptable, a broad consensus demanded instant mass privatization. At first, both the right and the left complained that privatization had not already been carried out, but after Russia had undertaken the largest and fastest mass privatization in world history, it was sharply criticized.

In December 1990, Russia had enacted a Law on Enterprises and Entrepreneurial Activity, and in the summer of 1991 the Russian parliament adopted one law on privatization and another on personal privatization accounts. Unfortunately, their drafters had not thought through the privatization, so these early laws could not possibly work.

An intense public debate on privatization took place in the first half of 1992. Since Russia was dominated by big enterprises, the debate focused on their privatization. All agreed that privatization had to be extensive and fast. The questions concerned primarily how to privatize and who would benefit. State managers were quickly taking over the nominally state-owned enterprises, because Russia's Enterprise Law of 1990 effectively left the managers as masters of state enterprises. A Soviet decree on leasing of April 1989 allowed them to "lease" their state enterprises, gradually seizing them as property. In February 1992, some 9,500 state enterprises were leased, and they accounted for 8 percent of total Russian employment (Frydman et al. 1993, 20–22). Between 1989 and 1991, a plethora of associations, concerns, and corporations were set up as ministerial officials attempted *nomenklatura* privatization. By the end of 1991, Russia harbored more than 3,000 such associations. Against this backdrop, Yeltsin (1991) stated in his big reform speech:

> For impermissibly long, we have discussed whether private property is necessary. In the meantime, the party-state elite has actively engaged in their personal privatization. The scale, the enterprises, and the hypocrisy are staggering. The privatization in Russia has gone on for [a long time], but wildly, spontaneously, and often on a criminal basis. Today it is necessary to grasp the initiative, and we are intent on doing so.

Russians talked about *prikhvatizatsiya*, a Russian pun combining the words for grabbing and privatization. A strong sense prevailed that what was not privatized would be stolen by the old elite. Chubais (1999, 29) noted: "At the end of 1991, the spontaneous privatization was steam-rolling all over. It was the theft of the common property, but this theft was not illegal, because legal schemes of de-statization did not exist."

A major aim of privatization was to ensure that managers did not usurp everything. Another threat was that the old industrial ministries or their subsidiaries would replace themselves with holding companies. State managers proposed that enterprises be given to the workers, presuming they could exploit their workers. Democrats and reformers hoped for mass privatization through vouchers distributed to all to give every Russian a share. Unlike in Central and Eastern Europe, restitution to former owners was not an issue.

Chubais' advisors, Maxim Boycko, Andrei Shleifer, and Robert Vishny, were the main thinkers behind the Russian privatization, and they published a forceful book, *Privatizing Russia*. Their view was that:

> [A]t least in Russia, political influence over economic life was the fundamental cause of economic inefficiency, and…the principal objective of reform was, therefore, to depoliticize economic life. Price liberalization fosters depoliticization because it deprives politicians of the opportunity to allocate goods. Privatization fosters depoliticization because it robs politicians of control over firms. (Boycko, Shleifer, and Vishny 1995, 10–11)

Under communism, managers had been selected and promoted by political criteria. The only cure was to separate politicians from property:

> In our view, controlling managers is not nearly as important as controlling politicians, since managers' interests are generally much closer to economic efficiency than those of politicians. Once depoliticization is accomplished, the secondary goal of establishing effective corporate governance can be addressed. (Boycko, Shleifer, and Vishny 1995, 65)

Another key idea was to unify cash rights and control rights to align the incentives of owners and managers and stop the rampant asset stripping. Managers should be made interested in profits and asset values rather than taking assets out of a company.

After extensive debates and negotiations, the government managed to persuade the Russian parliament to amend the Privatization Law and adopt a Privatization Program in June 1992. These were the last reform acts to be promulgated. The outcome was a compromise with three different options for privatization. First, importantly, enterprise associations were to be broken up and enterprises were to be privatized individually, which was done quite consistently. Then, large enterprises were transformed into joint stock companies. The property rights would not be collective but individual and transferable. The Russian privatizers pragmatically appealed to a spectrum of stakeholders to make sure that real privatization was possible. The managers were coopted by the reformers, and the most popular option gave 51 percent of the shares to managers and workers. The industrial ministries, however, were hostile to privatization, because it would deprive them of their control over state enterprises, but they were defeated.

For Chubais, the main goal of privatization was "to form a broad stratum of private owners." Other important aims were to improve the efficiency of enterprises, to create a competitive market, and to pursue rapid privatization.[16] Realizing the limits of their power, the Russian privatizers kept auxiliary objectives short. State revenues were not even a consideration, because no improvement in the functioning of enterprises could be expected until they had been privatized. Václav Klaus in Czechoslovakia sold privatization as an ideological program, while Chubais emphasized its material benefits to various stakeholders. In hindsight, Klaus' approach was more beneficial in the long run, but both countries got privatization done (Appel 2004).

In August 1992, Yeltsin made privatization the centerpiece of his speech on the anniversary of the coup. He advocated the benefits of capitalism for ordinary people: "We need millions of owners rather than a handful of millionaires." He emphasized equality of opportunity and freedom of choice. His big news was that Russia would undertake a voucher privatization: "The privatization voucher is a ticket for each of us to a free economy."[17] These two statements were to come back to haunt him.

The idea of voucher privatization for Russia was born relatively late, at a conference at Harvard University in Cambridge, Massachusetts, in February 1992 in a conversation among Chubais' main advisors on privatization.[18] The inspiration came from Czechoslovakia, whereas Poland and Hungary showed problems with privatization to be avoided. The Russian scheme was simpler than the Czechoslovak one. Every Russian received one privatization voucher for free before the end of January 1993. Unlike in Czechoslovakia, the vouchers could be traded, because the privatizers wanted to encourage an early concentration of ownership. They worried that the vouchers would disperse ownership too much to allow effective owners' control. Chubais exaggerated the material benefits Russians would gain from the voucher privatization, arguing that such a voucher would be worth a Volga car. This would cost him a great deal in the future, but his goal was not egalitarianism but a normal market economy based on predominant private ownership.

Yeltsin issued a decree on the issue of privatization vouchers in August 1992. Enterprises were privatized through auctions, where anybody with vouchers could bid for stocks of a specific company. The first voucher auctions were held in December 1992, and they continued relentlessly despite

---

16. "State Program for the Privatization of State and Municipal Enterprises of the Russian Federation for 1992," *Rossiiskaya gazeta*, July 9, 1992.

17. *Rossiiskaya gazeta*, August 20, 1992.

18. The advisors were Maxim Boycko, Andrei Shleifer, and Dmitri Vasiliev. I attended that conference.

considerable political tumult. The last voucher auctions took place in the summer of 1994. Meanwhile, 16,500 large enterprises (with more than 1,000 workers each) had been privatized in this way.

The voucher privatization was more successful than anybody had dared to hope. This was the largest privatization the world had ever seen. The distribution of shares, however, was not quite as expected. Only 20 percent of the shares of the companies were actually sold at voucher auctions, largely to outsiders, whereas 18 percent of the stocks belonged to managers and 40 percent to workers in 1996, and the managers often controlled their employees' shares. A critical mass of private enterprise had been built, because Russia claimed 920,000 private enterprises in 1995 (Blasi, Kroumova, and Kruse 1997, 189, 192–93).

Russia had hardly any small, private firms. "According to official statistics, as of January 1, 1992, in all of vast Russia only 107 retail stores, 58 cafeterias, and 56 service enterprises had been privatized" (Gaidar 1999, 167). Yet, small-scale privatization was neither innovative nor complicated, and it was swiftly done. Experimental sales of shops had started in St. Petersburg in 1991, and that city's privatizers were given the chance to apply their skills to the whole country. The lesson was clear: let the local authorities sell small enterprises at auctions and encourage them to do so quickly.

After Chubais had become minister of privatization in November 1991, he quickly established a new privatization apparatus throughout the country, and it started with the sale of small enterprises. In February 1992, the first shops were auctioned off in Nizhny Novgorod in a theatrical televised auction in the presence of both Gaidar and Chubais. Exploiting the old communist mechanisms, Chubais set up stiff monthly plan targets for the small-scale privatization by which officials were assessed.

Small-scale privatization gained full speed in July 1992, and an average of 5,000 to 6,000 small firms were sold each month until July 1993. By August 1994, the government assessed that no fewer than 106,000 small firms had been privatized. Quantitatively, the small-scale privatization was an unmitigated success, and it was not very controversial. Qualitatively, however, it was not all that great. In fact, few auctions were held and most shops were sold cheaply to their managers. Often, many liens and regulations persisted for years, rendering it difficult to distinguish between a privatized and state-owned shop. New private shops looked far better.

Housing was privatized with relative ease. By and large, it was given away almost for free to its tenants, who enjoyed quasi-property rights. Commercial real estate was a nightmare because usually about five different agencies had claims to the same property. One agency used the premises, whereas it formally belonged to another, and a third was entitled to rent income, and a fourth to possible sales revenues. It took years to align all these dispersed property rights. In agriculture, the old communist establishment ruled, and most peasants were old, conservative, and fearful, rendering land privatization nearly impossible.

Chubais' privatization was the greatest success of Russia's reform. In late 1994, the European Bank for Reconstruction and Development assessed that half of Russia's GDP originated in the private sector (EBRD 1994). Most of Russia's large, medium-size, and small enterprises had been privatized, while large sectors, such as agriculture, infrastructure, and the military-industrial complex, remained completely public.

Abortive Financial Stabilization

The appointments of three state enterprise managers as deputy prime ministers in June 1992, and of Viktor Gerashchenko as chair of the Central Bank in July, marked the end of the first attempt at macroeconomic stabilization. The money supply (M2) increased by a monthly average of 28 percent between June and October, and inflation rose to 26 percent a month from November to February 1993 (figure 3.1). Russia was approaching hyperinflation, which starts at 50 percent a month (Cagan 1956). The velocity of money was rising, which means that the inflation tax plummeted, because people and enterprises escaped from rubles to dollars or goods.

Gerashchenko maintained the extreme position that no monetary overhang had existed. He insisted that the prior ratio between money and GDP had to be restored through massive monetary emission:

> Could the economy manage with the former money supply when the prices were rising[?]. . . . [W]ere the previous monetary resources really sufficient to exist at the present price level, when the wholesale prices have risen 16 to 18 times? According to my view, they were inadequate. (Gerashchenko 1992)

The concern of Gerashchenko and the industrialists was rising interenterprise arrears. Partly, the nonpayments signaled a healthy capitalist instinct to care about money, but the centralized state payment system could not cope with the large number of new enterprises, and no collection system existed, but if so desired that could be resolved through advance payments. The industrialists easily colluded in demands for the issue of more money to net out the debts and to "index" their working capital. For some time the government and Central Bank complied (Sachs and Lipton 1993). Jeffrey Sachs assessed Gerashchenko as "the worst central banker in world history," which was a fair judgment.

A Bonanza for Rent Seeking

The reason for the failure of financial stabilization was that rent seekers made fortunes on the rent-seeking machine built by Gorbachev's partial reforms. In 1992, Russia's rents were possibly the greatest the world has ever seen. The four main sources of rents were regulated commodity exports, subsidized grain imports, subsidized credits, and state subsidies.

First, total export rents were no less than $24 billion or 30 percent of GDP in 1992. State-controlled, domestic prices of commodities were at most one-tenth of world market prices, and more than 70 percent of Russia's exports were commodities subject to export quotas (Aven 1994, 84). Total Russian exports outside the CIS amounted to $42.2 billion. Collected export tariffs were some $2.4 billion, while GDP was only $79 billion in 1992, because of the very low exchange rate (World Bank 1996b).

Another large source of rents was subsidized imports, which the IMF (1993, 133) calculated at 17.5 percent of GDP in 1992. Because of the fear of starvation, Russia maintained special exchange rates for so-called critical imports until 1993, subsidizing such imports to 99 percent. The Russian importers of grain bought hard currency for only 1 percent of the going exchange rate in 1992, allowing them to pay only 1 percent of the world market price for imported grain, while bread was sold at ordinary domestic prices. Ironically, $12.5 billion of foreign credits designated as humanitarian aid did not support but rather undermined economic reform efforts, whereas the outside world did not provide any support for the economic reforms in the first half of 1992.

A third source of rents was the emission of subsidized state credits. The Central Bank of Russia issued new credit equivalent to 31.6 percent GDP in 1992 (Granville 1995b, 67). As these loans were largely given at an interest rate of 10 to 25 percent a year, while inflation that year was 2,500 percent, they were sheer gifts. These gifts rendered Gerashchenko very popular among the Russian elite, although the banking sector was rampant with crime thanks to his largesse.

The fourth source of rents was direct enterprise subsidies provided by the state budget amounting to 10.4 percent of GDP in Russia in 1992 (EBRD 1997, 83).

From these four sources, total gross rents amounted to an incredible 90 percent of Russia's GDP in 1992. And that does not include some rents such as tax exemptions. Presumably, rents have never been larger as a ratio of GDP anywhere in the world than they were in the former Soviet Union in 1992. Select citizens became conspicuously wealthy when they transferred these rents and subsidies from state enterprises to their private accounts through transfer pricing or outright theft.

By the end of 1992, it was easy to despair. Russia appeared a state captured by rent seekers, ranging from state enterprise managers, state officials, bankers, and new entrepreneurs to organized crime. Could this rent-seeking machine be broken? Strangely, in the course of 1993, most of these rents disappeared, in part because of policy, in part due to a normalization of the market.

Although Gaidar had been ousted as acting prime minister in December 1992 and replaced by the industrialist Chernomyrdin, a strong reformer became minister of finance, the young and forceful economist

Boris Fedorov, who had been one of the authors of the 500-day program. With authority and militancy akin to that of Chubais, Fedorov started systematically sorting out macroeconomic policies. Energetically, he bombarded everybody with sensible policy initiatives. Sometimes he succeeded, sometimes not.

The End of the Ruble Zone

The most fundamental flaw was the ruble zone, which had to be broken up. At the beginning of 1992, 15 republican central banks competed in issuing ruble credits. If one country issued more credits than the average, it gained a disproportionate share of the common GDP, but it condemned itself to hyperinflation.

The collapsed Habsburg Empire had faced a similar dilemma after World War I. One single country, Czechoslovakia, had swiftly abandoned the common currency zone, and established its own national currency. It was the only Habsburg successor country to avoid hyperinflation and maintain democracy until World War II. All the others faced high inflation, which contributed to their political destabilization and the failure of democracy (Pasvolsky 1928). These lessons were well understood and discussed in the West at this time (Sargent 1986, Dornbusch 1992). Unfortunately, the CIS countries did not heed these lessons.

In the summer of 1992, the three Baltic countries broke out of the ruble zone and established their own national currencies. Kyrgyzstan followed in May 1993. The other 11 countries stayed in the notoriously inflationary common currency zone. From the outset, Gaidar (1993) and other Russian reformers had advocated the "nationalization" of the ruble. Fedorov pushed this line with great fervor, because the cost to Russia was enormous—22 percent of GDP in 1992 (IMF 1994b), which was part of the cost of the credit emission. However, the IMF considered this a political question, on which it preferred to be neutral, and it advocated coordination of monetary policy (Odling-Smee and Pastor 2002). But that could not have worked (Granville 1995b, 2002).

In July 1993, Gerashchenko, until then the greatest cheerleader of the ruble zone, suddenly finished it off by declaring Soviet rubles null and void, characteristically without consulting the minister of finance. A chaos of exchange queues outside all banks erupted again and lasted for several days, exactly as after Pavlov's unsuccessful currency reform in January 1991. In 1993, the 10 other countries remaining in the ruble zone experienced hyperinflation, that is, more than 50 percent inflation in the course of one month, while Russia escaped with an inflation of "only" 840 percent. By September 1993, the ruble zone broke up, and a basis for monetary stabilization had been created (Granville 1995b).

An Effective IMF Agreement

Apart from breaking up of the ruble zone, another major improvement facilitated by Fedorov was that Russia concluded an agreement with the IMF on a Systemic Transformation Facility in April 1993, which provided Russia with a framework for macroeconomic policy. This agreement established quarterly credit ceilings and compelled the Central Bank to raise interest rates, which Gerashchenko actually did. By November 1993, Russia had attained a positive real interest rate, and monetary emission started moderating.

A third important measure was that Fedorov managed to unify the exchange rate, which reduced import subsidies from 17.5 percent of GDP in 1992 to some 4 percent of GDP in 1993. He also minimized the destabilizing foreign commodity credits (IMF 1994a).

Fourth, Fedorov tried to raise or liberalize energy prices, and he was partially successful. Oil and coal prices were actually liberalized, and the prices of natural gas and electricity were hiked substantially. In addition, energy taxation rose through the imposition of VAT and increased excise taxes.

Many factors contributed to these policy improvements. Through their own suffering, the Russian people had learned the social costs of high inflation, and that it did not boost but disrupted production. The price distortions abated as the real exchange rate rose sharply. As a result, the average Russian wage rose from $6 a month in December 1991 to $114 a month two years later (figure 3.2). As arbitrage helped alleviate distortions, rents declined. The inflation tax dwindled when people and enterprises learned not to hold more rubles than absolutely necessary, which led to high velocity and demonetization (Åslund, Boone, and Johnson 1996). The IMF had finally become seriously engaged in the Russian stabilization, and it imposed some international norms on Chernomyrdin and Gerashchenko. Yeltsin, however, remained aloof from macroeconomic stabilization policy. As a consequence, in 1993 these rents were halved from their 1992 level, and they fell even more in 1994, but they started rising again from 1996 to 1998 (figure 3.3).

Although much of the groundwork for financial stabilization had been laid, stabilization remained elusive. Monthly inflation stayed in the double digits throughout 1993 and only halved from 26 percent in January to 13 percent in December 1993.

Failure of the West to Act

The Soviet political and economic crisis and postcommunist transformation were dominant topics across the world in 1990. Everybody who was

Figure 3.2 Monthly average wage, 1992–93

US dollars per month

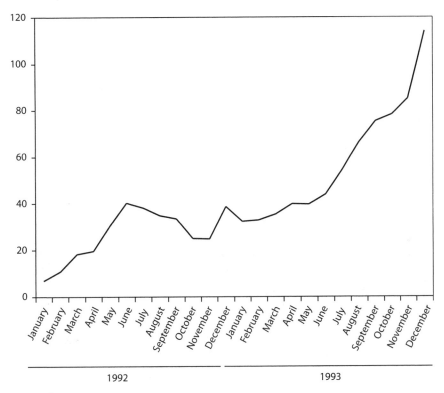

Source: Åslund (1995, 185).

anybody took a clear position. At their summits in the summers of 1990 and 1991, the leaders of the G-7, the world's seven leading industrialized democracies, discussed whether and how to support the collapsing Soviet Union economically. But they abstained from any decision. Admittedly, Gorbachev arrived to the G-7 summit in London in July 1991 with a contradictory economic memorandum, showing that he had no clear idea about what he wanted, and his economic policies were in shambles.

The situation changed completely with the abortive August 1991 coup, which marked Russia's democratization. The three big question marks were eliminated: the Soviet Union, the CPSU, and Gorbachev. They were replaced with Russia and Yeltsin. Yeltsin's big reform speech in October 1991 was as clear, market-oriented, and West-oriented as anybody could have asked for. Russia's intention to undertake a radical market economic reform was abundantly evident. Yeltsin (1991) exhorted the West to help Russia at length and in no uncertain terms:

Figure 3.3   Rent seeking, 1991–98

rents as share of GDP

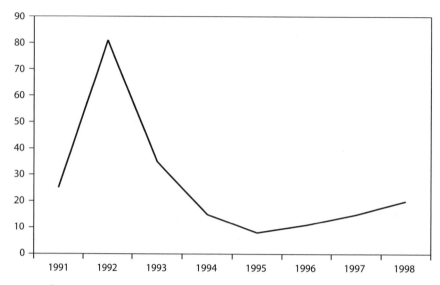

Sources: Åslund (1999); author's estimates.

We turn officially to the IMF, the World Bank, the European Bank for Reconstruction and Development and invite them to elaborate detailed plans in cooperation with and participation in the economic reforms.

We appeal to the developed countries and international organizations for technical assistance first of all for the training of personnel, analysis and elaboration of recommendations on principal economic, ecological, and regional questions. . . .

I appeal to the world community. Russia carries out its reforms in its own interests, and not under external pressure. Help from the world community can facilitate our movement along this road considerably and accelerate the reforms.

Alas, the West ignored his call. Throughout 1991, US officials avoided any speculation about the possible breakup of the Soviet Union, although it had been abundantly clear from August. Infamously, as late as August 1, 1991, US President George H. W. Bush warned of the dangers of a breakup of the Soviet Union in his "chicken Kiev" speech in the capital of Ukraine (Goldgeier and McFaul 2003, 28). The US Treasury harbored only a narrow interest in the Soviet Union serving its debt, which it was obviously unable to do without major reform.[19]

---

19. The exception was Secretary of Defense Dick Cheney, who was a dissident in the Bush administration. He favored Yeltsin, the breakup of the Soviet Union, and democracy and market reform in Russia (Goldgeier and McFaul 2003, 33).

Rarely has such a great historical opportunity arisen, and seldom has it been so evident in its coming. The young Russian reformers were working night and day to prepare their reforms, and a strong informed Western opinion urged their governments to support Russian reform. The *New York Times* (November 12, 1991) editorialized: "The challenge for the West is to encourage Mr. Yeltsin's real, radical program by giving attentive assistance now." On December 17, 1991, the *Financial Times* concurred: "Now is the first and, perhaps, the last chance for the West to promote radical economic reform in the former Soviet Union." They could not have been more right.

In mid-November 1991, the deputy ministers of finance of the G-7 descended on Moscow. The Russian reformers happily welcomed them, presuming they wanted to discuss the Russian reform plans and Western assistance. Alas, they did nothing of the kind. The G-7 representatives were interested in only one thing, that the soon-to-be former Soviet republics guarantee their "joint and several" responsibility to service the Soviet foreign debt. The Soviet republican representatives agreed, although it was evident that they could not guarantee anything in the rampant financial crisis. During four days in Moscow, the G-7 representatives ignored the Russian reform plans and refused to discuss assistance. They left the Russian reformers in a state of shock. Gaidar (1999, 141) noted, "The initial response of Western political and financial elites toward Russian economic reform was extremely wary and cool."

The next Western initiative was a sheer diversion. US Secretary of State James Baker convened a high-level international conference on humanitarian aid to the former Soviet Union in Washington in late January 1992, just after Russia had launched its daring reforms. The US administration designed the conference to discuss only humanitarian assistance and not support for reform. Incredibly, the United States did not invite anybody from the former Soviet Union, as if to avoid a reality test. In February 1992, the well-informed *Washington Post* columnist Jim Hoagland concluded that the United States did not provide any support to Russia because President Bush reckoned that Boris Yeltsin was a transitional figure.[20] Bush just could not get Russia right.

On April 1, 1992, five months after his dramatic appeal to the Western governments, Yeltsin received an answer of sorts. In the face of a coming onslaught from the opposition in the Russian Congress of People's Deputies, Bush and German Chancellor Helmut Kohl declared their intent to mobilize a $24 billion Western aid package for Russia, but they never substantiated their April Fools' claim.

The West took a very tough position in the Paris Club, which was to renegotiate Russia's excessive debt service, although Russia generously accepted responsibility for the whole debt of the Soviet Union (Gaidar

---

20. *Washington Post*, February 11, 1992.

1999, 119–21). The Russian reformers suffered from the parliament's attack, and by June 1992 their first reform attempt was effectively finished. The demonstrative absence of Western support contributed to the fall of the Russian reform government.

The amounts discussed were minor in comparison with the potential benefits. The total request for financial assistance for Russian economic reform in 1992 was about $25 billion, of which $6 billion was intended for a stabilization fund. Almost all the "assistance" would have been in the form of credits. A reasonable bilateral US contribution would have been $3 billion.

Meanwhile the United States reaped $69 billion in a peace dividend in terms of saved military expenditures in 1992 (Åslund 2002, 400–401). In comparison, the Marshall Plan accounted for 2 percent of US GDP at the end of the 1940s, which would have meant $125 billion for the United States in 1992 dollars (Milward 1984; US Census Bureau 1999, 459). The West did give Russia credits of $12.5 billion in 1992, benefiting Western agricultural interests. These bilateral loans were commodity credits, which actually blocked reform, because they became rents for commodity traders and their corrupt conduits. They were not conditional on any reform measures and not coordinated with international financial institutions.

The window of opportunity of "extraordinary politics" when the West could help Russian economic reform was brief, lasting only five months from October 1991 until March 1992. But the West turned its back on Russia's Western-oriented and democratic reformers, providing solely humanitarian assistance. This was the only big chance for the West to support reform in Russia, and the responsibility for missing it rests squarely with then-President Bush. This was a folly comparable with that of Georges Clemenceau at Versailles or Neville Chamberlain at Munich. Sachs' (1994, 1995) argument that early Western aid was critical for the success of economic reform, and that its delay could lead to both political and economic destabilization, was fully substantiated.

The only significant US interest was in denuclearizing the other former Soviet republics, either by destroying their nuclear arms or transferring them to Russia. This was the obsession of Secretary of State Baker, and he accomplished it because of effective Russian cooperation (Goldgeier and McFaul 2003). Even so, the Bush administration ignored Russia's hardship, which could do nothing but breed future Russian resentment against the United States.

Russia became a member of the IMF and the World Bank, as did most other former Soviet republics, in the spring of 1992. Both organizations had started working intensively in Russia from the fall of 1991, but they were not formally entitled to provide financing until Russia became a member. Alas, by that time Russia's economic reforms were already failing. As if to apologize for having missed the chance, the IMF gave Russia a loan of $1 billion in August 1992 without serious conditions. In June

1993, Russia applied for membership in the General Agreement on Tariffs and Trade, which became the World Trade Organization (WTO) in 1995. But accession to the WTO is a slow process, and in the 1990s it was no priority of the Russian government, which focused on managing its finances.

Yeltsin was primarily interested in becoming a full-fledged member of the G-7. He had a very positive view of the West, arguably naïvely so, but he did not quite know what to do with it. The Western leaders treated him with undue reserve because he was very Russian and an outsized hero. Unlike Gorbachev, he was not inclined to small talk, and Western leaders preferred the personable Gorbachev to the great Yeltsin.

Oddly, the most notable Western presence in Russia in 1991 and 1992 was independent economic advisors, the most prominent of whom was Harvard Professor Jeffrey Sachs.[21] Yeltsin and Gaidar invited foreign advisors, and they listened to them to a surprising degree. The foreign advisors were greatly inspired by the Polish radical economic reform, which most of them had worked on. They persistently argued for more radical, comprehensive, and consistent reforms, and they wrote analytical notes on various problems. To an amazing extent, the recommendations they made in 1991–93 were eventually carried out.

Dissolution of the Parliament and Shootout at the White House

The strife between the parliament and the president only escalated. Russia maintained the cumbersome Gorbachev model, with an outer parliament, the Congress of People's Deputies of slightly more than 1,000 deputies, who selected a smaller bicameral parliament, the Supreme Soviet, among themselves. Each session of the Congress amounted to a new onslaught on Yeltsin, his economic reforms, and his presidential powers. Originally, the Congress had been convened once every half year, but Speaker Khasbulatov called in the Congress ever more often to foment his irreconcilable opposition to Yeltsin.

Yeltsin could not stand the Congress. He spent as little time as possible there, which infuriated the parliamentarians. Before each congressional session, Yeltsin held a few consultative meetings and sacrificed a few of his most loyal and effective—and consequently most disliked—ministers, which demoralized his administration. From time to time, Yeltsin hinted about taking his own proposal for a new constitution and the dissolution

---

21. Sachs, David Lipton, and I operated an official economic advisory team to the Gaidar government financed by the Ford Foundation and the Swedish government. From the outset, we worked closely with the reform ministers, who had invited us, and with a large number of young and able Russian economists, most of whom have enjoyed impressive careers. In 1993, we had a total of 30 employees.

of the Congress to a referendum (Murrell 1997). This was a lose-lose strategy. Yeltsin neither stood up to the Congress nor reached any tenable compromise. Each session of the Congress brought major setbacks to Yeltsin and economic reform.

In December 1992, the Congress of People's Deputies demanded the ouster of Acting Prime Minister Gaidar, and Yeltsin had little choice. He had not put Gaidar up for confirmation by the Congress because he realized it would not approve him. Instead, Yeltsin nominated Viktor Chernomyrdin as his candidate for prime minister. He was the most prominent state enterprise manager, who accepted a market economy, although he was not committed to macroeconomic stabilization. He was easily confirmed on December 14. In his brief acceptance speech, Chernomyrdin stated ambiguously that he favored deepening market reform as long as people were not impoverished, but that the market must not be allowed to turn into a "bazaar." His first decision was a decree on general price regulation, but it was quickly revoked and its author sacked (Yasin 2002, 198). The outstanding British Foreign Office analyst of Russia's domestic politics, Geoffrey Murrell, passed his judgment after the December 1992 Congress:

> Yeltsin's handling of the Congress had been dogged . . . by indecision and misjudgement. He had wavered between two courses—appealing to the people over the heads of an unpopular Congress with a dubious mandate, and appeasing his congressional enemies with tactical sacrifices. Either course pursued with energy and consistency might have worked. Yeltsin's failure to choose between them and the timing of his belated attempt at confrontation ensured his defeat. (Murrell 1997, 126)

Unfortunately, Yeltsin continued in the same manner. The December 1992 Congress saw the last compromise between Yeltsin and Khasbulatov. They agreed on a referendum in April 1993 on the basic principles of the new constitution, and that the Congress would not introduce constitutional amendments to undermine the president's power. The chairman of the Constitutional Court, Valery Zorkin, was also part of this compromise, because the court participated as part of the Khasbulatov political camp, which seriously discredited the Constitutional Court.[22]

The first four months of 1993 were devoted to this ever more heated strife over the constitution and referendum. The threat of impeachment of Yeltsin was first raised in November 1992, and soon it became a major theme in congressional attacks on the president (Murrell 1997, 119). The Congress underwent quite a metamorphosis. In mid-1992, the moderate industrialists' party, the Civic Union, set the tone. From the end of 1992, a "red-brown" majority of unreformed communists and extreme Russian nationalists dominated, while democrats abandoned this madhouse. Some democrats converted to hard-core nationalism, seemingly out of op-

---

22. In 2003, the Constitutional Court elected Zorkin its chairman once again.

portunism to promote their careers. By the spring of 1993, the red-brown had achieved a two-thirds majority, allowing them to appoint the inner parliament, the Supreme Soviet, at will. Yet, the red-brown did not develop any grassroots organizations or popular support, becoming ever less representative. Yeltsin succeeded in having a referendum accepted on April 25, although the questions were largely set by the Congress.

The referendum was a huge victory for Yeltsin. He won on all of the four questions posed, and the turnout was high at 64.5 percent (Murrell 1997, 153):

1. Do you have confidence in President Yeltsin? 58.7 percent voted yes.
2. Do you approve of the socioeconomic policy carried out by the president and government since 1992? 53 percent voted yes.
3. Do you consider it necessary to hold preterm elections for the president of the Russian Federation? 49.5 percent yes (of those who voted, but only 31.7 percent of the whole electorate).
4. Do you consider it necessary to hold preterm elections of the people's deputies of the Russian Federation? 67.2 percent yes (of those who voted, but only 43.1 percent of the whole electorate).

The most important question was the final one about the dissolution of the parliament. A two-thirds majority was impressive, but Khasbulatov had cleverly imposed the requirement of a majority of the whole electorate for the last two questions. Yeltsin had the moral right to dissolve the parliament on the basis of this referendum, and he should have called for immediate new parliamentary elections. Instead, he did nothing. This was Yeltsin's final opportunity to resolve the conflict with the Congress in a peaceful manner, and he missed it.

By August, Khasbulatov and the parliament rebounded. The parliament took the position of "the worse, the better." In August, it adopted a budget for 1994 with a deficit of 25 percent of GDP, which would have sent Russia into severe hyperinflation. Minister of Finance Boris Fedorov refused to abide by such a budget, and the political stalemate over economic policy alone made a political explosion inevitable (Åslund 1995, 198).

The constitution offered no way out of the crisis. Facing a completely irresponsible and unrepresentative, but sovereign, parliament, Yeltsin had no choice but to disband it. He finally did so with a decree on September 21, complaining that the Supreme Soviet majority was flouting the will of the people, as it had been expressed in the April referendum. The political paralysis could only be resolved through new elections for a new parliament, based on the draft constitution that had been approved by the Constitutional Conference convened by Yeltsin. The new parliamentary elections were scheduled for December 12. This approach seemed the most sensible at hand, but it was much too late.

Yeltsin had not secured loyal troops. Nor did he have a clear action plan. Speaker Khasbulatov and Rutskoi, who had been deposed as vice president because of alleged corruption, led the White House opposition. They were aware of Yeltsin's plans, because the security services were not loyal to Yeltsin, and they had gathered hard-line Russian nationalists with plenty of arms. The government tried to isolate the White House and turn off its electricity, and it demanded that everybody leave by October 4, but the police force that surrounded the parliament was weak and demoralized. The parliament impeached Yeltsin and named Rutskoi president. It also replaced three power ministers with its own hardliners, two of whom had recently been sacked by Yeltsin for corruption. These appointments were a key mistake by Rutskoi and Khasbulatov, because they left the incumbent power ministers with little choice but to support Yeltsin. Together with Rutskoi, the parliament's power ministers tried to appeal to the men in uniform, but they failed to gather support. Even so, several thousand armed extreme Russian nationalists and communists made a few attacks, killing several people. However, street demonstrations were quite limited in size (Murrell 1997).

The real revolt erupted on October 3. Rutskoi emerged on the balcony of the White House and ordered his armed followers to attack the mayor's office nearby and the Ostankino television station in northern Moscow. Khasbulatov called for the seizure of the Kremlin. A full-fledged armed uprising was under way. The insurgents swiftly took the mayor's office. Intense shooting broke out at Ostankino, but the insurgents only partially occupied it, and at least 20 people were killed. The government had managed to defend the TV station and no further attacks on official buildings followed, although snipers indulged in wild shooting from rooftops in central Moscow. The red-brown forces barricaded themselves in the White House, and on the night of October 3–4, Russian special forces attacked with tanks. About 150 people were killed and more than 1,000 injured, but no parliamentarian was even injured. The leaders of the revolt, including Khasbulatov and Rutskoi, were arrested (Aron 2000, 552–53).

After the failed uprising, Yeltsin held a simultaneous parliamentary election and constitutional referendum on December 12, 1993, as he had promised. As after the August 1993 coup, he treated the rebels with amazing leniency. Rutskoi even made a political comeback as regional governor. Yeltsin's shortfalls lay in other areas. He should have dissolved the parliament much earlier, when his legal justifications were stronger. The armed uprising had to be quelled, but Yeltsin could have nipped it in the bud with minimal bloodshed. Yeltsin (1994, 269) provided his own candid criticism:

> Now that the bloody events are over, it can probably be said that we were tragically mistaken. If the police had been armed, if the Interior Ministry officers had had the chance from the start to react properly to the armed attack, the ferocious barbarism of the night of October 3–4 in Moscow would have been avoided.

Great Achievements but Mixed Results

The Russian revolution of 1991–93 included both great achievements and shortfalls. Rarely had a country fallen in as dire straits as Russia in late 1991. Hardly any elementary condition of state order existed. The borders of the state were not determined. No tenable political system was in place. Law and order were absent, with crime skyrocketing. The Soviet Union still had some 4 million men under arms and 30,000 nuclear warheads. Hyperinflation was around the corner, while shortages were unbearable, and output in free fall. The West sent emergency food supplies to forestall starvation. Russia's fate lay in the hands of one man, Boris Yeltsin, and he had a strong sense of his responsibility and direction. Intelligently and boldly, he drew radical conclusions.

Possibly Yeltsin's greatest achievement was that he finished off the Soviet empire effectively and peacefully. Such an act is never popular, but it was necessary, which Yeltsin understood. Dankwart Rustow (1970) emphasized the importance of securing the borders of a state before any democracy could be built. A state without secure borders cannot be stable (McFaul 2001, 9). Yeltsin understood that no Russian recovery was possible as long as the Soviet empire persisted. With an extraordinary sense of timing, he acted at the optimal time, one week after the Ukrainian vote for independence. One week earlier or later might have resulted in failure. Immediately after this daring move, Yeltsin secured the support from the Soviet general staff for Russia. He also established all basic state institutions. It was quite a feat that civil war did not erupt and that chaos was averted.

Domestically, Yeltsin concentrated on economic reform and left political reforms for later. It is easy to understand why. The economic crisis was rampant, whereas basic political institutions were in place. Yeltsin received eminent economic advice but no relevant political advice. He never showed any clear concept of how to build democracy, although accusations of him being authoritarian were greatly exaggerated. His greatest error was not to dissolve the predemocratic Russian parliament in August–November 1991, when he still had the authority to do so. Later on, he could have called a referendum on the dissolution of the parliament, but for too long he vacillated between compromise and confrontation, while his opponents grew more militant. In April 1993, he sensibly insisted on a referendum on the dissolution of parliament, but he still failed to dissolve it even after having won a two-thirds majority, only because Khasbulatov had imposed an absurd standard of assessment. That was the last chance for a peaceful resolution of the conflict between president and parliament. Since the parliament no longer represented anything, it had no reason to compromise. Yeltsin's dissolution of the parliament on September 21 came as a relief, because simultaneously he announced early parliamentary elections and a constitutional referendum three months later. His failure was not to head off the parliament's armed uprising.

Gorbachev is often accused of having started his democratizing reforms too early, but his real blunder was that he did not go far enough to real democracy. Yeltsin went all the way to truly democratic elections, notably the Russian presidential election in June 1991 and the parliamentary elections in December 1993. Alas, he stopped short of completing the democratic institutions over 1991–92. Because Russia did not hold any early founding election after the democratic breakthrough, its party system was never cemented (McFaul 1993). There was nothing fatal or peculiarly Russian in this misstep. Poland and Latvia did the same and Ukraine did even worse. The roots of the later demise of Russia's democracy lay not so much in the shootout of the parliament in October 1993 as in Yeltsin's failure to act decisively early on to dissolve the illegitimate parliament in the fall of 1991 and establish constitutional order.

These conclusions run counter to the thinking of transitologists that there should be negotiated solutions and a separation and spreading out of economic and political reform (O'Donnell, Schmitter, and Whitehead 1986; Karl and Schmitter 1991). It is difficult to blame Yeltsin, given that the leading political scientists of the day recommended his course of action.[23] Yeltsin rightly saw an early window of opportunity, but he chose to focus on the dissolution of the USSR and economic reform rather than on building democracy. Yet the extensive bloodshed in October 1993 did stain Russia's budding democracy.

In the fall of 1991, Yeltsin wanted to undertake radical market economic reform, and he did not shy away from talking about shock therapy. His basic strategy was sensible and delivered at least six major successes through reforms that proved viable and irreversible. First, price deregulation, the basic precondition for a market economy, was extensive. Second, imports were almost completely liberalized, rendering Russia an open market economy. Third, Russia unified its exchange rate. Fourth, by attempting to cut military procurement by 85 percent, Gaidar single-handedly beat once and for all what had long been considered an unbeatable military-industrial complex. Fifth, mass privatization established predominant private ownership, which provided the basis for subsequent economic recovery. Finally, in 1992 and 1993, the number of small private enterprises mushroomed as never before or after, with a critical mass of nearly a million private enterprises legally registered. Near hyperinflation was less harmful to small private firms than the resurgent bureaucracy that subsequently strangled their expansion. In sum, most, although not all, preconditions for a market economy had been created. In each case, reforms

---

23. The only success in democracy building in the postcommunist world has been the wholesale emulation of European Union institutions. None of the 12 CIS countries has consistently been democratic. At present, Freedom House (2006) rates only Ukraine as free.

worked because they were simple and radical. The unwieldy, extensive, and corrupt Russian state could not carry out any piecemeal reforms.

Within the economic reform, all problems arose from the failure to be sufficiently firm and radical (Dąbrowski 1993b). The main shortcoming was the inability to control inflation, which was primarily caused by the permissive monetary policy of the Central Bank and the persistence of the ruble zone. The Gaidar government opposed both but it was defeated. Without any restraint on monetary policy, inflation prevailed.

The strong energy lobby convinced Yeltsin that he must not liberalize energy prices, which kept their rents huge in 1992 and 1993. An early liberalization of energy prices would have solved this problem, but that might not have been politically possible given the extraordinary price discrepancy.

The big state enterprise managers spearheaded all these destabilizing acts, while also extracting subsidies from the state. Fortunately, none of these rent-seeking activities was tenable in the long run. People learned about the harm of high inflation from their own suffering. Many rents dissipated over time, but fundamentally macroeconomic stabilization was a political question: Would a small elite be allowed to thrive on inflationary gains or not?

The politics of transition turned out to be the opposite from what had been expected. The reformers feared, and their opponents hoped for, strikes from the coal miners and other workers who had been so militant from 1989 to 1991, but strikes ceased with reform, even though real wages fell precipitously and wage arrears proliferated. Another widespread worry was that the public would take to the streets when prices were liberalized, but, again, nothing happened. When prices of key consumer staples are hiked, people often protest, but not when prices are liberalized on a broad scale. The whole economic paradigm changed, and people could see that no specific group was singled out.

The population posed no obstacle to radical economic reform, contrary to the prevalent assumptions in political science and political economy. Not only Yeltsin but also his economic reform strategy enjoyed strong popular support until the summer of 1993, as recorded in a steady stream of high-quality opinion polls. The April 1993 referendum showed that a majority of the Russian population supported radical economic reform in the midst of economic hardship. Ordinary Russians wanted systemic change and they realized that hardship was inevitable, but the Russian government did not reform fast enough.

The political problem was not the losers, but the winners. The title of a seminal article by Joel Hellman (1998) formulated the dilemma: "Winners Take All: The Politics of Partial Reform in Postcommunist Transitions." The state enterprise managers and their accomplices were the main culprits, opposing early and radical reforms because they could make fortunes on delaying and distorting the reforms, and under the fragmented political system only small interest groups could successfully pursue collective action (Olson 1971). The political dilemma of Russia's postcommunist transition was that the ineffective budding democracy could not mobilize the people against the rent seekers in favor of more radical reform, as in Central Europe and the Baltics (Åslund 2007a).

Unfortunately, the reformers did not realize that the seemingly moderate state enterprise managers would be their main opposition. Many managers had opposed the August 1991 coup and welcomed Yeltsin. Reformers thought them progressive, but the managers simply wanted to make money on the collapse of the old system. They could enjoy freedom and control their state enterprises as their own property (Dobbs 1997).

After the transition to a market economy had started, the interests of the state enterprise managers diverged from the reformers because the managers favored a protracted and socially costly transition, with a maximum of rents being diverted to them. Yeltsin never understood this and damaged his reforms by veering over to their side in the spring of 1992. But the leading reformers did not understand, either—they tried to coopt and divide the state enterprise managers rather than defeat them.

On macroeconomic stabilization, no common ground existed between the reformers and the rent seekers, and any attempt by the reformers to reach a compromise just delayed stabilization and aggravated inflation. Fedorov's aggressive stabilization policy in 1993 was more successful than Gaidar's attempts to find compromises in 1992, but Fedorov benefited from the reforms already undertaken, the diffusion of rents, and the presence of the IMF. By contrast, Chubais succeeded because privatization allowed room for compromise: the state managers could accept giving away some of their quasi property rights to other stakeholders in exchange for legal guarantees for the rest of their ownership.

Although the assessment of the initial Russian transition from Soviet communism is mixed, it is impressive how many aspects of the transition were done right. In a revolution, many institutions are suspended and a few leaders play an immense role in confronting a small but fierce elite that is politically engaged (Mau and Starodubrovskaya 2001). The Russian capitalist revolution bears the imprint of one giant, Boris Yeltsin. Both successes and failures were direct consequences of his personal insights and frailties.

Yeltsin's strengths and weaknesses were reflections of his character. He was a hero who needed a monumental crisis to be at his best. At such times, he was invincible, like Winston Churchill and Charles de Gaulle. Ordinary governing, however, left him depressed, and he eased his depression with drinking. As a consequence, he did not play much of a role in day-to-day governing apart from in foreign and security affairs.

Russia's fundamental dilemma was that the greater magnitude of its economic and political quandary made it necessary to undertake a more comprehensive "big bang" reform than in Central Europe, but these arduous preconditions also made such an undertaking far more difficult. The opportunity missed was the failure to make the initial "big bang" in January 1992 even bigger by liberalizing energy prices and commodity exports, while imposing a stricter monetary policy and ending the ruble zone. That might have been possible, because resistance at the time was unorganized. The Russian reformers were very close to taking that step. What was missing was the West, which did nothing to help Russia's reformers at a most critical moment in the country's history.

4

The Rise and Fall of State Enterprise Managers: 1994–95

The conventional wisdom about Russia in the 1990s may be summarized: "Russia had embraced big-bang market reforms but collapsed in a corrupt mess."[1] A group of Russian communist economists and American Nobel Prize winners stated: "In spite of the hopes of the reformers for a flourishing private business which supports the economy, their program generated economic collapse, a strengthening of the mafia and growing political instability, which is destructive for the business climate." Their key point was "the necessity to reinforce the role of the government in the process of transformation" (Bogomolov 1996, 17–18).[2]

This view is tainted by at least three serious misconceptions. First, as argued in chapter 3, Russia did not launch a comprehensive radical reform. Only some reform measures were radical, but virtually all of them were successful, while all "moderate" policies failed.[3]

Second, the reformers were in power for only half a year, from November 1991 until May 1992. How can all of Russia's problems be blamed on them? This is a baseless accusation. From June 1992 until March 1998, the

---

1. Sebastian Mallaby, "Finishing What Wolfowitz Started," *Washington Post*, May 18, 2007, A23.

2. The five Nobel Prize winners were Kenneth Arrow, Lawrence Klein, Wassily Leontief, Douglass North, and James Tobin. They were joined by John Kenneth Galbraith and Marshall Goldman (Bogomolov 1996, 21–23; Klein and Pomer 2001). Their joint declaration in apparent support of Gennady Zyuganov, the presidential candidate of the newly formed Communist Party of the Russian Federation, was published in *Nezavisimaya gazeta*, July 1, 1996, just before the presidential elections on July 3 (Mau 1999).

3. Aven (2000); Dąbrowski, Gomułka, and Rostowski (2001); Fedorov (1999a, 1999b); Mau (1999); and Yasin (2002).

government was dominated by state enterprise managers. They did issue more subsidies and impose more regulation in the name of industrial policy, which delayed economic growth in Russia until 1999.

Third, critics failed to realize that the Soviet Union had collapsed in a complete crisis and revolution, which is the ultimate state failure and made the country largely ungovernable. As Yasin (2002, 219) noted: "In 1993–94, we had in reality a 'big and weak state' with enormous obligations but it was unable to carry them out."

True, Russia may be described as a corrupt mess in the mid-1990s, but it would be rash to draw any causality between "big bang" reforms and corruption. Soviet society had been a lawless kleptocracy kept in check by a ruthless police state controlled by the CPSU (Zemtsov 1976, Simis 1982, Vaksberg 1991). When the CPSU was prohibited, the repressive organs lost their authority and crime skyrocketed in the absence of order.

Reforms continued until late 1993, but then enterprise managers took over the Russian government, minimizing reforms for nearly five years. Privatization was the only reform that continued. The problem was not that reforms were too radical, but that they were partial and halted halfway, and that the dominant policy aimed at rent seeking, not radical market reform. The financial crash in August 1998 made the social costs of delaying fiscal and regulatory reforms obvious to a broad Russian elite.

This book divides the half decade of minimal reforms in 1994–98 into two periods: 1994–95, when the state enterprise managers dominated Russian politics and economy, discussed in this chapter. The period 1996–98, when the new big businessmen—the oligarchs—got the upper hand is discussed in chapter 5. This chapter first discusses the new 1993 constitution. It examines the December 1993 elections and argues that their main outcome was the formation of a government dominated by state enterprise managers. Next, we look at how the state managers ruled, noting that they were inveterate rent seekers who paid little attention to anything but material gains for their narrow interest group. Gazprom, the state-dominated natural gas monopoly, was the managers' commanding height.

Although this was a somber period, two major reform policies advanced. One was mass privatization, which was concluded in 1994 (discussed in chapter 3). The other was temporary financial stabilization, which was accomplished in early 1995. This period also saw two repulsive developments: the rise in organized crime, and the first Chechnya war, which was initiated at the end of 1994 by the "Party of War" close to Yeltsin.

The New Constitution

The shootout at the White House was a serious trauma for the new Russia.[4] Yeltsin's rationale for his actions was comprehensible, but the bloodshed

---

4. The main sources for this section are McFaul (2001), Remington (2006), and Sheinis (2004).

seemed excessive. Democracy was supposed to be peaceful, and Yeltsin was ultimately responsible for having failed to maintain law and order. During the last quarter of 1993, Russia was ruled by decree, which became a free-for-all. The reformers pushed through many reforms that they had long prepared. Yegor Gaidar, who was back as first deputy prime minister, saw this as a great opportunity lost: "We might swiftly, without fear of organized opposition, have begun a reform of the armed forces, reduced the size of the standing army. . . . We should have seized the lever of control at the KGB, which had not been working for Russian democracy. And we should have made radical personnel changes. . ." (Gaidar 1999, 266).

The rent seekers took care of their own interests. Prime Minister Viktor Chernomyrdin took the opportunity to pass an omnibus decree giving Gazprom all imaginable benefits. Rule by decree broke down government coordination. Many presidential decrees, often contradictory and easily changed or forgotten, were not respected. Because the decrees were not discussed in any broader community, as is the case when a law is prepared in a parliamentary committee, they often lacked support. Through its shortcomings, rule by decree showed the efficacy of the alternative— legislation by parliament (Remington, Smith, and Haspel 1998).

This was the obvious moment for Yeltsin to choose between democracy and authoritarianism. Between World Wars I and II, several fledgling Eastern European democracies collapsed at such moments. Yeltsin, however, unequivocally chose democracy. Despite, or perhaps because of, the many accusations that he had dissolved parliament to become a dictator, Yeltsin held parliamentary elections exactly as he had promised when he dissolved the Congress of People's Deputies. He proposed a presidential system with a bicameral parliament called the Federal Assembly, consisting of the State Duma and the Federation Council. Although the atmosphere was bitterly divisive, Russia held a referendum on a new constitution and elections to the new State Duma and Federation Council on December 12, 1993. Yeltsin no longer saw any need to negotiate the electoral rules, and imposed them by decree instead.

The presidential system put in place by Yeltsin gave the president strong powers, exceeding those of the US president, especially because they were less firmly regulated. This system is commonly called superpresidential. The president had the right to nominate the prime minister, but the parliament must approve him. If it refuted the president's candidate three times, the president had to dissolve the Duma. If the Duma passed two votes of no confidence in the government within three months, the president must either dismiss the cabinet or dissolve the Duma. The president could veto a law passed by the parliament, but the parliament could override a veto by a two-thirds vote in each chamber. The new constitution also limited the scope of impeachment to high crimes (Remington 2006, 58).

The prime minister appointed the ministers, who did not require Duma approval. In addition, the president named the so-called power ministers:

the minister of defense, the minister of interior, and the chairman of the Federal Security Service (FSB, the old KGB). He also appointed the minister for foreign affairs. These ministers reported directly to the president. In effect, the president was responsible for foreign and security policy, while the prime minister took care of economic policy. This division of labor worked well with Yeltsin and Chernomyrdin. Scared by the many problems he had had with his earlier vice president, Aleksandr Rutskoi, Yeltsin abolished that post altogether (McFaul 2001, 211–13).

The lower house of the new parliament, the State Duma, had 450 members. Half were elected in a proportional election every four years through party lists, with a threshold for representation of 5 percent of the votes cast. The other half was elected in one-mandate constituencies through a first-past-the-post system. The reason for this mixed system was a fear that Moscow would be too dominant in a purely proportional system.[5] The proportional elections were designed to support the development of parties. The Duma confirmed the prime minister, legislated, and adopted the budget, performing the functions of a normal parliament. Its size was customary, and Gorbachev's strange innovation with indirect election to an inner parliament was terminated.

The upper chamber, the Federation Council, was never taken seriously. It was somewhat inspired by the US Senate but probably more by the German Federation Council, and its aim was to reinforce the representation of the regions. Yeltsin had created this body in the summer of 1993 in an endeavor to gain regional support. It was composed of 178 members, two from each of the 89 regions. The constitution did not specify whether they would be elected or appointed, and the system changed all the time. In 1993, two representatives from each region were elected, but hasty elections in parallel to the far-more-important Duma elections virtually guaranteed the dominance of the regional rulers over the Federation Council. From 1995, the regional governors and the chairs of the regional legislative assemblies were automatically members of the Federation Council. In 2000, President Putin usurped the right to appoint them (Remington 2006, 68).

The Federation Council never had much of a role, functioning more as a house of lords than a legislature. Usually, its members did not represent parties but rather their regions, or, in reality, certain business groups, and usually it voted obediently with the Kremlin. Consequently it attracted little interest. It met about one day every two weeks to obediently approve legislation passed by the Duma.

The federal system was replicated at the regional level. Governors were elected, and they played the role of president in each region. Regional Dumas were also elected, with all the regional deputies being elected in

---

5. Such a system was introduced in 2007, when the threshold for representation was raised to 7 percent, but then its prime purpose was to block the entry of new parties and independent candidates.

one-man constituencies, where parties played no role. They tried to check the governors, but not very successfully, because the governors controlled all resources.

Russia's Constitutional Court had sided with the Supreme Soviet in 1993, which Yeltsin bitterly deplored. He accepted the formation of a new Constitutional Court, but he wanted safeguards. The court was enlarged to 19 members. The president nominated all the judges, and the obedient Federation Council, rather than the oppositional Duma, was to approve them. Just in case, Yeltsin delayed its formation so that it could hold its first meeting only 15 months after the first Duma elections (McFaul 2001, 212).

The locations of the new institutions clarified the real distribution of power. The president sat in the Kremlin and his administration in the old Central Committee headquarters at the Old Square. The government was far away in the grand White House, which had been evacuated by the parliament. The State Duma moved into the old Gosplan headquarters close to the Kremlin, making evident that pure politics was to be pursued between the Kremlin, the Old Square, and the Duma. The Federation Council moved between two not very prominent places on the Boulevard Ring, indicating its insignificance.

The Yeltsin constitution was a great improvement over the dysfunctional Brezhnev constitution. It contained all the requisite institutions and a reasonably clear division of power, even if it was tilted to the president, and it provided reasonable constitutional stability. All branches of government were allowed to introduce legislation, and normal legislative work started as intended in the new Duma.

Yet, the new constitution left much to be desired. Worst of all, the presidential administration reproduced the Central Committee apparatus of the CPSU in whose premises it sat. Similarly, the gubernatorial administrations behaved like the old regional party committees, in whose buildings they were housed. The same people returned to their old offices, and they worked with the same old methods, commanding people through phone calls without legal basis, transparency, or accountability. The strong presidential system led to the preservation of many of the worst features of Soviet political management.

The presidential administration was very wealthy because of its confiscation of the real estate of the CPSU. Pavel Borodin, a former party official from Yakutsk in Eastern Siberia, was the Kremlin's long-time property manager (1993–2000). He was also a drinking pal of Yeltsin and long seen as the master of corruption in the Kremlin. At the end of the 1990s, Borodin boasted about its property being worth $600 billion. Although this was an exaggeration, it was worth billions of dollars and it was used at the discretion of Borodin, who was the focus of major Swiss money-laundering charges in 1999 because of accusations of having taken kickbacks of $25 million for the renovation of the Kremlin. Every year, the Kremlin distributed some 2,000 luxurious apartments in the center of

Moscow worth anything from a quarter of a million to a million dollars and 14,000 dachas (Baker and Glasser 2005, 48, 91; Klebnikov 2000, 219, 295). A senior official could obtain such a once-in-a-lifetime apartment for free, but Borodin's administration used this for blackmail, corrupting the government from within. At the regional level, the governors indulged in the same corrupting practices.

The best feature of the new constitutional order was probably the new State Duma, which became an ordinary parliament, but the persistence of single-man constituencies undermined the development of normal political parties. The Federation Council never found any useful function and it has stayed superfluous, which has inspired repeated experiments with a consultative State Council, a Public Chamber, and other futile consultative bodies. The Constitutional Court has been too subordinate to the president to be taken seriously. The legal immunity of parliamentarians was attractive to some hard-core criminals who bought seats in both chambers of parliament for up to $10 million in the late 1990s.

The December 1993 Elections and the End of the Reform Government

The December 1993 elections were perfectly democratic and campaign expenditures modest, although the electoral rules were dictated in presidential decrees. Yeltsin's highest priority was the ratification of his new constitution, and he had decreed that it must be adopted through a popular referendum. To boost participation in the referendum, Yeltsin favored the holding of parliamentary elections at the same time. During the election campaign, Yeltsin made only one appearance on national television for 10 minutes, and he spoke about nothing but the constitution (McFaul 2001, 215–16). Yeltsin's constitution was approved in the referendum with 58.4 percent of the 54.8 percent who voted, according to the official figures that were disputed (Remington 2006, 58).

The first parliament was perceived as provisional, because it was elected for only two years, whereas future terms would last for four years. Before the December 1993 elections, a large number of new parties were formed. Opinion polls predicted a healthy majority for the two liberal parties, Russia's Choice (Yegor Gaidar) and Yabloko (Grigori Yavlinsky), but the results were a rude surprise.

The winner was Vladimir Zhirinovsky, whose misnamed Liberal Democratic Party won 22.8 percent of the proportional vote. Russia's Choice came second with 15.4 percent, the newly formed Communist Party of the Russian Federation (Gennady Zyuganov) third with 12.4 percent, and Yabloko obtained a paltry 7.8 percent (see table 4.1).

The first impression was that the elections dealt a big blow to the reformers, but that reflected exaggerated expectations. The new Duma was

Table 4.1   Results of election to the State Duma, December 12, 1993

Party	Percent of votes
Liberal Democratic Party of Russia	22.8
Russia's Choice	15.4
Communist Party of the Russian Federation	12.4
Women of Russia	8.1
Agrarian Party	7.9
Yabloko	7.8
Party of Russian Unity and Accord	6.7
Others or against all	18.8
Voter turnout	54.8

Sources: Åslund (1995, 200); Colton (2000, 231).

fragmented, with 11 different factions. Closer scrutiny revealed that it was most of all centrist. It was approximately equally divided between three camps: a red-brown communist and nationalist bloc (40 percent of the seats), liberals (30 percent), and centrists (29 percent), although some deputies changed factions, and the factions shifted political positions (Åslund 1995, 200–201).

The shock was the electoral success of the previously obscure Zhirinovsky and his seemingly hard-core nationalism. His party had been one of the first independent political parties to be registered in the Soviet Union, and it was widely known to be a KGB creation (Klebnikov 2000, 57). He campaigned as a hard-line Russian nationalist, but he did not hide that his father was Jewish, and he performed like an eminent stand-up comedian appealing to the cruder part of the male working class. Zhirinovsky soon made clear that his votes were for sale and the government was his preferred customer. Over time he became a steady supporter of any government, but for a solid fee. Later, he played a prominent role in the corrupt United Nations oil for food program in Iraq, which he took pride in as a matter of trade promotion.

Neither the liberals nor the communists or nationalists were to play much of a role in the future government, which reflected the balance point of the new Duma. This was a coalition of state enterprise managers, who were the chief lobbyists of the dominant industries. Prime Minister Chernomyrdin, who had been confirmed by the old parliament in December 1992, just stayed in office, although he had not run in the election. He faithfully represented the energy industry. His first deputy was Oleg Soskovets, who supervised and lobbied for the metals industry. A third influential member of the government was Deputy Prime Minister for Agriculture Aleksandr Zaveryukha from the procommunist Agrarian Party, who represented the *kolkhoz* chairmen. These were the three strongest industrial lobbies at the time, and they dominated government policy. A lone reformer, Anatoly Chubais, stayed on as deputy prime minister and minister of privatization and was authorized to complete the voucher privatization. The other reformist deputy prime ministers (Gaidar and Boris Fedorov) were compelled to leave.[6]

Yeltsin respected Chernomyrdin as a serious professional and an able manager, but they were never close personally. When you met both of them together, the tall Yeltsin spoke and the small, round Chernomyrdin said politely nothing, knowing his master and patently loyal to the Quixotic Yeltsin. Chernomyrdin was a technocrat of the old school, a good manager who attracted devotion from his subordinates. He was a hard worker but a poor speaker, charmingly mangling his words. His most famous phrase, which unfortunately captured the essence of his long tenure as prime minister, was: "We wanted to do the best, but it turned out as always."

Chernomyrdin's challenger and first deputy, Soskovets, was a personal friend of Yeltsin, Yeltsin's chief bodyguard Aleksandr Korzhakov, and Korzhakov's KGB sidekick, Mikhail Barsukov, soon to become chairman of the Federal Security Service (1995–96). This tightly knit trio formed the central part of Yeltsin's *banya* team and of state power from 1993 until their ouster in June 1996. Soskovets had made his career as manager of the giant Karaganda metallurgical company in Kazakhstan and he was a successful rent-seeking businessman in the metals industry connected with the worst organized criminals in the bloody aluminum war (Dixelius and Konstantinov 1998, 137–39; Klebnikov 2000, 307–13). In early 1993 he surged as deputy prime minister of Russia and as a personal favorite of Yeltsin. Persistent rumors had it that Yeltsin was about to replace Chernomyrdin as prime minister with Soskovets. This trio dominated the military and law enforcement, over which Chernomyrdin held no sway. Korzhakov built up a powerful and independent presidential security service using all secret police methods. In his business, Soskovets made use of Korzhakov and Barsukov's forces and taught them how to transform their power into money. The story about their deeds remains to be written, and it will be one of the most unsavory parts of Russia's post-Soviet history.

Pavel Grachev, minister of defense 1992–96, was one of their close friends. As a paratroop general, he had won Yeltsin's heart by refusing to attack Yeltsin and the White House in August 1991. However, he was nicknamed "Pasha Mercedes," because he was considered to have led the looting of the huge Soviet arms depots in East Germany. A journalist with the newspaper *Moskovsky Komsomolets*, Dmitri Kholodov, was killed by a

---

6. In January 1994, Gaidar, Fedorov, Chernomyrdin's economic advisor Andrei Illarionov, and foreign economic advisors Jeffrey Sachs and myself resigned from our posts. We tried to make a maximum amount of noise in order to alert people about the unfortunate course of the new government.

bomb in a briefcase in October 1994 when investigating these charges (Klebnikov 2000, 41–42). Several military officers were prosecuted for this murder, but they were acquitted, and their superior, Grachev, escaped unscathed.

The State Enterprise Managers

The first half of the 1990s marked the peak of the power and status of state enterprise managers. They had everything going for them. Within the old *nomenklatura*, they were the most reformist, devoid of ideology and opposed to violence. Ryzhkov had replaced most enterprise managers in 1985–87 with professional engineers in their 50s. They had an air of competence, being pioneers in adjusting to the market, and they accepted privatization.

The managers were also the best-organized interest group. Their chief organization was the Russian Union of Industrialists and Entrepreneurs (RSPP), which was founded and chaired by Arkady Volsky, one of the most liberal and savvy senior officials of the Central Committee of the CPSU. Another important organization was the Association of Russian Banks. In a time of nearly complete fragmentation of society, the managers were perfectly organized, just as Mancur Olson (1971) predicted of small groups with much to gain from collective action.

The state enterprise managers were the masters of the transition period, enriching themselves at the expense of state and society. As the foremost rent seekers, they were the main obstacle to financial stabilization, because they fought for subsidized credits and large subsidies from the state budget, which destabilized Russia's state finances. Chernomyrdin led them in declaring in July 1994 that while it was good that inflation had fallen to 5 percent a month (80 percent a year), stabilization policies bringing down inflation to 2 to 3 percent a month were unacceptable. According to Chernomyrdin, such a decline would have harmed the investment climate (Institute of Economic Analysis 2004). He supported Viktor Gerashchenko, chairman of the Central Bank, and his loose monetary policy.

The enterprise managers had a rational but complex approach to price regulation, being interested in any price distortions on which they could make money through arbitrage. Usually, they favored high prices on their output, but state managers in energy and agriculture called for low state-regulated prices for their produce, because they were traders, making their fortunes on buying these products cheaply and selling them at high international prices for personal benefit. Meanwhile, they claimed they protected the living standards of the population.

The RSPP sponsored a political party called the Civic Union, which was one of the strongest factions in the center of the Russian parliament in the second half of 1992. When it faced the electorate in 1993, however, the

Civic Union received no more than 2 percent of the popular vote, showing that the RSPP's strength lay in the political establishment, not in popular support.

The people in the countryside, by contrast, supported the Agrarian Party. After the parliamentary elections in December 1993, it used its newly won parliamentary strength of 12 percent of the seats to lobby for an omnibus decree on the agro-industrial sector, which Chernomyrdin signed. It prescribed subsidies and regulations: large centralized credits, plan targets for 10 major agricultural products (giving the agrarians bargaining chips against the state), and some trade monopolies. Still, marketization proceeded, and soon Russia's chronic grain shortage was history. Eventually, the producers revolted against the semi-state procurement companies and their artificially low state procurement prices. Russia introduced substantial import tariffs for agricultural goods in July 1994. Market developments were sufficient even in agriculture to break the unity of the strong agrarian lobby (Åslund 1995, 165–66).

Soskovets pampered the metallurgical industry, for which he secured substantial tax exemptions of about 2 percent of GDP. His main trick was to exempt metal trade from the value-added tax and foreign trade taxes through barter deals. Metallurgical companies used transfer pricing, buying inputs abroad for a higher price than the ruling world market price and selling them at a lower price, leaving their profits in a trading company in an offshore tax haven (Bagrov 1999).

Initially, mass privatization had aimed at containing the power of state enterprise managers. The privatizers' slogan—"what is not privatized will be stolen"—had been directed against the managers who controlled the state enterprises since the Law on State Enterprises had come into force in 1988. Although Chubais managed to limit their share of ownership to about one-fifth after the voucher auctions, the managers still controlled most enterprises by acting as proxies for the 40 percent of shares usually held by their employees.

In early 1994, the managers appeared to have won a complete victory. They controlled the government and the strongest interest organizations. They had conditional ownership of most big enterprises, and they had manipulated fiscal, monetary, and regulatory policies to their benefit. Yet, their weakness was that they were the masters of transition, which could not last forever.

Their most profound problem was that they did not know how to manage their enterprises in a market economy. Output continued to fall, and the official slump actually accelerated to 13 percent in 1994, almost as bad as in 1992, because hard budget constraints were not imposed (figure 4.1). The idea of financial stabilization was that money would become scarce, so that managers had to cut costs, sell off inventory and surplus supplies, cut prices in competition, and expand sales by producing more of their best products.

Figure 4.1   Decline in Russia's GDP, 1992–98

percent

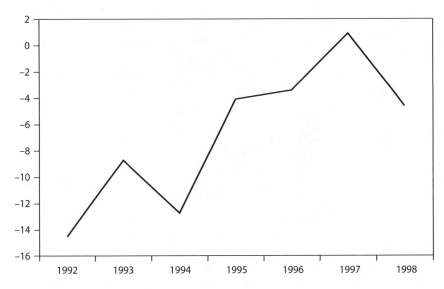

Source: Goskomstat (2000, 16).

Now, the opposite was happening. The managers trusted their friends in government to keep them afloat with subsidies. As the prospect of financial stabilization became more distant, they delayed enterprise restructuring. Increasingly, managers paid neither their taxes, bank loans, nor suppliers, accumulating large arrears. They hoarded workers as in Soviet times to extract more subsidies, which impeded the expected unemployment, but they cut real wages and caused chronic wage arrears and poverty. Many state-owned and insider-privatized enterprises came to a standstill in spite of large capital investment financed with subsidized state credits.

This irresponsible and parasitical mismanagement could not go on forever. Over time, many managers lost out. After several years little remained of their enterprises, and many failed completely. This was desired creative destruction (Schumpeter 1943/1976), because Russia had far too many industrial enterprises, with too large a physical capital, and most of them were obsolete. Production needed to be concentrated and expanded at the best companies (McKinsey Global Institute 1999).

In public utilities, telecommunication firms, and metallurgical companies, however, the asset values were great and the stock prices of the companies rose. Outsiders tried to buy such companies. They approached embryonic local stock dealers, who parked a bus outside the factory gates and announced that they would buy the workers' stocks at a good price. Workers sold their shares en masse, and outside raiders could mount a hostile takeover with majority ownership. Often, the raiders needed to enter the company with their own security guards and seize the assets physically to stop the incumbent managers from destroying the plant. Between 1992 and 1996, 33 percent of Russian's large and medium-sized enterprises changed management and underwent substantial restructuring (Blasi, Kroumova, and Kruse 1997, 203). Voucher privatization worked, but the positive effects were often delayed by several years. Young outside entrepreneurs, or raiders, gradually undermined the dominance of the old managers.

The Making of Gazprom

Gazprom was the mightiest of all Russian corporations, and it was ruled by its managers.[7] In 1985, Prime Minister Ryzhkov had appointed an outstanding young (47-year-old) gas engineer, Viktor Chernomyrdin, as Soviet minister of the gas industry. When the ministry was abolished in 1989, it was transformed into the state gas concern Gazprom, which was the customary first step in a spontaneous privatization. It kept all its assets, and Chernomyrdin remained its head.

When Yeltsin appointed Chernomyrdin as deputy prime minister for energy in May 1992, he had to leave Gazprom, but he passed on the top job to his protégé, Rem Vyakhirev. As deputy prime minister and later as prime minister, Chernomyrdin continued to protect Gazprom's interests to quite an extraordinary extent. In November 1992, a presidential decree transformed Gazprom into a joint stock company, strengthening its legal status.[8]

Almost all other old industrial ministries and enterprise associations were divided into individual enterprises as an initial step toward corporatization and privatization, but Gazprom was exceptionally corporatized as one company that included literally all enterprises and institutions dealing with gas: producing companies, refineries, pipelines, trading companies, the gas foreign trade company, all regulatory agencies, teaching and research institutes, and even 200 state farms. It employed about 400,000 people.[9]

After the Congress of People's Deputies was dissolved in September 1993, the reformers carried out all kinds of deregulation that had previously been politically impossible, but Chernomyrdin sponsored a decree that guaranteed Gazprom a complete monopoly on the production, sale, transport, and export of natural gas. The gas industry was the most mo-

---

7. A general source for this section is Stern (2005).

8. Information from Gazprom's website, www.gazprom.ru (accessed on May 31, 2007).

9. The railways and the nuclear industry remained ministries without corporatization for years. Telecommunications and public utilities were divided by regions and partially privatized. The oil and coal industries were divided into enterprises.

nopolized and regulated industry in Russia, while all other industries had undergone substantial liberalization. Natural gas exports were subject to licenses and quotas, but Gazprom itself was exempt from the export tax, some import tariffs, and the value-added tax (VAT) (Åslund 1995).

All Russian energy prices were regulated and extremely low in 1992. As head of Gazprom, Chernomyrdin did not advocate higher gas prices. Nevertheless, in 1994, he stated that a fundamental mistake of the first reform government was its failure to liberalize energy prices at the beginning of the reform. The price of natural gas remains regulated, and it has been raised only gradually, reaching one-fifth of the European import price by December 1993 (Åslund 1995, 158–61). After considerable fluctuation, the gas price remained about one-quarter of the European import price in 2007. Its pricing was nontransparent, and price regulation and discrimination persisted.

The value of the tax exemptions awarded in late 1993 amounted to 1 to 2 percent of GDP, when Gazprom's share of Russian net value added was about 8 percent of GDP (Bagrov 1999). Russia's wealthiest company was barely paying any taxes. Gazprom's gas production declined by only 4 percent (BP 2007), while the official decline in Russia's GDP was 44 percent from 1989 to 1998 (UN Economic Commission for Europe 2004, 80), although the real GDP decline was probably only about half of the official total (Åslund 2002). Consequently, Russia had a substantial surplus of gas in the mid-1990s. As a monopoly, it prohibited both domestic oil companies that produced associated gas and Turkmenistan from transporting their gas through Gazprom's pipelines. The oil companies had to flare about 20 billion cubic meters of gas each year, whereas Turkmenistan was subject to a complete embargo for a year and a half over 1997–98 and could export no gas until it built a pipeline to Iran. Given the monopoly and the arbitrary pricing, no domestic market could develop. Even in 2007, gas was allocated by administrative fiat as in Soviet times (Åslund 1995, 159; Olcott, Åslund, and Garnett 1999).

Gazprom was privatized in a unique order in 1993–94. Its management used the voucher auctions to privatize almost 40 percent of Gazprom shares for an implied price of about $100 million (Klebnikov 2000, 134–35; Stern 2005, 170–71). Of all Russia's privatizations, this was the biggest giveaway, because these shares cost one thousand times more, $100 billion, in 2006. In 1994, Prime Minister Chernomyrdin appeared to have time for nothing but Gazprom privatization. The stocks were given away for a nominal fee to Gazprom managers, senior officials, and employees—altogether half a million people—but not at all evenly.

At the time, it was rumored that Chernomyrdin and Vyakhirev each received 5 percent of the shares, which Chernomyrdin publicly denied. If that were actually true, and if they still possessed these shares in 2007, each would own about $13 billion. Cleverly, Gazprom gave stocks to many top people in the Kremlin, wedding them to the enterprise's interests.

To make sure that they did not lose control over the company, no stocks could be traded without permission from the Gazprom board, and they could be owned only by Russians. Furthermore, nearly 60 percent of the company stayed state-owned or owned by Gazprom subsidiaries. In 1996, 1 percent of the shares was sold in the West, where they traded at a much higher price until 2006, when domestic and foreign shares were unified. Lukoil and Surguteftegaz, two large oil companies, were also privatized by their skillful managers, Vagit Alekperov and Vladimir Bogdanov, respectively.

In spite of having powerful shareholders and a major international company as auditor, Gazprom management held shareholders in utter contempt until it was ousted in 2001. Instead of boosting the stock price, management focused on making money in unfortunate ways. In the second half of the 1990s, the biggest boondoggle was exports to other countries in the Commonwealth of Independent States (CIS), notably to Ukraine.

A private middleman, Itera, emerged to pursue this trade on behalf of Gazprom. Itera had originally been an independent company, but came to represent the interests of Gazprom management. Gazprom sold gas to Itera for $4 per 1,000 cubic meters (mcm) for export to Ukraine, which formally bought the gas for $80 per mcm. But the actual price Ukraine paid was about $42 per mcm. National sentiments were mobilized. Russians complained that Ukraine did not pay, while the Ukrainians lamented that the Russian price was outrageous. In reality, Itera cashed in on a couple of billion dollars each year and Ukrainian gas oligarchs made about as much in great friendship (Åslund 2001, Balmaceda 1998).

At the end of the 1990s, Gazprom management opted for large-scale asset stripping, transferring large properties such as gas fields to Itera and other companies owned by close relatives of the leading Gazprom managers (Stern 2005, 22–24). This took place after Chernomyrdin had been dismissed as prime minister in March 1998, and Gazprom management had good reason to fear losing control over the corporation.

Gazprom was Russia's foremost rent-seeking machine, but it remained respected for several reasons. It kept up production, allowing Gazprom to continue delivering gas to enterprises and households even when it was not being paid. It was Russia's largest exporter. When much of Russia's heavy industry plunged into murderous shootouts, Gazprom retained a veneer of peace and order. It was an idyllic Soviet theme park with wonderful holiday homes and social benefits.

Precarious Financial Stabilization

The dominant lobbies used the state treasury as a self-service boutique, keeping the ministry of finance weak. After their unpleasant experiences with the ebullient Boris Fedorov, they made sure that no permanent minister of finance was appointed, leaving First Deputy Minister Sergei Dubynin as acting minister. At the Central Bank, Gerashchenko was reliably accommodating. The budget balance was gradually undermined.

A shock hit on "Black Tuesday," October 11, 1994, when the exchange rate of the ruble fell precipitously by 27 percent in a single day. One year earlier, the exchange rate was of little concern, but now it had assumed real economic significance, because Russia had become a market economy. Powerful economic interests had become used to a reasonably stable and predictable exchange rate, and its mismanagement—or more likely, manipulation—aroused a popular outcry.

The currency crisis shook the Russian establishment out of its complacency with the stalled stabilization effort. The State Duma launched a vote of no confidence against the government, which the government survived by a slight margin. The main beneficiaries of a low exchange rate, the commodity traders, were no longer the dominant force in Russian business, as their rents were drying up, whereas the bankers were advancing. The leading economic policymakers, including Gerashchenko (but not Chernomyrdin), were sacked by President Yeltsin. Instead, Chubais was put in charge of macroeconomic policy as first deputy prime minister, and the old liberal reformer Yevgeny Yasin became minister of economy. Chubais attacked this task with his usual vigor and astuteness.

The key to macroeconomic stabilization was fiscal adjustment. Chubais focused on cutting enterprise subsidies, which were reduced by no less than 7.1 percent of GDP. The other important item to be slashed was regional transfers, by 2.5 percent of GDP, while socially important expenditures were maintained (Åslund 1999). As a consequence, the general government deficit fell from 10.4 percent of GDP in 1994 to 6.6 percent in 1995 (figure 4.2), but revenues declined by 3.6 percent of GDP as budget constraints tightened. For the first time, Russia concluded a full-fledged standby agreement with the IMF, with $6.8 billion in financing in one year. In the spring of 1995, macroeconomic stabilization was finally put on track. By the summer of 1996, financial stabilization had been attained. Inflation dropped to 22 percent in 1996 and to 11 percent in 1997 (figure 4.3).

The Russian financial stabilization appears a political paradox. How could the government undertake financial stabilization by cutting enterprise subsidies when it was dominated by these lobbies? The explanations are multiple. First, most of the old, large rents were gone. Subsidized credits and import subsidies had been eliminated, and export rents were small. The sharp cut in subsidies made profit seeking more lucrative than rent seeking, allowing a new profit-seeking lobby to defeat the rent-seeking lobby.

Second, at long last the government and Central Bank coordinated their economic policy and both aimed at macroeconomic stabilization. Third, for the first time, the IMF was considering substantial credits, and its standby loan for 1995 amounted to 2 percent of Russia's GDP, which gave the IMF

Figure 4.2 Consolidated state budget deficit, 1992–98

percent of GDP

Source: EBRD (2000, 68; 2003, 187).

real leverage in Russian politics. With strong IMF support, Chubais won over Soskovets within the government (Bagrov 1999). Fourth, the currency crisis of October 1994 greatly upset the Russian elite, which had developed an interest in economic stability, creating a political momentum for reform.

Fifth, the reformers in the government fought better than ever, because they hit all important interest groups hard and fast rather than negotiate with them or offer any trade-off. Enterprise subsidies and regional transfers were cut by two-thirds, delivering true shock therapy to those who lived on budget subsidies. Once again, reforms were more easily undertaken when they were straight, simple, and hard. The harshness of the government convinced the "victims," who were resourceful rent seekers, that they had better find a new strategy for making money. Sixth, Gaidar's party, Russia's Choice, was the largest parliamentary faction, providing the reformers with a strong base in the State Duma.

Treisman (1998) and Shleifer and Treisman (1998, 2000) have presented an additional explanation. Many bankers were enticed by a new rent, excessive yields on treasury bills, which turned their interest to low inflation and a stable exchange rate. Meanwhile loss-making enterprises started living on arrears, which were indirect and noninflationary subsidies instead of inflationary budget subsidies. The authors concluded that the Russian reformers lured the winners from inflationary partial reform with a less inflationary form of rent to give up their previous inflationary rents. How-

Figure 4.3   Inflation rate, 1994–98 (consumer price index, end year)

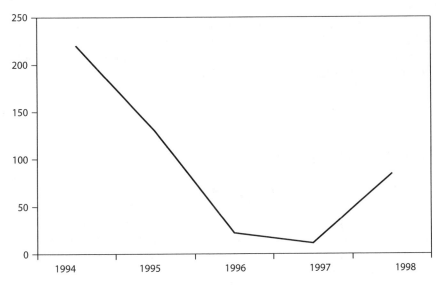

percent

Source: Goskomstat (1999, 547).

ever, this appears a rationalization in hindsight, because the timing does not match. In early 1995, the reformers divided the business community by driving rents down. The new rents mounted later, as the stabilization program was being undermined, and they were not part of the stabilization deal of March 1995. Still, Shleifer and Treisman rightly pointed to the rise of the bankers who thrived on the high yields of treasury bills, and to the decline of the state enterprise managers who lived on other forms of rents.

Alas, this cure was only temporary, because no lasting fiscal adjustment was accomplished. The yields on the treasury bills were moderate only briefly in 1997, and they were the direct cause of the financial crash in 1998. Rent seeking through extremely high treasury yields was no exit from fiscal jeopardy but a trap. Successful reforms, as in Poland and Estonia, beat rent seekers by changing the rules of the game once and for all, enticing businessmen to opt for profits rather than new rents. The purpose of reform is to defeat rent seeking and establish a more productive set of incentives. It would be both illogical and defeatist to think that one can make people honest only by bribing them, even if that were true of the stakeholder privatization. The Treisman-Shleifer hypothesis belongs to the popular political science idea of trade-off, against which stands the idea of a changed paradigm and ideology (Åslund 1992, Appel 2004).

The sudden and radical cut in subsidies was quite a blow to the old rent seekers. They were left in disarray, which demonstrated that the smaller their rents, the less their political power. Financial stabilization also divided the powerful Association of Russian Banks. When the interbank market dried up in the fall of 1995, financially strong banks did not call for state support but tacitly favored the bankruptcy of their competitors. A new generation of private bankers took over from the old state bankers, facilitating change (Dmitriev et al. 1996). Similarly, the old red directors lost ground to new businessmen. This is how shock therapy reforms should work. By changing the paradigm and the rules of the game, businessmen were enticed to switch from rents to profits, thus breaking up the rent-seeking lobbies.

The Rise of Organized Crime

To ordinary Russians, one of the worst shocks of the transition was the explosion of crime that started in 1989–90.[10] Initially, crime was not localized but erupted everywhere. Gangster shootouts occurred in local shopping centers all over the country. In 1992 and 1993, automatic gunfire could be heard every night in the center of Moscow. St. Petersburg was named Russia's crime capital. Seemingly meaningless murders became so common that everybody knew people who had been killed.

During the transition, crime was greatly redefined when communist crimes, such as "speculation" (that is, trade), were legalized, whereas corruption was criminalized. The reporting and registration of crime were poor. Therefore, only statistics on major and unequivocal crimes, such as homicides, are likely to reflect what actually happened. The numbers are truly shocking. Russia's murder rate doubled in three frightful years from 1991 to 1994, peaking at the internationally very high rate of 22 per 100,000, which is nearly four times the current US homicide rate (5.6 per 100,000 in 2005 [FBI 2005]; figure 4.4). Reality was even worse. About as many people disappeared each year, and the majority of them were probably murdered (Klebnikov 2000, 32).

Shocking as the rise in crime in Russia was, it was not exceptional. Most transition countries saw a doubling of their crime rates. This rise seemed related to how the old regime eased up. A more radical reform brought about an earlier peak in crime followed by stabilization, while the gradual reformers saw a longer but steady increase. Poland and Hungary experienced the sharpest surge in their crime rates in 1990, their first year of reform, after which they stabilized (Åslund 1997). Crime doubled in Rus-

---

10. Russian organized crime has attracted a huge literature, some of it serious, some fiction. The main sources for this section are Volkov (2002), Gilinskiy (2000), Handelman (1995), and Dixelius and Konstantinov (1998). Organized crime has been a dominant theme in Russian fiction, films, and TV programs. A favorite of mine is Latynina (2003).

Figure 4.4   Homicides, 1990–98

total in thousands

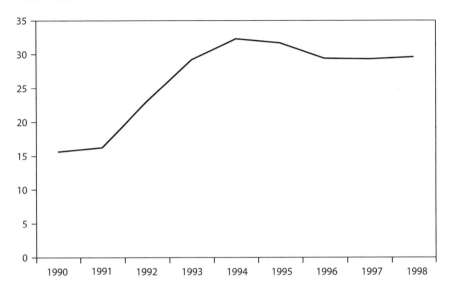

Source: Goskomstat (2000, 243).

sia and Kyrgyzstan from 1988 to 1992, while the crime rate grew more gradually in the most conservative countries, Turkmenistan and Uzbekistan (Mikhailovskaya 1994).

What was remarkable about Russia was that crime had been extensive under the old regime but not known. In the late 1980s, Soviet Russia had as high a murder rate as the United States. The Soviet Union had the largest prison population in the world as a share of its population. In addition, it held millions in exile in faraway provinces. Therefore, criminality was relatively limited in the big cities, which created an illusion of a law-abiding society (Mikhailovskaya 1994). This Soviet illusion was reinforced by strict censorship that prohibited the reporting of crimes in the media, which glasnost ended.

The explosion of crime was a natural consequence of the breaking down of the old order. The Soviet Union was a lawless society in the exact meaning of the word: there were few laws and therefore most actions were not regulated by law. The Soviet Union compensated with its totalitarian legal principle: Nothing is allowed that is not explicitly permitted. The CPSU had effectively established norms for how far officials and managers could diverge from the legal norms, because no state company could fulfill its plan targets without resorting to the illegal acquisition of vital inputs. The vagueness of informal norms blurred the line between the permitted and the prohibited.

Therefore, the Soviet state needed a huge law enforcement apparatus that pursued violators and meted out severe punishments with minimal court proceedings. Absurdly, in the Soviet legal system prosecutors were superior to judges and defense counsels were rarely permitted. Prosecution was nearly always successful. This arbitrary system was intolerable in a liberal society, and the repressive powers of law enforcement were curtailed in the early perestroika. But it would take a long time to build a new rule of law, because it required hundreds of new laws, a complete judicial reform, new court procedures, extensive training, and substantial financing. Even in the best-case scenario, the legal reforms would take more than a decade, and the masters of the old system, the prosecutors, had all the reasons to oppose legal reforms tooth and nail (Sachs and Pistor 1997; Anderson, Bernstein, and Gray 2005).

Another frightening feature of the late Soviet Union was its massive supply of criminals. The Soviet Union had well-organized criminal syndicates that had survived from tsarist times in the prison camps. In the late Soviet period, many hard-core criminals received amnesty and moved to the big cities. The collapsing Soviet society also harbored a large number of demoralized and brutalized war veterans from Afghanistan, disillusioned police and military officers, unemployed professional sportsmen, and tightly knit ethnic minorities. Rarely has a society had such a teeming reservoir of skillful and brutal criminals. This was a cynical society with a minimum of values, where neither church nor ideals could be expected to hold criminalization at bay (Volkov 2002, Handelman 1995).

The rise of disorganized individual crime became unbearable. New businessmen complained that they were visited by so many racketeers that they did not know whom to pay, although they had to pay protection fees to save their lives. Numerous entrepreneurs saw their premises burn, which was usually the second warning, and many were killed in the end. Law and order effectively broke down as the old police stayed passive, generating great demand for protection. During 1991–92, legal anarchy, a truly Hobbesian world, prevailed. Gambetta's (1993) economic analysis of the evolution of the Sicilian mafia appears perfectly applicable. The demand for private protection, or *krysha* (roof), was as great as the supply, while public law enforcement was worse than useless.[11]

Crime evolved in response to market forces and organized itself spontaneously. Through great violence, organized crime imposed its own order financed with racketeering fees, dividing cities into well-defined mafia districts. Each Russian city had its own distinct mafia gangs. They were well known, as were their leaders, and their names spoke volumes. Often they were named after an ethnic group (the Chechen mafia, the Georgian mafia, the Armenian mafia, etc.). One specific mafia was Afgantsy, Afghan

---

11. A young social scientist from St. Petersburg, Vadim Volkov (2002) has written an excellent analysis of the evolution of crime in Russia in line with Gambetta's analysis.

war veterans, who had their official nongovernmental organization as a formal base. Other groups were named after a sport club, and many after their specific region (Liubertsy, and the Solnechny and Izmailovsky groups in Moscow). Occasionally, a group was named after one leader (the Malyshev group in St. Petersburg) or for the origin of the leader (the Tambov and Kazan groups in St. Petersburg). The leaders sometimes became public personalities.

Businessmen actually appreciated the organization of crime that occurred in 1993–94. Now they knew whom to pay, which sharply reduced their risk of double-paying or being shot. At the same time, racketeering fees declined as the security business became standardized. Anecdotal evidence suggests that the standard fee fell from 20 to 10 percent of a businessman's turnover. The drawback, of course, was that most Russian businesses were still compelled to pay racketeering fees. The main exceptions were enterprises under solid state protection, such as those pertaining to the military-industrial complex and the Ministry of Interior. As Volkov (2002, 19) put it: "Since the actions of the state bureaucracy and of law enforcement remain arbitrary and the services provided by the state tend to have higher costs, private enforcers (read: the mafia) outcompete the state and firmly establish themselves in its stead." The state played a very small role in the early 1990s. Government officials, including policemen, were afraid and alienated, and they worked as little as possible.

The worst bloodbaths occurred in specific industries, primarily aluminum and banking. The gangster wars gave rise to a large number of detective stories, documentary "novels," and television series (e.g., Latynina 2001, 2003, 2005). One of the worst industrial battles was the "great aluminum war," which raged in 1993–94. When the Soviet Union collapsed, some traders secured control over and colluded with the managers of the state-owned aluminum plants by delivering raw materials to them through a barter arrangement. The managers felt cheated and tried to liberate themselves from the traders through privatization. Much of the bloodshed in the aluminum industry occurred when the parasitical traders tried to recuperate the plants by sending in their troops (Klebnikov 2000, 307–13; Dixelius and Konstantinov 1998, 137–39). But after privatization, these barter arrangements ended, and the traders lost out. Privatization cleansed even this most criminalized industry.

In banking, typical causes of murders were large unsecured loans that were not paid back on time. Russia's biggest car plant, Avtovaz in Togliatti, was completely criminalized in Soviet times. It has been the scene of no fewer than 500 murders, which unfortunately continue, as the enterprise has not been restructured and thus not cleaned up.

As so often in Russia's post-Soviet history, everybody threw up their hands and said that this is what Russia has become. But just as they resigned and said that nothing could be done, organized crime was about to be defeated by a combination of four forces.

First, in a masterstroke the Russian reformers legalized private security companies in 1992. Swiftly, organized crime legalized itself into private security companies, but it also exposed itself to more transparency, state supervision, regulation, and legitimate competition. Step by step, the private security companies became more orderly and legal in their activities (Volkov 2002).

Second, the dangers of organized crime were overwhelming. In 1993–94, the so-called great mob war eliminated most organized criminals. Many were killed by one another or by the police, while others were sentenced to long prison terms. The successful criminals who survived had the choice of selling out and retiring in the West or gentrifying, although few organized criminals were able to legalize themselves, and among the current 53 billionaires in Russia, only a few might have started as racketeers (Klebnikov 2000; Brady 1999, 60).

Third, the new big businessmen, the oligarchs, thought the fees of the protection rackets excessive, and they set up their own security and guard services. By the mid-1990s, 8 percent of the employees in a typical oligarchic corporation were occupied with security, either as guards or counterintelligence officers assigned to find out what their enemies were doing. The top oligarchs hired a "deputy minister of interior" to run their security and a "deputy chairman of the KGB" to manage their counterintelligence.[12] By the end of the great mob war in late 1994, the new businessmen "were powerful enough to ignore the old gangsters" (Klebnikov 2000, 44).

The new businessmen defeated organized crime also within their enterprises. A dirty secret of the old system was that Soviet enterprises were seriously criminalized (Simis 1982, Vaksberg 1991). Employees stole goods from every state enterprise and considered it their right. This was particularly true of an enterprise's transportation and construction departments, where valuable goods came in and out. A Russian corporate raider knew that to seize control of an unrestructured Soviet enterprise, he had to sack all the staff of these two departments, whereas the bookkeeping department was likely honest, because it only handled money, which was abundant in the Soviet system. Production and research and development were usually decent as well. Naturally, ruthless local businessmen with their own security forces were far superior to foreign investors in these actions.

The fourth force that contributed to the defeat of organized crime was actually the state, although it was less significant at this stage. New and more relevant legislation was being passed. The police were receiving increasing resources, and they possessed the legal monopoly on the use of violence. The return of state power was slow but relentless. "It will soon transpire, however, that public law and order is a 'public good,' and that it is better to pay taxes to keep an efficient municipal police than to run private or local security and guard services," as Sergei Vasiliev (1999, 52) noted.

---

12. Conversations at the time with two prominent oligarchs.

Notwithstanding of the many books written about post-Soviet organized crime, it lasted for only a brief period, approximately from 1992 to 1995, although it persisted in some places. As late as 2006, the Russian city of Novgorod was run by seven organized crime gangs, and supervised by one godfather without interference from the Russian state. In general, however, by 1995, the oligarchs had defeated the worst excesses of organized crime. Russia's murder rate peaked in 1994, and it fell by 9 percent from 1994 to 1996, but then the improvement stopped, and the murder rate stabilized.

The First Chechnya War

In spite of Yeltsin's words in Tatarstan in 1990, when he told Russia's constituent regions to take as much sovereignty as they wanted, he was greatly preoccupied with the cohesion of Russia in early 1992.[13] He aspired to define the legal and financial powers of the 89 constituent regions of the Russian Federation through a Federation Treaty signed in March 1992. Three strong autonomous republics requested special rights: oil-rich, Muslim Tatarstan and Baskhortostan (Bashkiria) on the Volga, and diamond-rich, vast Sakha (Yakutia) in East Siberia. Eventually, these three republics were accommodated in the Russian Federation after having extracted substantial privileges, and 88 of 89 regions accepted the Russian Federation. The exception was Chechnya.

Chechnya stood out for many reasons. The Chechens were Muslims and quite numerous at 1 million. They lived compactly in their own mountainous autonomous republic on Russia's border with Georgia, which made their demands for independence feasible. The Chechens were legendary for their prolonged and ferocious resistance against the Russian Empire in the 18th and 19th centuries, as detailed by the classical Russian writers Lev Tolstoi and Mikhail Lermontov. In 1944, all Chechens were deported by Stalin to Siberia and Central Asia. Nikita Khrushchev permitted them to return in 1957.

In 1991, Chechnya had its own revolution, overthrowing the Chechen communist leader. In October 1991, Chechnya held presidential and parliamentary elections. Dzhokhar Dudaev, a retired Soviet general, won the presidential elections with 85 percent of the vote and Chechen nationalist groups captured all the parliamentary seats. The new Chechen parliament declared full independence from Russia, which it confirmed in a new constitution passed in March 1992. The prior Chechen-Ingush Republic was formally divided into Chechnya and Ingushetia. Russia was faced with a full-fledged secession on its southern border. Russia refused to recognize

---

13. This section is primarily based on Dunlop (1998), Lieven (1998), Trenin and Malashenko (2004), and Gall and de Waal (1998).

the legitimacy of the Chechen election, fearing that ethnic separatism could lead to the disintegration of the Russian Federation, but it did not devote much attention or resources. In November 1991, Yeltsin declared emergency rule in Chechnya, and sent troops to the capital of Grozny, but they were forced to withdraw.

After this initial humiliation, the Chechen issue was put aside, but recognized as a potential cancer that could metastasize in other limbs of the country. Chechnya was poorly developed, although it possessed some oil. Many Chechens lived in Moscow, and several were quite prominent businessmen, but Moscow also harbored a large and brutal Chechen mafia. Ordinary Russians associated Chechens with violent crime.

The unresolved Chechen attempt at secession lay simmering in Russian politics. In the fall of 1994, the Kremlin tried to instigate an armed Chechen uprising against President Dudaev. Clandestinely, the Federal Security Service contributed with financial support, military equipment, and troops to opposition forces, which tried to attack Grozny in vain. Until November 1994, Moscow's military provocations in Chechnya appeared half-hearted, but then Yeltsin issued an ultimatum to Dudaev's government in Grozny to disarm and surrender. When Dudaev refused, the Russian air force started bombing Grozny, and on December 11, 1994, Russia launched a full-fledged military attack on Chechnya to restore "constitutional order," sparking the first Chechen war.

The decision to invade Chechnya was ultimately made by Yeltsin, but a distinct "Party of War" had evolved in the Kremlin. It included Yeltsin's *banya* pals, Soskovets, Korzhakov, Barsukov, Grachev, and other power ministers. Prime Minister Chernomyrdin and the civilian part of the government were hardly involved in this decision. Strangely, the oft-quoted rationale for the war was a remark by the tsarist minister of the interior, V. K. Plehve, in early 1904 before the disastrous Russo-Japanese war: "We need a small victorious war" (Gall and de Waal 1998). The first Chechnya war would prove as unsuccessful as the Russo-Japanese war. The "Party of War" thought the war would be popular because of Russians' dislike of Chechens, but they were mistaken. Only six years earlier, the Soviet Union had withdrawn from Afghanistan, and the Russian public opposed getting bogged down in another bloody quagmire in a mountainous, Muslim republic.

The Russian campaign was bungled from the beginning to the end. It was led by Minister of Defense Grachev, who promised an early and easy victory. Shortly before the invasion, Grachev boasted that "a battalion of paratroopers can take Grozny in two hours" (quoted in Klebnikov 2000, 42). But it took two months, because the Chechens unified and put up fierce resistance, while Grachev had deployed too few Russian troops, whose morale was deplorable. A horrendous bloodbath ensued. The Russian troops proved as incompetent as brutal. On the Chechen side, fundamental Islam was gaining popularity. The Chechens declared jihad (holy war) on the Russian aggressors, committing atrocities that matched those of the Russian forces. The embarrassment for the Russian government was all the greater because Vladimir Gusinsky's TV network NTV showed the war in all its gruesome details, arousing public opposition.

In June 1995, a startling incident occurred. Chechen rebels, led by the radical Islamic commander Shamil Basaev, seized 1,500 hostages in a hospital in the town of Budyonnovsk in southern Russia. Untypically, Chernomyrdin took charge and pursued telephone diplomacy with Basaev. Basaev and his guerilla troops were offered free passage to Chechnya, and the remaining hostages were saved, but about 120 people had already been killed. This was the first of several aggressive Chechen terrorist attacks in Russia proper (Klebnikov 2000, 43).

Meanwhile, substantial Russian troops had managed to gain control of most urban areas around Grozny, but not the mountainous regions of southern Chechnya, and Chechen warlords roamed at will. A few hundred Arab fighters led by veterans from the war in Afghanistan had joined the Chechens in their jihad. Up to 100,000 people, most of them civilian, are estimated to have been killed in this war. According to the official data, around 4,300 Russian soldiers were killed (Trenin and Malashenko 2004, 156).

The war in Chechnya was an unmitigated disaster, and the June 1996 presidential elections were approaching. Politically, the war harmed Yeltsin's popularity, while it strengthened the power of the secret police, military, and his *banya* team. The war in Chechnya undoubtedly undermined the future for Russia's democracy.

Halt of Reform Exacerbated Social Costs

Both in Russia and the West, the arrival of the regime of state enterprise managers was greeted with relief. At long last, the immature, irresponsible, and theoretical radical reformers were replaced with experienced, professional industrialists, such as Chernomyrdin and Soskovets, not to mention Gerashchenko, who were supposed to know how to build a market economy without the unnecessary social suffering characteristic of Gaidar's shock therapy. Yeltsin kept a low profile after the shootout at the White House, and the general impression was that he had fallen into a deep depression and tried to console himself with heavy drinking with his *banya* team.

The reality, however, was very different. Chernomyrdin, Soskovets, Zaveryukha, and Gerashchenko ignored the common good of Russian society, but they cared about their industrial lobbies, which they pampered with far more subsidies than the state could afford. The population, by contrast, did not benefit, although the worst hardships caused by the collapse of the old system had abated. Rather than proceeding with market reforms, the Chernomyrdin government tried to halt the transition halfway, which maximized the social costs.

The rule of the state enterprise managers was accompanied by an unparalleled rise of organized crime, which was connected with the half-transformed economic system, in particular the aluminum war and the bankers' war. Law enforcement was widely considered to be complicit in organized crime, and the government did little to contain crime.

Yeltsin spent much of his time meeting Western and CIS leaders, but little came out of it. The most memorable interaction with the West was the 1995 financial stabilization program, which was based on standard IMF conditions and supported with substantial IMF credits. Yeltsin devoted considerable attention to the annual G-7 meetings, each year edging closer to full membership, but these overpublicized meetings resulted in nothing substantial. US President Bill Clinton liked Yeltsin and wanted to help him, but in Russia the window of opportunity had been closed, and Yeltsin did not deal with economic policy, so the United States could not do much. The West had missed its chance to promote economic reform in Russia, which would never come back.

Relations with the CIS countries posed a constant conundrum that remained the reserve of old Gosplan hands. The most important decision was the formation of a free trade area of all 12 CIS countries on April 15, 1994, but it was never quite implemented. In early 1994, Russia and Belarus agreed to form a union, designed to be a real federation, but it never evolved in spite of innumerable top-level meetings.

On January 20, 1995, Russia, Belarus, and Kazakhstan established a purported Customs Union, which never became even a free trade area. Later, Kyrgyzstan and Tajikistan acceded, but when it became obvious that the Customs Union was a sheer diversion its members renamed it the Eurasian Economic Community in 2000 (Michalopoulos and Tarr 1996, 1997; Olcott, Åslund, and Garnett 1999).

A large literature on Russia's economic reforms condemns the economic policy of this period for having been too radical, but that literature tends to be more emotional than factual.[14] Chapter 3 showed how few and limited the radical reforms were in 1992, and in 1993 a number of catch-up reforms in deregulation and fiscal policy proved surprisingly effective. Over 1994 and 1995, Russia pursued no radical economic reforms whatsoever. The government contained no reformers with the exception of one single minister, Chubais. The economic results of this period were poor: The decline in output continued, officially totaling 17 percent in these two years (figure 4.1).

The only two significant acts of reform in 1994 and 1995 were spearheaded by Chubais. The first was the voucher privatization that was

---

14. Bogomolov (1996), Cohen (2000), Goldman (1996, 2003), Klein and Pomer (2001), Reddaway and Glinsky (2001), and Stiglitz (1999a, 2002).

successfully completed in 1994. By 1995, the EBRD (2000) assessed that 55 percent of Russia's GDP originated in the private sector, and Russia's privatization had become irreversible. Yet after the completion of mass privatization, it was politically difficult to proceed. The managers of the remaining big state enterprises refused to accept privatization for less than nearly complete ownership.

The other reform instigated by Chubais was the stabilization program adopted in March–April 1995 as a standby program with the IMF. This was Russia's first successful stabilization program, because it involved the first serious cut in the fiscal deficit since the beginning of the reforms in 1992. It had become possible thanks to an abatement of rent seeking, which had been prompted by the accumulated reforms in 1992 and 1993 as well as by attrition caused by rising market forces. Still, the fiscal adjustment was neither sufficient nor sustainable, because nothing had been done to the tax system or fiscal federalism.

On the whole, the policies of the government of state enterprise managers amounted to a massive failure. This was a period of larceny, organized crime, and irresponsibility, as the managers turned their back on all reforms. It was a low point in Russia's post-Soviet transition. Fortunately, so many of the pillars of a market economy had been installed in 1992–93 that a critical mass of market forces and private enterprise was about to emerge.

5

The Oligarchy: 1996–98

At the turn of 1995, Russia underwent a quiet but distinct change. The state enterprise managers lost out to younger big businessmen, who were known as oligarchs.[1]

The old managers failed for many reasons. They did not know how to run their companies under the new market conditions. Output continued to fall, and many of them were able to adjust only by cutting costs. They ran up notorious wage and interenterprise arrears. The ample rents of 1992 and 1993 had abated, and direct budgetary subsidies were insufficient to keep the managers afloat. Most of them knew little about finance and they were contemptuous of marketing. They failed to keep up with the changing nature of rent seeking. Insider privatization had given them ownership control over their companies, but mostly through minority posts. Gradually, one after the other, these substandard managers were ousted by outside raiders, exactly as the privatizers had hoped.

The rookies who rose to the apex of economic power were as colorful as the managers were gray. They were the first products of transition, and Russians received the oligarchs with awe and fascination. Their outstanding talent was financial magic: to make money out of anything, by any means, and they changed their techniques of enrichment almost as often as their beautiful women changed clothes. They made money on stocks and bonds and of course also on the state rather than on production. The old managers were no paragons of virtue, but the oligarchs were the

---

1. This period has received the best coverage in the literature because Russia was more open than ever before and the drama was fascinating. Excellent journalistic books are Brady (1999), Freeland (2000), Klebnikov (2000), and Hoffman (2002). A scholarly Russian book, Pappe (2000), adds facts and structure.

paragons of vice. Their only criterion of success was profit. A wave of jokes swept across the country about the "new Russians," who boasted about their expensive habits. The oligarchs bought old palaces in Moscow and restored them to a splendor greater than in the days of the tsars. In a few years, the patently gray Soviet Moscow turned into a colorful city of casinos and wild nightlife.

Who were these spectacular oligarchs and how did they attain their summit? Their rise was gradual, but the loans-for-shares privatizations in late 1995 signified their arrival. In the presidential elections of June–July 1996, Yeltsin won with the joint support of reformers and oligarchs. After Yeltsin had defeated the revitalized communist challenge, the reformers hoped for a new reform wave, but the dawn of new reforms turned out to be false because the oligarchs and reformers did not share interests in economic policy. Instead, "the bankers' war" erupted in the summer of 1997, and the acrimony between reformers and oligarchs contributed to the financial crash in August 1998. In conclusion, the oligarchs are assessed.

Who Were the Oligarchs?

The oligarchs were everything that the Soviet Union was not. They were fast and innovative, unconventional and conspicuous. They were the ultimate opportunists prepared to do whatever it took to become truly wealthy. The sky was no limit for these men. The only thing they had in common with the Soviet system was the contempt of law.

"Oligarch" is an ancient Greek concept, and an "oligarchy" is defined as "government in the hands of a few." In Russia, "oligarch" became a popular label for big businessmen around 1994 when the first truly rich people emerged, meaning a very wealthy and politically well-connected businessman, a dollar billionaire, or nearly so, who was the main owner of a conglomerate of enterprises and had close ties with the president. It would be more appropriate to call them plutocrats, because they focused on making money rather than ruling the state, and they did not maintain steady alliances, but the term "oligarch" stuck. Since the mid-1990s, the oligarchs have been a fixture on the Russian stage, but their personalities and activities have changed more than anybody seems to realize.

In October 1996, one oligarch, Boris Berezovsky, boasted that he was one of seven oligarchs who had been meeting weekly since February 1996. They maintained close contacts with the president's office, and they owned half of Russia (Freeland et al. 1996). The other six oligarchs were Mikhail Khodorkovsky, who controlled Bank Menatep; Aleksandr Smolensky, with Stolichny Bank; Mikhail Fridman and Petr Aven, with Alfa Bank; Vladimir Potanin, with Oneximbank; and Vladimir Gusinsky, with Most Bank and a media empire, including the independent television channel NTV.

In terms of business, Berezovsky was the odd man out, because his main company was Russia's biggest car dealership, Logovaz, whereas the other oligarchs were bankers. Berezovsky had only a minor bank (Obyedinnyony), and he was a minority shareholder in Smolensky's Stolichny Bank. Berezovsky's specialty was to tap the cash flow of state enterprises, such as the car company Avtovaz, the dominant state TV channel ORT, and Aeroflot. He was more of a courtier and financial operator than an entrepreneur. Moscow talked about *semibankirshchina*, the rule of seven bankers, but that was a gross exaggeration, as was Berezovsky's claim about their wealth. It would be more appropriate to talk about a dozen oligarchs, including Vladimir Vinogradov of Inkombank, Vitaly Malkin of Rossiisky Kredit, and Vagit Alekperov of Lukoil.

Something had happened to Russian business. Virtually all these early oligarchs were bankers, and their rise signified the defeat of the industrialists by the bankers. They were all Muscovites, because the financial sector was concentrated in Moscow. Russians noticed that all but one (Potanin) of the seven bankers were Jewish. Some were very young—in their early 30s. All had higher education from Moscow's best universities, and most came from intellectual families. Only Potanin belonged to the old *nomenklatura* as a hereditary foreign trade official.

All the oligarchs were impressive personalities. They were very sociable people, because networking was their *métier*. They could penetrate any locked door. Aven, who had been minister for foreign trade in Yegor Gaidar's government in 1991–92, knew everybody worth knowing. Their actions took as much courage as ingenuity. According to an unconfirmed story, Aven and the then-unknown oil trader Roman Abramovich met for the first time at the White House on October 3, 1993. Each arrived independently on their own initiative with a suitcase full of cash, which they dished out to the special forces to convince them to fight for Yeltsin, promising them as much after the job was done. The Yeltsin family was apparently so moved that they made Abramovich, their new acquaintance, family treasurer, although he was an unknown oil trader and an orphan from a small town in the Urals.

Nobody was more busy-bodied than Berezovsky. He made friends with everybody who was useful and provided them with whatever they needed. Early friends were Yeltsin's bodyguard Aleksandr Korzhakov and Yeltsin's daughter Tatyana Dyachenko, to whom Berezovsky gave a Niva, a Russian jeep, in 1994 and later a Chevrolet Blazer. He got close to the president when he published Yeltsin's memoirs in 1994, which generated amazing revenues. In 1997, when Berezovsky controlled Aeroflot, he hired Valery Okulov, one of Yeltsin's sons-in-law, as CEO. Yeltsin's other son-in-law, Leonid Dyachenko, was an oil trader working with Berezovsky's partner Abramovich (Klebnikov 2000, 117–18, 178, 201). All these actions were completely legal.

As a foreign trade official, Potanin managed to privatize one of the old banks from the Soviet-era Council for Mutual Economic Assistance (Comecon) in some mysterious way that seemed not to require any capital, which made him an oligarch overnight in 1993. Most of the oligarchs had a team of close partners with whom they shared their wealth, but usually their decision making was as centralized as it was fast. Whatever one may think of these men's morals, their ingenuity, imagination, speed, and charisma were second to none.

Vagit Alekperov of Lukoil was different. He was no banker but he was determined to become Russia's John D. Rockefeller. In late 1995, he stated: "We want to make Lukoil into the biggest oil company in the world—in both production and profits," making clear that he intended to overtake Exxon (quoted in Klebnikov 2000, 192). In 1990, he had risen through the ranks to become deputy Soviet minister of fuel and energy at the age of 40. After the August coup he became acting minister. He utilized this opportunity to seize some of Russia's finest oil properties and incorporated them as Lukoil. In 1994, Lukoil participated in the voucher auctions and later in several small cash auctions, enabling Alekperov and his partners to accumulate 28 percent of the shares. This was an uncommon model, because most oligarchs claimed nearly full ownership, but Alekperov was older and closer to the old establishment than most of the other oligarchs and therefore more cautious.

The bankers surged with the stabilization in the spring of 1995, because the new bonanza was to buy treasury bills (known as GKO in Russian). Their real yield hovered around 100 percent a year until 1998. The bankers were not interested in inflation as the industrialists had been, but they favored a large budget deficit that maintained the government's hunger for credits and kept the real interest rates high (Treisman 1998). They also made money as "authorized banks," handling the accounts of state agencies that did not claim adequate interest for their deposits.

The oligarchs were products of the prevailing conditions, which changed at an infuriating speed. Most of them had set up early cooperatives in 1988, doing all kinds of trading. Some had taken off with the importation of computers from the West, and most of them had become millionaires by exporting oil. Next, they entered banking. They usually established new banks and attracted some capital from old state banks. Invariably, they benefited from cheap credits from the Central Bank of Russia. Only to a very limited extent did they engage in the spontaneous privatizations before 1993. In the early 1990s, successful businessmen traded and "sat on the pipe," tapping the cash flow of state enterprises rather than managing or owning companies.

They all used the Marxist concept of "primary accumulation of capital." To them it meant that anything was allowed. The law was at best relative. One of the oligarchs told me in 1999: "There are three kinds of businessmen in Russia. One group is murderers. Another group steals from other private individuals. And then you have honest businessmen like us who only steal from the state."

Everything changed with privatization. The budding oligarchs were pioneers who bought hundreds of thousands of privatization vouchers that they used at voucher auctions to buy whatever stocks they could get. At this stage, it would have been foolish to have a strategy. It was difficult enough to keep up with when and where voucher auctions were held, how much would be sold, and at what price. Small bands of treasure hunters chased good stocks all over the country. By necessity, stock prices were ludicrously low at the voucher auctions. After the auctions were completed in 1995, the new enterprise owners looked at their catch and started considering business strategy. Conspicuously, Bank Menatep ended up with control over 200 sundry industrial companies. Not knowing what to do, Menatep established a holding company, which the Menatep owners with characteristic self-confidence named Rosprom (Russian industry).

The Loans-for-Shares Privatization

The voucher privatization had been completed in 1994, but a large share of the Russian economy remained in state hands, notably, some of the country's most valuable companies. The big state-owned corporations were frightfully mismanaged and criminalized, because the incumbent managers were stealing their companies bare. In some companies a few hundred million dollars a year were siphoned off.

For political reasons, the state was compelled to move toward cash auctions, but Russians had so little money. Russia had returned to its initial dilemma—too many enterprises to sell and too little demand backed by real money. Yet it was politically impossible to sell many of these enterprises to foreigners (Kokh 1998, Chubais 1999). The government's fiscal deficit remained a serious concern, and privatization was increasingly seen as a fiscal solution.

Potanin took the initiative in 1995. He proposed a debt-for-equity swap. He formed the Consortium of Russian Commercial Banks, which included six leading oligarchic banks. They offered to lend the cash-strapped Russian government $2 billion for one year against a collateral of big stakes in some of the country's best companies. The banks would manage the companies in trust, and if the state did not repay the credits one year later, the bankers would be entitled to sell their collateral, also to themselves. The proclaimed intention was that they would compete in auctions about offering the largest credit for each company. Yeltsin signed the decisive decree on August 31, 1995, and the auctions took place during November–December 1995 (Kokh 1998, 104; Klebnikov 2000, 198).

I discussed the impending loans-for-shares auctions with Chubais in September 1995. His primary goal was to continue privatization, and this was the only possible option. He was anxious to replace the criminal state managers who blocked all progress and he held great hopes for Russia's new big businessmen. However, he had been forced to make two concessions: These auctions were not open to foreigners, and the prices would by necessity be very low. He reassured me that the auctions would be open to Russian competitors, but that did not work out either.

Originally, the bankers proposed 43 lucrative corporations for privatization, but most of them resisted ferociously. Eventually, 16 companies were put up for auction, of which four attracted no bid. The 12 companies sold included five oil companies (Yukos, Sibneft, Sidanko, Lukoil, and Surgutneftegaz), Norilsk Nickel, two steel corporations (Novolipetsk and Mechel), two shipping companies, and the oil-products trader Nafta Moskva (Kokh 1998, 108–10).

Several of these auctions did not change control. The managers of Lukoil and Surgutneftegaz used this opportunity to expand their ownership. In reality, only three companies were controversial—Yukos, Norilsk Nickel, and Sibneft (Kokh 1998, 115–30)—and all the writing about the loans-for-shares auctions discusses these three corporations. Oneximbank bought Norilsk Nickel for $170 million. Menatep acquired 86 percent of Yukos' shares for $309 million. Berezovsky and the new oligarch, Abramovich, bought a majority of Sibneft for $100 million (Kokh 1998, 121, 123, 126; Freeland 2000; Hoffman 2002).

These sales aroused sharp criticism from the outset. As usual, the oligarchic banks were divided. Oneximbank, Menatep, and Stolichny were on the inside, being challenged by Rossiisky Kredit, Inkombank, and Alfa Bank on the outside. The banks that bought these companies organized the auctions themselves. Russian competitors offered higher bids, but they were disqualified with the argument that they could not pay as much as they promised. The rivals were powerful and discredited the winners. Many Russian reformers parted with Chubais over these auctions. Western organizations that had participated in prior Russian privatizations stood aside and took exception, and the Russian reformers lost their luster in the West. Naturally, the communists and nationalists in the Duma seized upon these controversial privatizations. The communists set up a special Committee to Investigate Privatization and Punish the Guilty (Blasi, Kroumova, and Kruse 1997, 75).

Part of the problem was that these privatizations were actually the most transparent Russian privatizations, and everybody could see all the details. Nobody knew who had bought how many shares at what price in insider privatized companies such as Lukoil and Surgutneftegaz, which rendered them much less controversial. Forty percent of Gazprom had been sold for $100 million, as much as Sibneft, although that share of Gazprom was worth about 10 times more than Sibneft (Klebnikov 2000, 135). But unlike the taciturn Viktor Chernomyrdin, the ostentatious and demonstrative Berezovsky could not keep quiet about his wealth.

The loans-for-shares privatizations were qualitatively important, because they marked the demise of the state enterprise managers and the rise of the oligarchs. As Chrystia Freeland (2000, 170) pointed out: "Loans-for-shares was revolutionary because it…took companies away from their red directors and gave them to a handful of thrusting entrepreneurs."

The incumbent managers resisted this privatization, and they were ousted in short order by the oligarchs. Vladimir Bogdanov of Surgut-neftegaz realized that the oligarchs were too strong to be beaten, so he joined them, letting Surgut's pension fund purchase 40 percent of the company for a mere $88 million. Bogdanov was the presumed real owner, and he became recognized as an oligarch. Alekperov of Lukoil, who had the habit, as the Russian saying goes, to dance at every wedding, did not get too deeply involved in this scheme, but he picked up another 5 percent of his company (Freeland 2000, 178; Klebnikov 2000, 209).

This privatization formed a new political alliance between reformers and oligarchs: "At heart, the loans-for-shares deal was a crude trade of property for political support. In exchange for some of Russia's most valuable companies, a group of businessmen—the oligarchs—threw their political muscle behind the Kremlin" (Freeland 2000, 169).

The oligarchs were neither liberals nor reformers. They had made their money on rent seeking, opportunism, and ruthlessness. An underlying rationale in the loans-for-shares scheme was that the oligarchs would hold the enterprises in trust for one year. Only after the presidential elections in mid-1996 would the oligarchs be allowed to buy the shares. These privatizations were a tool to ally the quixotic oligarchs with Yeltsin in the upcoming presidential elections (Freeland 2000, 180–81).

The government's defense was that the loans-for-shares auctions generated state revenues of more than $1 billion. No other privatization had generated such large state revenues. Potanin refuted complaints that he had bought Norilsk Nickel too cheaply: "And how much does a firm cost on the market with guaranteed losses, billions of dollars in fixed capital and sales, but with many years of negative cash flow of several tens of millions of dollars?" (quoted in Pappe 2000, 21). Khodorkovsky told Chrystia Freeland (2000, 178): "These were companies that the government was simply unable to sell," because they "were run by very powerful directors."

Initially, the oligarchs had to struggle to gain control over their new assets because the old managers did not give them up voluntarily. Many stocks were dispersed and it took some time to consolidate ownership. The oligarchs did so partly by diluting minority owners' holdings and partly by continuing to tunnel profits out of the companies through transfer pricing. But by 1999 a remarkable recovery started, recorded by Andrei Shleifer and Daniel Treisman: "Between 1996 and 2001, the reported pretax profits of Yukos, Sibneft, and Norilsk Nickel rose in real terms by 36, 10, and 5 times, respectively" (Shleifer 2005, 167). The stock market valuation of Yukos and Sibneft surged more than 30 times in real terms. Contrary to frequent allegations that the oligarchs indulged in asset stripping (Goldman 2003, Stiglitz 2002), their assets increased sharply after 1999. Yukos' assets trebled from 1998 to 2002, while asset stripping proceeded at Gazprom (Shleifer 2005, 167–68). Yukos and Sibneft led the spectacular recovery of Russia's oil production. By 2000, Yukos paid $6 billion a year in taxes,[2] which is more than it would have cost if the company had been auctioned internationally in 1995. At a maximum, Yukos could have caught a price of $5 billion, which was the market value of the Menatep stake in August 1997 after the stock market had quintupled (Klebnikov 2000, 209).

The oligarchs had been accused of lacking industrial knowledge, but they brought in the needed skills. They used international auditing companies to sort out the finances. They hired the American oil service companies Schlumberger and Halliburton to improve the poor exploitation techniques in the Russian oil fields. International management consultants helped them to rationalize their companies. To combat criminality, the oligarchs deployed their own security forces. However, success was never a given: the oil company Sidanko went bankrupt, underlining the commercial risks involved.

A decade after the loans-for-shares privatizations, it is difficult to understand the great emotions they aroused. After all, only three significant companies changed management and all became stunning successes of industrial restructuring. Conversely, only three prominent oligarchic groups benefited, and the loans-for-shares scheme did not make them oligarchs because they were already known as such. All the oligarchic banks involved have actually gone bankrupt and vanished. The Russian privatization scheme was never designed to be moral or egalitarian but to be functional, to privatize and generate able owners. The loans-for-shares did exactly that. Hardly any privatization scheme in world history can record such great economic success.

The loans-for-shares privatizations marked a divide. Private enterprise had already shown its superiority over state ownership. Now, the new oligarchs took over from the state enterprise managers. Chubais and his reformers had lost their political virginity in the eyes of the West and Russian liberals. The stage had been set for the presidential elections in 1996. The oligarchs and the reformers would unite against the communists, but the communists would campaign more intensely than ever against privatization.

The 1996 Presidential Elections: Oligarchs and Reformers United

The Russian government looked miserable in the winter of 1995–96. It was failing both in the war in Chechnya and in the battle for economic re-

---

2. See www.yukos.com (accessed on December 15, 2005).

Table 5.1   Results of election to the State Duma, December 17, 1995

Party	Percent of votes
Communist Party of the Russian Federation	22.7
Liberal Democratic Party of Russia	11.4
Our Home Is Russia	10.3
Yabloko	7.0
Others or against all	48.5
Voter turnout	64.4

Source: Colton (2000, 36, 232).

vival. The loans-for-shares privatizations were seen as corrupt. The regime looked all the worse because Gusinsky's NTV criticized the war in Chechnya and the economic policy every evening in excellent analytical television programs. Yeltsin was physically ailing and was rarely seen. In January 1996, his poll rating hit a low of 3 percent.

The first test of the government was the State Duma elections on December 17, 1995. Chernomyrdin, who had benefited from not standing in the elections in December 1993, made the mistake of heading a new government party, Our Home Is Russia (which was appropriately nicknamed "Our Home is Gazprom"). The assumption was that it would win the Duma elections, making Chernomyrdin a plausible candidate to replace Yeltsin in the presidential elections scheduled for June 1996.

If the election results in December 1993 had been a shock, the election results in December 1995 were devastating. None other than the old, unreformed Communist Party came roaring back, winning 22.7 percent of the votes cast, Vladimir Zhirinovsky's misnamed Liberal Democratic Party of Russia (LDPR) obtained 11.4 percent, and Chernomyrdin's Our Home Is Russia came third with merely 10.3 percent. Only one more party passed the 5-percent hurdle for representation, namely Grigori Yavlinsky's liberal opposition Yabloko Party with 7.0 percent. Gaidar's Russia's Democratic Choice did not even cross the threshold for representation, but neither did many socialist and nationalist parties. Russia's Duma had a solid red-brown majority for the next four years (table 5.1; Colton 2000, 232).

Chernomyrdin remained prime minister, but he was demoralized. The election results showed that he could not win a presidential election. Rather than blaming Chernomyrdin, Yeltsin sacked his most loyal servant Chubais as first deputy prime minister, insulting him publicly with the much-quoted words: "Chubais is guilty for everything." Especially, he blamed Chubais for "grave mistakes in privatization" (Freeland 2000, 192). For the first time since November 1991, Chubais was outside the government, which no longer contained any major reformer.

The implausible favorite to become Russia's next president was Gennady Zyuganov, an unreconstructed communist and ardent Russian nationalist. In January 1996, his poll rating was already 20 percent. As a former mid-level party official, he had surged when more able communists had been ousted or resigned. No viable alternative to Yeltsin had emerged, and however ill he seemed in January 1996 his advisors agreed that he was the only viable candidate. The reformers were reluctant to support Yeltsin because of the war in Chechnya. Eventually, the Gaidar team supported him, while the always oppositional Yavlinsky insisted on standing in the presidential election.

After Chernomyrdin took a political back seat, Soskovets became the government's political leader. Together with Yeltsin's bodyguard Korzhakov and Mikhail Barsukov, chairman of the FSB, he set up Yeltsin's official campaign staff. But these old-fashioned, Soviet-style bureaucrats knew neither how a democracy worked nor how to organize an election campaign. They stood for nothing but power. Their idea of an election campaign was to order senior officials to command their subordinates to vote for the ruler (Klebnikov 2000, 216).

Several of the oligarchs, as well as Chubais, attended the World Economic Forum in Davos, Switzerland, in early February 1996. The oligarchs were truly frightened by Zyuganov's forceful appearance, and they were impressed by Chubais, because of his sharp attack on Zyuganov: "If Zyuganov wins the Russian presidency in June, he will undo several years of privatization and this will lead to bloodshed and all-out civil war" (quoted in Freeland 2000, 193). The oligarchs worried about their newly won property and decided to unite behind Yeltsin. They chose Chubais as their secret campaign manager, running an alternative Yeltsin campaign. The loans-for-shares construction had worked. From February 1996, the leading oligarchs started meeting regularly, and Yeltsin's daughter Tatyana Dyachenko became their liaison with Yeltsin (Freeland 2000, 195).

On February 15, Yeltsin went to his hometown Sverdlovsk/Yekaterinburg to announce that he would run for reelection. At first, nobody took his candidacy seriously. It seemed just embarrassing. But the old Yeltsin, the vote-getter and fighter, had woken up. Amazingly, this infirm man traveled around the country and even danced with pop bands full of vigor. He had revived and seemed to do everything right again, showing what a campaign animal he was. His poll rating started rising, and it surged relentlessly, as inflation fell.

In practice, the secret Chubais team took over the Yeltsin campaign from the president's democratically challenged "Party of War." The Chubais campaign was abundantly financed and it ran a modern Western election campaign with all conceivable tricks. The official ceiling for campaign financing was $3 million, but one of the oligarchs told me afterwards that they put up a total of $600 million to finance the elections.[3] This was about as much as the George W. Bush presidential campaign cost in 2004.

The state undoubtedly helped the oligarchs with this funding by allocating cheap treasury bills to them. Gusinsky's NTV stopped criticizing Yeltsin and joined Berezovsky's ORT in providing positive television coverage. Since Gusinsky had the best journalists, his support was most important. An official Yeltsin campaign clip showed a documentary film of how Bolsheviks executed White cadets and burned a church, ending with the words: "Never Again! Vote for Yeltsin!" A campaign poster with Zyuganov's face announced: "This may be your last chance to buy food!" Another poster showed an empty food store in 1991 in black and white, while its other half showed the colorful grocery store with plenty of food (Klebnikov 2000, 234). Russia had not gone through real decommunization, which made raw anticommunist propaganda feel fresh. Yeltsin stood for freedom and modernity.

"If the Yeltsin campaign was hopelessly corrupt, the Communist candidate, Gennady Zyuganov, was hopelessly dull," observed Klebnikov (2000, 224). The communists reinforced their threat. On March 15, 1996, when the election campaign was gaining momentum, they instigated a vote in the Duma overwhelmingly repealing the 1991 agreement on the dissolution of the Soviet Union, substantiating the fears that they wanted revenge (Hoffman 2002, 337). Naturally, they suffered from poor media coverage and limited financial resources, but they could have done so much more with half a million active members.

The campaign was full of drama, but the battle between Yeltsin's two campaign teams was as prominent as their struggle with Zyuganov. In mid-March, the Soskovets-Korzhakov-Barsukov team had drawn their logical conclusion: Yeltsin could not win a democratic election. They almost convinced Yeltsin to undemocratically postpone the elections for two years, but during two dramatic days Chubais, Chernomyrdin, and Minister of Interior Anatoly Kulikov persuaded Yeltsin not to do so (Hoffman 2002, 337–40). And Yeltsin continued to advance in the polls, overtaking Zyuganov.

The first round of the presidential elections took place on June 16, 1996. The excitement was unbearable. Yeltsin won 35.8 percent of the votes cast against 32.5 percent for Zyuganov. In third place came General Aleksandr Lebed with 14.7 percent. He had made a stellar military career, having been a paratroop commander in Afghanistan, the commander of the fourteenth army in Transnistria in Moldova, and one of the rebels swinging behind Yeltsin during the August 1991 coup. Lebed had a strong popular appeal with his deep authoritative voice and habit of speaking in proverbs.

---

3. Klebnikov (2000, 220) cited "easily over $1 billion," which I think was an exaggeration.

Table 5.2   Results of presidential election, 1996
(percent of votes)

Candidate	First round, June 16, 1996	Second round, July 3, 1996
Boris Yeltsin	35.8	54.4
Gennady Zyuganov	32.5	40.7
Aleksandr Lebed	14.7	—
Grigori Yavlinsky	7.5	—
Vladimir Zhirinovsky	5.8	—
Others or against all	3.8	4.9
Voter turnout	69.8	68.9

Sources: Colton (2000, 234–35); McFaul (1997, 59).

Yavlinsky came fourth with 7.5 percent. Gorbachev decided to stand again, but he received a pitiful 0.5 percent of the votes cast (table 5.2; Colton 2000, 234–35).

The internal drama in the Yeltsin camp was even greater between the two rounds. Lebed was won over to Yeltsin's side, and on June 18, he was appointed secretary of the Security Council, whereas Yavlinsky refused to endorse either candidate. On that day, Korzhakov arrested two of Chubais' collaborators carrying a box with half a million dollars in cash out from the government headquarters. The chips were down. Through his action, Korzhakov forced Yeltsin to choose which team to oust. With their new ally Lebed, Chubais and the oligarchs won and Yeltsin sacked his closest collaborators and friends, First Deputy Prime Minister Soskovets, Head of the Presidential Security Service Korzhakov, Chairman of the FSB Barsukov, and Minister of Defense Grachev, turning an important political page. At the same time, Yeltsin abolished Korzhakov's Praetorian Guard, the Presidential Security Service.[4] However, for Yeltsin it was a serious personal setback to sack his closest drinking buddies. Soon afterward he suffered a severe heart attack that was not publicly acknowledged until after the elections. In the second round on July 3, Yeltsin won convincingly with 54.4 percent against Zyuganov's 40.7 percent (table 5.2).

The threat of a communist revanche was averted by largely democratic means. The voting results concurred with underlying popular opinions (McFaul 1997, Colton 2000). After the elections, however, little happened, because in the fall of 1996 Yeltsin was out of action for several months be-

---

4. In the fall of 1996, Korzhakov held a press conference to accuse Berezovsky of having repeatedly asked him to assassinate Gusinsky, but Korzhakov said that he thought Gusinsky was a nice man, so he saw no reason to murder him. Seemingly, Korzhakov did not realize that by making this accusation he presented himself as in the business of contract murders, as was widely rumored at the time (Klebnikov 2000, 256). In his scandal-mongering memoirs, Korzhakov (1997) published extensive records from his eavesdropping, as if that was normal.

The CPSU Politburo on the Lenin Mausoleum, November 7, 1985.
Photo: ITAR-TASS

Mikhail Gorbachev's début as public politician, Leningrad, May 17, 1985.

Photo: ITAR-TASS

Gorbachev tells Ronald Reagan that time is short, Reykjavik, October 1986.

Photo: Yuri Lizunov and Alexander Chumichyov/ITAR-TASS

Margaret Thatcher: "I like Mr. Gorbachev. We can do business together."
Photo: ITAR-TASS

Andrei Sakharov speaks at the First USSR Congress of People's Deputies. Gorbachev chairs, June 1989.

Photo: ITAR-TASS

The Berlin Wall is torn down, November 9, 1989.
Photo: Gerard Malie/AFP/Getty Images

The coup leaders hold their only press conference, Moscow, August 19, 1991.
Photo: Vladimir Musaelyan and Alexander Chumichyov/ITAR-TASS

Boris Yeltsin on a tank in front of the White House, Moscow, August 19, 1991.
Photo: Diane-Lu Hovasse/AFP/Getty Images

Yeltsin tells Gorbachev to dissolve the CPSU.
Speaker Ruslan Khasbulatov listens without enthusiasm,
August 23, 1991.
Photo: Alexander Chumichyov/ITAR-TASS

Anatoly Chubais and
Yegor Gaidar are
taking on a tough job,
October 1992.
Photo: ITAR-TASS

Chubais promotes
privatization vouchers,
August 21, 1992.
Photo: ITAR-TASS

Attack on the White House, October 4, 1993.
Photo: ITAR-TASS

Yeltsin works hard to attract votes, June 1996.
Photo: Laski Diffusion-Wojtek Laski/Getty Images

Yeltsin with his
closest confidant,
his daughter Tatyana,
July 1997.
Photo: Sentcov, Chumichev/
ITAR-TASS

Yeltsin leaves
the Kremlin to Putin.
Chief of staff
Aleksandr Voloshin
is in the middle,
December 31, 1999.
Photo: ITAR-TASS

Is this really my successor?
Vladimir Putin's Inauguration,
May 7, 2000.

Photo: Vladimir Rodionov and Sergei Velichkin/
ITAR-TASS

Soulmates: Jacques Chirac, Putin, and Gerhard Schröder,
Sochi, August 31, 2004.
Photo: Vladimir Rodionov/ITAR-TASS

George W. Bush
immediately decided
he could trust Putin,
APEC Summit, Hanoi,
November 19, 2006.

Photo: Jim Watson/AFP/Getty Images

The Beslan tragedy, September 4, 2004.
Photo: Andrei Yugov/ITAR-TASS

Youth meeting
with Big Brother:
"Forward Putin's generation,"
March 2007.

Photo: Alexander Nemenov/
AFP/Getty Images

cause of illness and heart surgery. Chubais became his chief of staff, but in Yeltsin's absence Chernomyrdin became more powerful than ever. The government changed little, but it bore Chernomyrdin's imprint, being dominated by his gray men of upper middle age. An exception was one oligarch, Potanin, who became first deputy prime minister for economic affairs, but he accomplished little apart from restructuring more than $1 billion of tax debts to the benefit of his Norilsk Nickel (Klebnikov 2000, 253). The hope of further economic reforms was elusive.

Lebed, however, acted fast. He used his status as a military hero to conclude a cease-fire in Chechnya with new Chechen President Aslan Maskhadov in August. In effect, Chechnya became independent in all but name. Russia withdrew its troops from Chechnya and let the Chechens manage themselves. To the Russian public, this was a great relief. Lebed behaved as the new heir apparent, being outspoken and even insulting to Yeltsin, who predictably sacked Lebed for insubordination on October 17. Two weeks later, Berezovsky was appointed deputy secretary of the Security Council with special responsibility for Chechnya (Hoffman 2002, 363; Klebnikov 2000, 236, 256). After Lebed had brokered the armistice in Chechnya, he alleged that Berezovsky told him: "What a business you have ruined. Everything was going so well. So, they were killing each other, but they've always been killing each other and always will be" (quoted in Klebnikov 2000, 258).

False Dawn of Reform: The Bankers' War, 1997

The year 1996 had been devoted to defeating the communist threat, and no reforms were undertaken. During his election campaign, Yeltsin promised every conceivable group some benefits, which undermined the budget, although the most excessive promises were reversed after the elections. Suddenly, Moscow realized that apart from privatization minimal reforms had been undertaken since 1993. Once again, the mood was: "We can no longer live like this!"

By early 1997, Yeltsin was back in good health, drinking less after his heart surgery and the departure of his drinking buddies. Full of energy and confidence, he wanted to complete his economic reforms, in which he had not been so interested since the fall of 1991. The election campaign had brought the reformers closer to Yeltsin, and his daughter Tatyana provided them with a strong personal link to the president.

In early 1997, Yeltsin replaced the ineffective Potanin with Chubais as first deputy prime minister for the economy. In addition, one of Yeltsin's favorites, Boris Nemtsov, the young and charming governor of Nizhny Novgorod, was lured to become another first deputy prime minister. At the time, Nemtsov was Russia's most popular politician. Once again Yeltsin revitalized the government with young reformers in their 30s, but

Chernomyrdin was left as prime minister. US Deputy Secretary of Treasury Lawrence Summers, who followed the Russian reforms closely, exclaimed that this was a "dream team."

The government's idea was that big complicated reforms that could not be undertaken in 1991–93 should be carried out. Nemtsov and Chubais declared that the period of "bandit capitalism" was over and that the time had arrived for a normal, honest market economy or "people's capitalism." Yeltsin promised them full support. They put the emphasis on structural reforms (Hoffman 2002, 366; Klebnikov 2000, 269–70).

Because of Yeltsin's support and Nemtsov's popularity, the reformers thought that they could overrule the oligarchs. They also reckoned that the oligarchs understood that the rules of the game had to be normalized. As in 1991, the reformers talked about themselves as a kamikaze government, which could do nothing but undermine their credibility.

Fearless, Nemtsov attacked Gazprom, Russia's wealthiest company, which was finally registered as a monopoly, and the reformers tried to tax it normally. They also questioned the management's right to vote for the government's shares (Slay and Capelik 1997). An equally unpopular idea was to force the oligarchs to pay taxes. Some of them were already paying millions of dollars in personal income taxes, but most did not (Fedorov 1999a, 199–200). The reformers insisted that Russia would hold open privatization auctions for the remaining big state companies. Nemtsov also wanted to deprive the oligarchic bankers of their privileges as authorized banks to hold state funds for minimal interest payment.

The oligarchs, however, knew they had helped Yeltsin to win the presidential elections. Now it was payback time. The tension between the reformers and oligarchs came to a crunch in July 1997. The government had decided to privatize one quarter of Svyazinvest, a state holding company that held controlling stakes in all Russia's regional wireline companies. Gusinsky, who had been left out of the loans-for-shares deals, had long eyed Svyazinvest and considered it promised to him. He formed a consortium with Fridman from Alfa Bank, who had also been excluded from loans-for-shares. Fridman asked: "Why did [privatizations] have to become fair at this particular moment?" (quoted in Freeland 2000, 280). Their consortium was supported by Berezovsky, although he had no direct commercial interest. He opposed the reformers because Nemtsov had blocked him from becoming chairman of Gazprom, and he favored corruption. In addition, he wanted to be the senior oligarch.[5]

However, Potanin decided to compete in the Svyazinvest auction, and he was not deterred by all the other major oligarchs ganging up against him. The auction took place in Moscow on July 25, 1997, and Oneximbank with partners won with a bid of nearly $1.9 billion. This was several times

---

5. Interview with Nemtsov, June 30, 2007.

more money than the government had received for any prior privatization, and it was the most transparent and honest large privatization auction Russia ever held. One of Potanin's partners, George Soros, later exclaimed: "It was the worst investment of my professional career" (quoted in Klebnikov 2000, 282), clarifying that the price was too high.

The other major oligarchs, however, were teeming with fury, ganging up behind Gusinsky and Fridman and launching "the bankers' war." Gusinsky and Berezovsky's media empires alleged that this most honest privatization auction had been one of the most shady, and the Russian public needed little convincing that a privatization had been corrupt. Gusinsky's muckrakers dug and in August they found that Chubais' protégé, Minister of Privatization Alfred Kokh, had received a hefty advance of $100,000 for a book about Russia's privatization from a company related to Oneximbank.[6] In addition, he was personally entertained by Potanin. Yeltsin sacked Kokh in short order.

On August 18, Chubais' chief ally in his native St. Petersburg, Deputy Mayor for Privatization Mikhail Manevich, was shot dead by a sniper in his car on Nevsky Prospekt, the city's main street. The murder shocked Chubais, who saw it as a warning to himself. As usual, the murder was never solved, so its meaning remains uncertain. The reformers took their revenge and had Berezovsky sacked from the Security Council on November 5 (Freeland 2000, 288–90; Klebnikov 2000, 273–74).

It was going to get even juicier. Yeltsin called six leading bankers to the Kremlin for a meeting in September 1997, telling them to make peace (Hoffman 2002).[7] The oligarchs just laughed it off. On November 12, Gusinsky's able muckrakers revealed another book contract. Five of the young reformers, including Chubais himself, had received advances of $90,000 each for a book on Russian privatization.[8] The generous publisher was controlled by Oneximbank.

These book contracts were undoubtedly legal, but of course ethically dubious.[9] Yeltsin himself had established this standard. The budding authors knew of Yeltsin's book contract with Berezovsky, but the public did not. By contemporary Russian norms, few violations or payments to officials were as small as these, but they were evident and concrete. For ordinary Russians, the sums were not small, and NTV and ORT hammered the young reformers. Kokh's successor as minister of privatization, Maxim Boycko, was forced to resign after only three months in office, as were two other senior Chubais allies (Freeland 2000, 291–92). For Chubais, who had

---

6. This substantial book was published one year later, Kokh (1998).

7. The bankers were Khodorkovsky, Gusinsky, Smolensky, Potanin, Vinogradov, and Fridman.

8. Also this excellent book was published in due order, Chubais (1999).

9. They would have been legal also in the United States.

the reputation of being as severe—but personally clean—as a Jesuit, this affair was highly damaging. Gusinsky and Berezovsky had successfully brought the reform offensive to a screeching halt.

The reform government had been devastated, before it managed to get anything done. The reform attempts of 1997 turned out to be a false start, although a substantial reform agenda had been set. All the big economic and social issues had been analyzed and plenty of sound policy advice had been elaborated upon. The professional reform debate of 1997 set the stage for Russia's economic revival, but it had to wait for a few years. It laid the intellectual foundation for the reforms of 2000–2003 (chapter 6).

The media oligarchs defeated the young reformers in the fall of 1997, but they were not alone. Prime Minister Chernomyrdin was not part of this reform offensive, and his beloved Gazprom was not weakened. A coalition of communists and nationalists held a majority in the State Duma, and they did not accept any reform legislation. The regional governors, who were powerful and deeply entrenched in corruption, could also block any reform legislation.

It is curious that the reformers thought anything could be done in 1997. Once again, they overestimated Yeltsin's strength and his support for market reform. But they felt that the time had matured. The state was growing stronger and making its comeback. After years of talk about the state having been privatized, the state was becoming nationalized. The reformers realized that the oligarchs could not survive if they did not adapt to a normal market economy, but most of the oligarchs, notably Berezovsky and Gusinsky, did not. Their opposition would cost them dearly. The reformers had expected some resistance from the oligarchs, but not that they would approach self-destruction. Gaidar passed the judgment: "We did not foresee how short-sighted the strategy of the so-called oligarchs would be, to what degree they would prove unable to understand their own self-interest" (quoted in Freeland 2000, 274).

The strife raged also among the oligarchs. The oligarchy was over after the presidential elections, and the usual ruthless competition had returned, even though murder was no longer perceived as a permissible means in Russian big business after 1994. The oligarchs were important, but the role of oligarchy was much exaggerated. The Russian chronicler of the oligarchy Yakov Pappe (2000, 22) assessed Russia's "oligarchy":

> Russia has had no economic oligarchy . . . coalitions of big Russian companies or individual businessmen were local, opportunistic, and short-term. They cooperated for one political or economic purpose and simultaneously they fought one another over other issues. The only broad coalition of big business emerged for the presidential election in 1996 . . . [but] it existed for only half a year before the elections and three-four months afterwards.

The unintended consequence of the bankers' war was that Yeltsin's second term was effectively over. Only a year into his second five-year term in office, he was a complete lame duck. The two groups of protagonists that had fought for him in the elections—the reformers and the oligarchs—had self-destructed through internecine struggle. The red-brown majority in the parliament wanted nothing but to impeach him, an issue that popped up from time to time. Yeltsin was left alone with limited abilities to act in spite of his purported superpresidential constitution. Russia was rudderless.

The Financial Crash of August 1998

The late Rudiger Dornbusch used to say that a financial crisis usually starts later than anybody could imagine, but when it starts, it goes faster than anybody had imagined.[10] That was true of Russia's financial crash in 1998. The country had violated so many rules of macroeconomic policy for so long that the culprits who had benefited from the loose fiscal policy felt nothing but secure.

Russia's standby agreement with the International Monetary Fund (IMF) in the spring of 1995 brought down inflation, but fiscal policy remained too loose, whereas monetary policy was very strict. This unfortunate combination forced the government to borrow extensively to finance its large budget deficit, primarily through domestic treasury bills at outrageous real interest rates lingering around 100 percent per annum. Access to the treasury bill market was limited to privileged Russian banks, excluding both foreigners and households, making it a bonanza of rent seeking. The IMF insisted on opening this market to foreign investors, which lowered treasury bill yields, but it also exposed Russia to a dangerous dependence on short-term foreign capital, attracted by the abnormally high yields.

Despite the large budget deficit and continued output decline, Russia's economy looked too inviting. The freely floating exchange rate showed a tendency to rise, so in the summer of 1995 the authorities introduced a currency band for the ruble exchange rate to impede its rise, prescribing a moderate devaluation instead. This band inspired a false sense of security.

As Russia entered 1996, the communist victory in the parliamentary elections in December 1995 cast a dark shadow. With the presidential elections in June 1996 approaching, the fear of communist revenge dominated Russian politics. Nobody paid much attention to economic policy. The West was enamored with desire to do whatever it could to keep Yeltsin in power (Talbott 2002). Distributing preelection gifts, the government let the budget deficit rise from 6.6 percent of GDP in 1995 to 9.4 percent of GDP in 1996 (figure 4.2). The real yields of the treasury bills peaked at 150 percent a year before the presidential elections, as the government tried to sell more bills than the market was prepared to buy given the political

---

10. This section draws on Åslund (1998, 1999, 2000).

risks. Almost 4 percent of GDP went to the payment of yields on treasury bills (Illarionov 1998b).

Although nobody in the government was concerned about reform, in the spring of 1996 the IMF concluded a three-year loan program with Russia, an Extended Fund Facility with $10.2 billion in financing. This program lacked all credibility, because it demanded that the budget deficit be slashed to 4 percent of GDP, which was never a serious proposition. This was all too obviously a G-7 political decision to secure President Yeltsin's reelection. Germany and France gave Russia substantial additional credits, allowing the Russian government to increase the budget deficit further.

Yeltsin survived, but these unconditional credits harmed Russia's economic policy. The soft IMF agreement convinced foreigners and Russians alike that Russia was too big and too nuclear to fail. In September 1996, the IMF delayed one credit tranche, but from that time and throughout 1997 the IMF had little leverage, because the election results and the IMF agreement had unleashed an extraordinary inflow of private foreign portfolio investment (Odling-Smee 2004, 25). Russia was set for a stock market boom that could only lead to a bust.

Foreign portfolio investment skyrocketed from a respectable $8.9 billion in 1996 to an incredible $45.6 billion in 1997, or 10 percent of GDP (RECEP 1999). Roughly half of the foreign portfolio investments went into federal government bonds and the other half into other bonds and stocks. At the peak of the stock market in 1997, foreigners might have owned as much as 30 percent of the market capitalization of some $100 billion. The stock of treasury bills in the summer of 1998 amounted to some $70 billion, of which foreigners held some $30 billion. In addition, substantial amounts of corporate, regional, and municipal bonds had been issued. In July 1998, the accumulated foreign portfolio holdings were at least $65 billion or nearly 15 percent of GDP. In addition, international financial institutions had provided the Russian government with more than $20 billion, or 4.5 percent of GDP, in loans. Ironically, Russia was flooded with foreign financing mainly private but also intergovernmental—after serious attempts at economic reform had faded.

Until October 1997, foreign investors had no reason to complain. Russia was the best performing stock market in the world in both 1996 and 1997 with the stock indexes increasing more than six times from January 1996 to October 1997 (figure 5.1). For foreign investors, Russia had become a magic money-making machine.

Russian capital, however, flew in the opposite direction. After having shrunk in 1994 and 1995, net capital outflows amounted to about $20 billion annually in 1996, 1997, and 1998. Russian businessmen wanted to escape the arbitrary Russian taxation, and they trusted their country's economic policy less than foreign investors did.

The foreign portfolio investments contributed to the magnitude of the Russian financial crash, and these loans to the Russian government di-

Figure 5.1 Russian stock market index (RTS), 1996–98

RTS index

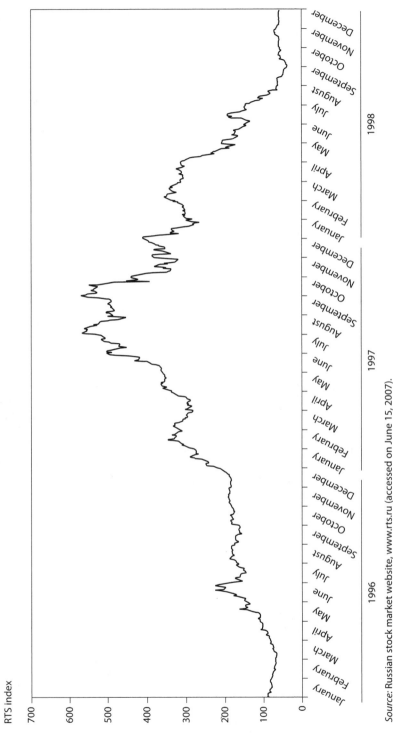

Source: Russian stock market website, www.rts.ru (accessed on June 15, 2007).

175

Figure 5.2 Barter payments in sales of industrial enterprises, 1992–2004

share of barter in total sales, percent

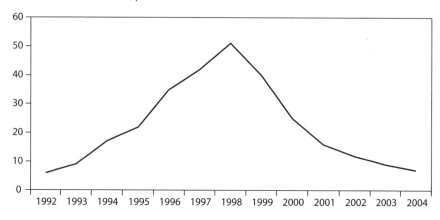

Source: IMEMO (2004).

minished the need for the state to collect taxes or cut subsidies. The conditionality of the IMF loans was ineffective in the presence of such large, unconditional private portfolio investments. The Russian bankers focused on the domestic treasury bill market, and encouraged by the World Bank and the European Bank for Reconstruction and Development (EBRD) they borrowed heavily in foreign currencies, exposing themselves to serious currency imbalances. This was a fools' paradise, and only fools did not buy treasury bills and Russian stocks.

Strangely, barter and nonpayments did not go away in this surplus of money but proliferated. By 1998, about half of all interenterprise payments were made in barter, about one quarter in money surrogates, and only one-quarter in money (figure 5.2). This was not the desired monetization of the Russian economy. The proliferation of barter was confusing and challenging, and many alternative explanations were presented. Communists complained about a shortage of money, requiring additional emissions, but the issue was not scarce supply of money but a lack of demand. Clifford Gaddy and Barry Ickes (1998, 2002) provided the most convincing explanation. They showed that a well-entrenched system offered many actors strong incentives to use barter, because barter and other noncash payments facilitated tax avoidance and evasion.

Barter and offset prices were about twice as high as prices in cash, and businessmen could extract tax discounts by paying with offsets (Commander and Mumssen 1998). If a construction company had not paid its taxes, it offered to build something for the regional government, thus winning an often unplanned public investment project. Offsets were by their nature discretionary negotiations between big businessmen and government officials about large amounts of money, imbued with corruption.

The masters of the barter economy were the big state monopolies, Gazprom and Unified Energy Systems, the state-owned holding company for regional public utilities. In 1996–97, only 7 percent of retail gas purchases were paid in cash, and arrears abounded (Slay and Capelik 1997). Big industrial enterprises used barter to subdue small enterprises. Forty percent of the barter trade was perceived as involuntary, meaning that an enterprise was compelled to accept a payment in products it did not want (Aukutsionek 1998). A second group of beneficiaries were regional governments, which used offsets to divert tax revenues from the federal government to themselves, receiving 60 percent of taxes in money surrogates, compared with 25 percent for the federal government (OECD 1997, Illarionov 1998a). Third, old loss-making, Soviet enterprises that were reluctant to adjust to market conditions were kept alive by subsidies extracted through barter.

The post-Soviet nonmonetary economy was a complex relations economy, benefiting big enterprises, old Soviet enterprises, and regional officials. The losers were the national economy, the consumers, small and medium-sized enterprises (which lived in the overtaxed cash economy), and the federal government (which was starved of revenues). A monetized economy is transparent and competitive, offering fewer advantages to large and old enterprises. Barter was an important structural cause of the financial crash of 1998.

The Asian financial crisis erupted in the summer of 1997, and in late October it hit Russia. On October 28, the Russian stock market suddenly fell from its near peak by 19 percent, and the international credit market tightened. The government was completely unprepared. During that month, Berezovsky worked with the communists in the State Duma and with Prime Minister Chernomyrdin to *increase* the budget deficit to over 8 percent of GDP in 1997 (figure 4.2), not least to undermine the reformers in government. Given that the government had just expanded the deficit, it failed to tighten its fiscal policy until February, and real interest rates shot up to over 100 percent a year again.

On March 23, 1998, President Yeltsin sacked his loyal but passive Prime Minister Chernomyrdin. At the same time, Yeltsin dismissed Chubais and his rival Anatoly Kulikov as deputy prime ministers. Chubais was soon appointed CEO of Unified Energy Systems and started a major reform of Russia's public utilities. Once again, Yeltsin rejuvenated the government. He appointed a 35-year-old bright reformer, Sergei Kirienko, who was seen as a Nemtsov protégé and had been minister of energy. The State Duma was not amused and it approved of Kirienko only one month later on Yeltsin's third attempt, facing the threat of dissolution. It took Kirienko another month to form a government. Mikhail Zadornov, the young

Yabloko deputy and initiator of the 500-day program, had become minister of finance in November 1997, and he was to stay on his post for the next two stormy years as one of the few pairs of steady hands.

The only mystery about Russia's financial predicament was that it had not resulted in a serious crash earlier. For years, the country had maintained a budget deficit of 8–9 percent of GDP. Even in 1998, it was 8.2 percent of GDP (figure 4.2), because the government had refrained from cutting enterprise subsidies. A study by Pinto, Drebentsov, and Morozov (1999) estimated that total Russian budget subsidies amounted to a staggering 16.3 percent of GDP in 1998, of which 10.4 percent of GDP was extracted through barter and nonpayments and 5.9 percent was direct enterprise subsidies. Federal-regional fiscal relations aggravated these problems because most of the revenues stayed with the regional governments that provided the bulk of the enterprises subsidies, whereas the federal treasury was responsible for all debt service on the fast-growing and unsustainable short-term government debt.

By late May 1998, the creditors finally got scared and withdrew on a large scale, and the dollar-pegged exchange rate came under severe pressure. Russian bankers started withdrawing their funds from the country, while foreigners were still attracted by the extraordinary bond yields. Even so, the central bank was swiftly losing its limited currency reserves defending the exchange rate. At this stage, a devaluation would have bankrupted half the banks because of their adverse currency balances.

The Kirienko government was neither fast nor resolute in handling the financial crisis, and it did not possess the necessary political clout to undertake the necessary fiscal adjustment. Politically, it was as isolated as Gaidar's government had been in the spring of 1992. Acknowledging his lack of experience, Kirienko called in Chubais as a special envoy to negotiate with the international financial institutions. The IMF pressured the Russian government to cut the budget deficit, and by July 1998 the government agreed to substantial expenditure cuts and new tax laws to raise federal revenues, not least by transferring taxes from the regions to the federal government. The IMF, the World Bank, and Japan granted Russia a uniquely large additional credit package of $23 billion on July 13. However, the State Duma refused to adopt most of the federal revenue measures proposed by the Russian government and the IMF in the next few days. As a consequence, the IMF issued only a first tranche of $4.8 billion on July 20. The US government passed the judgment that no salvation was possible and did not propose any new measures. Arguably, no amount of credit could have saved the Russian finances at this stage, only substantial and instant budget cuts, and they were not politically feasible (Kharas, Pinto, and Ulatov 2001).

The Russian government was by no means passive, and some of its acts were quite heroic. As the head of the State Tax Service in 1998, Boris Fedorov, the former minister of finance, tried to force Gazprom to pay taxes. He reckoned it necessary to beat the biggest company to convince other big corporations to do so. He found out that Gazprom had made a formal agreement with his predecessor at the tax service that illegally relieved Gazprom from half of its tax liability. When Fedorov went after Gazprom, its management reduced its tax payments, claiming that the federal budget owed it more money than it was supposed to pay in taxes. The government responded by threatening a change of management of Gazprom, and it let the police raid Gazprom's headquarters and its holiday homes. Gazprom CEO Rem Vyakhirev responded by going to Yeltsin and Kirienko. Gazprom's many supporters in the Duma protested against the government's supposedly malign actions. These attempts laid the ground for breaking the power of the big companies and for their effective taxation (Fedorov 1999a, 204–08).

The Russian finances could no longer be saved without devaluation or a default. On August 17, 1998, the government did both. It defaulted on its domestic debt of some $70 billion, and the value of the ruble soon fell by three-quarters. In addition, the government declared a moratorium on Russian banks' foreign payments, which in effect became a general freeze of bank accounts. Once again, ordinary Russian bank savers lost their money, usually about two-thirds of their deposits, and they had to wait in humiliating lines outside the banks for days hoping to rescue some of their savings. Inflation that had fallen to the single digits surged to 85 percent for 1998 as a whole. The Russian stock market hit bottom with a staggering fall of 93 percent from its peak in October 1997 until early October 1998 (figure 5.1). One Western investment banker said that he would rather eat nuclear waste than invest in Russia again (Freeland 2000), but this was of course the ideal time to invest.

About half of Russia's commercial banks went bankrupt, including all the big oligarchic banks save Alfa Bank.[11] The oligarchs' spell as bankers was over and their very survival was under a cloud. The big questions for the country were whether the market economy was over, whether the communists would come back, and whether hyperinflation would erupt. The shock was enormous and so was the sense of national failure. In Moscow, somebody put up unsigned posters with the words: "Nobody will save Russia apart from ourselves." In jest, one of the posters had been signed, "Michel Camdessus," the managing director of the IMF. Russia's self-confidence had hit a new low, but Russians realized they had to take their responsibility.

---

11. Menatep, Oneximbank, SBS-Agro, Inkombank, Rossiisky Kredit, and Most Bank went bankrupt. The owners of SBS-Agro, Inkombank, and Rossiisky Kredit disappeared from the big business scene.

Three major interest groups pushed their country into this abyss. The main culprits were the oligarchs. The bankers had encouraged the large budget deficit and thrived on the treasury bills, although many of them now suffered badly themselves. Berezovsky had even been talking down the Russian market (Klebnikov 2000, 281). Some oil barons, including Berezovsky, had campaigned for devaluation, although they knew that this would lead to the bankruptcy of most banks. The oil producers wanted lower production costs in rubles and thought little about other consequences (Alekperov 1998).

Second, the Russian State Duma, which was dominated by the communists, refused to accept a government proposal to move from a value-added tax based on payments to accrual basis in July 1998, which would have taxed barter. Nor did the Duma agree to transfer any regional revenues to the federal treasury. These two votes by the Duma triggered the financial collapse.

Third, behind these decisions by the Duma stood the regional governors, who resisted any transfer of their funding to the federal government, although regional revenue was almost one and a half times as large as the federal revenues, and much of it was spent on discretionary enterprise subsidies.

The behavior of all these three groups was socially irresponsible, but based on their own recent experiences, their actions appeared rational. They had learned that the most reckless rent seekers were the most successful. They seized any possibility instantly, considering it better to be seen as cunning and dangerous than honest.

An additional nuisance was that Siberian coal miners had gone on strike in May because they had not been paid their wages. Although the federal government was not responsible, the miners organized protest actions, from blocking railroads to camping outside the White House and beating on their helmets. ORT and NTV covered them so intensely that the suspicion arose that the protesting miners were paid by Berezovsky and Gusinsky.

In his Annual Address to the Federal Assembly on March 30, 1999, President Yeltsin (1999a) sadly summed up the situation: "We have got stuck half-way in our transition from the planned and command economy to a normal market economy. We have created . . . a hybrid of the two systems." It was evident that Russia had to change profoundly, but it was unclear how.

NATO and G-7 Enlargement

Despite Russia's weakness and friendliness, in 1997 the North Atlantic Treaty Organization (NATO) was enlarged to include Poland, the Czech Republic, and Hungary. In order to make sure that Yeltsin was not hurt, the West made Russia a full member of the G-7 at the same time (Talbott 2002). Yeltsin (2000, 131) reported in his memoirs:

> Russia was finally granted full-fledged status [as a member of G-8] in June 1997, at a summit in Denver, Colorado. . . . Paradoxically, I think our tough stance on the eastern expansion of NATO . . . played a role in gaining us this new status.

However, Russia's membership in the G-8 was not all that important. The exclusion from NATO, by contrast, meant that Russia was not included in the Western world, to which it had arguably belonged for two centuries from Peter the Great to 1917 (Malia 1999). Russian liberals felt wounded. Their dream of becoming a part of the West had been pushed aside for the foreseeable future.

Russia's policy toward the members of the CIS did not really evolve. It was characterized by bluster and a lack of realism. Russia came up with one harebrained scheme after the other. The CIS countries closest to Russia obliged by signing, whereas the other half did not. Hardly any country ratified any agreement, and even if they ratified they did not implement them. All these meetings and agreements cost time and effort, and they were utterly unproductive.

Major initiatives were a Russian-Belarusian Union broached in early 1994, a common free trade area for all CIS countries in 1994, and a Customs Union for, first, Russia, Belarus, and Kazakhstan in 1995, and later for Kyrgyzstan and Tajikistan. When the Customs Union did not work, it was renamed the Eurasian Economic Community in 2000 (Olcott, Åslund, and Garnett 1999). In April 1999, Berezovsky was appointed executive secretary of the CIS, and for a year he flew around trying to make sense of the organization until he failed. The CIS was a waste of time, diverting the CIS leaders from more serious international engagements such as their accession to the WTO.

Assessing the Oligarchs

To understand the implications of the Russian oligarchs, a comparative historical perspective is useful. The oligarchs, or Russia's "big business" or "big capital," as they preferred to call themselves, were not real oligarchs in the sense that they ruled Russia. The "rule of the seven bankers" or *semibankirshchina* of 1996 was brief and not characteristic of big business in Russia. Only for nine months in 1996 did the top bankers meet regularly with Russia's top politicians. The bankers played this prominent role and stayed united only because of the virulent communist threat.

The Russian oligarchs changed both their actual persona and their behavior rapidly. They took over from both the state enterprise managers and organized crime. They were more skillful than the old managers, especially in the financial and international sphere, and they proved generally more flexible and entrepreneurial. Tired of paying off racketeers, they set up their own security forces and cleansed their enterprises of organized crime, which old managers usually failed to do.

The oligarchs had enriched themselves as traders, primarily trading oil and metals. At the end of communism, they were all bankers and benefited from inflationary profits. In 1993–94, they thrived on the voucher auctions, opportunistically accumulating stocks in a large number of enterprises. From 1995 until June 1998, they made huge fortunes on domestic treasury bills with high yields. A breakthrough for the oligarchs was the loans-for-shares privatizations, even if only three significant companies—Yukos, Norilsk Nickel, and Sibneft—changed controlling owners. The newly rich entrepreneurs showed that they could beat the most powerful old state enterprise managers. The rise of the oligarchs marked the ascendance of ownership over the management of assets, which profoundly changed the nature of the Russian economy.

Two men stood out, Boris Berezovsky and Vladimir Gusinsky, because they were showmen and each possessed a media empire. As a businessman, Berezovsky belonged to the early stage of rent seekers, when state enterprises were tapped on funds and money was extracted through political contacts. An article in the business newspaper *Kommersant Daily* offered an accurate assessment of Berezovsky's business:

> To destroy Boris Berezovsky's "empire" is easy, primarily because it is based on the fallacious principle "not to own but manage." Berezovsky did not buy control packages of stocks. . . . With support of the Kremlin, he simply put his people on key posts in a company, and they helped him to manage the firm as was necessary for Berezovsky. (Zavarsky 1999)

In a conversation with the late Paul Klebnikov (2000, 170), Berezovsky himself put it similarly: "Privatization in Russia goes through three stages. The first stage is the privatization of profits. The second is the privatization of property. The third is the privatization of debts." Like the state enterprise managers, Berezovsky was best at the first type of privatization, which he exercised at state-dominated Avtovaz, Aeroflot, and ORT. The other oligarchs focused on real privatization of property. Corporate raiders purchased debts of companies to put them into bankruptcy and buy them cheaply.

Vladimir Gusinsky was a very different creature. Although he probably made most of his money on banking and real estate, he was an outstanding media entrepreneur, creating Russia's most interesting television channel, radio channel, and print media. Even if he sometimes used his media for political purposes, the quality of his journalism was eminent.

The financial crash of August 1998 brought about fundamental changes for the oligarchs. Their banks were most exposed to the financial collapse because they were heavily invested in treasury bills that defaulted and they had taken large foreign loans that they could not pay back after the devaluation. Of the big banks, only Alfa Bank and MDM had sold their treasury bills in time and survived. Another effect was the rise of the commodity producers, that is, oil and metals. Out of 26 Russian billionaires identified by *Forbes* magazine in 2005, 12 had made most of their money on metals, nine on oil, and two on coal (Kroll and Goldman 2005).[12] Another major change was that the oligarchs developed lucid corporate strategies. Their corporations remained conglomerates, but most of them concentrated on approximately three core industries. They sold off accidental assets that they had assembled during the privatization.

The ideal business strategy was to have been a banker thriving on treasury bills until May 1998 and then sell the treasury bills and sit on foreign cash until after the August crash. In the fall of 1998, the trick was to buy commodity-producing companies cheaply on the secondary market. Some rising oligarchs did exactly that, notably the owners of MDM Bank, Andrei Melnichenko and Sergei Popov, who were only in their 20s. In June 1998, they smartly sold all their treasury bills, and after the crash they started buying up privatized coal mines, eventually accumulating one-third of Russia's coal production in their company SUEK. They turned their coal mines around in no time, decriminalizing them, laying off workers, boosting coal output, and thus achieving good profits without state support in an industry that had lived on subsidies.

In late 1999, Oleg Deripaska and Roman Abramovich, both in their early 30s, bought most of Russia's aluminum production from the infamous brothers Mikhail and Lev Chernoi (victors of the bloody aluminum wars), and they formed Rusal. Thus, a new generation of even younger oligarchs emerged who did not suffer from the (unjustified) stigma of the loans-for-shares privatizations. Purchases of already privatized enterprises were politically much more acceptable than purchases directly from the state, which were invariably seen as corrupt.

The development of Khodorkovsky's Menatep group is fairly representative. Initially, it was Bank Menatep. In 1994–95, it became the industrial conglomerate Rosprom with 200 mismanaged enterprises. After the collapse of Bank Menatep in 1998, it became the oil company Yukos, which in 2000 became the best managed Russian oil company together with Sibneft, whereas most of Rosprom was sold off.

Fridman's Alfa Group offered another clear-cut strategy. Uncharacteristically, Alfa Bank remained the heart of this group. Only after the loans-for-shares did Alfa buy an oil company, TNK, which became its main money spinner. Alfa also bought a large part of Vimpelcom, an excellent start-up mobile phone operator. Alfa's purchase boosted Vimpelcom's share price, because Alfa could help this squeaky-clean company to obtain licenses in regions outside Moscow. Alfa's fourth major business line was retail trade.

---

12. Yukos, Lukoil, Surgut, TNK, and Sibneft in oil; Rusal, SUAL, Norilsk Nickel, Severstal, Evrazholding, NLMK, MMK, Mechel, and UMMK in metals.

Other large business groups looked similar. Usually, they had an oil or metals company as their cash cow. They poured the cash into manufacturing, consumer industry, or retail trade.

Comparing integrated business groups in Russia and the United States, Aleksandr Dynkin and Aleksei Sokolov (2002) found that big American business groups before the US stock market crash of 1929 tended to be as diversified as Russia's groups before its 1998 crash. In a similar fashion, business groups in both countries were streamlined after the respective financial crashes. Randall Morck, Daniel Wolfenzon, and Bernard Yeung (2005, 693) surveyed recent literature on ownership around the world and concluded: "Control pyramids effectively entrust the corporate governance of the greater parts of the corporate sectors of many countries to handfuls of elite, established families, who can quite reasonably be described as *oligarchs*." Rather than considering oligarchs an exception, as most of the Anglo-American literature about Russia does, we must accept them as the international norm. The two exceptions without concentrated enterprise ownership are the United States and the United Kingdom (La Porta, Lopez-de-Silanes, and Shleifer 1999).

Economically, the oligarchs went through a gradual transformation from rent seekers to profit seekers, from parasites tapping the assets of the state to full-fledged owners and investors. As conditions stabilized, their time horizon grew from one day to the long term. Until 1998, many of them could be criticized for asset stripping and the dilution of minority shareholders' ownership, but since 1999 that has hardly been true. The oligarchs have invested heavily; they have displayed large profits; and many of them have paid substantial dividends to minority shareholders. True, they have been more greedy and aggressive than most businessmen, but isn't that what capitalists are supposed to be? Increasingly, the Russian oligarchs have become more like big businessmen in Western countries, only more dynamic, successful, and colorful.

Almost all the oligarchs were not only owners but also managers of their big enterprises.[13] They turned around Russia's old heavy industry, especially the oil and metallurgical industries, using many talents. A first precondition for the successful management of a big Soviet enterprise was good relations with the Kremlin, that is, the federal government, as well as with the regional governor.

Another important skill was to be able to clean out an enterprise of organized crime. The oligarchs sent in their security forces and secured the plants, sacking pervasively criminalized parts of the company such as the transportation department and the construction department, whereas bookkeeping, production, and research were usually decent. The old man-

---

13. The exceptions were Potanin, whose partner Mikhail Prokhorov was the manager, and Abramovich, who, uncommonly, used hired managers.

agers were contemptuous of financial management and marketing, but the newcomers brought in the big international auditing companies.

Foreign investors are usually afraid of laying off labor, but the revival of a Soviet plant required that the chronic overstaffing was eliminated, and nobody could slim labor forces faster and with less public outcry than Russia's young entrepreneurs. The old Soviet social legislation persisted. Most of it was ignored, but some acts were honored. Russians mastered the real social legislation, which remains an enigma for most foreigners. Similarly, the local authorities posed many demands on major corporations, and able Russian businessmen knew what to do and what to avoid. For instance, when is a charitable donation necessary?

A typical Soviet factory was clogged with superfluous equipment, much of it obsolete, and quite a lot new but never installed. Western investors usually gutted factories, scrapping all the old equipment. Russian engineers, by contrast, knew what made sense in the old machinery and used it, while cleaning out the rest. To them, capital was scarce, making them keen on utilizing the viable physical capital. They often used second-best, but sturdy, Russian equipment, costing a fraction of Western equipment but performing only slightly worse. McKinsey and other Western management consultants were hired to identify bottlenecks, because small investments usually could swiftly raise capacity and quality. Finally, Russian businessmen understood the old management and how to sort it out. Many underwent the best of Western business training at their own expense.

As a consequence of all these peculiarities of big Soviet enterprises, Western business consultants typically advised foreigners to stay away from unrestructured Soviet enterprises with more than 1,500 employees, because they did not know how to manage them. Many big Western investors who did not heed this advice failed miserably. At least at the initial stage of the restructuring of big Soviet plants, Russian oligarchs were far superior to Western businessmen. Fortunately, Russia found ways to transfer large factories to natives who could revive them, in contrast to Central Europe. There, most of the big factories have been closed down because they were either bought by foreigners who failed to manage them, or they were mismanaged by the state for too long and rusted away.

By 2007, the social features of the oligarchs are easy to identify. Most of them are young, just over 40 years of age. They were about to graduate from university when the Soviet Law on Cooperatives was adopted in 1988, which usually formed the legal basis of their first enterprise. Almost all of them are engineers, and several have doctorates in engineering from the best Soviet universities, primarily in Moscow. Their social origins are mostly humble, and many come from the provinces, but the Soviet education system gave them the opportunity thanks to their outstanding mathematical skills. Initially, the dominance of Jews was striking, but ethnically the oligarchs have become more varied. Nearly all the oligarchs manage huge companies. All but one of the current Russian billionaires are men.[14] By all standards, Russia's oligarchs are outstanding self-made entrepreneurs, most of whom made their fortunes on revitalizing existing Soviet mastodons rather than developing new enterprises.

The similarities between the contemporary Russian oligarchs and the American robber barons of the late 19th century are greater than most recognize. Some industries, such as oil and metals, possess great economies of scale, which is a strong reason for concentration of production. The economies of scale are greater in large countries, such as Russia and the United States. Postcommunist Russia was characterized by even more rapid structural change than America during its industrialization and the reconstruction after the Civil War, which promoted the robber barons. In Russia, privatization delivered large assets cheaply to the daring purchasers, and US robber barons benefited from the free distribution of state assets as well, notably land around the railways, and cheap state credits, since multiple early railway investments ended up in bankruptcy because of insufficient state support to reach the desired economies of scale (DeLong 2002).

The US legal system was deplorable in the 19th century (Steele Gordon 2004), and so was the situation in post-Soviet Russia. In the precise meaning of the phrase, post-Soviet Russia was a lawless state. In the early 1990s, Russia lacked most of the necessary laws for a capitalist economy, ranging from property legislation to bankruptcy. To build strong legal institutions takes a long time, and without any forceful legal reformer around, such reforms were always on the backburner.

Poor judicial systems breed poor corporate governance, impeding the evolution of financial markets. Without strong corporate legislation and a potent judicial system, partners find it difficult to agree or resolve conflicts. "When institutions are weak, doing business with strangers is dangerous and unreliable" (Morck, Wolfenzon, and Yeung 2005, 672). Nor can principals (owners) control their agents (executives). But an economy can develop before a strong legal system has evolved. Russia's oligarchs knew how to handle these problems. The concentration of ownership of old Soviet corporations in the hands of a few oligarchs offered great comparative advantages and was often a precondition for the survival of these companies.

An early empirical study of Russian financial-industrial groups in the mid-1990s found that they were already more efficient in their real investment than independent owners (Perotti and Gelfer 2001). Businessmen with concentrated ownership were more successful than those who had to deal with many minority shareholders. Because of difficulties controlling

---

14. The single woman is Yekaterina Baturina, the wife of Moscow Mayor Yuri Luzhkov; she has proved highly skillful in Moscow real estate.

managers, owners were compelled to manage their companies themselves. Businessmen avoided concluding too many contracts that they could not secure in court by rationally opting for vertical integration; that is, they preferred corporate hierarchies to horizontal markets (Williamson 1975).

The oligarchs arose as an economically and legally rational response to adverse conditions to business. They could influence the conditions and sometimes caused considerable damage. Some leading oligarchs, notably Berezovsky, bore some responsibility for the financial crash of 1998. However, considering how diverse the oligarchs were, how swiftly they altered their behavior, and the extent to which their names changed, they were much more takers from than creators of the business environment. Of the seven dominant oligarchic banks in 1998, only one survived, and only two of the seven leading oligarchs, Fridman and Potanin, are still important in Russian business. The oligarchs' absence of staying power shows how dangerously they lived and consequently how limited their power really was. Yet, they salvaged and transformed the giant Russian factories, and enabled these companies to lead Russia's economic revival.

6

Postrevolutionary Stabilization: 1999–2003

Moscow was awful in September 1998.[1] The financial system had stopped functioning. Credit cards and the many ATMs could no longer be used. I was organizing an international conference in Moscow, and we had to pay for everything with cash. The ruble had collapsed, and hyperinflation was an evident threat. The talk of the town was whether Russia's market economy experiment had failed. The *New York Times Magazine* carried an article by John Lloyd (1998) titled "Who Lost Russia?" Russia's postcommunist transformation looked like a complete failure.

On August 23, 1998, six days after Russia's financial crash, President Yeltsin sacked Prime Minister Sergei Kirienko and his cabinet. The public mood called for old, experienced hands. Yet, when Yeltsin nominated Viktor Chernomyrdin, whom he had dismissed five months earlier, Moscow laughed in sad disbelief. Had Yeltsin lost his senses? Few were as guilty for the August crash as Chernomyrdin. The communist-dominated Duma turned Chernomyrdin down twice. On September 10, Yeltsin reconsidered and nominated his minister for foreign affairs, Yevgeny Primakov, who had previously been head of SVR, Russia's foreign intelligence service. Primakov was the single survivor from Gorbachev's time and close to the communists, who happily confirmed his appointment the next day.

Primakov formed a cabinet tainted by Soviet nostalgia. Nikolai Ryzhkov's old chairman of Gosplan, Yuri Masliukov, an unreformed communist, was appointed first deputy prime minister for economic affairs. Viktor Gerashchenko became chairman of the central bank for the third time, as if

---

1. Overall references for this chapter are Baker and Glasser (2005), Shevtsova (2005), and Jack (2004) for politics; and Åslund (2004) for economics.

he had not done enough damage already. Gennady Kulik, my old antire-form friend from the Soviet Ministry of Agriculture, became deputy prime minister for agriculture. The prime minister and the Duma had taken over power, marginalizing Yeltsin. Yet, quite a few ministers remained in office, notably Mikhail Zadornov as a sensible minister of finance.

Rarely has a situation turned into its opposite faster than after August 1998. Russia's market economy had not failed but graduated. Its apparent devastation was nothing but a catharsis. Finally, Russia attained sound financial stabilization and steady economic growth started.

The last year of Yeltsin's presidency, 1999, saw no fewer than three prime ministers, and Yeltsin selected the last of them, Vladimir Putin, as his successor. Putin started a relentless rise in popularity and power. His advance was driven by dark events—the bombing of apartment houses with hundreds of victims, and a large armed incursion into neighboring Dagestan by Chechen rebels. The Kremlin used these tragedies to justify a second war in Chechnya that was as brutal and bloody as the first one. Putin used this war as his election campaign.

The Duma elections in December 1999 and the presidential elections in March 2000 were nothing but Putin's coronation, and the newly elected president used this mandate to impose major changes. Politically, Putin favored centralization and authoritarianism. He broke the back of the media oligarchs, chasing them into exile, while gradually consolidating his power. The Russian federal-regional relations had never worked well, and Putin chose a far-reaching recentralization, which he called strengthening the "vertical of power." Economically, however, Putin promoted market reforms. The many unfulfilled reform projects were put into a comprehensive reform program, and many impressive reforms were undertaken. Putin also launched an extensive judicial reform that he called "the dictatorship of law." Russia undertook serious attempts to join the World Trade Organization (WTO) as well.

The Russian state was back. Putin had turned the tables on the oligarchs, and he had consolidated power, but the question remained: What kind of Russia did he want to build?

Finally Financial Stabilization

During the first half-year after the crash of August 1998, the new Primakov government did not really have any policy. It was governed by necessity and prior reform proposals, especially the substantial program the Kirienko government had concluded with the IMF and the World Bank in July 1998.

The default forced vital fiscal reforms upon the country. As no financing but tax revenues was available any longer, the budget deficit had to be eliminated. Renewed external default loomed if the government failed

Figure 6.1   Consolidated state revenues and expenditures, 1992–2005

percent of GDP

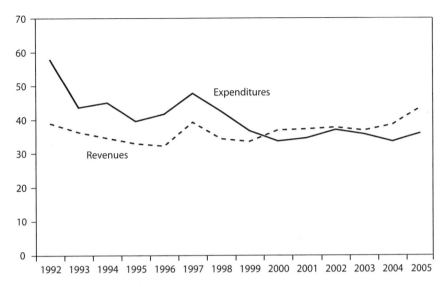

Sources: EBRD (2000, 205; 2003, 187; 2005, 173; 2006, 169).

to service the country's foreign debt. Russia's apparent political inability to balance its budget disappeared because the only alternative was hyperinflation, which nobody wanted. Hence, no money was available for the expensive public investment program or for industrial subsidies, which Masliukov spoke about, or even for prior social transfers. The government imposed new controls over both revenues and expenditures.

First, the Primakov government undertook a major fiscal adjustment entirely through expenditure cuts, slashing Russia's consolidated state expenditures by no less than 14 percentage points, from 48 percent of GDP in 1997 to 34 percent of GDP in 2000. All arguments about the impossibility of reducing public expenditures fell by the wayside. Enterprise subsidies of little or no social benefit were eliminated, which leveled the playing field for Russian business. Much more controversial was the reduction of real pensions by about half from the summer of 1998 to early 1999, by not allowing them to rise with inflation.

Revenues, by contrast, varied little (figure 6.1). The previously chronic budget deficit turned to the opposite. Since 2000, Russia has had persistent budget surpluses (figure 6.2).

Second, the financial crash reinforced central state power. The watershed was the budget of February 1999. It stipulated that offsets could no longer be used for payments to the federal government, which hit big corporations and regional governments (Owen and Robinson 2003, 37–38).

Figure 6.2 Budget surplus, 1999–2007

percent of GDP

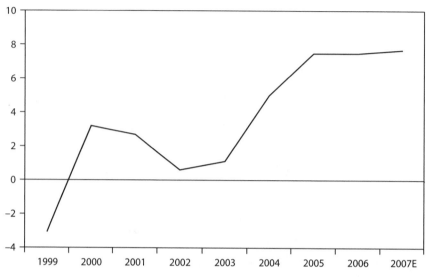

E = estimate

Sources: EBRD (2005, 173; 2006, 169); Bank of Finland Institute for Economies in Transition, Russia statistics, www.bof.fi (accessed on July 31, 2007).

From 2000, the requirement of only cash payments was imposed at the regional level, and the government ordered public utilities to do so as well. Bankruptcy legislation had long been on the books, but helped by a new aggressive bankruptcy law of 1998, the government started pursuing its claims with rigor. Barter and offsets were eliminated, clearing up chains of arrears. Barter payments between Russian industrial enterprises fell from a peak of 54 percent of all interenterprise payments in August 1998 to 14 percent in the fall of 2001, because barter had become unprofitable (figure 5.2). Large enterprises could no longer extract tax rebates through offsets, and regional governors could not divert federal funds. Arrears of pension and state wages dwindled. The monetization also leveled the playing field. As a result, many enterprises changed ownership, which revived them. Typically, old managers were forced to sell to hungry young entrepreneurs at rock-bottom prices.

Third, the Primakov government continued the tax war on the oligarchs that the reformers had launched in 1997–98, and the newly strengthened state could beat the weakened oligarchs. The government started applying the tax laws to big enterprises, especially the oil and gas companies, which had previously enjoyed individually negotiated taxes.

Figure 6.3   Total and federal state revenues, 1998–2002

percent of GDP

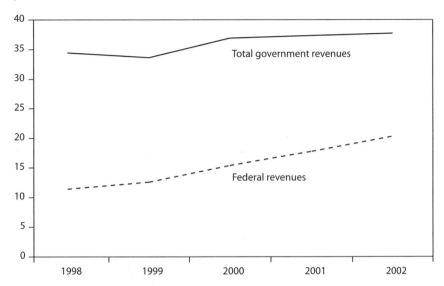

Sources: Bank of Finland Institute for Economies in Transition, Russia statistics, www.bof.fi (accessed on June 20, 2007); EBRD (2006, 169; 2004, 169).

A fourth measure was a radical centralization of government revenues to the federal government from both the regions and extrabudgetary funds. Federal revenues almost doubled from 11 percent of GDP in 1998 to 20 percent in 2002 (figure 6.3). The powers of the federal treasury were reinforced through the adoption of the new budget code in 2000. All state agencies had to make all their transactions through accounts with the federal treasury (Diamond 2002). Some extrabudgetary funds were abolished and all were put under federal treasury control. The previously sizable road fund and the small employment fund were eliminated, while three social funds (pension fund, medical insurance fund, and social insurance fund) were financed by a unified social tax collected by the new tax ministry, which further enhanced the federal government's leverage (Owen and Robinson 2003, 34–39). Russia's fiscal dimensions became reminiscent of the United States, with total fiscal revenues of about one-third of GDP and federal revenues of some 20 percent of GDP.

The federal treasury was also reinforced by the vagaries of the world market. With the devaluation, foreign trade taxes, which were valued in foreign currency, increased sharply. In addition, the government introduced high export tariffs to tax the natural resource companies. The windfall gains from rising world oil prices went to the federal treasury. The international oil price that had touched $10 a barrel during Russia's misery

Figure 6.4 Spot crude oil price, 1985–2006

Brent, US dollars per barrel

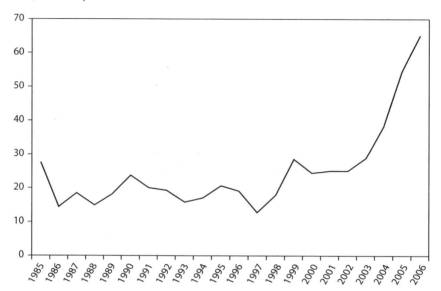

Source: BP historical data, www.bp.com (accessed on July 18, 2007).

in 1998, began a relentless rise to $70 a barrel in 2006 and 2007. However, it lingered around $25 a barrel until 2003, so high oil prices did not cause Russia's fiscal cleanup or economic growth (figure 6.4).

Trade and current account surpluses increased sharply and are still rising (figure 6.5). Russia's public foreign currency debt fell from 100 percent of GDP in early 1999 to 9 percent of GDP at the end of 2006, and its international reserves have reached a reassuring level exceeding $400 billion in the spring of 2007, the third largest in the world (figure 6.6). The sharp devaluation kickstarted the economy and helped put the foreign account right. Russia also received a windfall gain of about $60 billion as its default on its domestic treasury bills (GKO) left it with minimal liabilities.

The financial stabilization, monetization, and devaluation were the main catalysts for Russia's high and steady growth of nearly 7 percent a year from 1999 (figure 6.7). All the main requirements of economic growth that Gaidar had formulated were finally in place: "macroeconomic stability and low, predictable rates of inflation, and open economy plus access to promising markets, clear-cut guarantees of property rights and a respectable level of financial liability, high levels of individual savings and investments, and effective programs to aid the poor and to maintain political stability" (Gaidar 1999, 210).

Russia had a steady government budget surplus, but inflation continued apace in the low double digits until 2006 (figure 6.8), because of the

Figure 6.5 Trade and current account balances, 1998–2006

billions of US dollars

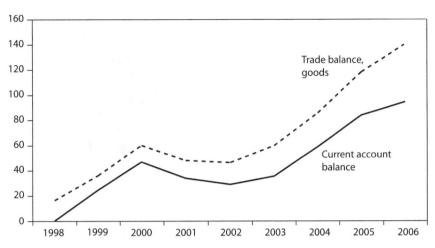

Source: Bank of Finland Institute for Economies in Transition, Russia statistics, www.bof.fi (accessed on May 30, 2007).

Figure 6.6 Public debt and international reserves, 1994–2006

percent of GDP   billions of US dollars

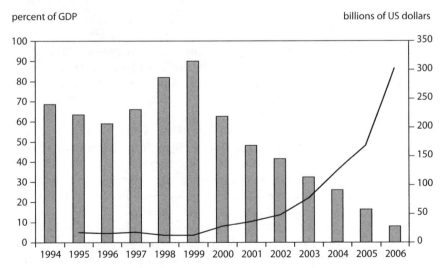

Note: The bars show public debt as percent of GDP (left axis). The line tracks international reserves in billions of dollars (right axis).

Sources: Bank of Finland Institute for Economies in Transition, Russia statistics, www.bof.fi (accessed on May 30, 2007); EBRD (2006, 169; 2005, 173; 2004, 169; 2003, 187; 2002, 193).

Figure 6.7 GDP growth, 1999–2006

percent

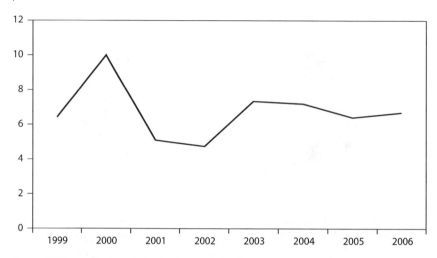

Source: UN Economic Commission for Europe online database, www.unece.org (accessed on May 23, 2007).

huge current account surplus, which boosted the money supply, and the Balassa-Samuelson effect, which states that the productivity of tradable goods rises faster than the productivity of domestic goods and services. Therefore, the prices of nontradable goods and services rise to compensate their producers on the common labor market. Frightened by the apparent overvaluation of the ruble in 1998, the government kept the nominal exchange rate low by buying international reserves, but it could do little about the real exchange rate, and the lasting high inflation reflected the real appreciation of the ruble.

After the crash of August 1998, all enterprises faced hard budget constraints and the playing field was leveled. The minimization of enterprise subsidies and the improvement of payment morals benefited small and medium-sized businesses as well as the federal government. The regional barriers that had been almost insurmountable even for the big industrial groups broke down after 1998 (Dynkin and Sokolov 2002).

Not everything was done right. Gerashchenko was back as Russia's central banker. He did not restart excessive monetary emission, but he nationalized most of the banking system by offering privileges to state banks. Initially, only the state savings bank (Sberbank) guaranteed deposits, and the state banks were offered substantial discretionary credits, whereas most big private banks collapsed. As a consequence, Russia's bank system would be state-dominated for the foreseeable future.

Figure 6.8   Inflation rate, 1999–2006 (consumer price index, end year)

percent

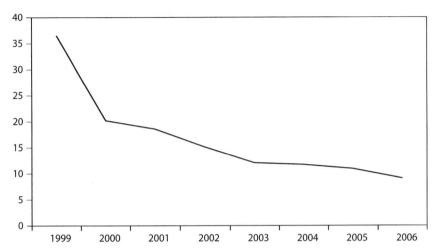

Source: Bank of Finland Institute for Economies in Transition, Russia statistics, www.bof.fi (accessed on May 30, 2007).

The financial stabilization shifted power over economic policy. The main losers were old managers and oligarchs, who had lived on subsidies and tax rebates extracted through barter or collusion with the government. The regional governors also lost both power and financial resources to the federal government. A third group of losers was the communists, who were marginalized by the Duma elections in December 1999. Their ideology of extensive government intervention had failed, giving way to a more liberal ideology. Before the Duma elections in December 1999, the communists revised their party program to embrace the market economy.

The August 1998 crash had broken the overwhelming resistance that had kept market economic reforms at bay since 1994, as suggested by Drazen and Grilli (1993). For the first time, a clear majority for a free market economy prevailed in the Duma. After years of vacillation, Russia started undertaking one big reform after another. Putin is often praised for these achievements, but the financial stabilization was undertaken in 1998–99 before Putin became prime minister, and Russia was already growing fast. Putin was lucky to arrive at a laid table.

President Yeltsin's Final Days

Yeltsin had been counted out many times, but he was an old fox, who did not give up. In the spring of 1999, when Russia's economic recovery became evident, conflicts between Yeltsin and Primakov were mounting. Primakov showed no loyalty to Yeltsin, whom he clearly intended to succeed as president, but his anti-Western and procommunist values were alien to Yeltsin. Primakov had also instigated corruption investigations against Berezovsky, publicly threatening him, and the investigation could touch the Yeltsin family.

In March 1999, the Kosovo crisis erupted. Yugoslav President Slobodan Milosevich invaded Kosovo, and NATO bombed Yugoslavia. Russian public opinion was pro-Serb and appalled. Primakov was more critical of the West than Yeltsin, who sent his loyal Chernomyrdin to persuade Milosevich to give up, which succeeded. Yeltsin had outflanked Primakov.

In the Duma, the communists wanted to impeach Yeltsin on purely political grounds, and Primakov did nothing to oppose them. This was the last straw for Yeltsin. On May 12, he sacked Primakov. As his replacement, Yeltsin nominated Minister of Interior Sergei Stepashin. He was a Yeltsin loyalist who had held numerous senior positions, including chairman of the FSB. Although he had made his career in the ministry of interior, Stepashin was relatively liberal and friendly with almost everybody. The Duma accepted his candidacy.

Stepashin was supported by Anatoly Chubais, but he was challenged by the Minister of Railways Nikolai Aksenenko, who was promoted by Berezovsky and Roman Abramovich. Aksenenko was seen as extremely corrupt. It was rumored that he had bought his post as minister of railways for $70 million in an outright auction organized by the presidential administration.[2]

At this time, everybody talked about "the family," which meant the Yeltsin family and a few close officials and businessmen. The backbone of the family was Yeltsin's daughter Tatyana Dyachenko and his former chief of staff Valentin Yumashev, soon to be Tatyana's husband. The two top businessmen in "the family" were Berezovsky and Abramovich, and the foremost officials were Yeltsin's new chief of staff, Aleksandr Voloshin, and the new minister of finance, Mikhail Kasyanov, but "the family" was a flexible concept. The reformers, led by Chubais, Boris Nemtsov, and Yegor Gaidar, were rivals of "the family," which was perceived as anticommunist but corrupt. Yeltsin himself was seen as close to "the family" but above the fray.

On May 15, 1999, the communist-dominated Duma impeached Yeltsin on five charges. He was accused of having unconstitutionally broken up the Soviet Union in 1991; illegally shelled the Supreme Soviet in 1993; permitted the deterioration of the military; allowed genocide through the massive rise in Russian mortality rates; and started the illegal war in Chechnya in 1994.

The communists failed to mobilize the necessary two-thirds majority, because the presidential administration resorted to gross bribery. Vladi-

2. Personal information obtained during a trip to Moscow, May 23–28, 1999.

mir Zhirinovsky had developed the habit of selling his LDPR faction's votes wholesale, and his large faction was absent (Klebnikov 2000, 291–92). It was rumored that individual deputies sold their votes for $30,000, a new record. The payments were made by private businessmen close to the presidential administration. Political corruption was becoming pervasive. This was the communists' last act of defiance.

At this time, Moscow Mayor Yuri Luzhkov emerged as the mainstay of opposition to Yeltsin. Luzhkov had been mayor since 1992 and largely loyal to Yeltsin. Until 1998, he had not engaged in national politics, gaining popularity as an effective, apolitical, and unscrupulous manager of Moscow City. Luzhkov secured his popularity by not allowing any criticism of himself, suing anybody who criticized him for libel, and he always won since he controlled the Moscow courts.

After Primakov's demise as prime minister, he and Luzhkov formed an alliance, calling their centrist political party Fatherland-All Russia. They mobilized numerous governors for their budding party of power. Yeltsin and "the family" felt threatened. On August 9, 1999, Yeltsin fired Stepashin and nominated Putin as prime minister, and he was swiftly approved by the Duma.

Vladimir Putin: KGB Lieutenant-Colonel

Vladimir Putin was everything that the Russian revolution was not. He had no clearly pronounced political views and his greatest loyalty was to the KGB. One of the great ironies of the Russian revolution was its hijacking by Putin, and that he was Yeltsin's choice. Like so many successful politicians, his greatest quality was his ability to make people underestimate him. Another skill was to flatter his superiors. The mystery is that this forgettable mediocrity of dubious reputation advanced to become president of Russia. His rise signaled that Russia's democratic revolution was over, and that the country had entered the stage of postrevolutionary stabilization, when people were tired of politics and wanted little but calm and economic growth (Mau and Starodubrovskaya 2001).

Putin's main claim to fame was that he had been first deputy mayor of St. Petersburg, 1991–96, under the democratic mayor Anatoly Sobchak. After Sobchak lost the mayoral elections in May 1996, Putin had little choice but to move to Moscow. He ingratiated himself with Pavel Borodin, the powerful Kremlin property manager and Yeltsin's drinking buddy, who had a reputation of being particularly corrupt. Borodin made Putin his deputy (Baker and Glasser 2005, 47–48). Klebnikov (2000, 295) observed: "Borodin's department seemed to epitomize the corruption of the Yeltsin government." From 1999, Swiss prosecutors sought him for kickbacks of $25 million in connection with the renovation of the Kremlin (Baker and Glasser 2005, 91). Putin was also helped to the

Kremlin by Aleksei Kudrin, another first deputy mayor of St. Petersburg under Sobchak.

In the presidential administration, Putin was noticed and appreciated by Yumashev, who became Yeltsin's chief of staff in 1997. Yumashev introduced Putin to Berezovsky. Putin's big break was when Yeltsin promoted him to chairman of the Federal Security Service (FSB) in July 1998. Putin had two features that were attractive to Yeltsin and the "family": he was loyal and tough. He had proved his loyalty by standing with Sobchak until the end. In early 1999, Prosecutor General Yuri Skuratov investigated corruption of Yeltsin's "family," opening several criminal cases, including one against Berezovsky. When Berezovsky's ORT responded by broadcasting a videotape with a naked Skuratov indulging himself with two equally bare prostitutes, Putin publicly vouched for its authenticity. He had proved his loyalty and firmness to Yeltsin.

Five people selected Putin: Yumashev, Tatyana, Berezovsky, Abramovich, and Voloshin, the heart of "the family." Chubais, by contrast, made a desperate attempt to retain Stepashin (Klebnikov 2000, 297; Baker and Glasser 2005, 50–53). In his last memoirs, which were considered largely ghostwritten by Yumashev, Yeltsin (2000, 327, 329) made these implausible statements:

> [T]he more I knew Putin, the more convinced I was that he combined both an enormous dedication to democracy and market reforms and an unwavering patriotism. . . . Putin was the man of my hopes. He was the man I trusted, to whom I could entrust the country.

Possibly, these sentences indicate that Putin was a capable influence agent, reflecting what people wanted to see, but during his last one and a half years as president Yeltsin was so ill that his "family" made many decisions for him (Tregubova 2003).

Putin's background is uncommonly devoid of attractive features and is outright frightening. Whereas both Gorbachev and Yeltsin had close relatives who had suffered under Stalin's repression, Putin's grandfather had been a cook at one of Stalin's dachas, which was an NKVD job. During World War II, Putin's father had served in the infamous NKVD troops, who killed Soviet soldiers that did not advance fast enough.[3] Putin was a lone, late child to old, austere, and poor parents living in a "communal" apartment, shared by several families, in Leningrad. He grew up as a semicriminal streetfighter not even accepted into the pioneers, which almost all Soviet children were. As a student, Putin was mediocre. His highest aspiration was to join the KGB, which he did as soon as he could. In its service, he participated in the persecution of dissidents in Leningrad and the spying on foreign visitors, which he described with delight in his interview book *First Person* (Putin 2000, 41–42, 49–50).

---

3. NKVD was the predecessor of the KGB.

In the KGB, Putin was no success. He was not sent to the challenging West, but to East Germany, and even there he was sent to the backwater of Dresden. After six years of undistinguished service, he was disposed of into the reserve as a mere lieutenant-colonel, a near failure (Baker and Glasser 2005, 40–43).

Back in his hometown, however, Putin made two masterstrokes. First, he turned to his old professor at the Leningrad State University, Anatoly Sobchak, who was about to be elected the democratic mayor of St. Petersburg. Putin rose with Sobchak, becoming first deputy mayor of St. Petersburg, 1991–96.

Second, Putin made good use of the many business opportunities in Russia's biggest port city after the collapse of communism. His responsibilities as first deputy mayor—foreign trade and foreign direct investment—were among the most corrupt spheres in Russia's criminal capital. A prominent liberal politician in St. Petersburg, Marina Salye, investigated Putin's licensing of exports of $92 million of oil products, timber, metal and other goods in exchange for imported food in 1992, alleging gross embezzlement. Her report was never made publicly available, and Salye has disappeared from the public eye (Baker and Glasser 2005, 47).

According to the Finnish government, Putin visited Finland 60 to 70 times during his five years as deputy mayor, and the Finns investigated his links with organized crime in Turku, Finland.[4] Both Swedish and Finnish businessmen complained about Putin squeezing out their companies, mainly through persecution by the lawless tax police, to the advantage of companies with which Putin was friendly.[5] Several of his close collaborators worked in the St. Petersburg Port, which was considered to be run by the Tambov group, the dominant mafia group in the city. Apparently, it merged with the city administration.[6] Several visitors noted with surprise that Putin did things without asking for a bribe, which was uncommon for such an official, but he appears to have focused on major deals.[7] Putin has never been prosecuted for corruption, but nor has any other Russian official that remains in a high position.

Yeltsin's selection of Putin was probably his greatest mistake. To the extent he made decision himself, he seems to have been preoccupied with loyalty to his family and the ability to win elections. Putin's values seemed

---

4. Personal information from four senior Finnish diplomats.

5. The most prominent example was Grand Hotel Europe, whose Swedish management company Putin forced out with the tax police.

6. Dixelius and Konstantinov (1998), Volkov (2002), and information on the Gazprom management board from Gazprom's official website, www.gazprom.com (accessed on June 30, 2007).

7. Personal information from annual visits to St. Petersburg.

to be a subordinate issue to Yeltsin, but as Yeltsin belatedly would realize, when he became healthier after retirement, they were the opposite of Yeltsin's.[8]

The Second Chechnya War

In the summer of 1999, Russia was marred by strange and tragic events. On August 7, several thousand armed men, led by the feared Chechen warlord Shamil Basayev and an Arab commander known as Khattab, staged an armed incursion from Chechnya into the neighboring Russian region of Dagestan. Their proclaimed goal was to unite the two republics as an Islamic state. They encountered little Russian resistance and quickly captured several villages. Two days later, Yeltsin replaced Stepashin with Putin as prime minister.

On September 4, an apartment building in the Dagestan town of Buinaksk was blown up, killing 58 people; on September 9, an apartment block in a working-class district of Moscow exploded, killing nearly 100 people; and four days later another Moscow apartment block was bombed, killing another 124 people. Finally, on September 16, a last apartment bombing occurred in Volgodonsk. More than 300 people died in these four residential bombings, which all occurred in the middle of the night to maximize the number of victims. These terrorist bombings were truly shocking, being so ruthless and unexpected. The otherwise calm Russians were close to panic. Nobody ever claimed responsibility, but Russian politicians blamed Chechen terrorists, arousing popular support for a second military campaign against Chechnya (Jack 2004).

After the Khasavyurt armistice was concluded in August 1996 by then-secretary of the Security Council Aleksandr Lebed, Yeltsin and Chechnya's President Aslan Maskhadov signed a formal peace treaty in May 1997. But Maskhadov failed to impose any state authority in Chechnya, which was outright criminalized, a hideout for criminals and illegal trade. Kidnappings and even slave trade proliferated. The promised Russian aid to repair the destruction from the 1994–96 war never arrived, or was stolen.

As a result, radical factions in the Chechen separatist movement grew stronger, and the Chechen independence movement fractured over the role of Islam and relations with Moscow. In early 1999, Maskhadov announced that Islamic shariah law would be introduced gradually, which aggravated tensions with Moscow. The official pretext for the second Chechen war was retaliation for the invasion of Dagestan and the Russian

8. Several confidants of Yeltsin reported that he had the most devastating things to say about Putin during his last years.

apartment bombings. Its goal was to eliminate Chechnya's de facto independence (Trenin and Malashenko 2004).

Chechen motivations for the attack on Dagestan remain unclear. Basayev might have tried to consolidate his influence in Chechnya and replace Maskhadov. Some suspect that Basayev's incursion into Dagestan was paid by Russia's FSB, which sought a pretext to launch an already planned invasion into Chechnya (Trenin and Malashenko 2004). In 2000, Stepashin told *Nezavisimaya Gazeta* that plans for invasion were drawn up in March 1999, and would have proceeded even without official pretext. Members of the Maskhadov government insisted that they repeatedly warned the Russian authorities of the upcoming attack. Although the Russian intelligence most likely knew about the raid in advance, they actually withdrew border guards just before the raid (Jack 2004, Baker and Glasser 2005).

The apartment bombings remain even more enigmatic. A number of *wahhabis* (fundamentalist Muslims) from Dagestan were sentenced to prison for the bombings, but innocent people are often jailed in Russia. Basayev usually claimed responsibility for his terrorist acts. Some suspect that the FSB carried out these bombings to create a populist wave of support for Putin that would sweep him into office (Jack 2004, 103–104).

In the Russian city of Ryazan, the authorities at first claimed that they had averted a similar terrorist bombing, but then police and journalists discovered that the preparations had been undertaken by nobody but the FSB. The hexogen explosives to be used in Ryazan were the same as in the Moscow, Volgodonsk, and Buinaksk bombings. Once the FSB involvement became known to the authorities, they confiscated all evidence, including the hexogen bags. The new Chairman of the FSB, Nikolai Patrushev, a friend of Putin from the Leningrad KGB, claimed that they contained only sugar and that the averted bombing was a training exercise (Baker and Glasser 2005, 55). According to David Satter (2003, 33), "it seems very plausible that the successful bombings of the buildings in Moscow, Volgodonsk, and Buinaksk, in which hundreds died, were also carried out by the FSB." After the Ryazan revelation, the bombings stopped as mysteriously as they had started.

In August 1999, Putin asserted, almost as foolhardily as Minister of Defense Pavel Grachev had in 1994 before the first Chechen war, that the second conflict "will be resolved within a week and a half or two" (quoted in Baker and Glasser 2005, 54). He turned the war in Chechnya into his election campaign.

Russia started a full-blown military offensive first in Dagestan and then on Chechnya. On September 24, Russia launched the second Chechnya war. Both sides committed widespread human rights violations during the conflict, as the civilian population got caught in vicious clashes between federal forces and rebels. Russian troops drew international condemnation for forced disappearances, extrajudicial, summary, and arbitrary executions, looting, torture, and other abuses. Russian soldiers regularly conducted *zachistki* (cleansing) operations in which many Chechens were summarily executed for the mere suspicion of sympathies with the rebels. The exact death toll from this conflict is unknown, but the likely losses were in the tens of thousands of Chechen civilians dead or missing. Official sources put the number of Russian military casualties at 4,249 dead, with the number of separatists killed at about 13,000, but human rights activists maintain that the losses were much greater (Shevtsova 2005, 251).

Putin developed a steely strongman attitude to the Chechen "terrorists." One statement came straight out of criminal jargon: "We will pursue the terrorists everywhere. . . . [I]f we catch them in the toilet, we'll wipe them out in the outhouse" (quoted in Baker and Glasser 2005, 55). Such crude and intemperate statements were to become Putin's hallmark. He prided himself on having led the war in Chechnya as prime minister, and he said about the war: "I do not have a second of doubt that we are doing the right thing. Maybe we should be even tougher" (Putin 2000, 142).

After relentless bombing, Russian troops took the Chechen capital of Grozny in early February 2000, and acting President Putin declared direct rule from Moscow. Later, he appointed former Chechen mufti Akhmad Kadyrov as the head of the Russian administration in Chechnya, as the Kremlin started a policy of "Chechenization," gradually transferring power to Chechens loyal to the Kremlin, using rigged elections to ratify its chosen leaders. Large-scale military actions ended in 2002, but guerilla war in Chechnya continues and casualties mount. What was supposed to be a "small, victorious war" turned into a long-lasting dirty war (Politkovskaya 2001).

During this war, Chechens started using suicide bombings in Russia proper, especially in Moscow. Chechen terrorists bombed trains, planes, subways, and other public places. Usually, the suicide bombers were "black widows," widows of fallen Chechen fighters dressed in black. About 1,000 Russians died in terrorist attacks over 2002–04 (Baker and Glasser 2005, 176).

Most spectacularly, in October 2002, a group of 50 Chechen hostage takers seized a theater in the center of Moscow, a mere three miles from the Kremlin, where the musical Nord-Ost was being performed. They held some 900 people hostage and demanded that Russian troops withdrew from Chechnya within one week, but Russian special forces poured a mysterious gas into the building and later stormed it, killing the hostage takers but also 130 hostages, who died because they did not receive adequate medical assistance in time. Television coverage was suppressed (Baker and Glasser 2005, 172).

Afterward Putin expressed his relief: "We achieved the nearly impossible, saving hundreds and hundreds of people. We proved that Russia cannot be brought to its knees." He remarked briefly: "We could not save everybody." Then, he profusely thanked the "special forces, who without hesitation, risked their own lives, while fighting for saving people" (Putin 2002b). Those "heroic" forces, secrecy, and mismanagement had just caused nearly 130 unnecessary deaths.

Putin's Assumption of Power: Elections of 1999 and 2000

In the summer of 1999, the Yeltsin era seemed to be over. The new party Fatherland-All Russia was gathering the regional elites under the experienced leadership of Primakov and Luzhkov. They expected to win the Duma elections scheduled for December 1999.

But in the fall of 1999, "the family"—Yumashev, Tatyana, Berezovsky, Abramovich, and Voloshin—who had promoted Putin, also decided to form a government party, Unity. This centrist party expressed as few political views as Fatherland-All Russia. Rather than experienced political leaders, it sought well-known and popular nonpolitical personalities as candidates, because Russians were no longer interested in politics. It was a feat of public relations specialists, who were convinced that they could sell anything after Yeltsin's victory in 1996 (Colton and McFaul 2003, 33–35).

The all-dominant theme during the fall of 1999 was the second Chechnya war, which amazingly turned out to be popular because Russians wanted the Chechens to be punished, in sharp contrast to 1994, when the war appeared to be a Russian mistake. Politically, the second Chechnya conflict was the desired "small and victorious war." Putin's popularity rating surged from nothing in August by a couple of percent each week (Shevtsova 2005).

Television dominated the campaign, which became a duel between Russia's two foremost anchormen, Sergei Dorenko at ORT and Yevgeny Kiselev at NTV. Every Sunday each presided over his own weekly political program. Like his master Vladimir Gusinsky, Kiselev supported Primakov and Luzhkov, and Dorenko promoted Putin and Unity, on Berezovsky's command. Traditionally, Kiselev had been the star, but this time Dorenko won.

Dorenko's great advantage was that Luzhkov had prohibited criticism of himself, and few had criticized Primakov. Dorenko dug some skeletons out of Luzhkov's closet, such as an unexplained murder of an American businessman in 1996 and his wife's fortune, and he presented Primakov as the retired apparatchik he was. Dorenko had a field day, goading Luzhkov into losing his temper in public and thus undermining his popularity. Neither side used political arguments, because the political consultants argued that Russians were tired of politics (Colton and McFaul 2003).

Table 6.1   Results of election to the State Duma, December 19, 1999

Party	Percent of votes
Communist Party of the Russian Federation	24.8
Unity	23.8
Fatherland-All Russia	13.6
Union of Right Forces	8.7
Yabloko	6.1
Liberal Democratic Party of Russia	6.1
Others or against all	17.0
Voter turnout	62.0

Sources: Colton and McFaul (2003, 8); Inter-Parliamentary Union, www.ipu.org (accessed on June 13, 2007).

The communists won the Duma elections on December 19, 1999, with 25 percent of the votes, but it was their last hurrah. The real duel was between Unity, which received 24 percent, and Fatherland-All Russia, humiliated with only 14 percent. Three more parties entered the Duma: Gaidar's Union of Right Forces (SPS) with 9 percent and Yavlinsky's Yabloko and Zhirinovsky's LDPR, each with 6 percent (table 6.1). The red-brown dominance was broken. For the first time, the Russian Duma had a solid centrist-liberal majority.

SPS and Yabloko expected that Unity would form Duma committees together with them, but Putin preferred an alliance with the communists. The opportunists in Fatherland-All Russia, including Luzhkov himself, soon joined Unity, and Putin had a big ruling party with a near majority in the Duma.

Previously, oligarchs had often bought specific votes from deputies. Now, the presidential administration monopolized its deputies and paid them all a supplementary salary that was initially $5,000 a month, no longer allowing competition from oligarchs. Zhirinovsky continued his practice of selling LDPR's votes wholesale, preferably to the presidential administration, for specific votes, but his bargaining position was weakened. Large-scale corruption of deputies by big businessmen continued but only when the presidential administration permitted. The highest payment I heard of was a gross total of $200 million for major structural legislation.[9]

Yeltsin reckoned he could relax and retire. His chosen successor had proven his electoral acumen. With his sense for the dramatic, Yeltsin de-

---

9. Multiple private conversations with Russian parliamentarians in 2000–2003; cf. Baker and Glasser (2005, 85).

cided to retire on the last day of the millennium and say farewell to his people with a very personal, televised speech:

> I want to ask you for forgiveness, because many of our hopes have not come true, because what we thought would be easy turned out to be painfully difficult. I ask you to forgive me for not fulfilling some hopes of those people who believed that we would be able to jump from the grey, stagnating, totalitarian past into a bright, rich and civilized future in one go. I myself believed in this. But it could not be done in one fell swoop. In some respects I was too naive. . . . But I want you to know that I never said this would be easy. (Yeltsin 1999b)

Russians cheered as they heard of Yeltsin's resignation. They were happy to see this drunken embarrassment go. His preterm departure made Prime Minister Putin acting president. Putin's first act was to sign a decree that granted Yeltsin and his family decent material conditions as well as legal immunity. He followed the example Yeltsin had set, by leaving the former president living well and peacefully in his land. He never reneged on his promise to Yeltsin, as Yeltsin had not abandoned his pledge to Gorbachev.

Putin's new position gave him a great advantage for the presidential elections, which were moved up three months to March 26, because the constitution stipulated they must be held within three months after the presidency had become vacant. The surprise change of the election date made it exceedingly difficult to mobilize any resistance to Putin.

Once again, Gennady Zyuganov was the main competitor in a field of 10 candidates, with Yavlinsky and Zhirinovsky coming next, but without a chance. Primakov chose not to run. They all looked tired and uninspiring. Putin made a point of not having any election program and of not campaigning, but only pursuing his ordinary work, showcasing his importance. As Lilia Shevtsova (2005, 70) wrote: "The vagueness of Putin's political image made him a tabula rasa." His main campaign performance was to fly to Chechnya in an SU-27 fighter plane in the copilot's seat. He won the first round with 53 percent, which corresponded to the opinion polls. Zyuganov obtained barely 30 percent (table 6.2). Since Putin had gained an absolute majority of the votes, no second round was required. Voter participation was respectable at 69 percent. Putin's approval rating hovered around 70 percent, as Russians were happy to see a young and energetic president who was sober and worked hard.

Alas, Yeltsin turned out to be wrong in his optimistic assessment of Putin's values. Yeltsin had talked about democracy without attributes, but soon after his inauguration on May 7, 2000, Putin's concept became known as, "managed democracy" (*upravlyaemaya demokratiya*). It did not sound good, nor was it. Like Gorbachev, Putin chose new words that did not have a clear ideological connotation and gradually altered their meaning. Gorbachev had made his concepts ever more liberal, but Putin did the opposite. Putin's favorite democracy was no democracy, and he moved on to the term "sovereign democracy," which seemed a synonym for authoritarian rule.

Table 6.2 Results of presidential election, March 26, 2000

Candidate	Percent of votes
Vladimir Putin	53.4
Gennady Zyuganov	29.5
Grigori Yavlinsky	5.9
Vladimir Zhirinovsky	2.7
Others or against all	8.5
Voter turnout	68.6

Sources: Colton and McFaul (2003, 10); Election Guide, www.electionguide.org (accessed on June 25, 2007).

Initially, Putin was vague and took a long time to make decisions because he was a micromanager who wanted to know all the details first. He acted slowly but deliberately. After a decision, Putin was adamant. He divided people into friends and foes, and he persecuted his foes without mercy. His psyche had been formed by the KGB. He was extremely suspicious and thought in terms of conspiracy theories. He did not believe in open sources, which he considered disinformation, but only in intelligence. He loathed any dissent, and acted in secret until he made his decision (cf. Shevtsova 2005, 81).

To begin with, he had selected a few themes for immediate action: the war in Chechnya, media control, centralization of federal power, and economic reform. During his first term, Putin continued to be everything to everybody, and he was an avid reader of opinion polls. His selection of national symbols was characteristic: He chose the tsarist double eagle as the coat of arms, the liberal Russian tricolor of 1896–1917 as the flag, and the Hymn of the Soviet Union as the national anthem. Their common denominator was that each of these national insignia enjoyed a popular majority support.

Muzzling of the Media

In the late 1990s, it was an intellectual delight to open one of Moscow's score of daily newspapers or watch the news and analytical programs on the three main TV channels. It was media competition at its best. Journalism had rarely been that good anywhere. Naturally, there were shortcomings. The analytical programs tended to be partisan and opinionated rather than objective, but they balanced one another. The circulation of the outstanding newspapers was limited, harming their finances. The worst shortcoming was that journalists often sold themselves to offer both good and bad publicity, blurring the line between advertising and journalism. But these were minor concerns.

Gusinsky was an outstanding media entrepreneur. The best TV channel was his NTV and the best radio channel was his Ekho Moskvy. However, Gusinsky was also highly political. He usually supported Moscow's Mayor Luzhkov and Yabloko leader Yavlinsky, and after 1996 he opposed the Kremlin. Thanks to his support during the 1996 presidential elections, the Kremlin granted Gusinsky's Media-Most company a few hundred million dollars of financing from Gazprom, in return for 30 percent of its stock. Gusinsky's Most Bank collapsed in the financial crash of 1998, and Gazprom helped him out with a loan of $262 million. Nevertheless, NTV provided critical coverage of the second Chechnya war and supported Luzhkov and Primakov during the 1999 election campaign.

Four days after Putin's inauguration, masked and armed tax policemen stormed Media-Most offices. They harassed Gusinsky, and on June 13 he was arrested on charges of embezzling funds from the state and kept in jail for three days. To regain his freedom, he had to give his media empire away to Gazprom and he fled from Russia for good. The official explanation was that Media-Most was bankrupt, although the company was not under serious duress. Putin, who was traveling in Spain at that time, claimed that he knew nothing (Remington 2006, 230). Yet, he seemed to order the repression in detail. He invited prominent NTV journalists for a meeting, revealing his detailed knowledge. Altogether Media-Most was raided 35 times, which can only qualify as harassment (Baker and Glasser 2005, 82–83, 91–93).

In short, Media-Most, Russia's finest media company, was confiscated for political reasons. Public protests were still possible at that time, but they were limited. Russians were tired of politics, and the confiscation process was so complex and gradual that it was not obvious when to mobilize for a protest. Cleverly, Putin muffled NTV step by step, sacking one manager and journalist after the other.

In 2004, the European Court of Human Rights in Strassbourg tried the case of Media-Most's confiscation in *Gusinsky v. Russia*. That court is attached to the Council of Europe, of which Russia is a member. It found that the prosecutor general of the Russian Federation had used power of incarceration to achieve economic objectives. It established that Gazprom asked Gusinsky to sign a commercial agreement when he was in prison and that a state minister endorsed it and "that a State investigating officer later implemented that agreement by dropping the charges strongly suggest that the applicant's prosecution was used to intimidate him." In sum, Gazprom and Russia's media minister colluded with law enforcement to seize Media-Most. The court ruled that the Russian state had to pay damages to Gusinsky.[10]

---

10. *Gusinsky v. Russia*, European Court of Human Rights, May 19, 2004 (Application no. 70276/01), http://cmiskp.echr.coe.int (accessed July 30, 2007).

The performance of the Russian state remained miserable. On August 12, 2000, the nuclear submarine Kursk exploded in the Barents Sea. Putin was on holiday in Sochi at the Black Sea, and he stayed there. A score of men had survived in the sunken submarine, but nothing was done to rescue them, and the whole crew of 188 men died. In traditional Soviet manner, the military presented one lie after another, but NTV and Berezovsky's ORT, which were still quite independent, exposed the military's and the government's incompetence and lies.

After the tragedy, Putin fumed about television, exclaiming: "They are lying, lying, lying." He attacked the media oligarchs: "There are people in television who bawl more than anyone today and who over the past ten years have destroyed the same army and navy where people are dying today. . . . It would be better for them to sell their villas on the Mediterranean coast of France [Berezovsky] or Spain [Gusinsky]. . . . We would then ask them where the money came from" (quoted in Baker and Glasser 2005, 89–90).

Berezovsky went to the Kremlin and saw Putin, who, according to Berezovsky, told him candidly: "I want to run ORT." In parallel, the authorities were going after his control of Aeroflot. Berezovsky, who had seen Gusinsky's fate and knew more than most, understood that he had better escape abroad. In October, he was forced to sell his shares in ORT to Abramovich, his erstwhile partner, who later passed them on to the state, and Berezovsky wisely left Russia for good (Baker and Glasser 2005, 90–91; Shevtsova 2005, 93–94).

Several excellent NTV journalists, especially Yevgeny Kiselev, made repeated attempts to maintain independent media. The first one was called TV-6 and its majority owner was Berezovsky, but 15 percent of the shares were owned by Lukoil's pension fund, which filed a suit to force TV-6 into bankruptcy, but obviously this was no financial issue (Remington 2006, 230). Kiselev's next attempt at independent television was called TVS and financed by a broad group of oligarchs, but they split under pressure from the Kremlin (Baker and Glasser 2005, 95). Putin also sorted out a few smaller TV channels.

Within a year or so, Putin had suffocated the independent television, and he continued his endeavors deliberately and conscientiously. One newspaper and magazine after the other was bought by businessmen close to the Kremlin, who knew how to please Putin. Not only publishers and editors but also ordinary journalists were persuaded to censor themselves.

Through a painful process, Russia's foremost journalists were excluded from the public eye. They tried one project after the other, which Putin closed down. The old celebrities were replaced by young, pugnacious journalists who entertained rather than informed. Superficially, Putin's dumbing down of the Russian public was reminiscent of the qualitative decline of Western commercial television, but its end result was confusingly similar to Soviet television. By 2007, the only serious electronic media outlet of significance was Aleksei Venediktov's independent radio channel Ekho Moskvy, which had a star-studded cast, being the only place left where outstanding journalists were allowed to work.

Putin's personal involvement and his aim of full censorship were evident, but he never said so. He always alleged that he knew nothing about the actions of state agencies and that they were independently acting according to the law. He always blamed something nonpolitical—a bankruptcy, a flawed privatization, a commercial takeover, or a lapsing license. Putin reestablished the public lie as the standard as in the Soviet Union.

Not everything is under Putin's control. The Russian blogosphere, serious journals, and books remain reasonably free of censorship, although the Kremlin controls many websites. The combination of the words "Putin" and "corruption" yields hundreds of interesting articles, not all of them true, on Russian search engines.

Ironically, Putin was a major beneficiary of the excellent Russian media that especially Gusinsky had developed, because the media maintained their credibility for years after their content had become "Soviet" again. Today, each newscast starts with several protocol clips about the president's glorious day. The lively commentary has turned into pro-Putin propaganda, often with militant nationalistic ingredients.

Centralization of Federal Power

Six days after his inauguration, Putin passed a decree imposing more central control over Russia's federal system. Since 1990, Russia's 89 regions had been freewheeling out of the Kremlin's control. The regional parliaments adopted their own laws, which often contradicted federal laws, to which the regional governors paid little attention. Although the regional governments were supposed to pass on most state revenues to the federal treasury, they did not. Nor did they deliver federal payments, whether subsidies to coal mines or pensions, to the intended beneficiaries. The regional governments were even less transparent and more corrupt than the federal government.

The Russian Federation was neither here nor there. The constitution told the federal and regional governments to share many obligations. The federal government demanded nearly complete centralized control as in Soviet days, but it no longer had the strength to enforce its formal powers. The imbalance of formal and actual powers was especially evident in the financial sphere. The regions and the center were supposed to share a score of different taxes, the ratios of which varied with tax and regions. The regional governments were the winners until 1998 (Shleifer and Treisman 2000, OECD 2000).

Regional and local taxes had proliferated. Although a handful of federal taxes reaped more than three-quarters of state revenues, Russia had

200 different taxes in the late 1990s because each region invented its own taxes to cover its needs. Usually, these taxes were licensing fees or penalties, burdening successful enterprises (McKinsey Global Institute 1999). The number of tax bases proliferated too, as did the tax collection services. As a result, profit-making enterprises without political protection were overgrazed, often fatally so. The disorder bred corruption (OECD 1995).

The World Bank initially favored revenue sharing in Russia because regional income inequality was so great that the World Bank reckoned that the federal government needed to serve as an equalizing force (Wallich 1994). This argument might have sounded laudable, but it presupposed an orderly government, while the all-dominant need in Russia was clear and simple rules to minimize corruption. The mixed Russian system of fiscal federalism was too dysfunctional to last.

The issues of federalism were the same in Russia as they had been in the newly independent United States. Some order was necessary, but the new system could be either centralized or decentralized. Shleifer and Treisman (2000) drew the logical conclusion, proposing a decentralized federal system with clear lines of responsibility. They took the division between the federal, regional, and municipal levels even further than in the United States, arguing that tax bases, taxes, and tax services should be clearly divided between the center, the regions, and the municipalities. Each level of government should be in full charge of certain taxes. Similarly, the responsibilities for various kinds of expenditures should be strictly divided between different levels of government.

Putin chose the opposite—far-reaching centralization. He justified his decision: "[F]rom the very beginning, Russia was created as a supercentralized state. That's practically laid down in its genetic code, its traditions, and the mentality of its people" (Putin 2000, 186). "Everyone was saying that the *vertikal*, the vertical chain of government, had been destroyed and that it had to be restored" (Putin 2000, 129). Here as everywhere, Putin advocated a strong *vertikal* of power, which meant all power to himself.

The prevailing mood favored centralization. On May 13, 2000, Putin changed Russia's federal order with a decree that mounted a full-fledged attack on the regional governors. Besides the oligarchs, they appeared to be the epitome of the corruption that had unleashed the financial crash of 1998. Putin eliminated them from the Federation Council, where they had been sitting ex officio since 1995, and reserved for himself the right to appoint senators, depriving the Federation Council of all political significance. He introduced a new administrative level, dividing the country into seven large regions, each headed by a new presidential envoy or supergovernor, appointed by himself. They were to supervise the still-elected governors and bring regional legislation into line with federal law. Putin assumed the right to sack governors who violated the law, which every governor had to do because Russian legislation remained so inconsistent. Putin attacked fast and hard, which was the most effective way to beat the governors, because they were more accustomed to subverting the implementation of the Kremlin's decisions than to organizing outright opposition (Shevtsova 2005, 91–93).

Minister of Finance Kudrin undertook many fiscal measures to bring the regions under federal control. Most regions received federal transfers, and the federal treasury was finally able to condition these transfers on the abidance of federal law by the regional governments. The Ministry of Finance imposed federal treasury control over all state budgets. Under Yeltsin, the three autonomous republics of Tatarstan, Bashkortostan, and Sakha (Yakutia) had managed to negotiate preferential tax deals. Under Putin, these agreements were dismantled. The City of Moscow had long benefited from receiving all the tax revenues from the corporations headquartered in the capital. Not least to punish Luzhkov, Putin made enterprises pay taxes in the regions of their activity instead (OECD 2002, Papernaya 2004, Gaidar et al. 2003).

Within a few years, most legal rights of the regional governments had been abolished. The old ambiguities in the distribution of federal-regional rights were eliminated, and instead a strictly centralized system had been chosen. It is doubtful whether Russia can be considered a federal state any longer.

Putin was reluctant to use his power to sack corrupt or criminal governors. Instead, the Kremlin worked hard manipulating and interfering in the gubernatorial elections in an illegal and heavy-handed fashion to gain full control. These elections were spread out over time. Most incumbents were reelected, usually after the incumbent governor himself had joined United Russia and become Putin's obedient servant. The Kremlin controlled most elections to such an extent that hardly any democracy remained (Fish 2005, Shevtsova 2005).

When Vladimir Lisin, the popular billionaire owner of the Novolipetsk Metallurgical Corporation, entered the Lipetsk gubernatorial elections in 2002, the Kremlin persuaded him to withdraw (Fish 2005, 65). In Primorsky krai, Kursk, North Ossetia, the Ingush Republic, and Rostov, Fish (2005, 66) reported: "Leading contenders were disqualified for purely political reasons in the waning hours of election campaigns on the basis of absurdly trivial or fabricated technicalities." They complained to the courts of justice, but nobody ever won a political case against Putin's state. Ruthlessly, the Kremlin seized full control over the governors by denying alternative candidates the right to run thanks to its reinforced federal control over law enforcement.

On the odd occasion, independent candidates still won. In October 2002, the raw material–rich Krasnoyarsk region held gubernatorial elections. The two dominant corporations in the region, Russian Aluminum (Oleg Deripaska and Roman Abramovich) and Norilsk Nickel (Vladimir Potanin and Mikhail Prokhorov), each put up their own candidate. The assumption was that Russian Aluminum would win because no businessman was closer to Putin than Abramovich and Russian Aluminum ruled Krasnoyarsk, the regional capital. The surprise was that Aleksandr Khloponin, Potanin's local manager, won.

Russian Aluminum let it be known that Potanin had spent $45 million on this election alone. When this was brought to Putin's attention, he reportedly responded sarcastically: "Olegu i Rome zhalko bylo?" ("Why were Oleg [Deripaska] and Roman [Abramovich] so stingy?") Norilsk Nickel paid more than half of all taxes in the region, while Russian Aluminum paid little, thanks to its political dominance. Russian Aluminum appealed to the regional election commission, which canceled the election because of alleged flaws, but the regional court surprisingly revoked that decision, after which the regional election commission renewed its cancellation. Then Putin stepped in and settled the embarrassment, decreeing that Khloponin had won.[11] The Krasnoyarsk elections showed that a minimum of pluralism persisted in regional elections, but the Kremlin regretted that it could still be beaten and that large sums were diverted to these elections.

The Gref Program: Second Generation of Economic Reform

In 1999, McKinsey Global Institute (1999) published a major study of Russian industry. It concluded that Russia had sufficient physical and human capital to have a potential growth rate of 8 percent a year. The main problems were a distortional tax system, a poorly functioning government giving large subsidies to inefficient companies, and the absence of a land market. The report found that neither the banking system nor the legal system were significant impediments at Russia's stage of development.

After the 1999 Duma elections, Russia for the first time had a legislature that approved of a normal market economy, and Putin forcefully concurred. He relied on German Gref as his chief economic reformer. Gref was a young liberal lawyer who had worked with Putin in St. Petersburg. Immediately after Putin had become acting president, he founded the Center for Strategic Problems with Gref as director. The "Gref Center" became the brain trust for Putin's reform program, gathering the best and the brightest from Moscow's liberal think tanks.[12] By April 2000, this elite group of liberal economists had compiled a "Gref Program" of economic reforms. In May 2000, after having become president, Putin appointed Gref as head of a new superministry, the Ministry of Economic Develop-

---

11. Personal information from contenders on both sides in Moscow, October 2002.

12. Gref drew primarily on economists from Yegor Gaidar's Institute of the Economy in Transition, the World Bank–financed Bureau of Economic Analysis, the Higher School of Economics, and Carnegie Moscow Center.

ment and Trade, and in July 2000, the Gref Program was adopted as the government's economic reform program.

Russia had seen many reform programs, but this was the most comprehensive and detailed, and it was the action program of the incoming president. It was a bureaucratic document of about 200 pages designed to instruct civil servants with proposals for hundreds of legal acts. Its goal was to boost economic growth to 8 percent a year through tax reform, bank reforms, deregulation, privatization, social reforms, accession to the WTO, judicial reform, and reform of the state. The program's weakness was that it was not very clear or concrete. Nor was it inspiring or even readable.

Gref's ministry became the center of reform, advocating comprehensive market economic reform. Strangely, Putin never made Gref deputy prime minister, which limited his bureaucratic leverage. The key powers in the government rested with Kasyanov and Voloshin, who were both liberal but considered members of "the family" and inclined to promote oligarchic interests.

In a typical bureaucratic fight over economic reform in Putin's first term, Gref advocated a reform, with sympathy from Kudrin and strong support from reformers in the Duma, but he was opposed by the branch ministry concerned and sometimes by oligarchic interests in the Duma. Eventually, Kasyanov or Voloshin mediated a decision. Often, Putin weighed in, usually tipping the decision in a more reformist direction, but cautiously avoiding technical details. The Federation Council rarely mattered, and the main strife took place within the government. A steady flow of reform legislation was adopted in 2000–2003.

Radical and Comprehensive Tax Reforms

After the government finances had been balanced, a radical tax reform became possible. The prior tax system was unwieldy, arbitrary, inefficient, and unenforceable. Of the 200 taxes, approximately 30 were federal and some 170 local or regional. Multiple tax agencies competed over the same revenues (Shleifer and Treisman 2000). The enforcement of the tax laws was as haphazard as it was brutal. The tax inspection and the competing independent tax police harassed businessmen. The more a businessman paid in taxes voluntarily, the more he could be extorted. For a businessman, the rational solution was to conclude a corrupt deal with the tax authorities.

The reform attempted to base the tax system on the sound principles of fairness, simplicity, stability, predictability, and efficiency. A draft tax code had been gathering dust in the Duma since 1997. Key provisions had been incorporated in the government-IMF crisis plan of July 1998, and the first part of the tax code was adopted and came into force in January 1999. It contained definitions, procedural laws and provisions, and regulated the tax administration. The second part of the code, which reformed key federal taxes, such as the value-added tax (VAT), personal income tax, and excise tax, and introduced the new unified social tax, became effective in 2001, and the new corporate income tax in 2002 (Owen and Robinson 2003, 82–84). The number of taxes was reduced sharply to 16 in 2004, of which 10 were federal, reflecting the strong trend toward centralization. Small and inefficient nuisance taxes, which generated more corruption and hazard than revenues, were abolished. The tax reforms liberalized and stimulated the Russian economy, but they also strengthened the federal authorities' power over the state.

The key tax reform was the replacement of the progressive personal income tax peaking at 30 percent with a flat income tax of 13 percent as of 2001, notwithstanding opposition from the IMF, which feared that tax revenues would fall. Estonia and Latvia had already introduced flat personal income taxes in the 1990s, but they were higher. Russia's introduction of the low flat income tax was a major breakthrough. It eliminated the disincentives to work and encouraged citizens to bring their earnings out into the open, reducing illegality and corruption. For the state, this reduction in shadow earnings expanded the tax base. It provided a positive shock, boosting the revenues from personal income taxes from 2.4 percent of GDP in 1999 to 3.3 percent in 2002 (Goskomstat 2006, 606).

The corporate profit tax was reduced in 2001 from 35 to 24 percent. Far more important was that most ordinary business costs became deductible. This tax reduction made it possible to abolish most tax exemptions, leveling the playing field. The social taxes were payroll taxes paid by the employer to four different social funds, which were poor at collecting them. In 2001, the payroll tax was cut from a flat rate of 39.5 percent to a regressive tax with a top rate of 35.6 percent and an average rate of 26 percent, which was set to decline. The four social taxes were transformed into a unified social tax, which was colleted by the federal tax ministry like other taxes. The greatest benefit to businesses was that the competition in tax collection ceased (Gaidar et al. 2003). As a result of the liberal tax reforms, tax collection improved, and the government could cut taxes further. The top VAT rate, which previously had been 20 percent, was reduced to 18 percent in January 2004.

The tax reforms reduced the threat to businessmen posed by tax inspection. The few, low, and simple taxes left less room for discretion for the authorities, making it possible to be an honest taxpayer. Small-scale tax violations were decriminalized, and became subject to civil rather than criminal law punished with moderate fines. The unification of tax collection by the tax ministry eliminated competition. Finally, the tax police (headed by Mikhail Fradkov), which represented arbitrary power of the bureaucracy over business, was abolished by presidential decree in March 2003, with the motivation that the tax police had not been "detecting, preventing or interdicting tax crimes" but instead extorting money from businessmen.[13]

Deregulation to Stimulate Small Enterprises

Russia finally woke up to its need for small and medium-sized enterprises. They were subdued by a madness of red tape and bureaucratic harassment. In 2000, an average small or medium-sized firm was inspected 37 times to check its licenses and 104 times to check certificates (Yasin 2002, 212). It was politically feasible to promote them because they threatened nobody. In July 2001, the Duma passed a package of laws that brought about major deregulation of small and medium-sized enterprises, by simplifying their registration, licensing, inspection, and certification (OECD 2002).

First, as before all enterprises in Russia were required to register with the state, but one new law simplified the registration of a business. Rather than having to be approved by several government agencies in a bureaucratic and time-consuming process, a businessman could register with one government agency. The mandated period of registration was sharply reduced from one month to a maximum of five working days, which reduced actual waiting time as well as possibilities for extortion by bureaucrats (CEFIR-World Bank 2003).

Second, about 2,000 business activities required government licenses from 37 federal agencies, and each agency had the potential to extort a bribe.[14] The new licensing law stipulated that a license would be extended from a maximum of three years to a minimum of five years. It also reduced the cost of a license and the number of business activities subject to licensing. When the licensing law came into effect in February 2002, it produced considerable improvements in the business climate (CEFIR-World Bank 2003).

Third, Russian businesses were plagued by inspections, which were another tool for extortion (INDEM 2001). The new inspections law stipulated that a government agency could not conduct more than one planned inspection of a firm once every two years, although any number of unplanned inspections was allowed. As a result, the number of inspections of small businesses fell by 27 percent between 2001 and 2002 (CEFIR-

---

13. Ukaz Prezidenta Rossiiskoi Federatsii N 306 "Voprosy sovershenstvovania gosudarstvennogo upravleniia v Rossiiskoi Federatsii" (Decree No. 306 of the President of the Russian Federation: Issues Concerning the Improvement of State Management in the Russian Federation), http://nalog.consultant.ru/doc46925.html (accessed on June 29, 2007).

14. Perechen' federal'nykh organov ispolnitel'noi vlasti, osushchestvliaiushchikh litsenzirovanie (List of Federal Executive Agencies which Carry Out Licensing), February 11, 2002, http://nalog.consultant.ru/doc35719.html#43 (accessed on June 29, 2007).

Figure 6.9 Number of registered enterprises, 1994–2006

millions

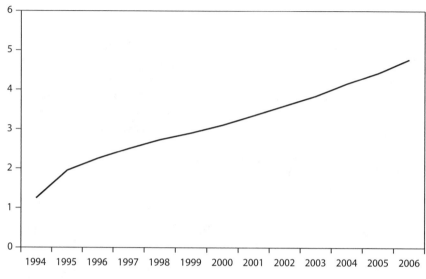

Source: Goskomstat (2006; 1999, 273).

World Bank 2003, 2–3). Yet, law enforcement agencies were excluded from these restrictions.

A fourth important law on deregulation tried to simplify standardization and technical regulation.

This broad effort at deregulation was impressive. The situation improved, and the amelioration has proved sustainable, although it has been greater in more developed and pluralist regions (Yakovlev and Zhuravskaya 2007). Small enterprises have grown steadily. The number of officially registered enterprises has steadily increased by more than 7 percent a year, and by 2006 the total number of registered enterprises in Russia had reached almost 5 million, quite a respectable number (figure 6.9). Still, the patriarchic surveillance system remains in place, and more radical deregulation is needed.

Land Reform and Privatization

The 1993 constitution proclaimed Russian citizens' right to own land as private property, but until 2001 the communists and agrarians in the Duma blocked the promulgation of a new land code, which aimed to legalize the private ownership of land. Putin avoided taking a public stand on this pivotal ideological question. Instead, the liberal Union of Right

Forces (SPS) repeatedly pushed it in the Duma. A new chapter in the civil code provided the legal basis for private transactions of land, and after a prolonged legislative battle a new capitalist land code was adopted on October 25, 2001, but it excluded farmland (Remington 2002).

The privatization of agricultural land was the last ideological barrier to break. On July 24, 2002, the Duma finally legalized the sale of agricultural land as well. It was a compromise, requiring each region to adopt a law to make the federal law effective. As a consequence, communist regions could withhold agricultural land from sale, while more liberal regions were allowed sell land (Kirchik 2004). In practice, the private ownership of agricultural land developed only gradually, and good connections with regional governors were vital for land purchases. As a result, big businessmen accumulated hundreds of thousands of hectares of agricultural land in huge estates, while family farmers often failed to acquire land.

In the aftermath of the financial crash of 1998, a strong public opinion demanded the nationalization of the oligarchs' properties. Putin did not adopt this line, but nor did he oppose it publicly. Privatization came to a near standstill. The only big privatization after 2000 was the oil company Slavneft, which was auctioned off in December 2002. In a rigged deal, two large private Russian oil companies, TNK and Sibneft, shared the company.[15] The state oil company Rosneft, whose privatization had been planned for years, was taken off the table. From 2003, the government emphasized what must not be privatized, notably the pipeline systems and majority ownership in big resource companies.

Formally, private property rights were reinforced through the promulgation of the civil code. In October 2002, a new bankruptcy law was adopted, because the old law had become a tool of corporate raiding of companies merely in a liquidity squeeze (EBRD 2003, 184).

Labor Market and Pension Reforms

The Russian social sector is highly inefficient, while the supply of resources may be appropriate. The social systems involve millions of employees and even more recipients, rendering any change as complicated as controversial. The social reform agenda was largely drawn up in 1996, primarily by Mikhail Dmitriev, who was first deputy minister of economic development and trade in Putin's first term (Åslund and Dmitriev 1996). Putin undertook two social reforms in his first term.

A new labor code was adopted in February 2002. It adjusted the regulation of the labor market to a market economy and reassured workers of their rights (EBRD 2003). It improved the old Soviet labor code and made

---

15. At the time, TNK was owned by Alfa (Mikhail Fridman), Renova (Viktor Vekselberg), and Access Industries (Len Blavatnik), and Sibneft by Abramovich.

Figure 6.10 Unemployment, 1998–2007

percent of labor force

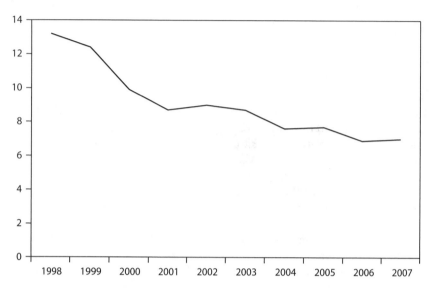

Note: 2007 statistics as of April 2007.

Source: Bank of Finland Institute for Economies in Transition, Russia statistics, www.bof.fi (accessed April 13, 2007).

it akin to an overregulated West European social democratic code rather than introducing the more liberal Anglo-American labor market philosophy. Old social benefits remained, even when their costs were excessive for employers, such as severance pay of three months' salary for employees laid off. In reality, however, Russia's labor market has persistently been quite flexible because of very limited unemployment benefits. Accurately measured, unemployment halved from 13 percent in 1999 to barely 7 percent in 2007 in spite of large-scale restructuring and considerable regional disparities (figure 6.10).

The biggest social reform during Putin's first term was the pension reform adopted in 2002. The old pension system was expensive and gave too small pensions to too many people. It was nearly egalitarian, leaving pensions barely above subsistence level, and everybody was dissatisfied. The new system was based on the World Bank (1994) model of "three pillars," that is, a minimal compulsory state pension for all, compulsory private pension insurance, and favorable tax treatment of voluntary private pension insurance. A minor share of the pension tax could be put into private accounts for the accumulation of pension savings. But the government deterred the public, successfully limiting private funds to merely 2 percent of those eligible (Aron 2007). In the end, little changed.

Other big social reforms were postponed until Putin's second term. The vast education and health sectors, together with housing services, remained among the least reformed parts of the Russian state, and hardly anything was done to improve them.

Dictatorship of Law

After communism, the demands on the judicial system steadily evolved and the number of court cases grew, as both the state and businesses increasingly sued one another (Hendley 2002). However, as the courts gained significance, they grew more corrupt, because the market value of their judgments rose, while judges were quite independent.

From the outset of his presidency, Putin gave priority to judicial reform, but he favored the ambiguous "dictatorship of law," which sounded like a contradiction in terms. A lawyer himself by training, Putin asked one of his closest aides, Dmitri Kozak, a deputy head of his presidential administration hailing from St. Petersburg, to lead a presidential working group on judicial reform. A package of new laws on judicial reform was adopted in December 2001. They included a law to enhance the status of judges, better financing of the courts, and the renewal of all legal procedural codes.

A key goal was to strengthen the independence of courts and judges. The judges' salaries were set to quintuple over five years, and the financing of the courts was greatly improved to make them independent of the regional authorities, which had provided supplementary funding. Judges already had steady tenure, but they needed to become accountable. The law on the status of judges of December 2001 weakened their protection from prosecution for criminal offences. Ordinary judges were still appointed without term limit, but they were forced to retire at 65 (Solomon 2002).

Under the Soviet system, judges had been subordinate to prosecutors. Their position improved greatly under Yeltsin, but prosecutors retained rights reserved for judges in Western countries, including the issuing of arrest and search warrants and the releasing of prisoners on bail. The 2002 criminal procedural code reinforced the powers of the judges and gave them the right to sign arrest and search warrants, and to decide on pretrial detention (Buchanan 2003). With the powers of the prosecutors' offices trimmed, the chances of frivolous arrest and detention were reduced. In the first year with the new code, the number of arrests fell by 33 percent (McDonald 2003).

Another boon for defendants was the spread of jury trials in serious criminal cases, such as murder, terrorism, and espionage, from nine regions to the whole country. The initial jury trials showed that juries were much more sympathetic to the defendants than judges were, acquitting many defendants. Prosecutors reacted sharply, appealing to higher courts or asking for new trials, and they often triumphed. The judicial reform

Figure 6.11 Homicides, 1998–2005

total in thousands

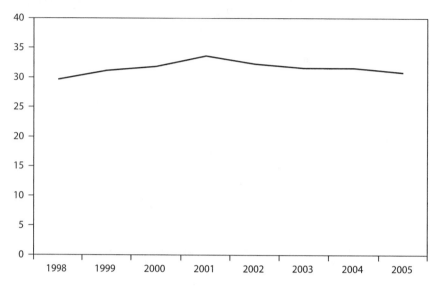

Source: Goskomstat (2006; 2000, 243).

stopped far short of the declared intentions. Still, the caseload of the economic (*arbitrazh*) courts increased substantially, as they became more independent, competent, even-handed, and efficient (Hendley 2004).

The essence of judicial reform, however, was that judges became dependent on the presidential administration rather than on regional governors. This reform was another centralization. The crime rate has stayed high, and the Kremlin has, characteristically, responded by demanding less reporting of crimes. Russia's homicide rate has actually been higher under Putin than under Yeltsin, reaching an all-time high in 2001 (figure 6.11). The purpose of ample financing for law enforcement is evidently not to improve law and order but to reinforce the power of the Kremlin (Taylor 2006).

Serious Efforts to Join the WTO

The Soviet Union was never a member of General Agreement on Tariffs and Trade (GATT), which it saw as no less capitalist than the IMF and the World Bank.[16] To join the IMF and the World Bank is easy, and Russia did so in 1992, but to accede to the WTO was much more complicated. In

---

16. This section draws on Åslund (2007b).

1993, Russia applied for membership of the GATT, which in 1995 became the WTO.

The WTO has three important functions. First, it is the forum for multilateral trade negotiations. Second, it is the depositary of numerous international trade conventions that are binding to all members. Third, it has an arbitration court for conflict resolution that is universally recognized. The chief reason for a country to join the WTO is to secure access to export markets. It is especially important for exporters of goods frequently subject to protectionist measures, such as steel, chemicals, and textiles.

In the 1990s, Russia's political leaders did not realize the importance of the WTO, devoting minimal political attention to it. One reason for this neglect was that 60 percent of the country's exports consist of oil and natural gas, which encounter minimal protectionism. After communism, however, Russia has become a major exporter of sensitive commodities, such as steel, chemicals, and grain, which accounted for 23 percent of its exports in 2005 (United Nations 2007). Even so, its losses from antidumping measures remain minimal.

Several studies sponsored by the World Bank and the Russian Ministry of Economic Development and Trade examined the potential effects of WTO entry on the Russian economy. Their overall assessment was that Russia's economic growth could be boosted by 0.5 to 1.0 percent a year in the medium term (Jensen, Rutherford, and Tarr 2004). These gains would come from the liberalization of barriers to foreign direct investment in service sectors, improved resource allocation because of lower Russian tariffs, and greater market access for Russian products (Yudaeva et al. 2002).

Russia's comparative advantage is overwhelmingly in hydrocarbons, other crude materials, and chemicals. Julian Cooper (2006a, 2006b) found that Russia had "revealed comparative advantage" (defined as a country's share of world exports of a particular good divided by its share of total world exports) in 70 product groups, of which only four were manufactured goods, namely nuclear reactors, condensers for steam boilers, rail freight wagons, and steam turbines. All were traditional Soviet products exported to former Soviet republics, showing that Russia was not breaking into new manufactured export markets.

The liberal economists had long advocated WTO membership but after Putin became president he energized Russia's efforts to join the WTO, committing himself to accession in 2003. In his annual address in April 2002, Putin (2002a) advocated the WTO at length: "The WTO is a tool. Those who know how to use it become stronger. . . . Membership in the WTO should become a tool to protect Russian's national interests on the world market." Russia was the only member of the G-8 that was not a member of the WTO, and China's entry in 2001 probably persuaded Putin to focus on WTO membership.

The Duma elected in December 1999 supported this endeavor. Little could happen, however, until the old Ministry of External Economic Relations, headed by the inert bureaucrat Mikhail Fradkov, was abolished. Putin merged it into Gref's new Ministry of Economic Development and Trade, and Gref has persistently been Russia's chief advocate of WTO accession. The big exporters, especially the steel producers, supported WTO membership, and public opinion was positive. According to a nationwide survey by VTsIOM, at the time still headed by the revered Yuri Levada, in 2002, 54 percent of Russians thought that it was in their nation's interest to join the WTO, with only 18 percent disagreeing (VTsIOM 2002).

Negotiations on accession to the WTO have been pursued on two parallel tracks. Russia had to conclude a bilateral protocol with each of 61 interested parties on market access.[17] Because the WTO decides everything by consensus, each member can veto the entry of a new applicant. Russia's bilateral negotiations with the European Union were concluded in May 2004 and with the United States in November 2006. The second track is a negotiation of a multilateral agreement in the working party in Geneva, which is far from finished.

WTO accession became one of the major themes in Putin's extensive institutional reforms from 2000 to 2003. A major Western concern was the weakness of the Russian legal system. Laws were not perceived as transparent, uniform, or enforced. This applied especially to customs. Many key laws were adopted during this period, including the tax code, a new customs code (which came into force in January 2004), and several parts of the civil code. The new customs code reduced the massive corruption and long delays in the customs. A whole new set of legislation on intellectual property rights was adopted. The legislative agenda was tense but well managed. By 2003, Russia was close to joining the WTO, but then the political focus faded.

In substance, Russia's problems in entering the WTO were smaller than China's, because unlike China, Russia is a relatively open market economy with average import tariffs of around 12 percent and few quotas and licenses. The required adjustments were many but not all that great.

In 2003, however, Putin came up with a new gimmick and his interest in the WTO weakened. On February 23, 2003, the presidents of Russia, Ukraine, Kazakhstan, and Belarus declared that they wanted to form a new Common Economic Space. It was supposed to be a free trade area, a customs zone, and eventually a currency union, but it was also intended to coordinate the four countries' entry into the WTO. Given that these countries already had a free trade zone that did not work, and that all but Ukraine also belonged to the dysfunctional CIS Customs Union, this proposal made little sense. Their key trade problem was the dearth of a mechanism for conflict solution for their mutual trade disputes. They could have solved that problem by joining the WTO to use its well-functioning

---

17. As of July 2007, protocols had not been concluded with Georgia, Cambodia, and Saudi Arabia.

arbitration. Yet, a four-nation agreement on the Common Economic Space was adopted in September 2003 and ratified by all four parliaments, and scores of agreements were concluded. Putin's real purpose for this new initiative appears to have been purely political—to woo Ukraine more closely to Russia before Ukraine's presidential elections in the fall of 2004.

Siloviki, Oligarchs, and Reformers: Who Is Mr. Putin?

The permanent question during Putin's first term was: Who is Mr. Putin? As a trained KGB agent, he was all things to all people. He appealed to Russian nationalists and the Orthodox Church, but he also saw and nurtured Western leaders. Unlike Yeltsin, Putin did not antagonize the communists, but he also appealed to economic liberals with more market reforms. His open-to-all attitude did not seem convincing. It looked like a waiting game. Everybody asked: What will Putin do when he has consolidated power?

Only in one regard was Putin completely clear: he was a political authoritarian, although he did not say so. He muzzled the media, starting with television and proceeding with one newspaper after the other. He had brought the Duma under control, partly through democratic means, partly through gross corruption. The regional governors were brought to heel. Putin's loyalty to the KGB and its predecessors was unwavering, demonstrative, and frightening.

The clearest indication of Putin's direction was his appointments. They all came from a very narrow stratum of former colleagues in St. Petersburg, mainly from the KGB. KGB people are called *siloviki* in Russian, which means people belonging to the power ministries—the KGB, the military, and the police. Putin's associates were from both the FSB and the foreign intelligence service (SVR), but the FSB people dominated.

KGB officers from St. Petersburg were appointed to a plethora of top positions in the Kremlin, the government, the Federal Assembly, and state-dominated corporations. Putin's top people became: Igor Sechin and Viktor Ivanov, who were deputy heads of the presidential administration, Minister of Defense Sergei Ivanov, FSB Chairman Nikolai Patrushev, First Deputy Railway Minister Vladimir Yakunin, and Minister of Communications Leonid Reiman. Vladimir Kozhin replaced Pavel Borodin as Kremlin property manager, while Borodin was given the honorific post of secretary general of the Russian-Belarusian Union. Lower down, the whole government administration was packed with KGB officers, many of whom left well-paid jobs in the private sector to pursue public service (Kryshtanovskaya and White 2003).

A minor group from St. Petersburg was made up of liberals, young economists and lawyers with whom Putin had worked in the mayor's office. Dmitri Kozak, Dmitri Medvedev, and Andrei Illarionov held senior positions in the presidential administration. Other prominent St. Petersburg liberals were Minister of Finance Kudrin, Minister of Economic Development and Trade Gref, and Gazprom CEO Aleksei Miller. They were a junior group in Putin's sphere, specializing in economic reforms, but they were a fixture. Putin left Chubais as CEO of UES, the Russian power company.

A dominant question during Putin's first term was what he would do about Yeltsin's "family," the senior officials with oligarchic connections. The surprise was that Putin acted very slowly and largely allowed them to stay. He let Minister of Finance Mikhail Kasyanov succeed him as prime minister, and Voloshin stayed as head of the presidential administration. Vladislav Surkov, who had worked for both Alfa and Menatep, remained first deputy head of the presidential administration, where he fought with Putin's favorite Sechin. Only people who had been closely connected with Berezovsky, such as Minister of Interior Vladimir Rushailo and Minister of Railways Nikolai Aksenenko, were ousted. A large number of quite prominent businessmen joined the state administration under Putin (Werning Rivera and Rivera 2006). It is impossible to say how many of them were originally KGB officers, but this stream indicated that businessmen were attracted by state service and found it lucrative.

Throughout Putin's first term this triumvirate of forces was at play: KGB men from St. Petersburg, oligarchs, and liberals from St. Petersburg. The balance between them was most evident in the presidential administration, which became the heart of state power, because Putin was a micromanager who wanted to decide ever more things as he gained insight and knowledge. The economic reforms were spearheaded by reformers and oligarchs together, whereas the *siloviki* paid little attention. Domestic politics was run by the presidential administration with assistance from outside consultants. Foreign policy was managed by Putin himself.

Another big issue was how Putin would handle the oligarchs. Berezovsky and Gusinsky were always seen as a separate matter, because they were just too ostentatious. Berezovsky wanted to show that he controlled the state, and these two men ran Russia's biggest and best television networks. Putin's elimination of them was primarily a matter of authoritarian media control.

On July 28, 2000, Putin held a long-awaited meeting with 21 oligarchs in the Kremlin. Conspicuously, three oligarchs were missing. Berezovsky and Gusinsky were no longer welcome, whereas Abramovich was so close to Putin that he avoided public events. Putin's message to the oligarchs was: "You stay out of politics and I will not revise the results of privatization" (Baker and Glasser 2005, 86–87). His unspoken point was that the Russian state was back and that the era of the oligarchs was over.

The first response by the oligarchs was to unite and organize. They looked around for a suitable organization, and they chose the old Russian Union of Industrialists and Entrepreneurs (RSPP), traditionally the fortress of the old state enterprise directors, as the strongest and broadest business association. The new big businessmen effectively bought the RSPP, put themselves on the board, and made it their central organization for advocacy and lobbying. But they kept old, wily Arkady Volsky as its president.

Until the end of 2003, the RSPP was a forceful body. The oligarchs met frequently in RSPP board meetings and discussed economic policy. Their views had changed as economic development had progressed. They had all become profit seekers, favoring a liberal market economy and providing forceful support for structural reforms. Their main concern was to secure their property rights.

The leadership of the RSPP reflected how Russian big business had developed. In June 2007, of its 24 businessmen, no fewer than nine were in metals (six in steel), five in finance, two in coal, two in high-tech, and one each in forestry industry, food processing, oil, gas, electricity, and railways.[18] Russia was still dominated by heavy industry, but also increasingly by the metallurgical industry and it was growing more diversified. Only four out of these 24 businessmen ran predominantly state-owned corporations.

Over time, however, the oligarchs differentiated also politically. The reclusive Abramovich, who had been close to the Yeltsin family, was one of the people who had selected Putin. He was closer to Putin than any other businessman, and he did everything differently. He was elected to the Duma in 1999.[19] Soon afterward he was elected governor of Chukhotka in northeast Siberia, spending vast amounts there, but he also benefited from the lowest taxes of all Russian oligarchs. Even so, he emigrated to London, while remaining governor of Chukhotka, and gradually sold off his holdings in Russia. Rising speculation had it that Abramovich shared his wealth with Putin as he was widely thought to have shared with the Yeltsin family.

Oleg Deripaska, co-owner of Rusal with Abramovich, was a real member of Yeltsin's family, because he married Yumashev's daughter from a previous marriage, and Yeltsin's daughter Tatyana married Yumashev. Abramovich and Deripaska were the main "family" oligarchs, but their

---

18. The RSPP bureau has changed very little over the years. In June 2007, its 24 businessmen were Aleksandr Abramov (Evraz), Vagit Alekperov (Lukoil), Andrei Bokarev (Kuzbassrazrezugol), Anatoly Chubais (UES), Oleg Deripaska (Rusal), Mikhail Fridman (Alfa Bank), Anatoly Karachinsky (IBS), Oleg Kiselev (banking), Andrei Kostin (Vneshtorgbank), Vladimir Lisin (Novolipetsk), Aleksandr Mamut (Ingosstrakh), Andrei Melnichenko (MDM), Aleksei Miller (Gazprom), Aleksei Mordashov (Severstal), Vladimir Potanin (Interros), Dmitri Pumyansky (TMK), Viktor Rashnikov (Magnitogorsk), Zakhar Smushkin (Ilim Pulp), Alisher Usmanov (Gazprominvest), Ruben Vardanian (Troika Dialog), Viktor Vekselberg (Renova), David Yakobashvili (Wimm-Bill-Dann), Vladimir Yakunin (Russian Railways), and Vladimir Yevtushenkov (Sistema). See www.rspp.ru (accessed on June 22, 2007).

19. Berezovsky also was elected to the Duma in 1999. Several business groups had a senior partner, but not the top person, in the Duma or the Federation Council to secure their interests.

behaviors contrasted greatly. Deripaska maintained a close relationship with the Kremlin and Putin, but he kept a high public profile, loudly defending his business interests.

Mikhail Khodorkovsky of Yukos chose the opposite strategy. More than any other oligarch, he opted for legalization and gentrification. He and his co-owners publicized their ownership. Yukos cleansed its corporate structures and financial system, abandoning transfer pricing. The company was richly rewarded on the international stock market, and Yukos became the Russian corporation with the highest market capitalization of $45 billion in 2003. Both Yukos and Khodorkovsky developed extensive charitable activities, donating some $200 million annually by 2003, supporting health care and civil society. Other oligarchs followed Yukos, becoming transparent, publicizing their ownership, and developing extensive charitable donations, estimated at $1.5 billion in 2006 (Finn 2006a).

Most of the oligarchs, however, preferred to lower their public profiles and be politically neutral. The old oligarchs who had participated in the loans-for-shares auctions were perceived as more suspect, notably Vladimir Potanin and Vagit Alekperov. The shares of their public and well-run companies Norilsk Nickel and Lukoil, respectively, traded with lasting "oligarch" discounts. The same was true of the joint venture TNK-BP for purely political reasons.

In the late Yeltsin period, the oligarchs had flocked to the Kremlin to gain commercial advantages. Putin turned the tables. All of a sudden, the oligarchs preferred not to go to the Kremlin, and they even stayed out of the country for extended periods not to be called there. Early in the Putin period, two oligarchs told me that when an oligarch was called to see one of the top figures in the Kremlin, he was asked to put up $10 million or $20 million in "donations," either for Putin's reelection campaign or for some charitable purpose. In the Yeltsin period, Mayor Luzhkov had persuaded the Moscow oligarchs to "donate" $500 million to the reconstruction of the Christ the Savior Cathedral. Now, Putin attracted $300 million in "donations" for the reconstruction of the Konstantinov Palace in St. Petersburg.

The state was back as the dominant power, but it was neither transparent nor democratic. The Kremlin treated the oligarchs as its self-service boutiques. A few major businessmen were rumored to make large-scale payments of hundreds of millions of dollars to the corporations belonging to Putin's circle in St. Petersburg.

The oligarchs looked at Putin and his KGB friends with increasing discomfort, recognizing their evident desire to make big money. To begin with, however, the Putin team did not know how to do it. A couple of St. Petersburg bankers close to Putin (Sergei Pugachev and Vladimir Kogan) were rumored to be coming oligarchs, but they never made it big. After two to three years, oligarchic representatives started talking of "the new family," meaning commercially inclined KGB officers close to Putin:

Sechin, Viktor Ivanov, Nikolai Patrushev, Patrushev's deputy Yuri Zaostrovtsev, and Prosecutor General Vladimir Ustinov, who had linked up with them. Zaostrovtsev was a major furniture trader in Moscow, and his oligarchic enemies leaked to the still-independent media that he imported furniture without paying import tariffs or the VAT. One of his major showrooms was bombed three times.[20] Pugachev was accused of racketeering in France and scrutinized in the French media. These oligarchs-in-waiting did not seem to be able to make it even with considerable state intervention. They needed another business model.

The alternative business model was evident: to take over the state-owned companies. After Chernomyrdin had been ousted as prime minister, the Gazprom management felt threatened and started massive asset stripping. Both minority shareholders and the Putin group cried foul. In the spring of 2001, Putin and his men carefully prepared the ouster of the Gazprom management, which controlled about 100 Duma deputies. Chernomyrdin was sent off as ambassador to Ukraine. The government owned the majority of Gazprom, and Putin sacked Rem Vyakhirev personally at a meeting in the Kremlin in May 2001. Putin appointed two of his closest collaborators to run Gazprom: His first deputy chief of staff Dmitri Medvedev became chairman of the supervisory board, and his former assistant Aleksei Miller was anointed chairman of the management board.

Usually, a Russian manager clears the deck and appoints his own people, but that did not happen in Gazprom. Its management board still consists of three mutually hostile groups. One is Miller's young economists, who had worked with Putin in the mayor's office in St. Petersburg and later in its infamous port. A second group consists of KGB men from St. Petersburg. Old Gazprom hands form a third group. Such a diverse group can hardly manage a major company, but that was Putin's intention. He runs Gazprom as his personal fiefdom, making all major decisions himself, with Miller and Medvedev as little but transmission belts. Russia's oligarchs dare not buy stocks in Gazprom because it would be perceived as a hostile act to Putin.

The litmus test of the Putin regime was how Gazprom would develop after the management change. Minority shareholders raised three issues. First, Gazprom was not run as a corporation but as a ministry. Considerable improvements were carried out for several years, resulting in Gazprom becoming Russia's most valuable company by 2005. Second, Miller focused on retrieving the assets that had been given away, and he managed to recapture most of them.

The third and most interesting test was what would happen to Itera, the trading company that skimmed off hundreds of millions dollars annually from the gas trade with Ukraine. The new management swiftly cut out Itera, but it did not clean up this trade. Instead, it established a similar

---

20. I happened to rent an apartment above that store.

new intermediary, Eural Trans Gaz, which was rumored to be connected with Semen Mogilevich, a major international organized criminal residing in Moscow, and top officials in Putin's administration. In 2004 Eural Trans Gaz was replaced with another intermediary, RusUkrEnergo, which was better formalized. On the Russian side, the same people were considered to be involved. The new trading system simply transferred the skimmed profits from the Ukrainian gas trade to other individuals. This was the old model of transfer pricing that Russian state enterprise managers had indulged in. The Putin administration had revealed itself. Its aim was not to clean up Russian business but to transfer the skimmed profits to its own people (Stern 2005).

As Putin's first term was drawing to its close, his public profile was that of an authoritarian modernizer straight out of Samuel Huntington's (1992–93) modernization school. His combination of authoritarianism and a private market economy stood out. However, unlike Prussian Emperor Friedrich II, Putin did not say: "I am the first servant of the state." Instead, he took his cue from Sun King Louis XIV of France and claimed: "L'état, c'est moi!" Berezovsky reported that in a private conversation with him, Putin, using the royal "we," exclaimed: "But we are the state!" (quoted in Baker and Glasser 2005, 85).

The Russian state apparatus had become more efficient and rational, but probably for the first time the higher levels of the Russian government were pervasively corrupt. With the oligarchic representation still intact, the prevalence of corruption could be blamed on the oligarchs. However, many oligarchs were gentrifying, whereas Putin made no attempt to demote even the most blatantly corrupt members of his own team. The balance between the oligarchs and the *siloviki* was precarious. Could it last?

Ideology was strangely absent. The economic liberals believed in private property and a free market economy, but few stood up to defend civil or political freedoms. Yet, neither socialism nor nationalism enjoyed significant support. The old Soviet cynicism had returned, but the new cynics were so much wealthier.

During his first term, Putin's relations with Western leaders were excellent, although not very important for anything but his domestic image. He pampered four Western leaders with whom he got on royally: German Chancellor Gerhard Schröder, French President Jacques Chirac, Italian Prime Minister Silvio Berlusconi, and US President George W. Bush. After their first meeting in Slovenia's capital of Ljubljana, Bush famously said of Putin:

> I looked the man in the eye. I found him to be very straightforward and trustworthy. We had a very good dialogue. I was able to get a sense of his soul, a man deeply committed to his country and the best interests of his country.[21]

---

21. The White House website, www.whitehouse.gov (accessed on July 3, 2007).

After the terrorist attacks on the United States on September 11, 2001, Putin telephoned Bush, and thanks to the old Cold War hotline he was the first international leader to get through, which Bush greatly appreciated. Putin allowed the United States to establish air bases in Central Asia for attacks on Afghanistan. He recast the conflict with Chechnya as part of the international war on terror, which he used as an excuse to reinforce his political repression.

In December 2001, Bush abrogated the Anti-Ballistic Missile Treaty of 1972. Putin called it a mistake but that was it. However, in 2002–03 Putin linked up with Chirac and Schröder, forming a strong international resistance against the coming US-led attack on Iraq, but the US criticism targeted France and Germany. Ironically, Russia benefited from the war in Iraq, because the Arab fighters who had fought the Russians in Chechnya preferred to battle the Americans in Iraq instead.

Although Bush embraced an international democracy agenda, he refrained from uttering a word of criticism of Putin's systematic dismemberment of democracy in Russia. On the contrary, on September 27, 2003, after having hosted Putin at Camp David, Bush stated: "I respect President Putin's vision for Russia: a country at peace within its borders, with its neighbors and with the world, a country in which democracy and freedom and rule of law thrive."[22]

Western leaders treated Putin as Yeltsin. They saw him as a man of similar values but unable to fully see their point of view and understand how things should be done. To a considerable extent, this had been true of Yeltsin, but Putin was the opposite. He was a man who knew the West quite well but opposed its values. Western leaders failed to notice the difference and misread Putin.

---

22. The White House website, www.whitehouse.gov (accessed on July 3, 2007).

7

Authoritarianism and Recentralization: 2004–07

Moscow was shining on a wonderful Indian summer evening. My good friend, Michael McFaul, took me along to Gleb Pavlovsky's private reception, the Kremlin's foremost political consultant. Everything was stunning. Pavlovsky had rented the Hermitage Theater and Park in central Moscow, entertaining 600 guests with dinner. Three orchestras played throughout the night.

The affluence reflected how profitable Kremlin politics had become. Pavlovsky himself was dressed in all black, a T-shirt under an Armani suit and round glasses, trying to look like Mephistopheles or Voland in Mikhail Bulgakov's novel *The Master and Margarita*, and quite successfully so. The composition of the guests showed how the elite had changed. The guests of honor were from the top of the presidential administration. Gone were the businessmen, elected politicians, and independent journalists, who had been replaced by bureaucrats and propagandists. The golden youth had taken over, and they were hardened cynics focusing on power and money. The Great Gatsby would have felt at ease.

This vignette shows how Russia had changed toward the end of Vladimir Putin's first term. Putin had tried to satisfy all kinds of constituencies to consolidate power. As Lilia Shevtsova (2005, 262) put it: "Putin was simultaneously a stabilizer, the guardian of the traditional pillars of the state, and a reformer. He was a statist and a Westernizer. He appealed to all strata in the society. . . ."

During his second term, however, Putin was going to show what he really stood for. The tipping point was the arrest of Mikhail Khodorkovsky, the wealthiest oligarch, on October 25, 2003. The crusade against Yukos constituted the campaign for the Duma elections in December 2003 and the presidential election in March 2004, which enabled Putin to consolidate power.

By the fall of 2004, however, everything seemed to turn against Putin. In September 2004, a school hostage drama in Beslan ended in a horrendous massacre. Later in the fall, Ukraine's presidential elections turned against him and became the Orange Revolution. In January 2005, an attempt to reform the social benefit system caused unprecedented popular protests. Frightened, the regime halted all reforms.

Putin exploited these events to justify further centralization of power and deinstitutionalization and allowed his underlings to indulge in large-scale renationalization. His economic policy veered toward state capitalism and he condoned corruption among his KGB friends. Putin's foreign policy was upset by the colored revolutions in Georgia, Ukraine, and Kyrgyzstan, and his policy toward the West turned hostile.

The Yukos Affair: The End of the Oligarchy

The last time I saw Mikhail Khodorkovsky was in Washington nine days before his arrest at an airport in Siberia on October 25, 2003. With extraordinary elegance and force, Khodorkovsky spoke at the Carnegie Endowment, advocating liberal democratic and economic reforms in Russia without antagonizing its ruler. The question everybody asked was: Are you not afraid of going back to Russia? Khodorkovsky denied that, but the large, spellbound audience breathed in sympathy: You should be afraid! I sat down with Khodorkovsky and asked him to elaborate. As the ultimate Russian chess player, he replied: "I do not understand how they can win, considering how many mistakes they make." In my dark mind, I thought of Nikita Mikhailkov's film "Blinded by the Sun" about the Stalin terror in the 1930s. The issue was not the number of mistakes, but pure power.

One week earlier, I had seen Putin speak at a business conference in Moscow, but he was delayed. Khodorkovsky was sitting in the center of the hall, and I was a couple of rows behind him. Suddenly, he picked up his mobile phone and rushed out. Then, Putin finally arrived. Later, I heard that Khodorkovsky had departed because prosecutors had raided a children's home run by his corporation, the Yukos oil company, as well as a school attended by Khodorkovsky's young daughter. The purpose of these raids seemed to be to get him out of the hall.

Putin read a stereotyped speech in favor of private business and foreign investment, which went down well. Only Western investors were allowed to pose questions, leaving journalists and Russians without a voice. Contemptuously, Putin poured scorn on Alexei Venediktov, the legendary head of the independent radio station Ekho Moskvy, refusing to accept any question from him. It was chilling.

The collision between Putin and Khodorkovsky was fundamental. It involved all the major issues of Putin's second term. Would Russia be democratic or authoritarian? Would it be dominated by state enterprises or private capital? Would it turn to the West or the East? Would Russia be ruled by law or by the vertical power of the Kremlin? Would civil society develop or would the authoritarian state prevail? All these profound questions were resolved through the Yukos affair.

Khodorkovsky had appeared to be the cleverest of all the oligarchs. A man of unlimited ability and adaptability, by 2003 he was the richest man in Russia with an assessed fortune of $15 billion and more than 100,000 employees. His Bank Menatep had failed, and he had sold off most of his industrial conglomerate Rosprom, but from 1999 his team started turning around Yukos, which they had acquired in the loans-for-shares privatization. Khodorkovsky was the foremost example of the gentrification of Russian capitalism.

The Yukos affair is best understood if we scrutinize its origins. In October 1999, I was called to Yukos' beautiful city palace in central Moscow for a lunch with one of Khodorkovsky's deputies, Leonid Nevzlin, whom I had never met. His direct question stunned me: What should Yukos do to become respectable in the West? I answered that it had to make an amicable deal with its Western minority shareholders. Nevzlin objected that these shareholders posed completely unreasonable demands. I responded that Yukos had committed so many sins (share dilutions, low transfer prices, and giveaways to offshore companies) that it could not win in any international court. Their only plausible escape would be friendly agreements. Grudgingly, Nevzlin accepted.

His next question was: What should Russia do to become respectable? I said that you cannot have a government in which virtually all ministers are corrupt and most massively so. You must sack a few senior ministers, sentence them to several years in prison, and keep them there. Nevzlin seemed to agree and asked: "Would Berezovsky be enough?" Admittedly, Berezovsky was no state official at that time, but I responded that it would be a good start. Suddenly, Nevzlin seemed relieved.[1]

Two months later, Yukos settled with its minority shareholders and launched all conceivable reforms. It introduced corporate transparency, adopted Western accounting standards, hired Western top management, and brought in independent directors on its board. It used international auditors and international consultants to improve its business and image. The owners of Yukos revealed their actual ownership and their corporate structures. Yukos stopped using transfer prices and paid substantial taxes from 2000.

Yukos led the revival of the country's old brownfields drawing on international technology and expertise that boosted Russia's oil production

---

1. Personal notes from Moscow, October 10–14, 1999.

Figure 7.1 Oil and gas production, 1985–2006

million tons or equivalent

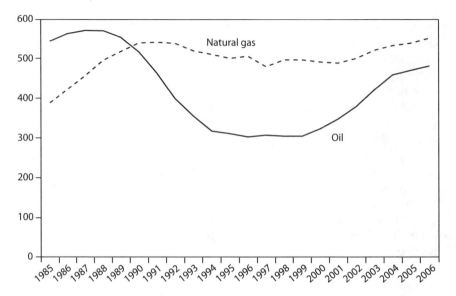

Source: BP historical data, www.bp.com (accessed on June 27, 2007).

by 50 percent from 6 million to 9 million barrels a day between 2000 and 2004. Meanwhile, the state gas production was nearly stagnant (figure 7.1). Yukos was one of the greatest success stories in the Russian economy.

Khodorkovsky made high-profile charitable donations and set up the nonprofit Open Russia Foundation in 2001. He promoted civil society, democracy, transparency, the rule of law, education, and economic development in Russia. He pursued numerous campaigns. Initially, Khodorkovsky demonstrated how Yukos had increased production and efficiency, while paying its taxes. He proceeded to advocate the construction of a private oil pipeline to China and another to Murmansk at Barents Sea, which would break the state-owned Transneft's monopoly. He criticized state-dominated Gazprom for its inefficiency and advocated a bigger role for Yukos in gas, complaining that Yukos was forced to flare billions of cubic meters of associated gas because of Gazprom's refusal to grant Yukos access to its monopolized gas pipeline system. In 2003, he conducted advanced negotiations with ExxonMobil about selling a majority of Yukos.

On February 19, 2003, an incident occurred that many think sealed Khodorkovsky's fate. Putin held his annual meeting with a score of oligarchs. The topic was administrative reform and corruption. Putin declared that his aim was "to liquidate the very basis of corruption." "During the last two years, new laws were adopted to de-bureaucratize the state apparatus. Unfortunately, so far we see no real improvement. . . . And today I would like to hear your views" (Putin 2003c). Khodorkovsky took Putin's words at face value. As Russian television viewers could hear, Khodorkovsky brought up the state-owned oil company Rosneft's purchase of the small oil company Severnaya Neft for $600 million, suggesting corruption, because Severnaya Neft had bought its main concession for $7 million two years earlier.

The talk of Moscow was that the Rosneft management, which was led by CEO Sergei Bogdanchikov and Putin's closest aide, Rosneft Chairman Igor Sechin, had extracted an unprecedented kickback of $200 million from the former owner of Severnaya Neft. Furiously, Putin explained that Khodorkovsky had no business to complain about corruption.[2]

Rosneft's purchase of Severnaya Neft was the first example of a new model for Putin's men to tap money from state enterprises. They realized they could pay high prices for private companies and ask for a substantial kickback. Putin's explosion made the Moscow elite wonder whether he was part of the deal. In any case, he evidently knew and approved of it (Baker and Glasser 2005, 282–83).

In May 2003, a Moscow think tank, the Council of National Strategy, published a report called "Russia on the Eve of an Oligarchic Coup." It accused the oligarchs in general and Khodorkovsky in particular of trying to buy Russia's politics. Since this small think tank was close to Putin, its report was seen as a Kremlin warning to Khodorkovsky.

Oligarchs had long bought a few deputies each for their lobbying in the Duma. Usually, Gazprom had about 100 deputies of its own placed in different factions. In early October 2003, I heard the allegation that Khodorkovsky had put up $100 million for the parliamentary elections, which should have rewarded him with about 100 deputies (out of 450). Khodorkovsky was financing the Union of Right Forces (SPS), Yabloko, and the Communist Party, receiving slots on each party list, but he was also paying substantial amounts to Putin's United Russia. The going price for a safe seat on a party list was $5 million, and the minimum was $2.5 million.[3] It was much cheaper to buy a seat in a single-mandate constituency because the average political campaign for one such seat cost $500,000 to $800,000, though seats in big cities were more expensive. Deripaska of Russian Aluminum was rumored to buy a similar number of seats, but in close cooperation with the Kremlin.[4]

---

2. Baker and Glasser (2005, 282). Private information from Moscow businessmen in March 2003.

3. My personal information in Moscow in early October 2003. Baker and Glasser (2005, 281–83) reported the same amount of $100 million but 130 seats. They reported the price of a guaranteed seat as $3 million to $4 million.

4. Personal information in Moscow in early October 2003.

In early July 2003, the Yukos executive Platon Lebedev was arrested and, on October 25, Khodorkovsky himself. He could have stayed abroad, but evidently he trusted Putin's judicial reforms. The actual accusations were long nebulous, but eventually he was charged with tax fraud. Yukos was the largest private taxpayer in Russia, and only Gazprom paid more taxes. Yukos minimized its profit taxes by legally registering its companies in low-tax regions in Russia, but so did many other companies. Putin's favorite, Roman Abramovich, did it much more aggressively in Chukhotka, where Abramovich is governor. The authorities reopened audited tax returns and denied the legality of the tax shelters. Initially, they slapped Yukos with $3.4 billion in back taxes, penalties, and interest for 2000. Then the biased tax authorities did the same for later years as well, ending up with the startling number of $28 billion, most of which was penalties (Baker and Glasser 2005, 345).

While denying that he had instigated Khodorkovsky's arrest, Putin explained to Western visitors that it was necessary because Khodorkovsky was buying up Russian politics. Putin's actual key motive was to enhance his political control by jailing the most politically active oligarch, while some of his aides wanted to seize Yukos assets.

In the ensuing process against Khodorkovsky and Yukos, Russia's legal authorities violated every rule in the book. No credible legal tax case existed to begin with. The Russian authorities dismissed the first two judges because of their impartiality. The offices of several defense counsels were raided, and they were harassed and punished. All rules regarding arrest, confiscation, and communication were violated. Khodorkovsky was denied bail, which was otherwise customary in nonviolent cases.

In the end, Khodorkovsky was sentenced to eight years in jail and sent off to East Siberia. Many other Yukos employees were condemned to lengthy prison sentences on the flimsiest of grounds (Amsterdam and Peroff 2007). Yukos' main asset, Yuganskneftegaz, was sold off in a fire sale in December 2004 to an unknown shell company, Baikal Financial Group, in an uncontested bid for $9.35 billion. This sale was premature; noncore assets did not go first as they should in an executive auction; no competitor was allowed; the bidder was a temporary shell company representing Rosneft; the sale price should have been about twice as high; and state banks financed Baikal's bid. The obvious purpose was to confiscate Yukos' finest oil field and give it to Rosneft. After the auction, Putin was the first to clarify that he knew who the owners of the shell company Baikal were.[5] His economic advisor Andrei Illarionov called this sale "the scam of the year," which caused his ouster (Baker and Glasser 2005, 352).

In a series of public statements throughout this process, Putin continued to deny any involvement. On October 27, 2003, two days after Kho-

---

5. "President Putin's Remarks on Results of Yuganskneftegaz Auction," NTV Segodnya, December 21, 2004, Federal News Service.

dorkovsky's arrest, he responded to protests: "There will be no meetings and no bargaining over the law enforcement bodies and their activities, so long, of course, as these agencies are acting within the limits of Russian legislation. . . . Neither the executive authorities nor even the Prosecutor's Office can deprive someone of their freedom, even for the period of pre-trial detention. Only the court has this power . . . and before the court, as before the law, all should be equal" (Putin 2003a). Yet he ignored the repeated declarations of the Moscow Collegium of Lawyers that the prosecutors violated the procedural norms in the investigation against the Yukos managers (Rumyantsev 2003).

In early November, Putin declared that the state did not want to destroy Yukos: "I am categorically against re-examining the results of privatization. . . . This is why there will not be a deprivatization or a re-examination of the results of the privatization, but everyone will have to learn to live according to laws" (Putin 2003d). In Rome, he stated with implicit reference to Khodorkovsky: "Having made their billions, they spend tens, hundreds of millions of dollars to save their billions. We know how this money is being spent—on what lawyers, PR campaigns and politicians it is going, and on getting questions like these asked" (Putin 2003b). The last words referred to the French journalist who posed the question.

On June 17, 2004, Putin told reporters: "The Russian administration, government and economic authorities are not interested in bankrupting a company like Yukos . . . the government will try to ensure that this company does not go bankrupt."[6] On September 6, he said: "I don't want to bankrupt Yukos. . . . Give me the names of the government officials who want to bankrupt Yukos and I'll fire them" (Belton 2004). On September 24, he reasserted: "We shall do this in strict accordance with the law. I want to stress it—in strict accordance with the law. . . . The state did not set before itself the task to nationalize this company or lay hands on it. And there is no such aim now . . ." (Putin 2004e).

In spite of his many unequivocal declarations to the contrary, Putin disregarded the law, successfully bankrupting and confiscating Yukos. He hardly ever said a true word about the Yukos affair. He insisted that the state must not interfere in the judicial process, but all the details indicated that prosecutors and judges received daily instructions from the Kremlin to be ruthless and lawless. He behaved exactly as he had done during the Gusinsky affair.

The Yukos case was Putin's most important political act, which framed his second term. In the summer of 2007, the last pieces of Yukos were auctioned off. Almost the whole of Yukos, which would now be worth over $100 billion, ended up with Rosneft, a poorly managed and nontransparent state company. This was confiscation through lawless taxation.

---

6. Interfax, Tashkent, June 17, 2004.

Khodorkovsky and Lebedev are sitting in prison in East Siberia and have been maltreated in numerous ways. All Khodorkovsky's appeals for the application of ordinary judicial rules have been dismissed. The other major Yukos owners and many managers wisely fled abroad around the time of Khodorkovsky's arrest. With characteristic vindictiveness, Putin made no concession. This legal case made a joke of his judicial reform and the supremacy of the state was reinforced. Like the CPSU, Putin's Kremlin acts with impunity and cannot be taken to court. Putin has demonstrated his strong approval of this miscarriage of justice by promoting many of its protractors. Now, the Kremlin is preparing the prosecution of Khodorkovsky for multibillion-dollar money laundering.

Khodorkovsky's arrest changed Russia's political system. Both Putin's chief of staff, Aleksandr Voloshin, and Prime Minister Mikhail Kasyanov, who had belonged to the Yeltsin "family," protested Khodorkovsky's arrest. They were relieved of their duties soon afterward. All other oligarchs heeded Putin's warning and withdrew from politics. The Russian Union of Industrialists and Entrepreneurs lost most of its influence. Putin's KGB officers had won over the oligarchs.

Although the Yukos affair attracted considerable international publicity, no major government tried to defend its shareholders. Foreign investors' belief in Putin's declarations was so great that the Yukos stock price held up well for nearly a year after Khodorkovsky's arrest, but then it collapsed. The stock price vacillated sharply with prosecutors' public statements, suggesting that insiders speculated on the basis of these allegations (Baker and Glasser 2005, 346). Foreign investors, who were naïve enough to believe in Putin's words, lost billions of dollars, but the biggest losers kept quiet not to reveal their folly to their shareholders. Russia's stock market took a break in 2004, but then it surged again.

Senior US officials intervened once—in October 2004—but only to say that they feared that Russia's oil production would decline during the then expected confiscation of Yugansk. Instead of condemnation, on October 18, 2004, US Secretary of State Colin Powell uttered his forceful support for Putin: "The Russian people came out of the post-Soviet Union era in a state of total chaos—a great deal of freedom, but it was freedom to steal from the state and President Putin took over and restored a sense of order in the country and moved in a democratic way."[7] Amazingly, Western governments accepted the confiscation of billions of dollars of their citizens' assets.

The Yukos affair also changed Russia's economic policy. The once-promising tax reform had become a joke as well. After all, the accusation against Yukos was that it followed the letter of the new tax code and utilized one of its loopholes. That the president let Yukos be confiscated through arbitrary taxation in kangaroo courts severely undermined Rus-

---

7. "Interview with the USA Today Editorial Board," October 18, 2004, US Department of State website, www.state.gov (accessed on July 15, 2007).

sia's property rights. Putin's program of structural reform came to a screeching halt. The Yukos affair showed the KGB men around Putin that they could seize Russia's biggest private companies if they just lied patiently. The road to large-scale renationalization through lawless government interference lay open.

In the spring of 2004, I asked Gusinsky over dinner how he could explain Khodorkovsky's daring challenge to Putin. Gusinsky answered with a sad smile: "It was the same with all of us: Hubris."

Elections of 2003 and 2004

According to the constitution, Russia was scheduled to hold Duma elections on December 7, 2003, and presidential elections on March 14, 2004. Considering Putin's persistent approval rating of around 70 percent, his victory in the presidential elections was a foregone conclusion. Because of the limited role of the Duma, the parliamentary elections were regarded as little more than primary elections.

The party of power was United Russia. It had been formed in December 2001 through a merger of Unity, Putin's hastily created party in 1999, and its erstwhile centrist rival, Fatherland-All Russia, which had been led by Yuri Luzhkov and Yevgeny Primakov. United Russia was a Kremlin party run by puppet-master Vladislav Surkov, deputy head of the presidential administration. Its formal leader was Minister of Interior Boris Gryzlov, one of Putin's KGB friends from St. Petersburg. Early on, in September 2003, Putin endorsed United Russia, which followed its precedent from 2003, presenting no program and refusing to debate other parties (Baker and Glasser 2005, 295–96; Shevtsova 2005, 287).

The Kremlin was experimenting with different new party projects to split the opposition. On the right, SPS and Yabloko did so themselves. On the left, however, the communists remained quite strong. The Kremlin put together a new party, with two attractive young politicians, communist Sergei Glaziev and nationalist Dmitri Rogozin, who formed the left-wing and nationalist party Motherland. The Kremlin ordered the oligarch Deripaska to finance its new creation and organized favorable official television coverage (Baker and Glasser 2005, 298–300).

The Kremlin needed some drama to excite the population about these elections, which looked both given and controlled. The Yukos affair became the election campaign of United Russia and Putin in the same way as the second Chechnya war was in 1999 and 2000. This was a political war against the oligarchs. Government media exposed Yukos' funding of SPS, Yabloko, and the Communist Party, but said nothing about its gifts to United Russia. Anybody who complained about the treatment of Yukos was accused of being paid by Yukos by the Putin propagandists, who ruled supreme on state-controlled television. The population was fed up with the oligarchs,

Table 7.1   Results of election to the State Duma, December 7, 2003

Candidate	Percent of votes
Communist Party of the Russian Federation	12.6
United Russia	37.6
Motherland	9.0
Liberal Democratic Party of Russia	11.5
Others or against all	29.4
Voter turnout	55.8

Source: Central Election Commission of the Russian Federation, www.cikrf.ru (accessed on July 10, 2007).

whom they blamed for the considerable corruption. Three-quarters of the public supported the Kremlin's antioligarchic campaign. Big businessmen understood that they could not win over the public, so they turned quiet and nurtured their personal relations with Putin. Moreover, no party could afford to stand in full opposition to Putin, because each of the existing parties harbored a majority supporting him (Shevtsova 2005, 281, 295).

The Duma elections worked out exactly as the Kremlin had planned. Participation was low as usual. United Russia received 37.6 percent of the votes cast, while the Communist Party lost half of its support and received merely 12.6 percent. Zhirinovsky's erratic but Kremlin-loyal LDPR gathered 11.5 percent, and new Motherland received 9.0 percent (table 7.1). The real losers were liberal SPS and Yabloko. Each received 4 percent, less than the 5 percent hurdle, and fell out of the Duma. In the one-mandate constituencies, "administrative resources," meaning manifold repressive measures, such as large-scale but brief arrests of election workers, gave United Russia almost all those seats (Fedorov 2004). Altogether, United Russia received a total of 305 out of 450 seats, that is, more than two-thirds majority.

Both the Council of Europe and the Organization for Security and Cooperation in Europe (OSCE) concluded that the elections were "free but not fair." The elections themselves were not notably falsified, but the election process was utterly biased. In particular, state-controlled television news was heavily tilted to the advantage of United Russia, Motherland, and LDPR, and against the communists, SPS, and Yabloko. These elections confirmed that Russia had become mildly authoritarian. The Duma ceased to play any essential role. Soon, Glaziev and later Rogozin were thrown out of Motherland by the Kremlin because they had become too independent. Demands of obedience were ratcheted up all the time (Baker and Glasser 2005, 311; Shevtsova 2005, 288).

In early February 2004, I had lunch with Moscow Mayor Luzhkov in Washington. I asked him about the Duma elections. Luzhkov, who was one of the leaders of United Russia, said that he had talked with the president, who was "concerned." That is how Russian officials now talk, letting their worries be reflected in the president. Luzhkov said that the new Duma was like a bird with too big and fat a bottom, a decrepit left wing and no right wing whatsoever. "Such a bird cannot fly."

After the Duma elections, Putin's victory in the presidential elections was a given. Surkov had problems persuading plausible candidates to run. To oppose Putin was both foolhardy and dangerous. Gennady Zyuganov and Grigori Yavlinsky refused to run to save themselves from another humiliation. Zhirinovsky, the outstanding standup comedian, nominated his bodyguard as presidential candidate. One of Putin's close FSB friends from St. Petersburg, Sergei Mironov, who was speaker of the Federation Council, became formally a candidate but declared his support for Putin. Eventually, the Kremlin managed to persuade the communists to put up a candidate, Nikolai Kharitonov, a decorated KGB colonel.

Yet, the Kremlin did not appreciate that Berezovsky supported a prominent politician, Ivan Rybkin. After Rybkin named three men he accused of being Putin's bagmen (Gennady Tymchenko, and the brothers Mikhail and Yuri Kovalchuk, all from St. Petersburg), he alleged that he was drugged and surfaced in Kiev under mysterious circumstances, and his candidacy was never registered.

Glaziev, who had broken with the Kremlin, became an independent opposition candidate. The liberal right could not agree on a candidate, as usual, but one of the leaders of SPS, Irina Khakamada, one of Russia's leading female politicians, put herself forward with the support of Leonid Nevzlin of Yukos, who had escaped to Israel. Khakamada ran a courageous and energetic campaign. The final list of registered candidates was short, only six people, of whom only Glaziev and Khakamada qualified as opposition (Shevtsova 2005, Baker and Glasser 2005).

As in the 2000 presidential elections, Putin thrived on the postrevolutionary contempt for politics and refused to debate any competitor. Still, this time he made a public policy declaration on television, surprising with a Jeffersonian declaration of freedom:

> We must continue work to create a genuinely functioning civil society in our country. I especially want to say that creating a civil society is impossible without genuinely free and responsible media. . . .
>
> I firmly believe that only a developed civil society can truly protect democratic freedoms and guarantee the rights and freedoms of the citizen and the individual. Ultimately, only free people can ensure a growing economy and a prosperous state. . . .
>
> I would like to stress once more that the rights and freedoms of our people are the highest value that defines the sense and content of the state's work.
>
> Finally, we will most certainly complete the transformations currently underway in the judicial system and the law enforcement agencies. I think this is a truly

important area that is decisive for building up real democracy in the country and ensuring the constitutional rights and guarantees of our citizens. (Putin 2004d)

Putin did none of this. As usual, when Putin said something, he was preparing to do the opposite. More tellingly, on February 24, only two and a half weeks before the elections, he sacked his competent and strong prime minister, Kasyanov, possibly to emphasize his struggle against oligarchs and arouse some interest in politics.

The presidential elections amounted to the expected cakewalk for Putin, who received 71.2 percent of the votes. Participation in the elections was much higher than in the Duma elections (table 7.2). In Ingushetia, Putin received 98 percent and in war-torn Chechnya 92 percent, reflecting that the less the freedom the higher the vote count for Putin (Baker and Glasser 2005, 333). Russia's democracy which, had never been full-fledged, was finished.

Inauspicious Start of Putin's Second Term

Putin's second term had an unfortunate start. Suddenly, everything seemed to go wrong. The government was caught in chaos because of poor reorganization. The most severe of all Chechen terrorist attacks, the Beslan school massacre, shook Russia. Toward the end of 2004, Ukraine turned against Russia in its democratic and West-oriented Orange Revolution. A mismanaged reform of the social benefit system led to massive popular protests.

Even before his own election, Putin had appointed Mikhail Fradkov as new prime minister. He had KGB connections and was considered close to Sechin. His appointment signified the victory of the *siloviki* over the oligarchs. Fradkov cut a most unimpressive figure, being bald, even shorter than Putin, and famously indecisive. He had made his early career as an expert on the WTO, when Russia did nothing about it. In 1993, he was appointed deputy minister for external economic relations with responsibility for the WTO, but he was completely passive.[8] Even so, he advanced to become minister for external economic relations in 1997. After one year, his ministry was abolished, which was celebrated as a major attack on bureaucracy and corruption. After another year, Fradkov became minister of trade. In 2000, that ministry was also eliminated because it blocked Russia's WTO entry and merged with German Gref's new Ministry of Economic Development and Trade. In 2001, Fradkov was given a new chance as head of the tax police, which had arisen out of the KGB. But the tax police was closed down two years later, because it was considered the most

---

8. His minister, Sergei Glaziev, told me that Fradkov was his only deputy who never prepared a single decision in the course of one year.

Table 7.2   Results of presidential election, March 14, 2004

Candidate	Percent of votes
Vladimir Putin	71.3
Nikolai Kharitonov	13.7
Sergei Glazíev	4.1
Irina Khakamada	3.8
Oleg Malyshkin	2.0
Sergei Mironov	0.8
Others or against all	4.3
Voter turnout	64.4

Source: Central Election Commission of the Russian Federation, www.cikrf.ru (accessed on July 10, 2007).

lawless and corrupt government agency. Finally, Fradkov was demoted to ambassador to the European Union in Brussels. On a visit to Brussels in early 2004, Gref publicly scolded Fradkov for being the most incompetent Russian ambassador he had ever encountered.[9] One month later, Fradkov became prime minister and Gref's boss.

Putin's choice of prime minister said everything about his second term. He wanted a weak and passive government that would not undertake major reforms. The *siloviki* were to dominate over the reformers (Gref and Kudrin). In one single appointment, Putin transformed his reform government into a nonreform government, although Kudrin and Gref remained ministers. Putin replaced Yeltsin's old chief of staff Voloshin with his close collaborator Dmitri Medvedev, who was considered as indecisive as Fradkov. Medvedev belonged to the St. Petersburg liberals, but that concept was about to lose relevance.

As Putin's second administration was formed, a substantial administrative reform was attempted. It was spearheaded by Dmitri Kozak, the liberal lawyer from St. Petersburg who had led the judicial reform. It had been prepared for two years by a working group led by Putin himself, and it was largely a revival of Yeltsin's government reform in November 1991. Its guiding principle was to organize the state administration by functions as in the West, and not by industrial branches as in the Soviet Union. Once again, the number of ministries was reduced—this time to only 15, as in a normal Western government. The many deputy prime ministers were reduced to one. Each ministry was supposed to have only two deputy ministers (Remington 2006, 63–64).

This reorganization caused lasting chaos. The deputy ministers were usually the real policymakers, while the heads of departments were sheer

---

9. This was the common view among eurocrats and diplomats in Brussels.

administrators. The reorganization squeezed out the policymakers, who tended to be young, bright reformers, whereas the older, more conservative heads of departments were left in place. The few remaining deputy ministers were overwhelmed with routine administration, and the reform agenda was effectively killed. The weakening of the government led to a big transfer of power to the presidential administration, where Putin's KGB men had reinforced their nontransparent and unaccountable administrative control.

On September 1, 2004, the traditional festive start of the school year, a new shock hit Russia. A band of heavily armed Chechen fighters seized a school in Beslan in Russian Northern Ossetia near Chechnya. They held more than 1,200 adults and children hostage, although the official government spokesman insisted there were only 354 hostages. Militants herded them into the school gymnasium, which they mined with explosives, threatening to blow it up if government forces attacked.

Russia's foremost special forces were sent there within hours, but the disarray was palpable. At no time was the school cordoned off. The regional governors of North Ossetia and neighboring Ingushetia, both recent Putin appointees (though formally elected), refused even to go to Beslan. The federal government ignored the crisis and minimized news coverage. On the third day, the special forces attacked the school with heavy arms, maximizing the losses. Brave local Ossetians were so exasperated with the incompetence of the federal troops that they took out *Kalashnikovs* from their closets and stormed the school themselves. The fire fight lasted for at least nine hours, although the government claimed that only 33 hostage takers participated, of whom all but one were killed. No fewer than 330 hostages, including 155 children, were killed. Chechen warlord Shamil Basayev claimed responsibility.

Again, the Russian government demonstrated itself both incompetent and callous, being most concerned about minimizing media coverage and concealing the real number of hostages. The government had no relevant intelligence. Once more, policemen accepted bribes to let the terrorists through. The refusal of the regional governors to show up illustrated how calcified Russia had become as a result of overcentralization. Putin, however, refused to accept any criticism for the catastrophe. He sacked none of the culprits, only the excellent editor of the private newspaper *Izvestiya*, Raf Shakirov, who committed the crime of accurate reporting.

Although the Beslan tragedy showed how poorly the overcentralized and authoritarian Putin regime reacted to crises, Putin's reaction was to roll back democracy even more. On September 13, he announced that he would eliminate the direct election of governors and appoint them himself. In his interview book *First Person*, Putin (2000, 183) had stated the opposite: "I think we have to preserve both local self-government and a system of election for governors." Since the governors' resistance had already been broken, this radical decision aroused no opposition. In effect, Russia was no longer a federal state but a unitary state, where all officials were appointed by the president officially or informally. Mayors are still elected, but their appointments are being contemplated (Petrov 2007).

Complex social reforms had been relegated to Putin's second term, and the priority was to change the misconstrued and costly social benefit system. Russia had myriad old social benefits primarily for the privileged, many of which were never paid out. Numerous nontransparent social benefits in kind needed to be transformed into cash payments, which was politically controversial because the beneficiaries suspected they would lose their benefits.

In January 2005, the social benefit reform was launched, but its implementation was remarkably inept. The reform was presented as the monetization of in-kind benefits, but in reality many benefits were abolished. Full compensation was promised for the actual in-kind benefits, but initially only about one-third of them were compensated for, because as usual the federal and regional governments did not agree on who should pay what. Although these reforms affected about 40 million people, they were not explained.

To add insult to injury, the 35,000 highest officials, including the president, had their salaries quintupled at the same time, and none of their substantial in-kind benefits were taken away. The social benefit reform seemed directed against the poor in the midst of Russia's oil boom, when the budget surplus reached record heights. To great surprise, widespread, spontaneous popular protests dominated by pensioners erupted against this reform in large parts of the country. For the first time, Putin was the center of public scorn.

To cool down the protests, the government reversed most of its actions and raised pensions substantially. The Kremlin got frightened and stopped most reforms in Putin's second term. The spectacular failure of the social benefit reform was another reason why liberal reformers lost out. There would be no more reforms worth mentioning during Putin's second term.

Consolidating Authoritarian Rule: Deinstitutionalization

Putin had already done much to turn Russia into an authoritarian country during his first term, and now he completed his accomplishments. He reinforced central control over law enforcement by appointing new regional heads of the ministry of interior, the prosecutor's office, and the security police throughout the country (Remington 2006, 234–35; Petrov 2004).

Whereas Yeltsin had split up the old KGB to weaken it, Putin put it together again to strengthen it. In March 2003, he decreed that the Federal Agency for Government Communication and Information (FAPSI) and the Federal Border Guard Service (FSP) were merged with the Federal Security Service (FSB) (Remington 2006). The old repression apparatus was now reassembled, and it proudly indulged in all the old KGB activities. The FSB was headed by Nikolai Patrushev, one of Putin's KGB friends from St. Petersburg.

In late 2004, the Ukrainian Orange Revolution shook the self-confidence of Putin and he hastened to fill all the holes in his authoritarian regime. In late 2005, he promulgated a restrictive law on nongovernmental organizations, which was impossible to comprehend, freeing the government to deprive at will any organization of its right to exist. Foreign grants were severely restricted and many required explicit government permission. The tax authorities were mobilized to audit and raid nongovernmental organizations. Public protests and demonstrations were restricted and often prohibited. Criticism of public officials was proscribed as "extremism." Electoral legislation was amended to give the government full control over the vote count and to minimize independent electoral monitoring. Almost all opinion poll organizations were brought under Kremlin control, and the last independent dailies were purchased by helpful businessmen close to the Kremlin.

The regime was legitimized by Putin's popularity, which stayed above 70 percent, bolstered by the strict prohibition of any public criticism of him. As the nuanced Russia analyst Thomas Remington (2006, 61) observed: "Vladimir Putin has quietly fostered a cult of personality through such methods as the use of official portraits that officials are encouraged to hang in their offices, and signals to the mass media to portray him in a flattering light." Russia had become a dictatorship (Fish 2005, Freedom House 2006).

One day as I walked along Arbat Street, a pedestrian shopping area, I realized that most of the sculptures in the stands were of four men: Lenin, Stalin, Putin, and Feliks Dzherzhinsky, founder of the secret police! But Russia is not ridden by any extreme nationalism, even if xenophobic Russian skinheads murder foreign students all too often. On the contrary, ideology is absent. This is posturing rather than extremism.

The Kremlin was not only repressive, but also proactive. In 2006, hardline KGB officers established a pro-Putin party called "A Just Russia" to capture dissatisfaction with corruption and inequality, providing a left-wing alternative to the purportedly center-right United Russia. The Kremlin formed a few youth "movements," notably Nashi ("Ours"). The common denominators of these popular initiatives were that they were populist and nationalist, based on careful studies of opinion polls and focus groups, and directed from above by the Kremlin. Nationalist, populist, and anti-Western commentators, such as Mikhail Leontiev and Alexei Pushkov, were promoted on state television.

Nor did Putin let up in the second Chechen war. His strategy was three-pronged. First, Russia continued a ruthless war and gradually killed off all the major warlords. In March 2005, former Chechen President Aslan Maskhadov, the last moderate leader, was killed by FSB special forces. In July 2006, Russian troops claimed the ultimate success killing of Shamil Basayev, after which the war slowed down.

A second strategy was "Chechenization," relying on the former mufti and warlord Akhmad Kadyrov. After 17 attempts on his life, he was finally assassinated on Victory Day, May 9, 2004, while watching a parade honoring the USSR's victory in World War II. He was succeeded by his ruthless son, Ramzan Kadyrov, whom Putin promoted to Chechen president in 2007. Kadyrov maintains a truly despotic regime.

The third strategy was to pour vast funding into Chechnya and rebuild it. Although violence continues, the calm is sufficient for the Kremlin to claim victory in the war in Chechnya. Ramzan Kadyrov is what Mancur Olson (2000) called a "stationary bandit," exploiting his republic but caring about its growth.

Most of the time, Putin's authoritarianism has been relatively soft. Because of its vast oil revenues, the Russian government can afford to tempt potential troublemakers with money rather than force them into silence. Putin has extended the concept of espionage to cover also innocuous contacts with foreigners, and seemingly innocent Russians have been sentenced to prison. But political prison sentences are rare. Far more common are beatings by unknown people, which may or may not be instigated by the authorities, since Russia's crime rates are so high.

Most chilling are the many murders of Russian journalists and opposition politicians. Russia ranks among the highest in the world in terms of murders of journalists (Fish 2005). Many murders have taken place in lawless Chechnya and most are probably connected with revelations about shady business dealings, but quite a few appear to have been purely political. Several bona fide politicians have also been murdered. On April 17, 2003, the impeccably honest liberal politician Sergei Yushenkov was murdered, presumably for having dug into military corruption in Chechnya, as did the Yabloko politician and investigative journalist Yuri Shchekochikhin, who was poisoned to death on July 13, 2003. On July 9, 2004, American journalist Paul Klebnikov, the editor of Forbes Russia magazine, was murdered in Moscow. He is a major source for this book. They all knew too much.

On February 13, 2004, Zelimkhan Yandarbiyev, the former president of the Chechen republic, was assassinated with a bomb in Qatar's capital of Doha.[10] The Qatar authorities sentenced two Russian agents from GRU, Russia's military intelligence, to life imprisonment for the murder, which they claimed was ordered by Russian top officials. Under heavy Russian pressure, the culprits were soon extradited to Russia, where they were

---

10. Steven Lee Myers, "Qatar Arrests Russian Agents for Murder of Exiled Chechen," *New York Times*, February 27, 2004.

supposed to serve their prison sentences, but they were released. This was the first time since the murder of a Ukrainian nationalist (Stepan Bandera) in Munich in 1959 that Russian agents were caught red-handed murdering people abroad on official orders.

Most shocking was the murder of the renowned journalist Anna Politkovskaya in the fall of 2006. She was one of Putin's fiercest domestic critics and her integrity was unsurpassed. Like Shchekochikhin, she worked for Russia's last independent newspaper, *Novaya gazeta*. Her murder took place on Putin's 54th birthday, which was noteworthy because Russian gangsters have a macabre tradition of making a birthday present of a murder. Putin's deprecating comment after her death was: "I think her impact on Russian political life was only very slight. She was well known in the media community, in human rights circles and in the West, but her influence on political life within Russia was very minimal" (Putin 2006d).

In November 2006, a KGB colonel who had defected and worked for Berezovsky, Aleksandr Litvinenko, was slowly poisoned to death with rare radioactive polonium in London. British magistrates requested the extradition of a suspect former KGB officer from Moscow, but the Russian government refused, while giving the accused ample TV time to defend himself. Putin commented:

> Aleksandr Litvinenko was dismissed from the security services. . . . But there was no need to run anywhere, he did not have any secrets. Everything negative that he could say with respect to his service and his previous employment, he already said a long time ago, so there could be nothing new in what he did later. (Putin 2007c)

As the oligarchs had done before them, Russia's liberal intelligentsia shivered. Had the Kremlin declared open season on them?

Renationalization: The Creation of Kremlin, Inc.

Throughout his first term, Putin spoke out loudly and clearly in favor of a free market economy and private enterprise. A typical statement of his was:

> A competent macroeconomic policy remains one of the state's most important regulatory functions. But . . . , the amount of direct administrative intervention in the economy must be reduced. Despite all the steps that have been taken to cut back bureaucracy in the economy, there is still too much intervention. We also need to optimise the amount of state-owned property. In any event, state-owned property should not exist simply to be a source of prosperity for the people running it in the state's name. I want to say once again that the state should manage only the property it needs to carry out its public functions, ensure state power and guarantee the country's security and defence capacity. (Putin 2004b)

Remarkably, the first sentence of this statement reflected Putin's actual policy, while the rest did not. Even at his big annual press conference in

Figure 7.2 Share of GDP from private enterprises, 1991–2006

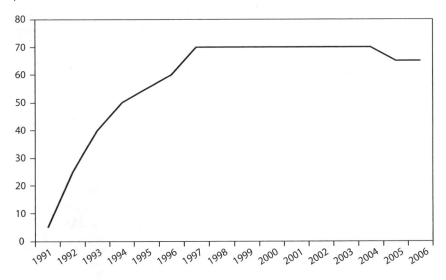

percent of GDP

Sources: EBRD (2006, 168; 2000, 204).

January 2006, Putin (2006c) stated: "We have about ten quite large private oil companies . . . . Nobody is going to nationalize them, nobody is going to interfere with their activities. They are going to develop according to market conditions like private companies."

Putin's policy sounded like a standard West European liberal-conservative policy, oriented toward gradual deregulation and privatization, but it was not after the Yukos affair. I have quoted Putin at length because of the great contrast between his words and actions. Despite his assurances, privatization stalled. The privatization of Rosneft had been discussed for years, but now it was abandoned. Although virtually all growth came from the private sector, while the state sector underperformed, state corporations were gobbling up successful private firms. According to the European Bank for Reconstruction and Development (EBRD), the share of Russia's GDP produced by private enterprise plummeted from 70 percent in 2004 to 65 percent in 2005 (figure 7.2).

Putin's economic policy statements did not embrace any socialist or nationalist ideology before renationalization was accomplished. The economic superiority of the private sector was just astounding, so the natural conclusion is that renationalization has been driven by state officials' interest to extend their power and wealth.

Renationalization occurred in steps. To begin with, Putin's men took charge of the main state enterprises in energy, transportation, military industry, and banking. Most of them were old KGB hands from St. Petersburg. This was the essence of the new Kremlin, Inc.:

- The non-KGB "liberals"—Dmitri Medvedev and Aleksei Miller—became chairman and CEO, respectively, of Gazprom, the jewel in Russia's industrial crown.

- Sergei Bogdanchikov, who was already CEO of Rosneft, linked up with Igor Sechin, Putin's closest collaborator, who became Rosneft chairman.

- Vladimir Yakunin, a KGB friend of Putin from St. Petersburg, became CEO of the new state company the Russian Railways.

- Viktor Ivanov, another KGB friend of Putin from St. Petersburg who was responsible for personnel in the Kremlin, became chairman of the arms manufacturer Almaz-Antei in 2002, after which three of its top executives were mysteriously murdered in the course of one year.[11] He also became chairman of Aeroflot, the Russian airline, in 2004.

- Minister of Defense and Deputy Prime Minister Sergei Ivanov, a former lieutenant-general in the Foreign Intelligence Service (SVR) and KGB schoolfriend of Putin, became chairman of the newly-amalgamated United Aircraft Corporation in 2006.

- Deputy Prime Minister Sergei Naryshkin, yet another KGB friend of Putin from St. Petersburg, was appointed chairman of the newly merged United Shipyards Corporation in 2007.

- Sergei Chemezov, who had served in the KGB in East Germany with Putin, was asked to lead the state arms trade agency Rosoboronexport.

- Leonid Reiman, another Putin friend hailing from foreign intelligence in St. Petersburg, is in charge of several telecommunication companies, some private and some state-owned.

- The KGB banker Andrei Kostin succeeded in getting close to Putin and is CEO of Vneshtorgbank (VTB).

Russia had a habit of appointing top officials to the boards of large state companies, and the new crop simply replaced ousted officials. Officially, public servants are not allowed to receive any fees as board members of state companies, but the law does not mean all that much in Russia. Most ministers appear to own corporations, which they do not declare as their property.

FSB friends of Putin do not have a monopoly on chairmanships of big state corporations. Chubais remains CEO of UES, with Voloshin as chair-

---

11. *Kommersant*, May 24, 2004.

man. Kudrin is chairman of Sberbank, the state savings bank, and Alrosa, the state diamond company. Minister of Industry and Energy Viktor Khristenko is the long-time chairman of Transneft, the oil pipeline company. Yet, non-FSB people are increasingly marginalized and their companies tend to be less predatory. UES even undertook a major regulatory reform in 2007, splitting it up in many competing corporations.

The first renationalization was Rosneft's purchase of Severnaya Neft in early 2003, which looked like a kickback. The biggest renationalization was Rosneft's seizure of Yukos, which added a net value to Rosneft of perhaps $60 billion.[12] Gazprom wanted to keep up with the competition. In September 2005, it bought the oil company Sibneft, paying a high market price of $13.1 billion for Kremlin-friendly Abramovich's dominant stake. Gazprom also forced Royal Dutch Shell and its partners to sell its 51 percent of the Sakhalin-1 project, and it compelled TNK-BP to give up its large gas field Kovykta in East Siberia for a symbolic price. A new medium-sized oil company, Russneft, appeared to be about to be given the Yukos treatment with prison sentences for its owners and managers and then confiscation, but its owner wisely escaped abroad.[13]

As a consequence of all these nationalizations, the private share of Russia's oil production fell from 90 percent in 2004 to 45 percent in the second half of 2007. The impact on Russia's oil production was immediate and drastic. From an average output growth of 8.5 percent a year from 1999 to 2004, the increment fell to about 2 percent a year for the ensuing three years (figure 7.1). Sibneft's production fell sharply, while the remaining big private companies (TNK-BP, Lukoil, and Surgut) understood the danger of investing significantly, or boosting production, and moderated their investment.

VTB has been particularly aggressive. Russian banking is still dominated by state banks, and therefore it is less developed than in Kazakhstan and Ukraine, as reflected in its low ratio of money supply (M2) to GDP. Rosoboronexport seized the unrestructured car giant Avtovaz for a nominal amount, and it forced the excellent titanium producer VSMPO-Avisma to give up ownership at a price amounting to one-quarter of the market price (Finn 2006b).

After Kakha Bendukidze, the owner of the large machine-building company OMZ, became minister of economy of Georgia in 2004, Gazprom forced a purchase at a price that was a mere 40 percent of the market price, according to what an insider told me.

The pattern is clear. State enterprises are buying good private companies either at a high price in a voluntary deal, which is accompanied by

---

12. Yukos would in all likelihood have been more highly valued because it was more transparent and better managed than Rosneft.

13. Irina Reznik, "Lichnoe delo Gutserieva (Gutseriev's Personal Matter)," *Vedomosti*, July 30, 2007.

rumors about sizable kickbacks, or the sale is forced and the price is low. No economic rationale is evident. The most likely purpose of renationalization is corruption.

As renationalization has evolved, a need has arisen to justify it. One idea is a purported need for "national champions," emulated from France, which means inefficient national monopolies. Gazprom is the model. A new national champion was the United Aircraft Corporation with three-quarters state ownership, created in 2006. Russia's oversized aircraft industry needed restructuring, but merging the few successful private companies with big dying state enterprises threatens to kill them all. Similarly, in 2007, the United Shipyard Corporation and the Atomic Energy Industry Complex were formed and monopolies are rarely beneficial for economic development.

Another official argument is that major national resources should be domestically owned. Russia has produced a number of drafts of a law on strategic assets that should be majority-owned by Russians, but it has not as yet adopted such a law. The most obvious examples are major oil and natural gas findings, but major infrastructure and the military industry are also included.

The ideological motive for nationalization is absent. Two of the most aggressive predators, Rosneft and VTB, carried out large international initial public offerings (IPOs) in London in 2006 and 2007, respectively. The purpose was not to privatize them but to endow them with new funds for enterprise acquisitions. Once more, Gazprom with its 51 percent public ownership was the model. Foreign investors happily buy these stocks, because they are reassured that companies with excellent Kremlin contacts can purchase valuable Russian assets cheaply. They pay little attention to limited transparency, corporate governance, or even poor economic results. The asset values are just too attractive.

The Russian state-dominated companies are remarkably focused on their stock prices. During the Yukos affair, Putin met repeatedly with foreign portfolio investors to reassure them. Apart from false promises about Yukos, he pledged that Gazprom's domestic stocks would become freely tradable. After Putin promised that in September 2004, it finally happened in January 2006. Putin (2006a) bragged in his annual address: "We already feel confident in the mining and extraction sector. Our companies in this sector are very competitive. Gazprom, for example, has just become the third biggest company in the world in terms of capitalization. . . ." Gazprom was helped by benign taxation. For oil companies, 88 percent of the oil revenues over $27 a barrel were taxed away, which depressed their stock prices and investment, but Gazprom suffered no such tax.

The main Russian stock index (RTS) rose no fewer than 11 times between January 2000 and July 2007, being one of the best performing stock markets in the world year after year, although 2004 was a lost year because of the Yukos affair (figure 7.3).

Figure 7.3 Russian stock market index (RTS), 2000–2007

RTS index

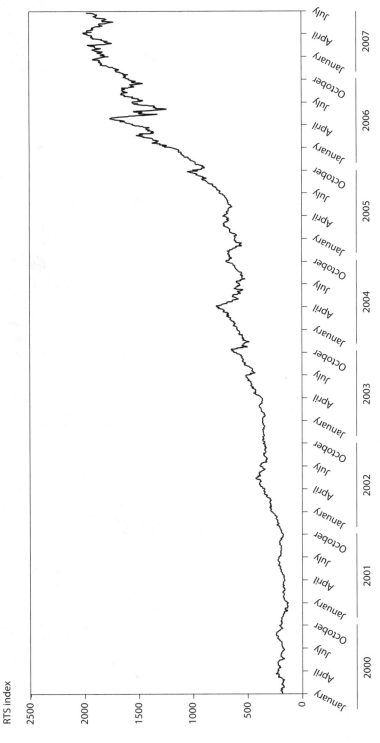

Source: Russian stock market website, www.rts.ru (accessed on July 6, 2007).

Figure 7.4   Gross fixed investment, 1991–2006

percent of GDP

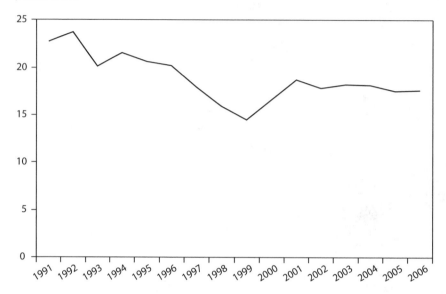

Source: UN Economic Commission for Europe online database, www.unece.org (accessed on May 30, 2007).

The Russian renationalization has had a limited negative impact on the economy. It has been evident only in oil and gas production, banking, and possibly machine building. Most of the Russian economy is still in private hands, including the metals, retail trade, and construction sectors. The aggregate indicator that has suffered the most is investment, with Russia's official investment ratio remaining rather low at 18 percent of GDP despite the economic boom (figure 7.4). Other successful transition countries have much higher investment ratios, with ratios as high as 35 percent of GDP in Estonia and Latvia (UN Economic Commission for Europe 2007).

SPS leader Boris Nemtsov did not mince his words when commenting on renationalization: "It is offensive that under Putin the state has taken on the role of plunderer and racketeer with an appetite that grows with each successive conquest. . . . But the greatest calamity is that nobody is allowed to utter a word in protest regarding all this. 'Keep quiet,' the authorities seem to say, 'or things will go worse for you. This is none of your business' " (Nemtsov 2007).[14]

---

14. He could publish this in the *Moscow Times* because it is not censored since it appears in English.

Figure 7.5 Exports and imports of goods, 1992–2006

billions of US dollars

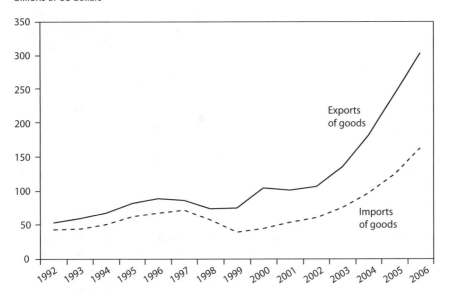

Sources: Bank of Finland Institute for Economies in Transition, Russia statistics, www.bof.fi (accessed on May 30, 2007); EBRD (2000, 205; 2003, 187).

Toward State Capitalism?

In 2004, the international oil prices took off (figure 6.4), filling the Russian state treasury. Russian exports started skyrocketing, mainly because of the rising commodity prices. In 2006, Russia's exports reached $305 billion compared with the pitiful $29 billion of Soviet exports to the West in 1990 (figure 7.5 and figure 2.2). Imports could not keep up with exports, leading to a steady current account surplus of about 10 percent of GDP (figure 6.5).

The government maintained an impressively conservative fiscal policy, with a budget surplus of 7.5 percent of GDP in the oil boom years of 2005 and 2006. The government established a stabilization fund on the pattern of Norway and Kazakhstan, in which windfall taxes from high oil prices were accumulated. By July 2007, its balance exceeded $120 billion. Russia was flooded with easy money, which made it difficult to justify arduous reforms. The huge revenue flows endowed Russian leaders with a deleterious sense of hubris.

The reformers no longer set the trend in Russian economic policy, having been muscled out by big state-dominated companies and the *siloviki* who controlled them. Time and again, Putin emphasized that his two key economic goals were macroeconomic stability and high economic growth of 7 percent a year, which were regularly achieved. No economic reforms were needed to accomplish the desired growth rate. Yet, even populist statements by the Russian officials specified remarkably small additional expenditures. Public expenditures showed no tendency to rise as a share of GDP, although revenues surged (figure 6.1).

By 2006, Putin's unrelenting advocacy of sound market economic policy suddenly wavered. His televised question-and-answer session with the nation on October 25, 2006 (on the third anniversary of Khodorkovsky's arrest), marked a radical departure from his prior rhetoric (Putin 2006b). He restored much of the old Soviet rhetoric.

The essence of Putin's three-hour marathon exposition was industrial policy, extensive state intervention, centralized micromanagement, state investment, subsidies, trade and price regulation, protectionism with higher customs tariffs, export taxes, and import substitution, as well as ethnic discrimination. As in the old days, the patriarchic state had authority over everything but responsibility for nothing. Conspicuously absent were his prior ideas of deregulation, the rule of law, and private property rights.

Putin's starting point was ethnic discrimination. Ethnic strife over market trade had flared up in the small Karelian town of Kondopoga in August 2006, and local Chechens had killed two Russians. Putin fanned the racist flames by siding with Russian farmers who complained that (Chechen) merchants paid them too little. Putin wanted to "categorically protect the priorities and interests of Russia's indigenous (korennoi) population both in the labour market and in trade." The Kremlin had long allowed aggressive Russian nationalism to rule the media. Here Putin himself came out as a Russian nationalist.

Putin also advocated more regulation. When a farmer complained about poor market access, he suggested further restrictions on the already heavily regulated kolkhoz markets. Traders should not be allowed "to sell processed goods such as smoked salamis" or "clothes brought in from China." For the first time since the battle against "unearned incomes" in 1986, a Russian leader raged against the sale of the "wrong products" in the collective-farm markets.

The president displayed a similar fondness for price regulation. He condemned "unprincipled manufacturers" who raised prices because of shortages. This was Soviet orthodoxy, the classic Marxist labor theory of value in the first chapter of Karl Marx's Das Kapital (1867/1981). Putin also called the disparity in prices between agricultural and industrial products the "most serious problem today," repeating, unwittingly or not, the Bolshevik argument about the "scissors' crisis" for collectivization that brought an abrupt end to the happy New Economic Policy in the 1920s (Nove 1969).

Putin's most dramatic turnaround concerned the WTO. In his annual address on May 10, 2006, Putin (2006a) had advocated accession to the

WTO because of the need for "more rational participation in the international division of labor" to make "full use of the benefits offered by integration into the world economy." This time, he omitted the WTO but proposed measures contradicting the organization's rules: increased subsidies for animal husbandry, higher customs duties for automobile production, and higher export tariffs for lumber. He proposed industrial policy, import substitution, and state subsidies for priority industries.

The only Soviet economic tenet missing was nationalization of the means of production, which was already well advanced. Not with a single word did Putin reassure private investors. A retired St. Petersburg actress complained about the condition of her retirement home, which a major company wanted to take over. Putin readily named that corporation, Sistema (owned by Kremlin-friendly billionaire Vladimir Yevtushenkov), and called on it to provide $5 million in financing to solve the pensioners' housing problem. "For this company this would represent a minimal amount of money," he said. This little show was designed to demonstrate Putin's concern for the elderly. What it revealed, instead, was his disrespect for private property rights.

To judge by his words, Putin reverted to the Brezhnev tradition, which had led to the Soviet economic collapse. Yet, as we have seen Putin tends to say the opposite of what he is intent on doing. The two tenets of Russia's economic policy appear to remain macroeconomic stability and 7 percent annual economic growth. The easier it is to achieve these two targets, the more leeway Russia's government has in its economic policy. If the price of oil were to fall precipitously, the regime would likely improve its economic policy, rendering the oil price the main determinant of Russia's economic policy.

Corruption: Rationalized but Pervasive

Throughout Russia's transition, corruption has been a major theme. Corruption is defined as "the misuse of public power for private gain" (Rose-Ackerman 1999, 91). It means the malfunctioning of the state, with politicians and civil servants selling public goods for private benefit rather than working for the goals of society. In the last decade, empirical studies have generated substantial empirical information, allowing us to assess how corruption has evolved in Russia.[15]

---

15. Transparency International was the pioneer, initiating its Corruption Perceptions Index in 1996 (Transparency International 2007). The most authoritative and specific studies have been the surveys by EBRD and World Bank (2002, 2005)—Business Environment and Enterprise Performance Surveys (BEEPS)—but they were done only for three years, 1999, 2002, and 2005. A third major source is the Russian INDEM Foundation run by Yeltsin's former political advisor Georgy Satarov (e.g., INDEM 2001). INDEM is best at establishing actual payment habits, but its aggregate numbers are too high to appear credible.

During the collapse of communism, corruption presumably exploded in parallel with crime. The Soviet Union had a strong tradition of corruption (Zemtsov 1976, Simis 1982). When the threat of the communist police and party state disappeared, the potential benefits of corruption greatly increased. Most corrupt practices involved in rent seeking were not even illegal. No conflict of interest rules existed, and during the final throes of the Soviet Union ministers boasted about owning enterprises to show how progressive they were. This tradition of ministers owning and running enterprises persists.

At the beginning of the transition, corruption attracted surprisingly little public attention, but the interest has increased sharply. Andrei Shleifer and Robert Vishny (1993) published a seminal article on corruption in Russia, comparing it with Africa: people paid bribes but they did not receive the requested services. Corruption was bad, but unreliable and anarchic corruption was worse. Moscow Mayor Gavriil Popov, a leading democrat at the end of communism, even proposed that public officials be allowed to charge a commission for their services since they did so in any case.

Extortion was exceedingly cumbersome because the bureaucrats did not know what to charge. They haggled forever, costing time and discomfort and often failing to conclude an agreement (Kaufmann 1997). The popular view arose that since all politicians were corrupt, it was better if the leaders remained the same, because new hungry office holders would demand more bribes. Yet, few Russian leaders ever seem to become satisfied.

Over the years, the Russian government has instituted many measures to regulate, control, and outlaw corruption. The early deregulation reduced officials' right to sell permits and licenses. Privatization took a major source of corrupt revenues out of their hands (Kaufmann and Siegelbaum 1996). Stabilization helped to cleanse the financial system. Cutting off enterprise subsidies reduced discretionary deals. Various forms of corruption have been outlawed. Since the mid-1990s, candidates for political offices have been forced to make public their incomes and fortunes, although their declared wealth has often been ludicrously small, and Russian officials talk freely about their foreign bank accounts. One proposal was that public officials would have to reveal the wealth of family members as well, but Moscow Mayor Luzhkov (with a billionaire wife) famously claimed that such a requirement would violate human rights. Transparency remains pitiful.

Fiscal reforms undertaken by Ministers of Finance Kasyanov and Kudrin in the wake of the financial crash of 1998 have probably been most effective in limiting corruption. These measures were designed to increase transparency, simplify the tax system, minimize discretion, eliminate competitive tax collection, but also to centralize the financial system. The elimination of offsets and barter was a fundamental breakthrough, because businessmen and officials could no longer make corrupt, discretionary deals about tax rebates. Another huge step forward was the tax reform, especially the introduction of the flat personal income tax of 13 percent that made it possible to be an honest taxpayer. Competitive tax collection was eliminated when the tax police were abolished and extrabudgetary funds were prohibited from collecting taxes (Åslund 2004).

A major problem was so-called unfinanced mandates, that is, government agencies were obliged to carry out certain tasks but did not receive state financing to do so. The agencies' standard solution was to invent new revenue sources, typically fees and penalties, which were extracted through cumbersome inspections. Naturally, inspectors put some of the poorly regulated revenues into their own pockets. The tax reforms prohibited most such inefficient nuisance taxes. Simultaneous budget reforms attempted to centralize additional revenues and provide full financing for required expenditures. Although not everything succeeded, the change was huge (Åslund 2004).

The overhaul of registration, licensing, and inspections in 2001–02 changed the business environment in Russia profoundly (see chapter 6). It primarily benefited small and medium-sized businesses. Millions of individual entrepreneurs had been shielded by simplified taxation all along, often in the form of lump-sum taxes that protected them from extortion by officials. Moreover, corruption tends to fall with rising incomes and expanding foreign trade (Treisman 2000).

All of these reforms had four positive effects. First, the average "bribe tax," that is, the percentage of annual revenue a firm pays in bribes, declined from 1.4 percent in 2002 to 1.1 percent in 2005 in Russia, according to the EBRD and World Bank Business Environment and Enterprise Performance Surveys (EBRD and World Bank 2002, 2005).

Second, corruption was rationalized. The frequency of bribery declined, prices were standardized, and people received what they paid for.

Third, nuisance extortion in taxation, customs, business licensing, and all kinds of inspections declined, although corruption increased in courts and government procurement.

Fourth, businessmen saw corruption as an increasing problem (Anderson and Gray 2006, 8). Yet, corruption has become standardized and more rational. Low-level officials are often asked to deliver a specified share of their booty to higher officials, rendering corruption more pervasive and lucrative.

These observations suggest that Russia is "just as corrupt as one would expect it to be, given the prominence of natural resources in its exports" (Fish 2005, 130; see also Treisman 2000, Shleifer and Treisman 2004). Russia's corruption is normal for a post-Soviet country, and it has always been less than in Central Asia and the Caucasus.

Especially, top-level corruption seems to be getting worse. During a trip to Moscow in September 2004, I was struck to hear from several senior Russians in private conversations: "I thought that corruption could never get as bad as it was under Yeltsin, but now it is far worse." The bribe frequency in Russia was the third highest among all postcommunist countries, and Russian businessmen reported that corruption increased significantly as a problem for business from 2002 to 2005, while the dominant postcommunist tendency was improvement (Anderson and Gray 2006, 8, 11).

It is hardly an exaggeration to say that everything is for sale in Russia. People pay bribes to enter university, to escape military service, to stay out of prison, and to land a good job. Until the late 1990s, the selling of top offices was not an issue, but then it took off, and by 2004 it had become endemic. One former senior official who had been fishing for a high appointment was told by friends in the administration that he could not possibly hope for any senior job since he was not ready to pay.

A senior Russian politician told me that one of the worst struggles in the Kremlin over Putin's appointment of governors was which top official in the presidential administration would be allowed to sell these offices. Transparency International in Russia found that deputy ministerial posts were sold for $8 million to $10 million.[16] Gubernatorial and ministerial posts must have been traded for multiples of this amount. In table 7.3, I have compiled some newspaper citations of prices, but they appear low.

Russian business is divided into four different administrative categories depending on which level of the state they need to deal with. Oligarchs deal directly with the Kremlin, that is, the federal administration. Businesses of regional importance do their business with regional governors, and enterprises of up to 250 employees only with mayors. Individual entrepreneurs without employees are free from the administrative yoke.

The lower down on the administrative ladder, the happier businessmen seem to be, and big businessmen are no longer anxious to become oligarchs. In September 2004, I heard one oligarch being quoted: "Nowadays, you do not really feel that you own anything but just have your money at your disposal for a limited time." The oligarchs were being forced to pay billions of dollars in extortion to the Kremlin that year, and they were increasingly afraid of saying that. With the centralization of power, corruption was centralized as well.

Although often complaining about corruption in public, Putin has allowed his own administration to become pervasively corrupt. Not a single member of his inner circle of KGB people from St. Petersburg, which is sometimes called the "Politburo," has ever been demoted, and even less prosecuted for corruption. Their legal immunity is complete. Top-level corruption has become extraordinary, and the lifestyle of the top officials hardly differs from that of the oligarchs.

The best documented case is Minister of Communications Leonid Reiman, a close friend of Putin from foreign intelligence in St. Petersburg.

---

16. Statement by Elena Panfilova, Transparency International, Russia, at the World Economic Forum Russia Summit in Moscow in October 2005.

Table 7.3   Prices of corruption in Russia, 2004–06

Good for sale	Going price	Source
Minister's post	$10 million	Mereu (2006)
Governor's post	$8 million	Mereu (2006)
Parliamentary seat	$2 million	Mereu (2006)
Senate seat	$1.5 million to $5 million	Belkovsky (2006)
Job in customs	$1 million	Mereu (2006)
Release in a criminal investigation, GUUR (Main Department of Criminal Investigation)	$100,000 to $150,000	"Main Graft" (2004)
Initiating or terminating a case, GUBNP (Main Department for the Combating of Tax Crimes)	$30,000 to $100,000	"Main Graft" (2004)
Admission to most prestigious universities	$30,000 to $40,000	Lee Myers (2005)
Terminating a case, GUBEP (Main Department for the Combating of Economic Crimes)	$25,000	"Main Graft" (2004)
Avoiding service in the military	$1,500 to $5,000	Lee Myers (2005)

In May 2006, Reiman lost a civil case in Zurich, Switzerland. The court established that Reiman had committed major crimes in Russia, that he owned large chunks of Russia's telecommunications that he oversaw as minister, and that he created a vast international money-laundering scheme to conceal his diversion of state assets.[17] The news was suppressed in Russian media and Reiman remains on his post. In 2007, his apparent assets were assessed at $5.9 billion, when Reiman capitalized his booty by selling it to a friendly oligarch.[18]

The overall evolution of corruption in Russia in the last decade is captured by a comparison of its Corruption Perception Index, empirically established by the independent and authoritative Transparency International (2007), with that of Ukraine (figure 7.6). Both countries are quite corrupt, but after a significant improvement in Russia from 2000 to 2004, its corruption has grown worse. Ukraine, by contrast, has become less cor-

---

17. Gregory L. White, David Crawford, and Glenn R. Simpson, "Why Putin's Telecom Minister is in Investigators' Sights Abroad; German and Swiss Probes Tag Leonid Reiman as Owner of Businesses He Oversees; Commerzbanks's Unusual Role," *Wall Street Journal*, October 17, 2006.

18. Neil Buckley, "Russian Phone Feud Is Settled," *Financial Times*, July 30, 2007.

Figure 7.6 Corruption Perceptions Index in Russia and Ukraine, 2000–2006

index (from highly clean = 10 to highly corrupt = 0)

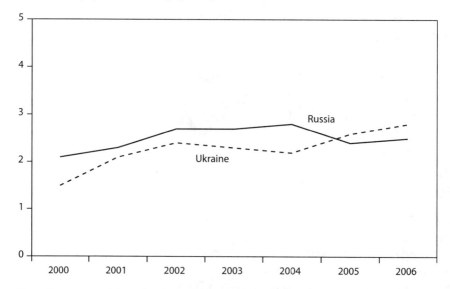

Source: Transparency International, www.transparency.org (accessed on May 30, 2007).

rupt than Russia after the Orange Revolution in 2004. The difference is that the Ukrainian media expose corruption and Ukrainian senior officials cannot be sure that they are exempt from punishment.

Colored Revolutions

All along, Putin expressed nostalgia about the Soviet Union. In *First Person* Putin (2000, 81) stated: "We would have avoided a lot of problems if the Soviet had not made such a hasty exit from Eastern Europe." He even expressed sympathy with the putschists in August 1991: "In principle, their goal—preserving the Soviet Union from collapse was noble . . ." (Putin 2000, 93). In his annual address in April 2005 Putin (2005) went all out: "the collapse of the Soviet Union was the biggest geopolitical disaster of the century. . . . Tens of millions of our co-citizens and compatriots found themselves outside Russian territory . . . old ideals [were] destroyed." Putin had declared himself a neoimperialist.

In his first term, Putin's policy toward the Commonwealth of Independent States (CIS) countries was passive. After September 11, 2001, he accepted that the United States established substantial air bases in Uzbekistan and Kyrgyzstan for the war in Afghanistan. In his second term,

Russia's policy toward the CIS was dominated by the so-called colored revolutions in Georgia, Ukraine, and Kyrgyzstan, and by gas trade.

Gorbachev's old Soviet Minister for Foreign Affairs Eduard Shevardnadze had returned to Georgia in 1993 and was elected president. Although Shevardnadze had muted Georgia's antagonistic relations with Russia, the Russian foreign policy elite disliked both him and Georgia. The Georgians had originally welcomed Shevardnadze, but they increasingly reacted against the corruption of his close relatives. In November 2003, Georgia held parliamentary elections, which Shevardnadze's party won through falsification, prompting mass protests. When a crowd attempted to overthrow Shevardnadze, his US-trained presidential guard refused to defend him, and he was forced to resign. The charismatic revolutionary leader Mikheil Saakashvili won a landslide electoral victory in a hastily scheduled presidential vote in January 2004. Russia did not mind Shevardnadze's demise and Minister for Foreign Affairs Igor Ivanov even mediated his resignation, but the popular Georgian Rose Revolution was the antithesis of Putin's managed democracy.

Ukraine was facing a similar situation to Georgia's in the fall of 2004. President Leonid Kuchma had reached his term limit, and his once-solid popularity had evaporated after sordid scandals. His regime was reminiscent of Yeltsin's—oligarchic and semidemocratic. A mixed opposition had almost won parliamentary elections in March 2002. Under the leadership of Viktor Yushchenko, the opposition was strong and well organized, and it enjoyed substantial support from the business community, while the oligarchs supported Kuchma.

Putin was intensely engaged in stopping a victory of the West-oriented and democratic opposition in Ukraine. One attempt was the Common Economic Space with Russia, Ukraine, Kazakhstan, and Belarus that Putin launched in February 2003. It was designed to keep Ukraine in Russia's orbit. Putin plunged deeply into Ukrainian politics, which he handled himself. He met President Kuchma once a month in 2004, and granted Ukraine substantial trade benefits.

Kuchma proposed Prime Minister Viktor Yanukovych from the largest Ukrainian oligarchic group as his successor. Putin agreed to support him and promised Russian enterprise financing of no less than $300 million for his campaign.[19] Russian TV, widely viewed in Ukraine, praised Yanukovych and slandered Yushchenko. Dozens of Russian political advisors, well paid by the Kremlin, descended on Ukraine to promote Yanukovych. Early in the campaign, Yushchenko was severely poisoned by an uncommon substance that probably originated in Russia. In the last month before the elections, Putin went to Ukraine twice to campaign for Yanukovych.

---

19. Personal information from the Yushchenko campaign in September 2004.

After the Yanukovych camp blatantly falsified the results of the second round of the elections, up to one million Yushchenko supporters poured into the streets of Kiev and the Orange Revolution was a reality. After mainly European mediation between Yanukovych and Yushchenko, they peacefully agreed to hold a third, fair round, which Yushchenko won (Åslund and McFaul 2006, Wilson 2006).

Putin's intrusive actions in Ukraine made him appear poorly informed, antidemocratic, anti-Western, and ineffective. In one stroke, he managed to unite the United States and the European Union, badly split over the war in Iraq, against himself. Putin seemed primarily worried about Ukraine as a democratic model for Russia. However intrusive Putin's policy was in Ukraine, its aim was domestic policy and it did not qualify as neoimperialist. When Yanukovych became prime minister in 2006, Putin lost interest in Ukraine.

The situation in Kyrgyzstan was reminiscent of Georgia and Ukraine. President Askar Akaev was approaching his term limit in October 2005, and his great popularity was slipping because of his family's conspicuous corruption. Like Georgia and Ukraine, Kyrgyzstan was semidemocratic and quite an open society. It had a strong, organized opposition with prominent leaders and some free opposition media. In March 2005, after a botched parliamentary election, the regime was overthrown. The unrest started in the south and moved to the capital Bishkek in the north. The presidential administration was stormed by a limited crowd and the Akaev family fled to Moscow. The Kremlin did not seem to mind and established somewhat closer relations with the newly-elected President Kurmanbek Bakiev than it had with Akaev.

In May 2006, a sudden armed uprising broke out in the Uzbek city of Andijan in the fertile but overpopulated Fergana Valley. Uzbekistan's President Islam Karimov sent in troops that killed a few hundred people, which stopped the uprising. Putin showed his appreciation of Karimov's resolute massacre, condemning the Andijan uprising as a terrorist act. The colored revolutions were over.

McFaul (2006, 166) has summarized the crucial conditions for the three colored revolutions: (1) a semiautocratic regime; (2) an unpopular leader of the *ancien régime*; (3) a strong and well-organized opposition; (4) an ability to create the perception quickly that election results were falsified; (5) enough independent media to inform citizens about the falsified vote; (6) a political opposition capable of setting in motion tens of thousands of demonstrators to protest electoral fraud; and (7) a division between intelligence forces, military, and the police. In addition, external actors can facilitate the development of many of these domestic factors.

The Kremlin appears to have drawn the conclusion that all these factors had to be dismantled in Russia, and Putin transformed Russia from a semiautocratic into a regular authoritarian regime.

Apart from the colored revolutions, Gazprom's interests dominated Russia's policy in the former Soviet space. Gazprom had two ambitions: to secure its monopoly over transportation and sales and to boost its export prices. It expanded its ownership and control over gas pipelines and sales of Central Asian gas to Europe, averting Western ideas of a new transcaspian gas pipeline to Europe. Often it extracted ownership in debt-equity swaps from countries, such as Moldova and Belarus, which had run up large arrears for gas deliveries.

The biggest strife concerned Gazprom's new ambition to extract full market prices also from CIS countries. Because of corrupt trading schemes and neoimperialist sentiments, Gazprom had charged as little as one-quarter to one-fifth of the European price, and Ukraine and Moldova refused to accept stark price hikes. In early January 2006, Gazprom's Chairman and Russia's First Deputy Prime Minister Dmitri Medvedev was shown on Russian television turning off the gas tap to both countries in a macho display. But 80 percent of Gazprom's exports to the European Union passed through Ukraine. Not only the Orange Ukrainian government but also the European Union and the United States protested. A reasonable deal for Ukraine was settled within days, and the disruption lasted only two days. Moldova, however, was no transit country, and it received no gas for 16 days, after which it was forced to accept Gazprom's ultimatum.

In January 2007, Belarus, the Kremlin's closest ally, suffered the same treatment as Ukraine one year earlier. With 20 percent of Russia's gas deliveries to the EU going through Belarus, EU leaders protested loudly against delivery disruptions, and Belarus got away with a mere doubling of the gas price. Yet, by 2007, Gazprom had largely achieved its aim of market-oriented prices, which greatly boosted its profitability and stock price.

An untidy, unfinished business from the collapse of the Soviet Union was the so-called frozen conflicts: unregulated, separatist territories outside the control of the national government. The Moldovan province of Transnistria refuses to recognize the Moldovan government, and the Georgian territories of Abkhazia and South Ossetia demand independence from the Georgian government. The leaderships in these three territories are pro-Russian, and the Kremlin supports them with troops, but it has stopped short of recognizing their independence.

The Moldovan and Georgian governments want to restore their national integrity, whereas Moscow seems to enjoy the complication. In 2006, these conflicts escalated, and Russia suddenly embargoed Georgia's and Moldova's large exports of wine and fruits to Russia. It also blocked most transportation to and from Georgia and even bank transactions. Georgia played hardball, revoking its bilateral protocol on Russia's accession to the WTO, thus blocking Russia's entry into that organization, of which Georgia was already a member.

As Putin's second term is nearing its end, Russia's policy in the former Soviet space is strikingly ineffective. Russia has cut lingering subsidies to its poorer neighbors, which are trying to reach out to reduce their dependence on Russia because it no longer offers any benefits and has proven highly unreliable through many sudden disruptions of Russian gas deliveries and embargoes on successful exports. No Russian free trade initiative can work without a mechanism for conflict resolution.

In sum, Russia has failed to develop good relations with its neighbors, but the Kremlin does not seem to care. If you visit a Russian embassy in a CIS country, you find no Russian diplomat who speaks the local language. The problem with Russia's policy in the former Soviet space is less neoimperialism than disinterest and disrespect.

A New Distance from the West

Like Gorbachev and Yeltsin, Putin has been anxious to be accepted by the leaders of the big, wealthy Western countries. His interest has been primarily ceremonial. The two most important international events during his tenure have been the celebration of St. Petersburg's tercentenary in 2003 and the G-8 meeting in St. Petersburg in July 2006. On neither occasion was any significant decision made. Putin wanted to demonstrate Russia's return as a great power and his own international standing.

Gradually, Russia has drifted away from the United States and the European Union, and Western influence over Russia has waned. In 2004, Putin turned outright hostile to the West. After the Beslan massacre, Putin made a vague but ominous statement about hostile forces, implicitly referring to the United States as wanting "to tear from us a 'juicy piece of pie' " (Putin 2004c).

The Orange Revolution provided the tipping point. Russia's policy united the United States and the European Union against Russia, which accused the West of subversion in Ukraine. It was followed by Western protests over the restrictive Russian draft law on nongovernmental organizations in the fall of 2005, and Gazprom's disruption of gas deliveries to Europe through Ukraine in January 2006. Official Russian spokesmen blame the enlargement of NATO to the Baltic states and the US failure to eliminate the Jackson-Vanik amendment's potential (but implausible) threat of trade sanctions. In 2007, Putin escalated his rhetoric after the US revealed plans to establish antimissile bases in Poland and the Czech Republic. Putin threatened to target European capitals with nuclear missiles and to withdraw from two arms control treaties, CFE and INF.

Putin's underlying worry was that the West would instigate an Orange Revolution in Russia. The *siloviki* around Putin dislike the West, and increasingly Putin has let them take over. Their idea is that Russia is strong enough on its own. Judging from his public statements, Putin is caught in "growth Darwinism," contemptuous of the slowly growing West, while enchanted with the dynamic (and authoritarian) China. Meeting with prominent international journalists before the G-8 meeting in Heiligendamm in Germany in June 2007, Putin clarified his international outlook:

> DER SPIEGEL: Mr. President, former Federal Chancellor Gerhard Schroeder called you a "pure democrat." Do you consider yourself such?
>
> VLADIMIR PUTIN: (laughs) Am I a "pure democrat"? Of course I am, absolutely. . . . The problem is that I'm all alone, the only one of my kind in the whole wide world. Just look at what's happening in North America, it's simply awful: torture, homeless people, Guantanamo, people detained without trial and investigation. Just look at what's happening in Europe: harsh treatment of demonstrators, rubber bullets and tear gas used first in one capital then in another, demonstrators killed on the streets. That's not even to mention the post-Soviet area. Only the guys in Ukraine still gave hope, but they've completely discredited themselves now and things are moving towards total tyranny there; complete violation of the Constitution and the law and so on. There is no one to talk to since Mahatma Gandhi died. (Putin 2007d)

No doubt this sarcastic tirade went down well with the Russian populist electorate, but it begs the question: About what does it make sense to talk to Putin?

US President George W. Bush, however, has not wavered in his confidence in Putin. On July 1–2, 2007, Bush honored Putin by inviting him to his father's summer house in Kennebunkport, Maine. At the ensuing press conference, Bush revealed: "But one thing I've found about Vladimir Putin is that he is consistent, transparent, honest and is an easy man to discuss our opportunities and problems with . . . . I know he's always telling me the truth."[20] As this book hopefully has shown, this statement was not quite true.

Putin has successfully divided the European Union for years. In 2004, when Poland and the three Baltic states became members of the EU, Moscow scolded them as "the new aggressive minority." Russia undertook sanctions against them, invoking alleged sanitary or environmental concerns. It prohibited meat imports from Poland and fish imports from Latvia, while refusing to deliver oil by pipeline to Lithuania. In early May 2007, Estonia was subject to a cyber war attack, which took out its e-banking and e-government, for moving a Soviet war memorial.

Meanwhile, Putin has nurtured his friendship with Schröder, Chirac, and Berlusconi, and the southern wing of the European Union—France, Italy, Spain, and Greece—has supported Russia against Poland and the Balts. As a result, the EU has neither a Russia policy nor an energy policy, although it accounts for over half of Russia's foreign trade and most of its gas and oil exports.

---

20. "President Bush Meets with President Putin of Russian Federation," White House press release, July 2, 2007, available at www.whitehouse.gov (accessed on July 13, 2007).

Controversially, Schröder obtained the lucrative post as chairman of a Russian-German consortium for North Stream, a gas pipeline from Russia to Germany through the Baltic Sea immediately after he was voted out as German Chancellor in the fall of 2005. In his last days as Chancellor, he gave German approval to that pipeline.

Poland forced a harder EU position in November 2006, by vetoing an EU negotiation mandate on a broad agreement with Russia because of Russia's refusal to allow meat imports from Poland. In May 2007, at the EU-Russia summit in the Russian city of Samara, Estonia and Lithuania added their support, and President of the European Commission José Manuel Barroso stated a newly found EU unity:

> The question of Polish meat is a difficult one for us. We had the opportunity to tell our Russian partners that difficulties for an EU member amount to difficulties for the entire EU. The European Union is based on the principle of solidarity. We now have 27 members. And Poland's problem is a pan-European problem. Just as Lithuanian or Estonian problems are problems for all of Europe.[21]

Under Putin, Russia's attitude toward the United States, the European Union, and the CIS countries has become tougher. However, the main goal of his foreign policy appears to be domestic image making: to show Russia's new strength and Putin's standing as an international leader. Russia's foremost international interest is that of Gazprom, and protectionist agricultural lobbies have been given a free rein. Senior Russian politicians habitually make unsubstantiated threats against other countries, but they are fortunately more aggressive than their follow-up. Sometimes vicious embargoes are suddenly being imposed, yet Russia is not reforming its military and only minor military provocations are attempted. Russian politicians can afford these jokes, because their country does not face any evident external threat and its exports enjoy ample market access.

Does Russia Suffer from an Energy Curse?

Russia's energy curse is evident, but in politics and structural policies rather than macroeconomic policy. In the 1970s, Brezhnev did not undertake any reforms because they did not appear necessary due to the USSR's abundant fortunes during the energy crisis. Although Russia today has a market economy, a similar vicious circle is apparent. The more the resource wealth is worth, the more latitude the president is afforded. Mistakes pass without correction, and ever worse malpractices are permitted.

Energy plays an enormous role in the Russian economy. According to Russia's official statistics, its contribution to GDP was only 9 percent even in 2006 (Goskomstat 2006, Deutsche Bank 2007). The national accounts, however, understate the importance of energy in Russia's GDP because of

---

21. Samara, May 18, 2007, www.kremlin.ru (accessed on July 13, 2007).

low domestic energy prices, especially for gas. Assuming normal market prices of energy in Russia, energy would have contributed almost 20 percent of GDP in 2006 (World Bank 2004). In 2006, energy accounted for 63 percent of Russia's exports and about 50 percent of its tax revenues. Gaddy and Ickes (2005, 562) found a strong positive correlation between oil and gas rents and GDP. The energy rents peaked at over 40 percent of GDP in 1981, while they were very low throughout the 1990s, when Russia reformed. They took off again from 2003, and Russia stopped reforming.

Is oil good or bad for Russia's economic development? In an important paper with multicountry regressions, Sachs and Warner (1996) found that countries that enjoyed an abundance of natural resources (measured as a share of their exports) had less long-term economic growth than countries with less natural resources. The question is why? Three categories of possible effects are: macroeconomic, structural economic, and political.

Macroeconomically, large resource exports influence the exchange rate and thus the wage level in dollars. Oomes and Kalcheva (2007) found that an increase in the Urals oil price of 1 percent led to a 0.5 percent appreciation of the real effective exchange rate. Russia's dollar wage increased an average of 30 percent a year from 1999 to 2006, boosted by large energy exports. Yet, given Russia's splendid economic performance, these effects do not appear to have had major negative repercussions.

Considering that Russia's GDP is increasing by almost 7 percent a year, while energy production has increased by 1 to 2 percent a year since 2005, the country's economy is swiftly diversifying. The service sector is expanding at the cost of industry, as it should. With Russia's comparative advantage in energy and metals production, manufacturing is inevitably impeded out. Why produce machinery in Russia rather than in Ukraine, when similar production facilities are available in both countries and Ukrainian wages are half as high?

Resources easily tempt governments to undermine their macroeconomic policies, but so far the crash of 1998 has kept the Russian government immune to this temptation as is evident from large budget surpluses, substantial international reserves, and a sizable stabilization fund (figures 6.2 and 6.6). Even if the Ministry of Finance is under pressure to spend more money, its resistance has been effective.

Still, Russia suffers from an energy curse in its structural policies. First, the renationalization wave began in 2003, when the international oil price was taking off (figure 6.4). State officials were overwhelmed by the temptation to seize oil companies because the high oil prices rendered production and cost control—that is, management skills—pretty irrelevant. It has been argued that the energy curse is a curse of state ownership, but Russia under Putin shows how the energy curse leads to state ownership (Tompson 2005, 355).

Second, Putin ended his economic reforms when Russia could achieve an annual growth of 7 percent without bothering with additional reforms.

If the oil price were to fall, by contrast, the government would probably pursue reforms again to maintain the 7 percent annual growth target.

Third, corruption, which declined during Putin's first years of structural reforms, started rising with the renationalization drive after 2004 (figure 7.6). State officials could not resist the temptation to transfer oil and gas wealth to themselves.

Fourth, Russia has become overly dependent on the taxation of oil. The marginal tax rate on oil production is no less than 88 percent (Gaddy and Ickes 2005, 564). A fall in oil prices would hurt Russia's state finances; the high oil taxes deter oil companies from investment in production and development; and the government pays little attention to other sectors of the economy, since it is financed by oil taxes.

The most important energy curse, however, is political. The resource wealth has greatly facilitated Putin's efforts to make Russia authoritarian. He does not need to ask the population for financing but can scare up two scores of immensely wealthy oligarchs. That is a reason for him to allow such a concentration of wealth. Acemoglu (2003) pointed out that oligarchies block entry but keep taxation down, which is Russia's current situation.

The question is how far economic policy can deteriorate. It can be halted by bottlenecks, falling output, and eventually by falling energy prices. It was not by chance that Russia undertook all its heroic reforms in the 1990s when the world oil price was so low (Gaddy and Ickes 2005, Gaidar 2006).

Putin's Model: Back to Nicholas I

The fundamental question is: What kind of Russia has Putin created? In his annual address in 2007, Putin (2007b) attempted an answer. First, he claimed to "achieve real democratisation of the electoral system . . . the proportional system gives the opposition greater opportunities to expand its representation in the legislative assemblies. . . . I am certain that the new election rules will not only strengthen the role of political parties in forming the democratic system of power, but will also encourage greater competition between the different parties." Yet, Putin has systematically eliminated democratic electoral competition.

Second, he said: "Decentralisation of state power in Russia is now at a higher point today than at any other time in our country's history." Yet, Russia is far more centralized under Putin than it was under Yeltsin.

Third, Putin stated that the "rapid expansion of our national information and media space is also having a beneficial effect on the development of democratic institutions and procedures." But he has suppressed the freedom of all major media.

Fourth, "it is impossible to imagine the democratic political process without the participation of non-governmental organisations, without taking into account their views and opinions. . . . This exchange of views, this dialogue with the NGO's, is developing consistently today" (Putin 2007b). Yet, Putin has stifled independent organizations with arbitrary regulations.

For eight years, Putin has talked about the reinforcement of democracy, and even after having abolished every bit of it, he cannot stop talking about his democratic ambitions. Apparently, Putin uses public statements as disinformation. He has restored the Soviet tradition of "newspeak," calling everything its opposite, as George Orwell (1949) described in his novel *1984*.

To understand what is happening in Putin's Russia, we must not believe Putin's public or private statements, but examine his actual policy. After eight years of Putin, it is evident that his main endeavor has been to dismantle all democratic institutions and build an authoritarian system. His vindictiveness has been extraordinary, which is untypical of Russians. If somebody crosses him once, Putin seems determined to annihilate him. Few politicians show fury and contempt so often and so publicly.

First, Putin strangled major media. Putin can still manipulate the population through television, although the political reporting of the two central state channels, ORT and Rossia, is perfectly Soviet. The strength of the Putin regime lies in its skill to manipulate the elite, the media, and civil society, but if this propaganda deviates too much from reality for too long, it will eventually lose credibility.

Putin's second step was to rein in the regional governors. He appointed presidential representatives to supervise them and enforce federal legislation. He deprived the governors of their seats in the Federation Council. As its members were appointed, the upper chamber lost significance. Next, Putin abolished gubernatorial elections, appointing all governors himself. Russia's traditional centralization of power has been restored.

Third, he stifled the political influence of the oligarchs through the long and tortuous Yukos affair. If not even the property rights of Russia's richest man were safe, all property rights were unsafe. Not only individual oligarchs but also their organizations, such as the Russian Union of Industrialists and Entrepreneurs, lost out.

Fourth, while Putin appeared to improve Russia's courts through judicial reform, he subordinated the judges to the presidential administration rather than to regional governors.

Fifth, the Duma elections have lost all democratic content. A wide range of means have been used—refusal to register parties, the disqualification of candidates, illegal harassment, temporary arrests, and prohibition against public meetings. Each measure in itself might not appear too arduous, but taken together they are overwhelming (Fedorov 2004, Fish 2005). As a consequence, both liberals and communists have been marginalized.

A sixth step was to transfer power from the Council of Ministers to the presidential administration. The two most important measures came in early 2004: the appointment of the weak Fradkov as prime minister, and the government restructuring that minimized its policymaking capacity.

All these profound institutional changes have gone in one direction. Putin has centralized power to the presidential administration and relied on FSB veterans to control the country. These secret policemen control much of the economy through the big state-owned corporations. Checks and balances have been minimized. Putin has deprived the formal institutions—the Federal Assembly, the Council of Ministers, and the regional governors—of any real power. As camouflage, he has set up informal advisory institutions, such as the State Council and the Public Chamber, which are of little or no consequence. As a result, Russia has suffered a far-reaching deinstitutionalization. Putin has concentrated power in his own hands, trying to micromanage everything. He and a handful of his closest aides in the Kremlin make far too many decisions about things that they know far too little about.

Paradoxically, Russia's economy is doing very well with a steady growth of 7 percent a year, and the standard of living is rising considerably faster. Thanks to the extensive market reforms in the 1990s and during Putin's first term, dominant private enterprises have driven growth, and the high oil prices have added impetus. No new reforms are in the offing, but the petrification of decision making has also safeguarded the survival of most reforms already adopted. Russia's market economy, solid macroeconomic stability, and focus on economic growth appear secure.

Putin is the master of good feelings. One of his outstanding political strengths is to reflect in himself everything that people want to see (Tregubova 2003). His main political achievement is that he has made Russians feel good about their country again. Gorbachev dug up all the tragedies in Soviet history and society. Yeltsin was perceived as drunk, corrupt, and just embarrassing. Putin is controlled and so is his media environment. Russia exudes strength and dynamism. In this scheme, foreign policy is not very important. Russia wants to be truly sovereign, and Putin plays with foreign policy as theater for the masses, providing amusement and projecting Russia's rising power, because Russia has no dangerous enemies. But nor does it have any real friends.

As Russia's political system and rulers change, so do its interests. Putin's KGB friends dominate the state administration and the big state enterprises, which badly need reform, but few reforms can occur contrary to the ruling interests. These hungry secret policemen accept few limits, least of all the private property of others. They take over one big enterprise after another. Sooner or later, the squeezing out of good enterprises by bad ones will be reflected in the growth rate. The threat is that inefficient state giants will gobble up efficient private corporations and promote old-style over-regulation and corruption.

In his excellent book on Russian conservatism, Richard Pipes (2005, 1) concluded: "The dominant strain in Russian political thought throughout history has been a conservatism that insisted on strong, centralized authority, unrestrained either by law or parliament." Along these lines, current First Deputy Prime Minister Sergei Ivanov (2006) published an article in *Izvestiya* in 2006. In a Soviet manner, Ivanov presented the world as a competition between different value systems. He drew on Count Sergei Uvarov's famous triad of "Orthodoxy, Autocracy, Nationality," which became the ideological foundation of Tsar Nicholas I (Pipes 2005, 100). He argued that the "new triad of Russian national values is sovereign democracy, strong economy, and military power."

Putin's new concept of "sovereign democracy" is no democracy but the autocracy in Uvarov's triad. Russia's new strong economy is for real, but state monopolies are on the offensive. The military, however, is weak, not least because Ivanov failed to reform it during his five years as minister of defense. Today's real triad is: "autocracy, secret police, and state monopolies," and it is difficult to see any spiritual value embedded in either that or Sergei Ivanov's triad.

This is a time of cynicism. No ideology or values are apparent. Putin pampers the Orthodox Church, but it remains a symbol and a privileged cast rather than a force. At one moment, Putin appeals to populism and nationalism, but in the next he criticizes nationalism and demonstrates ethnic tolerance.

The late Soviet comedian Arkady Raikin once said: "If it is better than in 1913 it is already good."[22] The Russian public agreed. One of the first private restaurants in St. Petersburg was named "1913." The period just before World War I is embellished in nostalgic Russian television advertisements. Putin seems to be returning Russia to this presumed ideal state. Fortunately, this is neither Soviet restoration nor fascism. Russia might need to return to the point where its development was so violently aborted. Yet, non-Russians would hardly regard the political system of the Russian Empire of 1913 as ideal or even viable. This reactionary project has been possible because Russians are tired of politics in their postrevolutionary stabilization. With its deinstitutionalization and dominant secret police, Putin's regime is more reminiscent of Tsar Nicholas I (1825–55) than Tsar Nicholas II (1894–1917). Neither regime ended well, and ill-fated wars were only one cause of their downfall.[23]

Russia has entered the 21st century professing the creed of long-gone tsars. Putin's Russia is marked by a profound contradiction between an obsolete, overcentralized, authoritarian state and a swiftly modernizing market economy. Politically, Putin has deprived Russia of all relevant institutions, which will leave him alone before the people in a severe crisis. This revival of the long-dead tsarism is a monstrosity of nostalgia.

---

22. Quoted in *Izvestiya*, October 12, 1986.

23. The Crimean War and World War I, respectively.

8

Conclusions: Why Market Reform Succeeded and Democracy Failed

As President Vladimir Putin's second term is drawing to a close, Russia is a market economy but no democracy. How did Russia end up in this situation, and how is it likely to develop?

Russia experienced a great revolution, which had many implications for its development. The revolution was carried out from above. It was formed by Russia's three consecutive leaders and their ideas. As shown in chapter 3, the empirical evidence suggests that early, radical, and comprehensive reforms worked best. Privatization was always controversial, and assessments have changed over time. At present, the respect for the resulting property rights seems crucial, which means that the political acceptance of privatization is key. Our investigation of Russia's policymaking in the last two decades leads to general conclusions on how policymaking is best done in the midst of a revolution. This is also a suitable occasion to review the role of the West in the Russian transformation.

Finally, we turn to Russia's future. Currently, the dominant picture is a contradiction between market economic success and reactionary politics. This disparity is widening with Russia's economic growth, and its politics are becoming increasingly authoritarian. This contradiction is not likely to last for long. Either authoritarianism or the free economy will have to give, and the obsolete political system is more likely to lose out.

Market Economy but No Democracy

The empirical evidence is strong: Russia has persistently grown less democratic since 1992, while it became a market economy after a couple of years of transition, with no significant reversal.

Figure 8.1 Civil and political rights in Russia and Ukraine, 1991–2006

index (from 1 = free to 7 = not free)

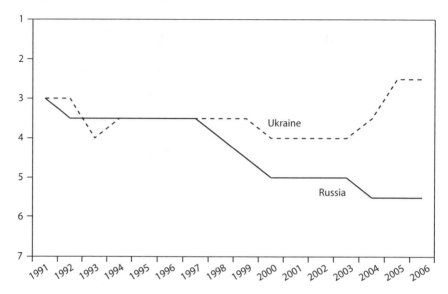

Source: Freedom House, *Freedom in the World Historical Rankings*, http://freedomhouse.org (accessed on May 28, 2007).

A country's degree of democracy, or civil and political rights, is authoritatively assessed by Freedom House (figure 8.1). It rated Russia as "partially free" from 1992 to 2003 and "not free" from 2004. Russia's political freedom has steadily deteriorated from 1992, when the country was close to free, to its present state of mild authoritarianism. Russia can be compared with Ukraine, which was similarly semidemocratic in the 1990s, but Ukraine did not suffer Russia's authoritarian degeneration in the late 1990s. Ukraine's freedom increased greatly after the Orange Revolution in late 2004.

The most relevant measure of a country's degree of market economy is the EBRD's transition index, ranking countries from no market economy (0) to normal Western market economy (1). From 1992 to 1995, Russia was an intermediary market economy, in the interval 0.5–0.7, and in 1996 it reached 0.7, the level of a full-fledged market economy. Figure 8.2 includes Poland for comparison. Its more far-reaching reforms are representative of Central Europe and the Baltics. Russia's rise was sufficiently sharp to qualify it among the countries that undertook "early, radical economic reform" from 1991 to 1993 (Åslund 2007a, 84–86).

The key feature of a market economy, according to the definition in the introduction, is that economic decisions are predominantly made by free

Figure 8.2   EBRD transition index, 1990–2006

index (0 = no market economy, 1 = free market economy)

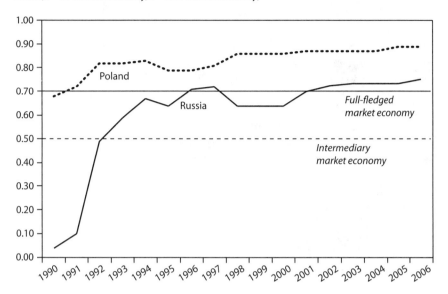

EBRD = European Bank for Reconstruction and Development

Notes: The formula of this index is 0.3 times EBRD's index for price liberalization and competition policy, 0.3 times EBRD's index for trade and foreign exchange liberalization, and 0.4 times EBRD's index for large-scale privatization, small-scale privatization, and banking reform. Thus this index represents liberalization to 73 percent, while the rest is privatization.

Sources: De Melo et al. (1997); Havrylyshyn and Wolf (2001); author's calculations from EBRD (1998, 1999, 2006).

individuals and independent firms. Russia's distribution is completely private and independent. No state planning committee tells enterprises what to produce. Nor does the state allocate goods. Prices and trade are predominantly free, and Russia's subsidies are small. Transactions are overwhelmingly monetized. All perceivable financial markets have evolved (Frye 2000).

The private sector is predominant, contributing 65 percent of GDP according to EBRD (2006) (figure 7.2). Russia has 5 million registered private enterprises (figure 6.9). Its stock market capitalization has reached $1 trillion, equaling its GDP, as is common in Western Europe. The World Bank and International Finance Corporation (2006) *Doing Business* index ranks Russia as 96th among 175 countries, that is, average. Russia receives its best rankings for enforcing contracts (25), starting a business (33), and registering property (44), which all concern property rights, while the regulatory environment is bad. Russian companies take the state and one another to court ever more often (Hendley 2002, 2004). Russia's negotiations on World

Trade Organization (WTO) accession clarify the problems. Subsidies have raised limited concerns, whereas regulations and intrusive state inspections are the dominant issues. The final proof of Russia's status as a market economy is that since 2004, the European Union and the United States recognize Russia as such according to exceedingly strict legal criteria.

Concerns about the oligarchs' domination of the Russian economy appear exaggerated. They do not own that large a share of the economy and they face severe market competition. Oligarchs dominate large-scale industry, primarily energy and metals, but in energy they are increasingly squeezed out by the state. Russia's industrial sector is still large by international standards, contributing 38 percent of GDP in 2005, compared with 27 percent of GDP in the euro area (World Bank 2007).[1] Currently, the state accounts for 85 percent of gas production and 55 percent of oil production. The approximately 30 oligarchic groups probably contribute about one-quarter of total GDP together. The biggest oligarchic sector is the steel industry with six major companies, and commercially more consolidation is needed. The production of a few metals—aluminum, nickel, and copper—is nearly monopolized, but these industries face strong international competition. Only in gas and aluminum are Russian corporations among the biggest in the world, and Gazprom is controlled by the state.

The threat of the state is greater, as the state is expanding its ownership through renationalization. Yet, many factors contain its expansion. The state tends to enter industries that are growing slowly, such as gas and oil, and state ownership depresses production growth further. Russia has no socialist ideology.

At present, Russia's big state corporations are moving from full state ownership toward 51 percent state ownership. Two major state companies—Rosneft and VTB—made initial public offerings (IPOs) in 2006 and 2007, respectively, to move in that direction. As a result, state-dominated corporations are exposing themselves to assessment by the stock market.

Although privatization has slowed down, it continues. Russia's power industry is being divided up and privatized. Some state forays into complicated industries, such as the automotive industry, are bound to result in spectacular failure and be reprivatized in the near future. Many officials want to transform their power into private fortunes, which they do through transactions, some of which are nationalizations, while others are privatizations.

Given that Russia's economic freedom holds firm, while its political freedom is declining, the disparity between them is rising. In 2004, Shleifer and Treisman (2004, 22) published a provocative article in *Foreign Affairs*, arguing that Russia was a "normal country":

---

1. Partly, Russia's large industry reflects insufficient market adjustment, and the industrial share in Russia's GDP should shrink further. Partly it shows Russia's comparative advantage in raw material–extracting industry.

> Russia was in 1990, and is today, a middle-income country with GDP per capita . . . comparable to Argentina in 1991 and Mexico in 1999. Almost all democracies in this income range are rough around the edges: their governments suffer from corruption, their judiciaries are politicized, and their press is almost never entirely free. They have high income inequality, concentrated corporate ownership, and turbulent macroeconomic performance. In all these regards, Russia is quite normal.

Their assessment rang true at the time, but the imbalance between economic and political freedom has grown worse over time, because of Russia's backsliding to authoritarianism. For the last decade, the world as a whole has become more democratic, while Russia's economic strength has grown substantially.

One excellent attempt to explain why Russia has failed to democratize is *Democracy Derailed in Russia* by Steven Fish (2005). On the basis of multicountry regression analysis, he singled out three causes: "too much oil, too little economic liberalization, and too weak a national legislature" (p. 247). First, Russia's abundance of raw materials has undermined democratization by fueling corruption and encouraging economic statism. Second, the "predatory regulatory environment has slowed the growth of an entrepreneurial class and the middle class more generally. . . . It has left society underorganized, inarticulate, and incapable of holding rulers accountable" (p. 248). Third, Fish argued that the imbalance between the presidential might and the limited powers of the legislature "damaged the legitimacy of the post-Soviet regime," "inhibited the development of political parties," and undermined state capacity (pp. 248–50). The unconstrained presidential power also stimulated corruption.

While Fish looked upon Russia in the aggregate, Kathryn Stoner-Weiss (2006) undertook an empirical study of why regional democratization failed in Russia. She found that the limitations of market reform impeded regional democratization, as local businessmen colluded with regional governors to thrive on corrupt revenues. Stunted party development weakened the linkage between the federal government and the regional governments (p. 112). With weak parties in the regions, clientelism evolved instead of institutions, and it encouraged corruption. Russia entered a vicious circle. Businessmen paid huge amounts to buy the elections of regional governors because they could benefit so much (p. 146).

Both Fish and Stoner-Weiss argue that authoritarianism benefits corruption, and therefore the beneficiaries of corruption favor authoritarianism. Apart from Fish's emphasis on the corrosive impact of oil, they do not offer any reason for Russia not becoming democratic in the longer term, if marketization and economic growth proceed.

Russia's Capitalist Revolution

The Soviet collapse and Russia's post-Soviet transformation from 1985 to 2007 become comprehensible only if we realize that this country went through a revolution. Revolutions have many peculiar features in common.

As early as 1984, Richard Pipes (1984, 50–51) considered the Soviet situation revolutionary, because the ruling elite could no longer rule, and the population did not accept to be ruled in the old way. In July 1986, Mikhail Gorbachev revealed that a revolution was under way: "I would equate the word perestroika with revolution."[2] Boris Yeltsin was intensely conscious of being part of a revolution and contemplated its logic at each step (Yeltsin 1994).

Since Russia experienced the Great Socialist Revolution in 1917, Russians were acutely aware of what revolutions were and how they functioned.[3] Major actors understood and used the revolutionary momentum, but sometimes they refused to accept revolutionary precedents. In particular, a broad consensus opposed the bloodshed and civil war of the 1917 revolution, which rendered Russia's capitalist revolution so peaceful.[4]

The literature on revolutions is immense. A major classic is Crane Brinton's (1938/1965) *The Anatomy of Revolution*. It analyzed four successful revolutions, the English revolution of the 1640s, the American revolution, the great French revolution, and the Russian revolution of 1917. Brinton established a chronology of revolutions: first stages, the rule of the moderates, the rise of the extremists, reigns of terror and virtue, and Thermidor (postrevolutionary stabilization). The literature on Russia's 1991 revolution is extensive.[5]

A schematic revolutionary paradigm frames the Russian development from 1985 to 2007 perfectly well. Mau and Starodubrovskaya (2001, 330–32) offer a stylized process of revolution, which guides the structure of this book. Gorbachev was the liberal reformer who inadvertently unleashed the revolution. Yeltsin was the revolutionary hero, who did not quite know what to do after the revolution, and Putin became the postrevolutionary dictator, a Napoleon or Stalin, who consolidated power in authoritarian rule when people had grown tired of politics.

When Gorbachev, the moderate revolutionary, came to power, both the elite and the population harbored a solid contempt for the old regime. It lacked legitimacy and Marxism-Leninism was a dead idea. People were passive, but only because they thought change was impossible. Gorbachev lit their hopes, and glasnost enlightened Russians about their relative economic backwardness. His early attempts at economic reform failed because of resistance from the party elite. The new party leadership became

---

2. *Pravda*, August 2, 1986.

3. In Soviet historiography, it is called the second Russian revolution, the first being the abortive revolution of 1905.

4. A theorist of revolution, Chalmers Johnson (1982, 7), has argued that a "nonviolent revolution" is "a contradiction in terms" (quoted in McFaul 2006, 191).

5. Three excellent sources are McFaul (2001), Mau and Starodubrovskaya (2001), and Aron (2000).

increasingly divided, with a profound rift erupting between the three leaders Gorbachev, Yeltsin, and Ligachev in November 1987. Their split represented a characteristic revolutionary divide between moderates, radicals, and reactionaries.

As Alexis de Tocqueville (1856/1955) observed on the time before the French revolution, old injustices became more intolerable. "For it is not always when things are going from bad to worse that revolutions break out. On the contrary, it oftener happens that when a people which has put up with an oppressive rule over a long period without protest suddenly finds the government relaxing its pressure it takes up arms against it" (p. 176). "Only consummate statecraft can enable a King to save his throne when after a long spell of oppressive rule he sets to improve the lot of his subjects" (p. 177).

The rule of Gorbachev's reform communists from 1988 to 1991 was characterized by impressive political liberalization, but it also drove radicalization and polarization, because a broad public realized that the Soviet system could not be reformed, only broken or conserved. The old institutions were too rigid to adjust to new demands, rendering revolution the natural outcome (Bunce 1999). Gorbachev, the reformer, stayed in a vanishing political center, being outflanked by both the liberal revolutionary Yeltsin and reactionary communists. The liberal intelligentsia and reformist enterprise managers joined Yeltsin, who was the master of radicalization and democratization. Because of the inadequacy of Soviet economic theory and strong pressures from rent-seeking interests, Gorbachev's reforms transformed the Soviet economic system into a rent-seeking machine that broke down the economy. In 1991, the Soviet Union had become ungovernable and the state collapsed.

The failed August 1991 coup delivered the revolutionary breakthrough, and Yeltsin assumed power. He dissolved the Soviet Union, making Russia somewhat manageable, and he launched a radical market economic reform. The liberal revolutionaries built new market economic institutions and started redistributing property from the state to the new elite, but the economic crisis was too deep to allow quick results. Political reform was left on the back burner, while society calmed down.

The radical reformers were split and became alienated from more moderate parts of the elite. First enterprise managers and then oligarchs seized power, as the revolution turned more moderate, and the redistribution of property to these new elites continued. The ideas of the market economic revolution were already taken for granted, signifying the ultimate success of the revolution: "when great revolutions are successful their causes cease to exist and the very fact of their success has made them incomprehensible" (de Tocqueville 1856/1955, 5).

Finally, a postrevolutionary dictatorship was established after Putin came to power. The economic reforms had succeeded, and people were happy to enhance their personal welfare. They were tired of politics and withdrew, allowing Putin to consolidate authoritarian power. Almost as suddenly as the state had collapsed, it came together again, which the population greeted with relief.

If we accept that a generalized revolutionary scheme fits the Russian transformation, several important observations follow:

- First, a revolution has its own internal logic that is not exclusive to any nation. In the last two decades, Russia's development has followed a normal revolutionary logic, and national peculiarities have been secondary.

- Second, a characteristic of a revolution is that the institutions of the old regime fall apart or stop functioning for some time. As a consequence, state failure has been greater than market failure (Shleifer 1997, Shleifer and Vishny 1998).

- Third, in the near absence of institutions, the latitude and impact of political leaders become all the greater. They can carry out much more profound changes than usual, as long as they understand the limits of administrative capacity.

- Fourth, during the period of radicalization, moderation is not an option. Russia's problem was not that the reforms were too radical, but that some key reforms, notably political reforms, were not undertaken during the short revolutionary window of opportunity.

The main achievements of Russia's capitalist revolution were the peaceful dissolution of the Soviet Union, the building of market economic institutions, and privatization. They were secured during the short window of opportunity that was at hand. The problem with Russia's democracy building was that no clear idea existed. Therefore, the period of extraordinary politics was not exploited. Since democratic institutions were never properly built, they could not withstand the postrevolutionary reaction.

The revolutionary dynamic delineates the main stream of events, but the determinism must not be exaggerated. Each leader had a great deal of leeway. One of the peculiarities of this Russian revolution was that it was antirevolutionary, as was the democratic revolution in Eastern Europe in 1989, being directed against the socialist revolution of 1917 (Dahrendof 1990). The revolutionaries did not long for utopia but for "a normal society," which meant a wealthy Western European society.

Through their reaction against the Russian revolution of 1917, a broad Russian consensus refuted the use of force and bloodshed. Revolutions have often led to war, but so far Russia's capitalist revolution has avoided that fate even if Russian statements are growing increasingly aggressive. Another reaction against 1917 was Yeltsin's conviction that the Soviet administration must not be dissolved and that lustration of old cadres was harmful. He wanted to avoid the Soviet classification of people as "class enemies." The 1991 revolution was not only antisocialist but also anti-ideological. Gaidar and Chubais were attacked for being too ideological and called "market Bolsheviks," mostly by communists who favored status quo, but they claimed to be technocrats and professional economists. This strong resistance against ideologies was an impediment not only to clear thinking and consistency but also to fanaticism.

Nearly everything that was identified with 1917 or the CPSU was condemned. The communists had always been rash, which made many praise gradualism or even slowness. The long-lasting dominance of the CPSU engendered a widespread dislike of political parties among all but orthodox communists, leaving the Communist Party as the only sizable political party.

Russia's History Is That of Its Leaders and Their Ideas

In two books about Soviet and Russian leaders, George Breslauer (1982, 2002) described a three-stage pattern of their rise, consolidation of power, and decline. He emphasized the importance of the leaders in Soviet/Russian politics, showing their extraordinary freedom of choice. This means that Soviet institutions were less of a straitjacket than is usually thought, particularly in this revolutionary time, when institutions and social forces were so weak.

Revolutions are times of ideas. The ideas of the leaders were extremely important and were to mold their policies, which John Maynard Keynes's (1936/1973, 383–84) noticed:

> the ideas of economists and political philosophers, both when they are right and when they are wrong, are more powerful than is commonly understood. Indeed the world is ruled by little else. . . . I am sure that the power of vested interests is vastly exaggerated compared with the gradual encroachment of ideas.

Political scientists, by contrast, often emphasize the restrictions imposed on policymaking by institutions and interest groups. An excellent example is Daniel Treisman's (1999–2000) article "After Yeltsin Comes . . . Yeltsin." Treisman argued: "The undesirable aspects of Russian politics and policies in the 1990s have resulted less from the bad decisions made by powerful central leaders . . . than from these leaders' extreme impotence" (p. 75). He foresaw that Yeltsin's unnamed successor would be as constrained by regional governors and oligarchs as Yeltsin had been and predicted that Russia would "remain a decentralized federation" (p. 83). Treisman's daring but incorrect prediction illuminates two theses. First, during the Russian capitalist revolution, the leader and his views were far more important than institutions. Second, during the postrevolutionary stabilization the leader could defeat strong interest groups with the re-assembled state institutions.

Gorbachev was a nice man who wanted to do good. He embraced the ideas of enlightenment, modernization, and internationalization. But his ideas were quite vague, which is evident from his memoirs (Gorbachev 1995). Gorbachev accomplished what he understood.

- Glasnost was his and Aleksandr Yakovlev's original contribution. The Soviet Union and the world were astounded by how fast and radically these two men broke down the age-old Soviet censorship. The freedom of speech and media that lasted in Russia from 1989 to 2000 was their accomplishment.

- Gorbachev loved foreign policy, and he concluded three important arms control agreements: INF in 1987, CFE in 1990, and START I in 1991. He also engineered the Soviet exit from Afghanistan.

- The Soviet evacuation from Eastern Europe and the reunification of Germany were Gorbachev's greatest international accomplishments. Sooner or later, the Soviet Union would probably have been forced to depart because of imperial overstretch, but the timing and the peacefulness were to Gorbachev's credit.

Gorbachev tried to introduce democratization, market reform, and federal reform, but he did not think clearly about any of these topics. Therefore, his confused actions unleashed the collapse of the Soviet political system, the Soviet economic system, and the Soviet Union.

Yeltsin and Gorbachev were the same age, and they came from the same kind of background and made similar careers, but they could not have been more different as persons. Yeltsin was a rebel and revolutionary, who was prepared to think and do the unthinkable. Although he was less close to intellectuals than Gorbachev, he was more interested in ideas. He shifted between manic periods and depressions when he drank heavily, and his drinking and illnesses stifled his reign. Yeltsin's high point was 1989–91, before and at the beginning of his tenure as Russia's president.

- By standing in elections in 1989, 1990, and 1991, and each time winning a resounding democratic victory, Yeltsin cemented democratic elections in Russia.

- On January 13–14, 1991, Yeltsin shamed Gorbachev to stop the bloodshed in Vilnius and Riga. He went to Estonia to meet with the Baltic presidents and signed a declaration for the Baltic nations' independence together with them. He issued an appeal of his own to the Russian soldiers in the Baltic republics, urging them to abstain from violence, securing the independence of the Baltic States (Aron 2007, 15–27).

- Yeltsin's most heroic deed was Russia's democratic breakthrough. He faced down the August 1991 coup, proving himself an outstanding revolutionary leader. His calmness, strength, and confidence inspired Russians to stand up for their rights as citizens.

- The prohibition of the CPSU immediately after the coup gave the democratic revolution a chance before the revanche of the old regime. Gorbachev and Yeltsin did this together, but Yeltsin was the driving force.

- Yeltsin's greatest achievement was to dissolve the Soviet Union easily and without bloodshed, in opposition to Gorbachev. He chose the optimal time, one week after Ukraine's referendum on independence, and he acted with the necessary speed, attaining a clear break of the no longer tenable union.

- Yeltsin's last great accomplishment was the radical economic reform he instigated in October 1991. Together with his economic reformers, Yeltsin built a market economy faster than anybody had dared to hope. He delegated most decisions to his young economic reform ministers.

- Gaidar successfully deregulated prices and imports.

- Gaidar also defeated the military-industrial complex through a draconian cut of arms procurement.

- Chubais succeeded in executing both a small-scale privatization and a large-scale mass privatization with vouchers.

Yeltsin was the revolutionary hero. The problem, however, was that he remained president until 2000, and he did not attain much positive after 1993. His greatest sin of omission was that he did not disband the old parliament early enough to avoid the bloodshed of October 1993 and thus failed to consolidate Russia's democracy.

Yeltsin made two major mistakes. First, he launched the first war in Chechnya in December 1994, which was brutal, costly, and unnecessary. Yeltsin's final mistake was to appoint Putin as his successor.

Putin is the opposite of Gorbachev and Yeltsin. He belongs to the cynical Brezhnev generation, while Gorbachev and Yeltsin came of age under Khrushchev's thaw. He comes from an NKVD family background, whereas Gorbachev and Yeltsin had family members who had been repressed by the NKVD. Putin made his career in the KGB, not in the party, and he was a near failure. Gorbachev and Yeltsin knew little about the West although they shared its values. Putin knows the West well and speaks German and English, but he detests Western values. Gorbachev and Yeltsin favored democracy, but Putin opposes it. Both Gorbachev and Yeltsin were revolutionaries, but Putin is a restorer. The only common denominator among these three men is that they all understood the need for a market economy.

- Putin should be recognized for one important achievement, the completion of the market reforms that he carried out in his first term.

- His main endeavor, however, has been a systematic centralization of authoritarian power in his own hands and a far-reaching deinstitutionalization.

- His first targets were the regional governors, whose power he eliminated.

- Next he minimized and marginalized independent media.

- Finally, he defeated the oligarchs through the confiscation of Yukos and the jailing of Khodorkovsky.

The rest was little but a mopping up operation. In its period of postrevolutionary stabilization, Russia was susceptible to an authoritarian reversal, but it was not a given. The authoritarian restoration was Putin's choice. He is an outstanding image maker. He has made the Russians feel good and proud of themselves, Russia, and its history again. Unlike Gorbachev and Yeltsin, he maintains a great popularity toward the end of his second term.

Naturally, the political leaders did not decide everything themselves, but when they focused on a goal, the effect was truly amazing.

Early, Radical, and Comprehensive Reforms Most Effective

In this book, a large number of attempts at reform have been discussed. It is easy to classify them as radical and gradual. To an extraordinary extent, radical reforms have been successful, while gradual reforms have failed.

Among the radical reforms, many stand out: the dissolution of the Soviet Union, price deregulation, import liberalization, unification of the exchange rate, cuts in military procurement, small-scale privatization, voucher privatization, the fiscal adjustment of 1995, and the cleansing of the financial system in 1998. By and large, every reform that was sufficiently radical succeeded in the sense that it achieved the intended results, was completed, and was not reversed.

The opposite can be said about gradual reforms. Invariably, they have failed. Four important examples are: the early monetary policy, the preservation of the ruble zone, the slow deregulation of energy prices, and the tardy democratization.

First, CBR Chairman Georgy Matiukhin's "moderate" monetary stabilization with an average expansion of M2 of 11 percent a month in the first five months of 1992 left everybody dissatisfied. No hard budget constraint or demand barrier was erected to force enterprises to restructure. Nor was output stimulated.

Second, the gradual dissolution of the ruble zone was a full-fledged disaster. All the dozen central banks within the ruble zone had strong incentives to issue more money to seize a disproportionate share of the common output. The defenders of the ruble zone argued that adjustment must be gradual and that fast change was undemocratic. Considering that the ruble zone led to hyperinflation and sharp output decline in all the countries concerned, and that none of them stayed democratic, we can conclude that gradual currency reform was a failure.

Third, the gradual hike in energy prices created one of the biggest sources of rent seeking the world has ever seen, and it delayed the necessary adjustment of the Russian economy. The energy lobby favored low energy prices because it could buy energy cheaply at home and charge world market prices abroad.

Fourth, the most gradual process in Russia was its democratization, and it appears the most unsuccessful. Political compromise was possible immediately after the August 1991 coup, but not later on. The problems lay not in knowledge or technicalities, but in interests that were diverging over time.

All these examples suggest that early, radical reforms were better than gradual, delayed, or partial reforms. So why did some scholars object to radical reforms as such? Only the main lines of argument in this wide-ranging discussion will be summarized here.[6] Some argued that the Soviet reformers should have followed the Chinese path of reform, but as discussed in chapter 1, the Soviet preconditions were completely different.

Second, many wanted to limit the shock of liberalization and stabilization, assuming that then the costs of transition would be smaller. However, these arguments have been empirically disproved by a large literature of regression analysis, which has shown that more radical reforms have caused less output decline, a faster return to economic growth, and less social suffering (De Melo, Denizer, and Gelb 1997; Berg et al. 1999; Havrylyshyn and Wolf 2001; Campos and Coricelli 2002).

A third gradualist argument was that institutions had to be built first, which requires time (Murrell 1992a, 1992b; North 1994; Yavlinsky and Braguinsky 1994; Braguinsky and Yavlinsky 2000). Empirically, however, no postcommunist country that delayed reforms built more or better institutions than those that launched more radical reforms (Havrylyshyn 2006). Critics disregarded the substantial institution building undertaken by the radical reformers, and they did not understand the revolutionary nature of events. Therefore, they recognized neither the existence nor

---

6. I have pursued this discussion at length elsewhere (Åslund 2002, 2007a).

importance of using a brief window of opportunity. Nor did they see the strength of the rent-seeking interests.[7]

Fourth, in political science, transitologists advocated a gradual and pacted transition because they noted that democratizations in Latin America that had been negotiated and agreed with the old elite tended to survive (Karl and Schmitter 1991). But the unrepentant and entrenched communist elite in Russia was not ready to compromise, as the two coup attempts made evident. Therefore, no evolutionary reform was possible in the Soviet Union. Any marketization or democratization had to be revolutionary. Otherwise the old communist establishment would prevail. Russia's obvious alternative was a restoration of the old system without communist ideology as happened in Belarus.

After the Russian financial crash, Joseph Stiglitz (1999a, 2002, 2006) became the most illustrious critic of the Yeltsin-Gaidar reforms. He attacked International Monetary Fund (IMF) policy on Russia, the Washington consensus, and privatization, while embracing all the prior gradualist arguments. Stiglitz even stated: "The Gorbachev-era *perestroika* reforms furnish a good example of incremental reforms," disregarding that they led to economic collapse (Stiglitz 1999a, 24). He thought Russia should have followed China's example, focusing on the growth rates, but he ignored the very different preconditions. He commended communist institutions: "Once dissipated, organizational capital is hard to reassemble . . ." (Stiglitz 1999a, 9). It is unclear whether he realized that he thus endorsed communist dictatorship (Mau 1999). Logically, Stiglitz praised nonreforming and tyrannical Uzbekistan: "Countries that were castigated a few short years ago for the slowness and incompleteness of their reforms, such as Uzbekistan and Slovenia, are performing rather well, whereas other countries heralded as models of reform, such as the Czech Republic, are now encountering difficulties" (Stiglitz, 1999b, 4).

The fundamental difference between gradualists and radical reformers was their view of market failure and state failure. Gradualists regarded the old communist economy and state as more viable than radical reformers did, and they downplayed the economic crisis after communism. They refused to accept that the communist state was highly corrupt and that rent seeking was rampant, focusing on market failures, such as possible monopoly effects, while radical reformers emphasized speed because they feared the transition to market economy would fail. Finally, gradualists wanted to stimulate output through demand management, while radical reformers saw a lack of supply as the prime problem. Many gradualists retained more socialist views than they wanted to reveal.

---

7. A lucid example is Stiglitz (1999a, 9), who complained about radical reformers who "blame the failure of the shock therapy reforms on corruption and rent-seeking at every turn . . . without recognizing any role of the institutional blitzkrieg in destroying but not replacing the old social norms. . . ."

The arguments for radical reform are many. Changes must be credible and the economic system consistent to function, which requires that the intellectual paradigm change. Critical masses of markets and private enterprise were required for economic recovery and irreversible transformation, since the danger of reversal was considerable. Quick macroeconomic stabilization has proven most effective.

Drawing on the Russian transformation, two groups of arguments for radical reform stand out. The first is that Russia was in a revolutionary situation. The old regime had not been finished off but was suspended for a brief time. The Russian leaders had only a short window of opportunity. They should be judged by how well they used this chance.

The other argument was best presented by Joel Hellman (1998) in his seminal article "Winners Take All." His fundamental insight was that rent seeking was the main game in town. Reformers had a brief chance to act against it. Otherwise rent seeking took over in both economics and politics. State managers and new entrepreneurs had won big through rent seeking in the transition. They "used their power to block new market entry" and "undermined the formation of a viable legal system." Hellman reckoned that the winners had "developed a stake in the very distortions that impede the realization of the efficiency gains of a fully functioning market" (p. 233).

Murphy, Shleifer, and Vishny (1993) explained that this was likely to happen because rent seeking generates increasing returns. The establishment of a rent-seeking machine required fixed costs, but when it had been established it favored the rich and powerful, and the risk of punishment diminished with their dominance over the state. The obvious policy conclusion was that the politics and economics of transition had to focus on beating the interests of the prime rent seekers, which meant both fast democratization and radical market reform.

I am not aware of any full-fledged prescription for what the building of democracy should entail, but Michael McFaul (1993, 1997, 2001) has probably said it all. After elementary political and civil rights had been established, several building blocks of democracy were necessary. First, the old parliament had to be dissolved and new parliamentary elections held within a year after the democratic breakthrough. Second, to encourage the evolution of normal political parties, those founding elections should be based on parties, preferably be proportional, and have a reasonable threshold for representation of 4 or 5 percent. Third, the old constitution, with the sovereign and undivided power of the parliament, should be replaced with a constitution containing a clear division of legislative, executive, and judicial powers. Fourth, a clear division of powers between the federal, regional, and municipal governments was also desirable. Fifth, a parliamentary system would have been much preferable to a presidential system, because of its greater transparency and accountability. These are the building blocks of a democracy that Russia lacked. All of them could have been introduced before April 1992, but none was even attempted.

Viktor Sheinis (2004, 60), a former Yabloko deputy and specialist on the Russian constitution, noted that the "surge toward democracy immediately after the events of August 1991 was the time when a democratic constitution was most likely to pass, and this moment was lost." The quality of the constitutional drafts did not improve but deteriorated over time: "The compromising nature of the draft was a weakness, not a strength." McFaul (1993, 89) concluded: "Russia's poor sequence of elections has inhibited the stabilization of democratic politics. . . ."

Essence of Privatization: Legitimate Property Rights

The discussion on privatization has been wide-ranging and intense. Initially, many observers were impressed by Russia's fast mass privatization. However, both enterprise restructuring and economic growth were delayed. The loans-for-shares privatizations and Russia's corruption made many dismayed over dubious morals, and the financial crash of 1998 all the more so (Stiglitz 1999a, 1999b; Black, Krakkman, and Tarassova 2000). Strangely, many blame all negative phenomena on privatization, which was the most consistent reform undertaken, as if privatization and not the dearth of other reforms was the problem.

The empirical evidence is vast and quite consistent. Multicountry regressions have invariably shown that privatization had a positive impact on GDP (De Melo, Denizer, and Gelb 1997; Berg et al. 1999). A multitude of enterprise surveys have been undertaken. Overwhelmingly, they show that private firms are doing better than publicly owned corporations. Start-ups and foreign-owned companies have done especially well. New outside owners are better than the original managers (EBRD 1999; Havrylyshyn and McGettigan 2000; Megginson and Netter 2001; Djankov and Murrell 2002; Brown, Earle, and Telegdy 2005).

Private ownership of enterprises has many positive effects on the economy as a whole. As early as 1999, the EBRD and the World Bank Business Environment and Enterprise Performance Surveys showed that private enterprises are rarely monopolies and extract much less subsidies than state corporations (EBRD 1999).

A concern has been that companies privatized by insiders or with vouchers were less efficient for many years (Brown, Earle, and Telegdy 2005). After 1999, however, the high growth rates in the former Soviet Union have changed the picture. Now, countries that undertook mass privatization have actually grown faster than those that carried out case-by-case privatization and mass privatization appears to be the key explanation (Bennett, Estrin, and Urga 2005). Russia has experienced a big wave of mergers and acquisitions, rendering both owners and managers fluid, which has driven enterprise restructuring and economic growth. Therefore, it is becoming less important how an enterprise was privatized, while private ownership is vital.

Today, the greatest economic concern is whether Russia will be able to secure property rights of big enterprises. The confiscation of Yukos set a bad example. Currently, one big private enterprise after the other is being renationalized, which has many harmful economic consequences. Renationalization is reportedly often connected with kickbacks. With little transparency or accountability, state enterprises are bound to corrupt top officials, offering them easy access to great wealth. Their insecure property rights compel big Russian businessmen to invest hundreds of millions of dollars in politics, further aggravating corruption.

Virtually all sales to outsiders have been highly controversial. Ironically, the most open and transparent auction of Svyazinvest in July 1997 was the most loathed privatization. Nor did it help that the highest price was attained and paid in cash. The second most despised privatizations were the loans-for-shares deals, which generated the second largest state revenues before 1998 and revitalized the enterprises excellently. Evidently, subsequent economic success makes a privatization more disputed because it arouses the impression that the enterprise was worth more than was paid.

Initially, mass privatization and insider privatization were significantly less successful economically, but politically they have been more easily accepted. Hence, their resulting property rights are more legitimate. If that is the vital value, a positive reevaluation of these forms of privatization is called for. The conclusion is that it is far more important that privatization is politically acceptable than that it is economically optimal, because private enterprises generate so many positive effects in any case. Anybody who buys a company from the state suffers, because the politicized state is unable to make a fair transaction.[8] The optimal business approach is to buy enterprises on the secondary market and leave the hazards of privatization to others.

To stave off renationalization, a sector needs to be completely privatized. Remaining state enterprises are so harmful that almost any privatization is better than no privatization. In 2003, only 10 percent of oil production occurred in state companies, but by summer 2007 that share had risen to 55 percent. If only the small state corporation Rosneft had been privatized, like had been planned since 1997, Russia's oil sector might still be private, as the entirely private steel and coal sectors. One remaining state firm in an industry is a cancer that can cause metastasis. If a big state

---

8. Alexis de Tocqueville (1856/1955, 101) noticed a similar phenomenon before the French revolution: "we constantly read of royal property being sold, then declared 'unsalable' and taken back; of broken pledges; of established rights being brushed aside. In every financial crisis the creditor of the State was victimized and the government broke faith with the governed."

company is allowed to dominate an industry, the danger is great that it will claim monopoly of the whole sector, as Gazprom has done.

Policymaking in the Midst of a Revolution

These observations lead us to more general conclusions about how policy should be made in the midst of a revolution. On the one hand, the state apparatus is suspended. On the other, many social forces are also paralyzed. This situation allows top policymakers to make more radical decisions than under normal conditions. At the same time, the capacity of government is sharply reduced, so it needs to focus on principles and cannot manage details. If policymakers do not use this window of opportunity, rent seekers will decide instead, and they will do so to their advantage.

Policymaking during a revolution can be divided into six subsequent steps: ideas, operative policy advice, political leadership, policymakers, parliamentary support, and policy implementation. We shall examine what was done to market reform and democracy at each stage.

First come *ideas*, as Keynes so rightly pointed out. A revolution means rethinking, the introduction of a new intellectual paradigm. The ideas of radical market economic reform came from the Balcerowicz (1992) program in Poland, which were a concretization and radicalization of the Washington consensus (Williamson 1990). Radical market reforms have been implemented in many countries, and they have stood the test of time. The dominant economic reform idea was economic freedom.

The Russian reformers were shy about being ideological because the communists had given ideology a bad name. Hilary Appel (2004) has rightly observed that Václav Klaus was politically more successful with privatization in the Czech Republic than Chubais because he sold it as an ideological mission, while Chubais tried to sell it on the basis of direct material benefits of various stakeholders.

Second, an idea needs to be translated into *operative policy advice* to be relevant. Yeltsin's (1990) big reform speech on October 28, 1991, could have been more detailed, but it clarified the design of the economic reform: Prices and trade would be deregulated, and the budget brought close to balance. Enterprises should be privatized. The Gaidar team should have worked out a more specific program, but the policy was reasonably clear.

Third, *political leadership and a clear policy declaration* from the top political leader are needed. Yeltsin's big reform speech was such a declaration about economic reform.

Fourth, *operative policymakers* or reform ministers are needed. Yeltsin appointed a reform government of young professional economists on November 6–8, 1991. Usually, major reforms are undertaken by young professional economists coming from outside, bringing in foreign knowledge (Williamson 1994).

Fifth, *parliamentary support* is vital. A market economic reform requires the adoption of hundreds of new laws, and only an orderly legislative process can generate high-quality legislation. Yeltsin put his reform speech to a vote and obtained nearly unanimous support. Alas, his extensive rights to rule by decree for one year alienated and circumvented the parliament and thus harmed economic reform. This and the absence of democratic reform were the greatest shortcomings in Russia's economic reform process.

Sixth, *policy must be implemented while ordinary politics is in suspension,* what Leszek Balcerowicz (1994) called the time of "extraordinary politics." In Russia, it lasted from late August 1991 until the end of March 1992. The two first months were understandably devoted to preparations of strategy, leaving an actual window of opportunity of only five months, when most of the important economic reforms were adopted. Considering that time was so short and policymaking capacity limited, decisions had to be simple. Another reason for simplicity was that the government apparatus was at best passive but usually actively sabotaged policies.

International organizations could support reforms in several ways. They could offer advice, suggest benchmarks or conditions, and they could provide financing. The IMF, the World Bank, and the US Agency for International Development (USAID) did so for marketization, financial stabilization, and privatization. The problem, however, was that their financing did not start during the first year of reform, when it was most needed. Timeliness is crucial for the efficacy of international assistance.

As for democracy, no clear idea was presented on how to build democracy in Russia. If you do not know what to do, you achieve nothing. Without any detailed idea of what democracy entailed, nobody could say how to build it.[9] Consequently, Yeltsin never made a big reform speech on democracy because neither ideas nor priorities were evident. As no political reform was under way, no political reformers were brought into the government. Nor could parliamentary support be mobilized, and there was nothing to implement.

No international organization is responsible for democracy building. Two international organizations, the Council of Europe and the Organization for Security and Cooperation in Europe (OSCE), organize election monitoring, which is an important but limited element of democracy building. Not surprisingly, political scientists assess several post-Soviet countries as "electoral democracies," meaning that they hold formally correct elections, but not "liberal" or full-fledged democracies (McFaul 2001; Zakaria 2003). The only postcommunist countries that have become full-

---

9. Michael McFaul (1993, 89) emphasized the need for early parliamentary elections after the democratic breakthrough to develop political parties, but that was just one dissenting voice. In his memoirs, Gaidar (1999, 265) singled out McFaul and me as proponents of early elections in 1991 (which he considered impossible).

fledged democracies are those that have been admitted to the European Union, because they have to adopt all EU laws, which include democracy. The failure of democracy in Russia and the whole of the former Soviet Union is the intellectual failure of the international community to conceptualize democracy building.

In sum, Yeltsin and Gaidar got the essentials right about economic reform, but the lack of political reform harmed it through the malfunctioning of the legislature. It took the catharsis of the financial crash of 1998 to complete Russia's market economic transformation. The fundamental shortfall of political reform was the dearth of any clear idea of how to build a democracy. Political scientists were more preoccupied with the politics of economic reform than with democracy building. Consequently, little was done. It was not economic "shock therapy" but the absence of decisive political reform that led to an exhausting political crisis, which culminated in the bloodshed of October 1993, which badly stained Russia's nascent democracy.

The key issue during a revolution is what trajectory is chosen. Russia's choice was between radical market reform and democratization, on one hand, and partial market reform leading to rent seeking and authoritarianism, on the other. If reformers did not fight for the first option, the alternative would win by default. The short explanation of why market reform succeeded in Russia, while democracy failed, is that the initial big bang of radical economic reform was sufficient, while democratic reforms were never designed.

These conclusions suggest that the IMF and the World Bank largely acted correctly. The World Bank formulated an excellent program of radical economic reform (World Bank 1991, Fischer and Gelb 1991). It holds up very well today, and the World Bank (1996a) rightly showed that it had worked. Ironically, the World Bank has become wobbly because of the criticism by Joseph Stiglitz (2002) and Dani Rodrik (2006), ending up in general confusion and hardly daring to advise anything (World Bank 2005). Such a posture renders the World Bank of little use. It needs to go back to its sound roots of the early 1990s, restoring a basic set of coherent policy advice based on coherent market economic ideas. It neither can nor should guard itself against every exception, as Rodrik argues, because then it cannot provide relevant advice.

For democracy building, the very ground stones need to be laid. Political scientists must dare to become normative and prescribe a set of relevant policy advice for how a democracy should be built. They need to lose their academic virginity. Such policy advice, with the components suggested above, would roughly correspond to the Washington Consensus or the World Bank program for radical economic reform. In addition, an international organization for the building of democracy is called for. Naturally, such an organization must assemble only democracies, for example, the Community of Democracies. Otherwise its purpose would be diverted. The world must not stand empty-handed the next time a democratic revolution erupts.

Foreign Aid: Limited but Important

In hindsight, it is difficult to comprehend why the West did so little in Russia in 1991–92, and it was equally mysterious at the time. During that winter, the West had an extraordinary opportunity to make Russia an eternal friend, but Western governments were thinking seriously only about legal guarantees for their old debts to the Soviet Union. US Secretary of State James Baker thought of the danger of nuclear proliferation.

The West could provide relevant short-term support to Russia in its time of hardship in three ways: through advice, international standards, and financing. Although it was slow in coming and amazingly small, Western aid was important. Yeltsin spent a lot of his time on relations with the West, especially the United States and the G-7. The Western leaders were all friendly, but Russia got little out of these many meetings.

In the early 1990s, a Western newspaper reader could easily get the impression that Russia's transition was run by the IMF, because it had taken a firm lead on Russia in the international community, as the G-7 asked it to do in 1990. Both the Bush and Clinton administrations respected the IMF, and the immediate concern was macroeconomic stabilization. In addition, the IMF controlled large funds that could be lent to Russia without any approval by Western parliaments. The IMF was also more aggressive and effective under the leadership of Michel Camdessus and Stanley Fischer than any other international organization. It acted faster and had competent staff.

The most important task of international assistance was to provide Russia with a normal market economic paradigm. This was an ideological task, and ideas came primarily from independent economic advisors financed by nongovernmental organizations. The leading nongovernmental organization was George Soros' Open Society Institute, which financed civil society activities, research, qualified education, and textbook writing and translation (Soros 1991). A market economic paradigm was transferred to Russia independently and at minimal expense. The IMF, the World Bank, and the EBRD provided important backup, but they were slower in coming.

The second assignment was macroeconomic stabilization. One element was to introduce decent financial and monetary policies. A second element was to regulate overwhelming Soviet debts, and a third to finance Russia's international reserves. This was the task of the IMF. Unfortunately, the first year was lost because Western initiative was lacking. The official excuse was that Russia was not yet a member of the IMF and the World Bank, but nor was anything done about debt relief. The IMF provided no financing in the five-month window of opportunity November 1991–March 1992, when everything seemed possible. Because of the complete absence of currency reserves, Russia's average wage fell to $6 a month in December 1991, which was a horrendous humiliation to the Russian people. There was never any economic advantage of letting it fall below $100 a month. The West could have helped, but it did nothing. This failure to act should be blamed on President George Bush rather than the IMF that lacked mandate.

The other major mistake by the IMF was its policy on the ruble zone. It was partly intellectual, partly political. The Russian reformers and their foreign advisors wanted to dissolve it as soon as possible drawing on the precedent of the dissolution of the Habsburg Empire. The IMF preferred to stay out of this battle, which it reckoned was political (Odling-Smee and Pastor 2002). Many IMF shareholders opposed breaking up the ruble zone, notably the European Union, which was building its own monetary union at the time. The IMF could have salvaged Russia and the other Commonwealth of Independent States (CIS) countries from hyperinflation, but it failed to do so.

When the IMF finally came to play a role, the reformers had already been marginalized, and a big early stabilization program was no longer possible. The IMF advanced through incremental steps. From 1993, it concluded more or less annually a stabilization agreement with Russia. Two of these were successful. In 1993, Minister of Finance Boris Fedorov concluded a soft Systemic Transformation Facility agreement with the IMF with a one-year credit of $3 billion. It helped Fedorov carry out important structural improvements, being conditioned on the elimination of import subsidies and subsidized credits. The IMF's finest achievement was its first full-fledged standby agreement with Russia in April 1995, with $6.8 billion in financing in one year. It led to substantial fiscal adjustment through cuts of enterprise subsidies and to a temporary stabilization (Odling-Smee 2004).

Two other IMF programs, however, were too political to be successful. In 1994, Chernomyrdin was fully in charge, and thanks to his diplomatic skills, the IMF concluded an agreement in April 1994. But the program never looked serious. The IMF staff opposed it, but they were overruled by the US Treasury. Because of political pressure from the G-7, Camdessus was "more willing to settle . . . for an economic program that was less strict than he would have liked, to preempt any undue pressure from the G-7. Perhaps more importantly, the U.S. statements produced a hardening of the Russian position" (Odling-Smee 2004, 13). In the spring of 1996, the IMF concluded a three-year Extended Fund Facility of $10.2 billion with Russia, which was quite a disaster economically. The US government and G-7's political interventions to help Yeltsin get reelected were evident and heavy-handed, convincing everybody that in Russia the IMF was only concerned about politics. After the summer 1996 elections, by contrast,

Russia's government ignored the IMF because of the large foreign currency inflows.

In 1998, the IMF came back with force. IMF staff knew what to do, when Russia's financial crisis turned rampant. With substantial credit commitments of $23 billion, the IMF and the World Bank showed that they cared about Russia's fate. But the Russian Duma blocked the necessary tax legislation to make Russia's stabilization viable. Russia's stabilization could no longer be salvaged, and the IMF, the World Bank, and the US Treasury let it sink. Through this act, the IMF restored its credibility, but this seemed a callous act that might have alienated Russians from the West and undermined their belief in democracy.

The frightful crash of 1998 taught Russians all they needed to know about macroeconomics. The IMF could have withdrawn and declared victory. Soon, Russia returned all its IMF credits of $20 billion, and the IMF could present Russia as a success story (Owen and Robinson 2003). After seven years, Russia's financial stabilization was completed, which was no mean feat, even if it ideally could have been done in two years.

The third big task involving foreign assistance was to build a market economy and privatize the economy. Here, the World Bank took the lead. Its greatest achievement was to facilitate the mass privatization, cooperating closely with the US Agency for International Development (USAID). The World Bank was also deeply involved in all other structural reform. A major success was the restructuring of the coal industry through privatization and deregulation. However, the World Bank could achieve little in social reforms, because of the dearth of serious Russian counterparts. The Bank contributed intelligently to the Russian economic discussion, and eventually much of its sound analysis was implemented.

The only big task that remains for the West is to welcome Russia into the World Trade Organization (WTO). Russia applied for membership in 1993, but the Russian leaders did not take negotiations seriously until 2000. Putin instigated great progress during his first term, but then he appears to have lost interest. Because of its dominant commodity exports and the world boom, Russia has had few problems selling its products without being a member of the WTO (Åslund 2007b). Yet Russia's growth should increase by 0.5 to 1.0 percent a year in the medium term when the country joins the WTO (Jensen, Rutherford, and Tarr 2004).

The West could have done much more for Russia in 1991–92. The amounts required were minor, approximately $25 billion in loans, but timeliness was vital, and the West held back because of poor analysis. Total Western grant assistance to Russia has been tiny: –$2.6 billion from the USAID in 1990–2000 and $1.4 billion in EU grant assistance. Total IMF loans amounted to $20 billion and World Bank commitments to $11.7 billion by 1999 (Åslund 2002, 420–29). This does not include military security spending, which benefited Western security, and food "aid," that is, credits supporting Western agricultural lobbies. In fact, Russia's servicing of the old Soviet debt exceeded all government and intergovernmental grants and credits by far, so Russia was actually financing the West in the midst of its hardship (IMF 2000, 62).

Yet, the West got what it cared about. The dominant G-7 interest was to secure claims on the Soviet Union, and they were paid back in full. The US cared about nuclear nonproliferation, which was accomplished. Multiple Western forces promoted market economy in Russia, which was successful. Few in the West bothered about democracy or Russia's future direction, so we should not be surprised if those achievements were minimal.

Russia's Future: Contradiction Between Economic Miracle and Reactionary Politics

Russia's future lies in the contradiction between fast economic modernization and a reactionary authoritarian political system.

In 1993, Daniel Yergin and Thane Gustafson (1993) published the book *Russia 2010* presenting four different scenarios for Russia in 2010. Their most positive scenario, *Chudo* (miracle), corresponds closely to Russia's current economic situation. The government has secured macroeconomic stabilization, and the economic growth reaches 9 percent, driven by private business. This economic miracle is modeled on the German and Japanese postwar miracles (pp. 162–65). Two early books on Russia's economic transformation realizing its positive impact were Granville (1995a) and Layard and Parker (1996).

Politically, however, Yergin and Gustafson's "Two-Headed Eagle" scenario fits better. The government is noncommunist but conservative and statist, with the exports of natural resources being brought back under the control of state monopolies. It is based on a coalition of managers of large industries, the central bureaucracies in Moscow, and the *siloviki*. Its key feature is "the reconstitution of a stronger central government" (pp. 134–36).

Russia's economic progress is impressive. Real growth has been nearly 7 percent annually since 1999. In current dollars, however, Russia's GDP has quintupled from $196 billion in 1999 to $979 billion in 2006, becoming the 10th biggest economy in the world (IMF 2007). This corresponds to an annual increase of 25 percent and Russia's leaders feel it. Russia's GDP per capita at current exchange rates is still four times higher than China's.

In a much-noticed paper, Goldman Sachs projected that even with an average annual growth of only 3.9 percent, Russia's GDP would overtake Germany's in 2028, and Russia would become the fifth biggest economy in the world after the United States, China, Japan, and India (Wilson and Purushothaman 2003).

The Goldman Sachs study preceded the current oil boom, which has boosted the Russian economy further. Peter Westin considered the effects of higher oil prices. Assuming stable oil prices at $50 per barrel, Russia's GDP would grow by an annual average of 5.9 percent until 2015 (Westin 2005). Then, Russia would become the fifth biggest economy in the world before 2020.

Three fundamental conditions make it possible for Russia to generate this steady and high economic growth. First, Russia has established a normal market economy based on predominant private enterprise. It has adopted a liberal tax system with moderate and relatively flat tax rates. The overall lesson from transition countries is that public expenditures must not exceed 35 percent of GDP, as is the case in Russia (Gray, Lane, and Varoudakis 2007). In general, a higher tax level is neither justified nor beneficial for economic growth (Tanzi and Schuknecht 2000).

Second, the financial crash of 1998 was so severe that Russia is likely to maintain strict macroeconomic balance for a generation. The current macroeconomic policy is if anything overly cautious with budget surpluses of 7.5 percent of GDP in 2005 and 2006 and current international reserves of 40 percent of GDP, though neither is likely to hold for long.

The third factor that underlies Russia's dynamism is the single-minded focus on economic growth of not only the president but also the intellectual establishment. Russian economists of all colors are preoccupied with economic growth (e.g., Gaidar 2005). The peer pressure from neighboring countries is strong as well. The whole Eurasian region from China via India to the Baltics has been growing steadily by 7 to 11 percent a year since 2000. Russia is actually comparatively less dynamic.

Of these three factors, Putin can claim the focus on growth and the conclusion of the economic reforms, but the systemic transformation was largely done in the 1990s, and the respect for macroeconomic stability resulted from the crash of 1998. Growth accounting shows that after 2000, half of Russia's growth arises from capital and half from rising total factor productivity, while labor has given a minor positive input (Iradian 2007).

In addition, several profound structural changes are under way and they should contribute to growth. One of the least noticed factors is the relentless rise in the number of registered enterprises of 7 percent a year. With 5 million registered enterprises (figure 6.9) and at least 4 million registered individual entrepreneurs, Russia has a total of 9 million firms, which means one enterprise per 16 people or approximately as many as in Western European countries.

Another indication of Russia's ambitions is that Russia is swiftly becoming a middle class society with a middle class of at least 20 to 25 percent of the population (Maleva 2003). Ever more young Russians opt for higher education. According to UNICEF statistics, the share of Russian college-age youth that pursue higher education nearly doubled from 25 percent in 1989 to 47 percent in 2005 (figure 8.3). With a broader definition of higher education, UNESCO (2007) arrived at 71 percent for 2005, more than the average for the European Union.

Figure 8.3 Share of college-age youth going to higher education, 1989–2005

gross ratio, percent of population aged 19–24

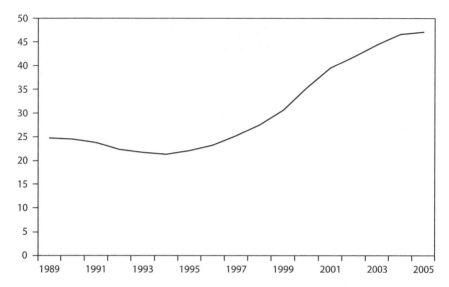

Source: TransMONEE 2007 Database, www.unicef-irc.org/databases/transmonee (accessed on May 28, 2007).

A common feature of the postcommunist economies is a large pent-up need for investment financed with the remonetization and releveraging of the economy. In 2005, Russia's M2 as a share of GDP was as little as 28 percent of GDP (EBRD 2006), while 70 to 80 percent of GDP would be a normal level for a European market economy. As long as private property prevails, Russia has plenty of collateral for more than twice as large a credit volume without any apparent financial risks. Considering that its investment ratio is still moderate, Russia has room for higher growth.

One more indicator that passes unnoticed is that since the financial crash, the profits share of GDP has been quite extreme, amounting to no less than 37 percent of GDP in 2005, if we believe the official statistics (Goskomstat 2006). This explains why Russia can have both 53 billionaires and substantial investment (Kroll and Fass 2007).

An additional factor stimulating Russia's growth is the country's fast integration in the world economy. Russia's total exports have surged from $42 billion in 1992 to $305 billion in 2007. Much of the increase has come from rising oil prices, but Russia's economy is diversifying, and the share of oil and gas in Russia's exports has fallen to 60 percent from 90 percent of Soviet exports to the West in the late 1980s.

Figure 8.4 Life expectancy for men (at birth), 1989–2005

total number of years

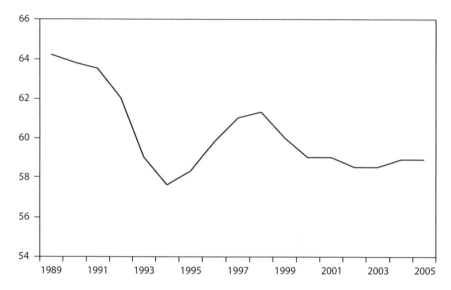

Source: World Bank, *World Development Indicators* database, http://devdata.worldbank.org
/dataonline (accessed on May 27, 2007).

Russia's labor market is tight, but the demographic situation is quite
flexible. For years, demographers have claimed that the Russian population will decline by one-third in 50 years, but the Russian population has
barely shrunk by 3 percent in the last 17 years (World Bank 2007). The explanation is that Russia has benefited greatly from the immigration of millions of people from former Soviet republics, many of them ethnically
Russian and all Russian-speaking.

A major concern, however, is that male life expectancy fell by 7 years
from 64.2 in 1989 to 57.6 in 1994 (figure 8.4). A quick recovery until 1998
suggested that this was a temporary phenomenon, but a subsequent decline showed that it was not. For years, Russia's life expectancy for men
has lingered around 59 years, which is extremely low. The main killer is
cardiovascular disease, followed by manifold violent deaths. The all-
dominant explanation is excessive consumption of alcohol. Russian men
have always been known to be heavy drinkers. With lower relative prices
of alcohol combined with the uncertainties of transition, they started drinking even more heavily, drinking themselves to death on a massive scale.
Russian women, by contrast, live 13 to 14 years longer than their men,
having a normal life expectancy for a relatively developed country (Shapiro
1995; Vishnevsky and Shkolnikov 1997; Brainerd 1998; Shkolnikov, Andreev,

Figure 8.5 Infant mortality, 1989–2006

per thousand births

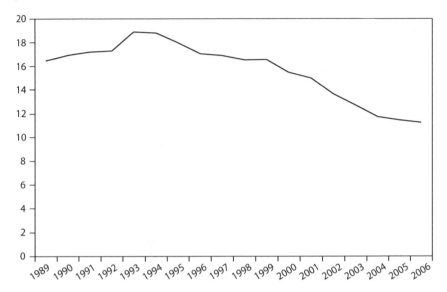

Source: US Census Bureau, international database, www.census.gov/ipc/www/idb (accessed on May 30, 2007).

and Maleva 2000). Strangely, the Russian government pays little attention to alcoholism and does hardly anything to improve the situation, even if Putin shows a good example by drinking minimally.

Russia's health care sector might not be great, but it is not the cause of the low male life expectancy. Infant mortality reflects the performance of the health care system. After a slight rise at the beginning of transition (which is probably explained by a change in definitions), infant mortality fell steadily by 40 percent from 1993 to 2006 and the decline continues (figure 8.5). After communism, health care is receiving much larger resources. Unlike in Soviet times, all kinds of medicines and equipment are now available, although the efficiency of public health care remains deplorable.

The worst economic threat is if renationalization were to make the state sector dominant again. Then the Russian state would kill the private geese that have been laying all the golden eggs it is living off. Yet, renationalization is likely to be contained for many reasons: the focus on economic growth, the absence of socialist ideology, and the faster growth of private enterprises and sectors dominated by them. Neither the dominant private sector nor the market economy appear to be in danger. However, the higher the oil price is, the worse Russian economic policy is likely to be.

A specific concern is that the output of key state enterprises, such as Gazprom and the transportation corporations, will fall short of demand and create major bottlenecks because of shortages of gas, power, or transportation. Again, this would harm economic growth, and the government would probably react pragmatically by letting in private enterprise. Still, the needed long-term investment could be much delayed.

The obsolete state is bound to preserve Russia's numerous state failures, as reflected in the patently flawed bureaucracy, law enforcement, public health care, public education, and public infrastructure. The common denominator of all these problematic sectors is public ownership. These state failures are expressed in endemic corruption, high murder rates, and high traffic deaths. These drawbacks have been lasting features of the new Russia, and they are not likely to go away until the country becomes democratic. An obvious corollary is that the Russian state should be small because it is likely to stay inefficient, ineffective, and corrupt for many years.

The worst political specter for Russia is fascism. The parallels between post-Soviet Russia and Weimar Germany are many and much discussed—an empire lost, hyperinflation, sharp output decline, a strong authoritarian tradition, spiritual vacuum, and fast, confusing transformation (Gaidar 2006). Many of the Kremlin's endeavors point in this direction, notably the formation of *Nashi* (Ours), a youth group reminiscent of both Hitler *Jugend* and Hitler's SA, his storm troopers (Buckley 2007). Russian state TV spews nationalist and anti-Western propaganda. The Kremlin has sponsored nationalist parties and movements, such as the LDPR and Motherland. Putin himself makes anti-Western speeches and calls for ethnic discrimination in favor of Russians (for example, Putin 2004c, 2006b, 2007a). Even so, the popular response to hard-core nationalism pushed by the Kremlin remains quite limited, and the fascist scenario looks unlikely.

Russia is simply too rich, too economically pluralist, too educated, and too open to be so authoritarian (Lipset 1959; Acemoglu and Robinson 2006, 358–60). This contradiction between an increasingly obsolete political system and a swiftly modernizing economy and society is likely to be untenable even in the medium term. No modern society can function without unbiased information or checks and balances. Putin cannot make decisions of high quality about everything after having abolished all feedback and concentrated so much decision making to himself. His regime is too rigid and centralized to handle crises, which always occur in Russia. Therefore, it can hardly be very stable.

Against this latter-day police state stands a rising middle class. Yet, Russia's current authoritarianism is quite sophisticated. While the middle class is being pampered with a high standard of living, political dissent is severely punished. Under such conditions, few are tempted to join the opposition. The costs are too high, and the probability of success too small.

The weakness of the political system lies elsewhere. It is likely to break from the top or the bottom. At the top, Putin has divided the elite in fierce competition to make sure that all need his arbitration. Each group of his KGB men sits on one or several state companies. Since these corporations pertain to different industries, they often have opposing interests and cannot collude. Considering that their struggle involves billions of dollars in contracts that cannot be legally secured, they are likely to protect their contracts by all means.

An important political weakness of Putin's system is that it does not have much to offer to the working class. Despite hikes, their wages remain relatively low; they die early from alcoholism; and they have no voice. Although Russia has experienced very few strikes, the current situation could easily breed strikes among elite workers, such as oil workers, while the system is too centralized to handle crises. Putin is continuously tightening his grip on information about all mishaps, but eventually some disaster may become too embarrassing.

Corruption has become more pervasive than ever, and it is difficult to escape the impression that it is a driving force in Putin's Russia. In East-Central Europe, corruption has been the main popular argument against every incumbent government (Krastev 2000), and it is worse in Russia. Even if corruption has been rationalized, it undermines the functioning of the state. Law enforcement, in particular, is unreliable, as evidenced by the successful entry of Chechen terrorists in the Moscow Nord-Ost and the Beslan hostage dramas. Prominent Russians often argue that Russians accept corruption, but it is never popular, even if elites hope so. In a survey in 2000, 70 percent of Russians said that taking a bribe is "never justifiable" (Fish 2005, 131–32).

Putin is supposed to end his presidency and a new president be elected in March 2008, but it is difficult to see how that could happen. Putin is healthy and young, immensely ambitious, and has no evident future post. He has systematically deinstitutionalized the political system, rendering it entirely dependent on himself. Several of his top aides have publicly called for a third term for Putin. They argue that the state would collapse without him. They might be right. If he had intended to retire, he would have been better advised to strengthen the rule of law, so that he could feel as secure as Gorbachev and Yeltsin did out of power.

Putin has vaguely implied that either of the first deputy prime ministers, Dmitri Medvedev or Sergei Ivanov, may replace him, but he has not anointed any candidate, and neither of these heirs apparent has declared his candidacy. Both are considered too weak to be president, and they have advanced only thanks to Putin. Admittedly, the constitution does not allow a president to stay for three terms, but considering that most other laws are disregarded, why take this article so seriously? Yelena Tregubova (2003, 55) reported a conversation with Putin in 1999, when he was FSB chairman. Then, the question was whether the Constitutional Court would rule in favor of a (clearly unconstitutional) third term for Yeltsin. Putin answered: "I tell you that the Constitutional Court will make such a decision as is necessary."

Putin could have changed the constitution already, but then he would have revealed his cards, and he loves to surprise. The current uncertainty allows him to keep everybody, including his closest associates, in suspense. He has said many times, both publicly and privately, that he intends to step down because the constitution says so. But given his record of doing the opposite of what he says and ignoring the law, his repeated statements are a strong indication that he will stay.

This book has focused on policymaking, emphasizing how much could have been done to build democracy, while few of these possibilities were used. In a broader historical perspective, however, it is not surprising that Russia's attempt at democratization failed. That is often the case, especially if the initial conditions are as adverse as in Russia (Linz 1978). Russians blame democracy for all their hardship in transition, not recognizing that communism had put them in jeopardy. Nor do they acknowledge the construction of a new economic system that was carried out in the 1990s. Many circumstances contributed to the backlash against democracy: It was seen as linked to corruption, lawlessness, financial instability, and insecurity. The absence of a strategy of democratization made this failure a near certainty, and democracy building will remain miserable if the world does not learn from the sins of omission in Russia.

In world history, economic and political pluralism have largely developed in parallel, with market developments usually preceding democracy. A market economy is often seen as a necessary but not sufficient condition for democracy, whereas no centrally governed economy without private ownership has been a democracy. Usually countries evolve toward political pluralism when their economies become wealthier, more open, and their populations more educated. A natural development would be that Russia in due time will throw off its authoritarian yoke and mature as a democracy, even if it needs to overcome a heavy authoritarian inheritance.

References

Abalkin, Leonid I. 1992. Ekonomicheskaya reforma: rezultaty i perspektivy (Economic Reform: Results and Perspectives). *Ekonomicheskaya gazeta*, no. 21 (May): 14–15.

Acemoglu, Daron. 2003. *The Form of Property Rights: Oligarchic vs. Democratic Societies*. NBER Working Paper 10037. Cambridge, MA: National Bureau of Economic Research.

Acemoglu, Daron, and James A. Robinson. 2006. *Economic Origins of Dictatorship and Democracy*. New York: Cambridge University Press.

Alekperov, Vagit. 1998. Nuzhno ispol'zovat' opyt Yaponii (It Is Necessary to Utilize Japan's Experience). *Kommersant-Daily*, November 11.

Allison, Graham, and Grigori Yavlinsky. 1991. Window of Opportunity: Joint Program for Western Cooperation in the Soviet Transition to Democracy and the Market Economy. Harvard University, Cambridge, MA, and the Center for Economic and Political Research, Moscow. Photocopy (June 29).

Amalrik, Andrei. 1980. *Will the Soviet Union Survive until 1984?* London: Harper Collins.

Amsterdam, Robert, and Dean Peroff. 2007. White Paper on Abuse of State Authority in the Russian Federation. Photocopy (February 7).

Anderson, James H., David S. Bernstein, and Cheryl W. Gray. 2005. *Judicial Systems in Transition Economies: Assessing the Past, Looking to the Future*. Washington: World Bank.

Anderson, James H., and Cheryl W. Gray. 2006. *Anticorruption in Transition 3: Who Is Succeeding . . . and Why?* Washington: World Bank.

Appel, Hilary. 2004. *A New Capitalist Order: Privatization and Ideology in Russia and Eastern Europe*. Pittsburgh, PA: University of Pittsburgh Press.

Arbatov, Georgi. 1992. Kuda poshli den'gi? (Where Did the Money Go?). *Nezavisimaya gazeta*, April 3, 4.

Aron, Leon. 2000. *Yeltsin: A Revolutionary Life*. New York: St. Martin's Press.

Aron, Leon. 2007. *Russia's Revolution, 1989–2006*. Washington: American Enterprise Institute.

Ash, Timothy Garton. 1990. *We the People: The Revolution of '89 Witnessed in Warsaw, Budapest, Berlin & Prague*. Cambridge: Granta Books.

Åslund, Anders. 1989. Soviet and Chinese Reforms—Why They Must Be Different. *The World Today* 45, no. 11: 188–91.

Åslund, Anders. 1990. How Small Is the Soviet National Income? In *The Impoverished Superpower: Perestroika and the Soviet Military Burden*, eds. Henry S. Rowen and Charles Wolf, Jr. San Francisco: Institute for Contemporary Studies.

Åslund, Anders. 1991. *Gorbachev's Struggle for Economic Reform*. Ithaca, NY: Cornell University Press.

Åslund, Anders. 1992. *Post-Communist Economic Revolutions: How Big a Bang?* Washington: Center for Strategic and International Studies.

Åslund, Anders. 1995. *How Russia Became a Market Economy.* Washington: Brookings Institution.

Åslund, Anders. 1996. Reform vs. 'Rent-Seeking' in Russia's Economic Transformation. *Transition*, no. 26 (January): 12–16.

Åslund, Anders. 1997. Economic Causes of Crime in Russia. In *The Rule of Law and Economic Reform in Russia*, eds. Jeffrey D. Sachs and Katharina Pistor. Boulder, CO: Westview Press.

Åslund, Anders. 1998. Russia's Financial Crisis: Causes and Possible Remedies. *Post-Soviet Geography and Economics* 39, no. 6: 309–28.

Åslund, Anders. 1999. Why Has Russia's Economic Transformation Been So Arduous? Annual World Bank Conference on Development Economics, Washington, April 28–30.

Åslund, Anders. 2000. Russia and the International Financial Institutions. Paper presented to the International Financial Institutional Advisory Commission on January 18, Washington.

Åslund, Anders. 2001. Ukraine's Return to Economic Growth. *Post-Soviet Geography and Economics* 42, no. 5: 313–28.

Åslund, Anders. 2002. *Building Capitalism: The Transformation of the Former Soviet Bloc.* New York: Cambridge University Press.

Åslund, Anders. 2004. Russia's Economic Transformation under Putin. *Eurasian Geography and Economics* 45, no. 6: 397–420.

Åslund, Anders. 2007a. *How Capitalism Was Built: The Transformation of Central and Eastern Europe, Russia, and Central Asia.* New York: Cambridge University Press.

Åslund, Anders. 2007b. Russia's Accession to the World Trade Organization. *Eurasian Geography and Economics* 48, no. 3: 289–305.

Åslund, Anders, Peter Boone, and Simon Johnson. 1996. How to Stabilize: Lessons from Post-Communist Countries. *Brookings Papers on Economic Activity* 26, no. 1: 217–313.

Åslund, Anders, and Mikhail Dmitriev, eds. 1996. *Sotsialnaya politika v period perekhoda k rynku: problemy i resheniya (Social Policy in the Transition to a Market Economy: Problems and Solutions).* Moscow: Carnegie Endowment for International Peace.

Åslund, Anders, and Michael McFaul, eds. 2006. *Revolution in Orange: The Origins of Ukraine's Democratic Breakthrough.* Washington: Carnegie Endowment for International Peace.

Aukutsionek, S. 1998. Barter v rossiiskoi promyshlennosti (Barter in Russian Industry). *Voprosy ekonomiki* 70, no. 2: 51–60.

Aven, Petr O. 1994. Problems in Foreign Trade Regulation in the Russian Economy. In *Economic Transformation in Russia*, ed. Anders Åslund. New York: St. Martin's Press.

Aven, Petr O. 2000. Ekonomichesky rost i obshchestvennaya moral' (Economic Growth and Public Morality). *Kommersant Daily*, February 29.

Bagrov, Andrei. 1999. MVF—glavny borets s korruptsiei v Rossii (IMF—the Main Fighter against Corruption in Russia). *Kommersant Daily*, March 4.

Baker, Peter, and Susan Glasser. 2005. *Kremlin Rising: Vladimir Putin's Russia and the End of Revolution.* New York: Scribner.

Balcerowicz, Leszek. 1992. *800 dni skontrolowanego szoku (800 Days of Controlled Shock).* Warsaw: Polska Oficyna Wydawnicza "BGW."

Balcerowicz, Leszek. 1994. Understanding Postcommunist Transitions. *Journal of Democracy* 5, no. 4: 75–89.

Balmaceda, Margarita Mercedes. 1998. Gas, Oil and the Linkages between Domestic and Foreign Policies: The Case of Ukraine. *Europe-Asia Studies* 50, no. 2: 257–86.

Belkovsky, Stanislav. 2006. How Do Ordinary Officials and Politicians Make Billions? *Argumenty y Fakty*, May 17.

Bell, John D. 1997. Democratization and Political Participation in 'Postcommunist' Bulgaria. In *Politics, Power, and the Struggle for Democracy in South-East Europe*, eds. Karen Dawisha and Bruce Parrott. Cambridge: Cambridge University Press.

Belton, Catherine. 2004. Putin: Tell Me Who Wants Yukos Broke. *Moscow Times*, September 9.

Bennett, John, Saul Estrin, and Giovanni Urga. 2005. Methods of Privatization and Economic Growth in Transition Economies. Paper presented at the WIDER Jubilee Conference, Helsinki, Finland, June 17–18. Available at www.wider.unu.edu (accessed on June 15, 2006).

Berg, Andrew, Eduardo Borensztein, Ratna Sahay, and Jeromin Zettelmeyer. 1999. *The Evolution of Output in Transition Economies: Explaining the Differences*. IMF Working Paper 73. Washington: International Monetary Fund.

Bergson, Abram. 1997. How Big Was Soviet GDP? *Comparative Economic Studies* 39, no. 1: 1–14.

Bergson, Abram, and Herbert S. Levine, eds. 1983. *The Soviet Economy: Toward the Year 2000*. Boston: George Allen & Unwin.

Berkowitz, Daniel M., Joseph S. Berliner, Paul R. Gregory, Susan J. Linz, and James R. Millar. 1993. An Evaluation of the CIS's Analysis of Soviet Economic Performance, 1970–90. *Comparative Economic Studies* 35, no. 2: 33–57.

Black, Bernard, Reiner Krakkman, and Anna Tarassova. 2000. Russian Privatization and Corporate Governance: What Went Wrong? *Stanford Law Review* 52, no. 6: 1731–805.

Blanchard, Olivier, Rudiger Dornbusch, Paul Krugman, Richard Layard, Lawrence Summers. 1991. *Reform in Eastern Europe*. Cambridge, MA: MIT Press.

Blasi, Joseph R., Maya Kroumova, and Douglas Kruse. 1997. *Kremlin Capitalism: Privatizing the Russian Economy*. Ithaca, NY: Cornell University Press.

Boettke, Peter J. 1993. *Why Perestroika Failed: The Politics and Economics of Socialist Transformation*. New York: Palgrave.

Bogomolov, Oleg T. 1992. Net ni vremeni, ni effektivnoi vlasti (There Is Neither Time, Nor Effective Power). *Nezavisimaya gazeta*, February 7, 4.

Bogomolov, Oleg T. 1993. Is Russia Threatened with Hyperinflation? *The Cato Journal* 12, no. 3: 593–602.

Bogomolov, Oleg T., ed. 1996. *Reformy glazami amerikanskikh i rossiiskikh uchenykh (Reforms in the Eyes of American and Russian Scholars)*. Moscow: Rossiisky ekonomichesky zhurnal.

Boycko, Maxim. 1991. Price Decontrol: The Microeconomic Case for the 'Big Bang' Approach. *Oxford Review of Economic Policy* 7, no. 4: 35–45.

Boycko, Maxim, Andrei Shleifer, and Robert W. Vishny. 1995. *Privatizing Russia*. Cambridge, MA: MIT Press.

BP (British Petroleum). 2007. *Statistical Review of World Energy 2007: Historical Data*. Available at www.bp.com (accessed on May 24, 2007).

Brady, Rose. 1999. *Kapitalizm: Russia's Struggle to Free Its Economy*. New Haven, CT: Yale University Press.

Braguinsky, Serguey, and Grigori Yavlinsky. 2000. *Incentives and Institutions: The Transition to a Market Economy in Russia*. Princeton, NJ: Princeton University Press.

Brainerd, Elizabeth. 1998. Market Reform and Mortality in Transition Economies. *World Development* 26, no. 11: 2013–27.

Brealey, Richard A., and Stewart C. Myers. 2000. *Principles of Corporate Finance*. New York: McGraw-Hill.

Breslauer, George W. 1982. *Khrushchev and Brezhnev as Leaders*. London: George Allen & Unwin.

Breslauer, George W. 2002. *Gorbachev and Yeltsin as Leaders*. New York: Cambridge University Press.

Brinton, Crane. 1965 [1938]. *The Anatomy of Revolution*. New York: Random House.

Brown, Archie. 1996. *The Gorbachev Factor*. Oxford: Oxford University Press.

Brown, J. David, John S. Earle, and Álmos Telegdy. 2005. *The Productivity Effects of Privatization: Longitudinal Estimates from Hungary, Romania, Russia, and Ukraine*. Upjohn Institute Staff Working Paper 05-121 (October). Kalamazoo, MI: W.E. Upjohn Institute for Employment Research.

Brzezinski, Zbigniew. 1983. The Tragic Dilemma of Soviet World Power: The Limits of a New-Type Empire. *Encounter* 61, no. 4: 10–16.

Buchanan, Elizabeth. 2003. *Start with a Level Playing Field: How CEELI Helped Bring About a New Criminal Procedure Code that Gives Russia's Defendants a Voice.* American Bar Association (February). Available at www.abanet.org (accessed in August 2007).

Buckley, Neil. 2007. "New Cadre Raises Campfire Song to Russia and Putin," *Financial Times*, July 19.

Bunce, Valerie. 1999. *Subversive Institutions: The Design and the Destruction of Socialism and the State.* New York: Cambridge University Press.

Cagan, Philippe. 1956. The Monetary Dynamics of Hyperinflation. In *Studies in the Quantity Theory of Money*, ed. Milton Friedman. Chicago: University of Chicago Press.

Campos, Nauro F., and Fabrizio Coricelli. 2002. Growth in Transition: What We Know, What We Don't, and What We Should. *Journal of Economic Literature* 40, no. 3: 793–836.

Carrèrre d'Encausse, Hélène. 1978. *L'empire éclaté: la révolte de nations en U.R.S.S. (The Exploded Empire: The Revolt of the Nations in the USSR).* Paris: Flammarion.

CEFIR (Center for Economic and Financial Research) and World Bank. 2003. *Monitoring administrativnykh bar'erov na puti razvitiia malogo biznesa v Rossii: rezul'taty vtorogo raunda (Monitoring the Administrative Impediments to the Development of Small Business in Russia: The Results of the Second Round).* Available at www.worldbank.org.ru.

Chernyaev, Anatoly. 2000. *My Six Years with Gorbachev.* University Park, PA: Pennsylvania State University Press.

Christensen, Benedicte Vibe. 1994. *The Russian Federation in Transition: External Developments.* IMF Occasional Paper no. 111. Washington: International Monetary Fund.

Chubais, Anatoly B., ed. 1999. *Privatizatsiya po-rossiiski (Privatization in a Russian Way).* Moscow: Vagrius.

CIA (Central Intelligence Agency). 1990. *Handbook of Economic Statistics.* Washington: US Government Printing Office.

Cohen, Stephen F. 2000. *Failed Crusade: America and the Tragedy of Post-Communist Russia.* New York and London: Norton.

Colton, Timothy J. 2000. *Transitional Citizens: Voters and What Influences Them in Russia.* Cambridge, MA: Harvard University Press.

Colton, Timothy J., and Michael McFaul. 2003. *Popular Choice and Managed Democracy: The Russian Elections of 1999 and 2000.* Washington: Brookings Institution.

Commander, Simon, and C. Mumssen. 1998. *Understanding Barter in Russia.* EBRD Working Paper 37. London: European Bank for Reconstruction and Development.

Conquest, Robert. 1986. *The Harvest of Sorrow: Soviet Collectivization and the Terror-Famine.* New York: Oxford University Press.

Cooper, Julian. 2006a. Of BRICs and Brains: Comparing Russia with China, India and Other Populous Emerging Economies. *Eurasian Geography and Economics* 47, no. 3: 255–84.

Cooper, Julian. 2006b. Can Russia Compete in the Global Economy? *Eurasian Geography and Economics* 47, no. 4: 407–25.

Dąbrowski, Marek. 1993a. Debate on the Guidelines of Russian Economic Reform at the End of 1991 and in 1992. In *The Gaidar Programme: Lessons for Poland and Eastern Europe*, ed. Marek Dąbrowski. Warsaw: Centre for Social and Economic Research and Friedrich Ebert Foundation.

Dąbrowski, Marek. 1993b. The First Half Year of Russian Transformation. In *Changing the Economic System in Russia*, eds. Anders Åslund and Richard Layard. New York: St. Martin's Press.

Dąbrowski, Marek, Stanislaw Gomułka, and Jacek Rostowski. 2001. Whence Reform? A Critique of the Stiglitz Perspective. *Policy Reform* 4: 291–324.

Dahrendorf, Ralf. 1990. *Reflections on the Revolution in Europe.* London: Chatto & Windus.

Davis, Christopher, and Murray Feshbach. 1980. *Rising Infant Mortality in the U.S.S.R. in the 1970's.* Washington: US Department of Commerce, Bureau of the Census.

DeLong, Bradford. 2002. Robber Barons. In *Ocherki o mirovoi ekonomiki: Vydayushchiesya ekonomisty mira v Moskovskom Tsentre Karnegie (Series of Lectures on Economics: Leading World Experts at the Carnegie Moscow Center)*, eds. Anders Åslund and Tatyana Maleva. Moscow: Carnegie Endowment for International Peace.

De Melo, Martha, Cevdet Denizer, and Alan Gelb. 1997. From Plan to Market: Patterns of Transition. In *Macroeconomic Stabilization in Transition Economies*, eds. Mario I. Blejer and Marko Skreb. New York: Cambridge University Press.

de Tocqueville, Alexis. 1955 (1856). *The Old Regime and the French Revolution.* New York: Doubleday.

Deutsche Bank. 2007. Russian Equities: Russia Morning Comment. April 5.

Diamond, Jack. 2002. *The New Russian Budget System: A Critical Assessment and Future Reform Agenda.* IMF Working Paper 02/21, February. Washington: International Monetary Fund.

Diamond, Larry. 1995. Democracy and Economic Reform: Tensions, Compatibilities, and Strategies for Reconciliation. In *Economic Transition in Eastern Europe and Russia*, ed. Edward P. Lazear. Stanford, CA: Hoover Institution Press.

Dixelius, Malcolm, and Andrej Konstantinov. 1998. *Maffians Ryssland (The Mafia's Russia).* Stockholm: Kommentus.

Djankov, Simeon, and Peter Murrell. 2002. Enterprise Restructuring in Transition: A Quantitative Survey. *Journal of Economic Literature* 40, no. 3: 739–92.

Dmitriev, M. E., M. Y. Matovnikov, L. V. Mikhailov, L. I. Sycheva, E. V. Timofeev, and A. Warner. 1996. *Rossiiskie banki nakanune finansovoi stabilizatsii (Russian Banks on the Eve of Financial Stabilization).* St. Petersburg: Norma.

Dobbs, Michael. 1997. *Down with Big Brother: The End of the Soviet Empire.* New York: Knopf.

Dornbusch, Rudiger. 1992. Monetary Problems of Post-Communism: Lessons from the End of the Austro-Hungarian Empire. *Weltwirtschaftliches Archiv* 128, no. 3: 391–424.

Drazen, Allen, and Vittorio Grilli. 1993. The Benefit of Crises for Economic Reforms. *American Economic Review* 83, no. 3: 598–607.

Dunlop, John. 1993. *The Rise of Russia and the Fall of the Soviet Empire.* Princeton, NJ: Princeton University Press.

Dunlop, John. 1998. *Russia Confronts Chechnya: Roots of a Separatist Conflict.* New York: Cambridge University Press.

Dynkin, Aleksandr, and Aleksei Sokolov. 2002. Integrirovannye biznes-gruppy v rossiiskoi ekonomike (Integrated Business Groups in the Russian Economy). *Voprosy ekonomiki* 74, no. 4: 78–95.

Earle, John S., Roman Frydman, Andrzej Rapaczynski, and Joel Turkewitz. 1994. *Small Privatization.* Budapest: Central European University Press.

EBRD (European Bank for Reconstruction and Development). 1994. *Transition Report 1994.* London.

EBRD (European Bank for Reconstruction and Development). 1995. *Transition Report 1995.* London.

EBRD (European Bank for Reconstruction and Development). 1997. *Transition Report 1997.* London.

EBRD (European Bank for Reconstruction and Development). 1999. *Transition Report 1999.* London.

EBRD (European Bank for Reconstruction and Development). 2000. *Transition Report 2000.* London.

EBRD (European Bank for Reconstruction and Development). 2002. *Transition Report 2002.* London.

EBRD (European Bank for Reconstruction and Development). 2003. *Transition Report 2003.* London.

EBRD (European Bank for Reconstruction and Development). 2004. *Transition Report 2004.* London.

EBRD (European Bank for Reconstruction and Development). 2005. *Transition Report 2005*. London.

EBRD (European Bank for Reconstruction and Development). 2006. *Transition Report 2006*. London.

EBRD (European Bank for Reconstruction and Development) and World Bank. 2002. Business Environment and Enterprise Performance Survey (BEEPS). Available at www.worldbank.org (accessed in August 2007).

EBRD (European Bank for Reconstruction and Development) and World Bank. 2005. Business Environment and Enterprise Performance Survey (BEEPS). Available at www.worldbank.org (accessed in August 2007).

Faltsman, Vladimir K. 1987. *Proizvodstvenny potentsial' SSSR: voprosy prognozirovaniya (Industrial Potential of USSR: Questions of Forecasting)*. Moscow: Ekonomika.

FBI (Federal Bureau of Investigations). 2005. *Crime in the United States 2005*. Available at www.fbi.gov (accessed on May 17, 2007).

Fedorenko, Nikolai, Nikolai Petrakov, Vladlen Perlamutrov, V. Dadayan, Dmitri Lvov. 1992. Shturm rynochnykh redutov poka ne udalsya (The Storm of Market Redoubts Has Not Succeeded So Far). *Izvestiya*, March 18, 3.

Fedorov, Boris G. 1999a. *10 Bezumnykh let (10 Mad Years)*. Moscow: Sovershenno Sekretno.

Fedorov, Boris G. 1999b. Vremya dlya liberalnykh reform v Rossii eshche ne prishlo (The Time for Liberal Economic Reforms in Russia Has Not Arrived As Yet). *Kommersant Daily*, February 4.

Fedorov, Boris G. 2004. Gryaznye vybory: Administrativny resurs po-moskovski (Dirty Elections: Administrative Resources Moscow-Style). *Russkoe ekonomicheskoe obshchestvo (Russian Economic Society)*, no. 2, January.

Finn, Peter. 2006a. In Russia, Cautious Generosity. *Washington Post*, September 22, A10.

Finn, Peter. 2006b. Kremlin Inc. Widening Control over Industry. *Washington Post*, November 19, A1.

Fischer, Stanley, and Alan Gelb. 1991. The Process of Socialist Economic Transformation. *Journal of Economic Perspectives* 5, no. 4: 91–105.

Fish, Steven. 2005. *Democracy Derailed in Russia: The Failure of Open Politics*. New York: Cambridge University Press.

Freedom House. 2006. *Freedom in the World 2006: Selected Data from Freedom House's Annual Global Survey on Political Rights and Civil Liberties*. Available at www.freedomhouse.org (accessed in August 2007).

Freeland, Chrystia. 2000. *Sale of the Century: Russia's Wild Ride from Communism to Capitalism*. New York: Crown Business.

Freeland, Chrystia, John Thornhill, and Andrew Gowers. 1996. Moscow's Group of Seven. *Financial Times*, November 1.

Frydman, Roman, Andrzej Rapaczynski, John S. Earle, et al. 1993. *The Privatization Process in Russia, Ukraine, and the Baltic States*. Budapest: Central European University Press.

Frye, Timothy. 2000. *Brokers and Bureaucrats: Building Market Institutions in Russia*. Ann Arbor, MI: The University of Michigan Press.

Gaddy, Clifford G., and Barry W. Ickes. 1998. Russia's Virtual Economy. *Foreign Affairs* 77, no. 5: 53–67.

Gaddy, Clifford G., and Barry W. Ickes. 2002. *Russia's Virtual Economy*. Washington: Brookings Institution.

Gaddy, Clifford G., and Barry W. Ickes. 2005. Resource Rents and the Russian Economy. *Eurasian Geography and Economics* 46, no. 8: 559–83.

Gaidar, Yegor T. 1990. Trudny vybor (Hard Choice). *Kommunist* 67, no. 2: 23–34.

Gaidar, Yegor T. 1993. Inflationary Pressures and Economic Reform in the Soviet Union. In *Economic Transition in Eastern Europe*, ed. P. H. Admiraal. Oxford: Blackwell.

Gaidar, Yegor T. 1999. *Days of Defeat and Victory*. Seattle, WA: University of Washington Press.

Gaidar, Yegor T. 2005. *Dolgoe vremya (The Long Term)*. Moscow: Delo Publishers.

Gaidar, Yegor T. 2006. *Gibel' Imperii: Uroki dlya sovremennnoi Rossii (The Collapse of the Empire: Lessons for Modern Russia)*. Moscow: Delo Publishers.

Gaidar, Yegor T., et al., eds. 2003. *Ekonomika perekhodnogo perioda: ocherki ekonomicheskoi politiki postkommunisticheskoi Rossii, 1998–2002 (Transition Economics: Essays on the Economic Policies of Post-Communist Russia, 1998–2002)*. Moscow: Delo Publishers.

Gall, Carlotta, and Thomas de Waal. 1998. *Chechnya: Calamity in the Caucasus*, New York: New York University Press.

Gambetta, Diego. 1993. *The Sicilian Mafia*. Cambridge, MA: Harvard University Press.

Gerashchenko, Viktor V. (Interview with). 1992. Tseny, den'gi, kredity (Prices, Money, and Credits). *Ekonomika i zhizn*, 46 (November). 1, 5.

Gilinskiy, Yakov. 2000. *Crime and Deviance: Stare from Russia*. St. Petersburg: St. Petersburg Branch of the Institute of Sociology of the Russian Academy of Sciences.

Goldblat, Jozef. 2002. *Arms Control: The New Guide to Negotiations and Agreements*. London; Thousand Oaks, CA: Sage Publications.

Goldgeier, James M., and Michael McFaul. 2003. *Power and Purpose: U.S. Policy Toward Russia after the Cold War*. Washington: Brookings Institution.

Goldman, Marshall I. 1996. *Lost Opportunity: What Has Made Economic Reform in Russia So Difficult?* New York: Norton.

Goldman, Marshall I. 2003. *The Piratization of Russia: Russian Reform Goes Awry*. London, New York: Routledge.

Gorbachev, Mikhail S. 1985. *Korennoi vopros ekonomicheskoi politiki partii (The Fundamental Question of the Party's Economic Policy)*. Moscow: Politizdat.

Gorbachev, Mikhail S. 1987a. *Izbrannye rechi i stati (Selected Speeches and Articles)*, volume 3. Moscow: Politizdat.

Gorbachev, Mikhail S. 1987b. *Perestroika: New Thinking for Our Country and the World*. New York: Harper & Row.

Gorbachev, Mikhail S. 1987c. *Izbrannye rechi i stati (Selected Speeches and Articles)*, volume 4. Moscow: Politizdat.

Gorbachev, Mikhail S. 1988. Excerpts of Address by Mikhail Gorbachev, 43rd UN General Assembly Session, December 7. Available at www.coldwarfiles.org (accessed in August 2007).

Gorbachev, Mikhail S. 1990. Krepit' Kluychevoe Zveno Ekonomiki (Strengthening the Key Link in the Economy). *Pravda*, December 10, 5.

Gorbachev, Mikhail S. 1995. *Memoirs*. New York: Doubleday.

Goskomstat SSSR. 1986. *Narodnoe Khoziaistvo SSSR v 1985 g. (The National Economy of the USSR in 1984)*. Moscow: Finansy i statistika.

Goskomstat SSSR. 1989. *Narodnoe Khoziaistvo SSSR v 1988 g. (The National Economy of the USSR in 1988)*. Moscow: Finansy i statistika.

Goskomstat SSSR. 1990. *Narodnoe Khoziaistvo SSSR v 1989 g. (The National Economy of the USSR in 1989)*. Moscow: Finansy i statistika.

Goskomstat SSSR. 1991. *Narodnoe Khoziaistvo SSSR v 1990 g. (The National Economy of the USSR in 1990)*. Moscow: Finansy i statistika.

Goskomstat. 1996. *Rossiisky statistichesky yezhegodnik 1996 (Russian Statistical Yearbook 1996)*. Moscow.

Goskomstat. 1997. *Rossiisky statistichesky yezhegodnik 1997 (Russian Statistical Yearbook 1997)*. Moscow.

Goskomstat. 1999. *Rossiisky statistichesky yezhegodnik 1999 (Russian Statistical Yearbook 1999)*. Moscow.

Goskomstat. 2000. *Rossiisky statistichesky yezhegodnik 2000 (Russian Statistical Yearbook 2000)*. Moscow.

Goskomstat. 2006. *Rossiisky statistichesky yezhegodnik 2006 (Russian Statistical Yearbook 2006)*. Moscow.

Granville, Brigitte. 1995a. *The Success of Russian Economic Reforms*. London: Royal Institute for International Affairs.

Granville, Brigitte. 1995b. So Farewell Then Rouble Zone. In *Russian Economic Reform at Risk*, ed. Anders Åslund. New York: St. Martin's Press.

Granville, Brigitte. 2002. The IMF and the Rouble Zone, Response to Odling-Smee and Pastor. *Comparative Economic Studies* 44, no. 4: 59–80.

Gray, Cheryl, Tracey Lane, and Aristomene Varoudakis, eds. 2007. *Fiscal Policy and Economic Growth: Lessons for Eastern Europe and Central Asia*. Washington: The World Bank.

Handelman, Stephen. 1995. *Comrade Criminal: Russia's New Mafiya*. New Haven, CT: Yale University Press.

Havrylyshyn, Oleh. 2006. *Diverging Paths in Post-Communist Transformation: Capitalism for All or Capitalism for the Few?* New York: Palgrave Macmillan.

Havrylyshyn, Oleh, and Donal McGettigan. 2000. Privatization in Transition Countries. *Post-Soviet Affairs* 16, no. 3: 257–86.

Havrylyshyn, Oleh, and Thomas Wolf. 2001. Growth in Transition Countries, 1991-1998: The Main Lessons. In *A Decade of Transition: Achievements and Challenges*, eds. Oleh Havrylyshyn and Saleh M. Nsouli. Washington: International Monetary Fund.

Hellman, Joel S. 1998. Winners Take All: The Politics of Partial Reform in Postcommunist Transitions. *World Politics* 50, no. 2: 203–34.

Hendley, Kathryn. 2002. Suing the State in Russia. *Post-Soviet Affairs* 18, no 2: 122–47.

Hendley, Kathryn. 2004. Reforming the Procedural Rules for Business Litigation in Russia: To What End? *Demokratizatsiya* 11, no 3: 363–80.

Hendley, Kathryn, Barry W. Ickes, Peter Murrell, and Randi Ryterman. 1997. Observations on the Use of Law by Russian Enterprises. *Post-Soviet Affairs* 13, no. 1: 19–41.

Hoffman, David E. 2002. *The Oligarchs: Wealth and Power in the New Russia*. New York: Public Affairs.

Huntington, Samuel P. 1992–93. What Cost Freedom? Democracy and/or Economic Reform. *Harvard International Review* 15, no. 2: 8–13.

Illarionov, Andrei N. 1998a. Kak byl organizovan rossiisky finansovy krizis (1) (How the Russian Economic Crisis Was Organized). *Voprosy ekonomiki* 70, no. 11: 20–35.

Illarionov, Andrei N. 1998b. Kak byl organizovan rossiisky finansovy krizis (2) (How the Russian Economic Crisis Was Organized). *Voprosy ekonomiki* 70, no. 12: 12–31.

IMEMO (Institute of World Economy and International Relations). 2004. *Russian Economic Barometer* XIII, no. 2 (Spring).

IMF (International Monetary Fund). 1993. *Economic Review: Russian Federation*. Washington.

IMF (International Monetary Fund). 1994a. *Economic Review: Financial Relations among Countries of the Former Soviet Union*. Washington.

IMF (International Monetary Fund). 1994b. *Economic Review: Trade Policy Reform in Countries of the Former Soviet Union*. Washington.

IMF (International Monetary Fund). 2000. *World Economic Outlook*. Washington (April).

IMF (International Monetary Fund). 2007. *World Economic Outlook*. Washington (April).

IMF (International Monetary Fund), IBRD (International Bank for Reconstruction and Development), OECD (Organization for Economic Cooperation and Development), and EBRD (European Bank for Reconstruction and Development). 1991. *A Study of the Soviet Economy*. Paris (February).

INDEM Foundation. 2001. Praktika delovoi korruptsii (The Practice of Business Corruption. In *Diagnostika rossiiskoi korruptsii: sotsiologicheskii analiz (Diagnostics of Russian Corruption: A Sociological Analysis)*, December. Available at www.anti-corr.ru (accessed in August 2007).

Institute of Economic Analysis. 2004. *Rossiiiskie ekonomicheskie reformy: poteryanny god (Russian Economic Reforms: A Lost Year)*. Moscow.

Iradian, Garbis. 2007. *Rapid Growth in Transition Economies: Growth Accounting Approach*. IMF Working Paper no. 164. Washington: International Monetary Fund.

Ivanov, Sergei. 2006. Triada natsional'nykh tsennostei (Triad of National Values). *Izvestiya*, July 13.

Jack, Andrew. 2004. *Inside Putin's Russia: Can There Be Reform without Democracy?* New York: Oxford University Press.

Jensen, Jesper, Thomas Rutherford, and David Tarr. 2004. *Economy-Wide and Sector Effects of Russia's Accession to the WTO.* Washington: World Bank. Available at http://siteresources. worldbank.org (accessed in August 2007).

Jentleson, Bruce W. 1986. *Pipeline Politics: The Complex Political Economy of East-West Trade.* Ithaca and London: Cornell University Press.

Johnson, Chalmers. 1982. *Revolutionary Change.* Stanford: Stanford University Press.

Johnson, Juliet. 2000. *A Fistful of Rubles: The Rise and Fall of the Russian Banking System.* Ithaca, NY: Cornell University Press.

Karl, Terry Lynn, and Philippe Schmitter. 1991. Modes of Transition in Latin America, Southern and Eastern Europe. *International Social Science Journal* 128: 269–84.

Kaufmann, Daniel. 1997. Corruption: Some Myths and Facts. *Foreign Policy*, no. 107: 114–31.

Kaufmann, Daniel, and Paul Siegelbaum. 1996. Privatization and Corruption in Transition Economies. *Journal of International Affairs* 50, no. 2: 419–58.

Kazmin, Andrei I., and Andrei V. Tsimailo. 1991. Toward the Convertible Ruble: The Case for a Parallel Currency. In *Currency Convertibility in Eastern Europe*, ed. John Williamson. Washington: Institute for International Economics.

Keynes, John Maynard. [1936] 1973. The *General Theory of Employment, Interest, and Money*. London: Macmillan.

Kharas, Homi, Brian Pinto, and Sergei Ulatov. 2001. An Analysis of Russia's 1998 Meltdown: Fundamentals and Market Signals. *Brookings Papers on Economic Activity* 1: 1–50.

Khasbulatov, Ruslan. 1992. Programma dlya Khasbulatova (Program for Khasbulatov). *Nezavisimaya gazeta*, April 3, 5.

Kirchik, Olesia. 2004. Zemel'naia reforma: 1990–2002 (Land reform: 1990–2002). *Otechestvennye zapiski (Notes of the Fatherland)*, no. 1: 16. Available at www.strana-oz.ru (accessed in August 2007).

Klebnikov, Paul. 2000. *Godfather of the Kremlin: The Decline of Russia in the Age of Gangster Capitalism.* Orlando, FL: Harcourt.

Klein, Lawrence R., and Marshall Pomer, eds. 2001. *The New Russia: Transition Gone Awry.* Stanford, CA: Stanford University Press.

Koen, Vincent, and Steven Phillips. 1993. *Price Liberalization in Russia: Behaviour of Prices, Household Incomes, and Consumption During the First Year.* IMF Occasional Paper 104. Washington: International Monetary Fund.

Kokh, Alfred. 1998. *The Selling of the Soviet Empire.* New York: Liberty Publishing House.

Konstitutsiya (Osnovnoi Zakon) Soyuza Sovetskikh Sotsialisticheskikh Respublik (Constitution [Main Law] of the Union of the Socialist Republics). 1985. Moscow: Yuridicheskaya literatura.

Kornai, János. 1990. *The Road to a Free Economy: Shifting from a Socialist System: The Example of Hungary.* New York: Norton.

Kornai, János. 1992. *The Socialist System: The Political Economy of Communism.* Princeton, NJ: Princeton University Press.

Kornai, János. 1994. Transformational Recession: The Main Causes. *Journal of Comparative Economics* 19, no. 1: 39–63.

Korzhakov, Aleksandr. 1997. *Boris Yeltsin: ot rassveta do zakata (Boris Yeltsin: From Sunrise to Sunset).* Moscow: Interbook.

Krastev, Ivan. 2000. The Strange (Re)Discovery of Corruption. In *The Paradoxes of Unintended Consequences*, eds. Ralf Dahrendorf, Yehuda Elkana, Aryen Neier, William Newton-Smith, and Istvan Rev. Budapest: Central European University Press.

Kroll, Luisa, and Lea Goldman, eds. 2005. The World's Billionaires. *Forbes*, March 10. Available at www.forbes.com (accessed on June 2, 2005).

Kroll, Luisa, and Allison Fass, eds. 2007. The World's Billionaires. *Forbes*, March 7. Available at www.forbes.com (accessed on July 9, 2007).

Kryshtanovskaya, Olga, and Stephen White. 2003. Putin's Militocracy. *Post-Soviet Affairs* 19, no. 4: 289–306.

La Porta, Rafael, Florencio Lopez-de-Silanes, and Andrei Shleifer. 1999. Corporate Ownership around the World. *Journal of Finance* 54, no. 2: 471–517.

Latynina, Yuliya. 2001. *Nich'ya (A Draw)*. Moscow: Olma-Press.

Latynina, Yuliya. 2003. *Promzona (The Industrial Zone)*. Moscow: Olma-Press.

Latynina, Yuliya. 2005. *Okhota na izyubrya (Elk Hunt)*. Moscow: Olma-Press.

Layard, Richard, and John Parker. 1996. *The Coming Russian Boom*. New York: Free Press.

Lee Myers, Steve. 2005. In Russia, Bribery Is the Cost of Business. *New York Times*, August 10.

Lieven, Anatol. 1993. *The Baltic Revolution: Estonia, Latvia, Lithuania, and the Path to Independence*. New Haven, CT: Yale University Press.

Lieven, Anatol. 1998. *Chechnya: Tombstone of Russian Power*. New Haven and London: Yale University Press.

Lieven, Dominic. 2000. *Empire: The Russian Empire and Its Rivals*. New Haven, CT: Yale University Press.

Ligachev, Yegor. 1985. Sovetuyas' s partiei, s narodom (Consulting with the Party, with the Nation). *Kommunist* 62, no. 16: 77–92.

Ligachev, Yegor. 1989. *Izbrannye rechi i stat'i (Selected Speeches and Articles)*. Moscow: Politizdat.

Ligachev, Yegor. 1993. *Inside Gorbachev's Kremlin*. New York: Pantheon.

Linz, Juan J. 1978. *The Breakdown of Democratic Regimes: Crisis, Breakdown, and Reequilibration*. Baltimore, MD: Johns Hopkins University Press.

Linz, Juan J., and Alfred Stepan. 1992. Political Identities and Electoral Sequences: Spain, the Soviet Union, and Yugoslavia. *Daedalus* 121, no. 2: 123–40.

Lipset, Seymour Martin. 1959. Some Social Requisites of Democracy: Economic Development and Political Legitimacy. *The American Political Science Review* 53, no. 1: 69–105.

Lloyd, John. 1998. Who Lost Russia? *New York Times*, August 15.

Main Graft Sources for Police. 2004. *Ekspert*, no. 39 (October).

Maleva, Tatyana. 2003. *Srednie klassy v Rossii: ekonomicheskie i sotsial'nye strategii (The Middle Class in Russia: Economic and Social Strategies)*. Moscow: Carnegie Moscow Center.

Malia, Martin. 1999. *Russia under Western Eyes*. Cambridge, MA: Harvard University Press.

Marsh, Peter. 2006. Sector Comes in from the Cold. *Financial Times*, June 14, 4.

Marx, Karl. 1867/1981. *Das Kapital: Kritik der politischen Ökonomie (The Capital: A Critique of Political Economy)*, volume 1. Berlin (East): Dietz Verlag.

Matlock, Jack F. 2004. *Reagan and Gorbachev*. New York: Random House.

Matiukhin, Georgy G. 1993. *Ya byl glavnym bankirom Rossii (I Was Russia's Main Banker)*. Moscow: Vysshaya shkola.

Mau, Vladimir. 1999. Rossiiskie ekonomicheskie reformy glazami zapadnykh kritikov (Russian Economic Reforms in the Eyes of Western Critics). *Voprosy ekonomiki* 71, no. 11: 4–23.

Mau, Vladimir, and Irina Starodubrovskaya. 2001. *The Challenge of Revolution: Contemporary Russia in Historical Perspective*. Oxford: Oxford University Press.

McDonald, Mark. 2003. Russia Begins New Twist on Trials: Juries. *Knight Ridder Newspapers*, February 17. Available at www.cdi.org (accessed in August 2007).

McFaul, Michael. 1993. *Post-Communist Politics: Democratic Prospects in Russia and Eastern Europe*. Washington: Center for Strategic and International Studies.

McFaul, Michael. 1997. *Russia's 1996 Presidential Elections: The End of Polarized Politics*. Stanford, CA: Hoover Press.

McFaul, Michael. 2001. *Russia's Unfinished Revolution: Political Change from Gorbachev to Putin*. Ithaca, NY: Cornell University Press.

McFaul, Michael. 2006. Conclusion: The Orange Revolution in a Comparative Perspective. In *Revolution in Orange*, eds. Anders Åslund and Michael McFaul. Washington: Carnegie Endowment for International Peace.

McKinsey Global Institute. 1999. *Unlocking Economic Growth in Russia*. Moscow: McKinsey & Company.

Megginson, William L., and Jeffry M. Netter. 2001. From State to Market: A Survey of Empirical Studies on Privatization. *Journal of Economic Literature* 39, no. 2: 321–89.

Mereu, Francesca. 2006. Bureaucrat Numbers Booming Under Putin. *Moscow Times*, April 13.

Michalopoulos, Constantine, and Vladimir Drebentsov. 1997. Observations on State Trading in the Russian Economy. *Post-Soviet Geography and Economics* 38, no. 5: 264–75.

Michalopoulos, Constantine, and David G. Tarr. 1996. *Trade Performance and Policy in the New Independent States*. Washington: World Bank.

Michalopoulos, Constantine, and David G. Tarr. 1997. The Economics of Customs Unions in the Commonwealth of Independent States. *Post-Soviet Geography and Economics* 38, no. 3: 125–43.

Mikhailovskaya, Inga B. 1994. Crime and Statistics: Do the Figures Reflect the Real Situation? *Demokratizatsiya* 2, no. 3: 412–25.

Milward, Alan S. 1984. *The Reconstruction of Western Europe 1945–51*. London: Methuen.

Montesquieu, Charles de Secondat. [1748] 1977. *The Spirit of Laws*. Berkeley: University of California Press.

Morck, Randall, Daniel Wolfenzon, and Bernard Yeung. 2005. Corporate Governance, Economic Entrenchment, and Growth. *Journal of Economic Literature* 43, no. 3: 655–720.

Murphy, Kevin A., Andrei Shleifer, and Robert W. Vishny. 1992. The Transition to a Market Economy: Pitfalls of Partial Reform. *Quarterly Journal of Economics* 57, no. 3: 889–903.

Murphy, Kevin A., Andrei Shleifer, and Robert W. Vishny. 1993. Why Is Rent-Seeking So Costly to Growth? *American Economic Review* 83, no. 2: 409–14.

Murrell, Geoffrey D.G. 1997. *Russia's Transition to Democracy: An Internal Political History, 1989–1996*. Brighton: Sussex Academic Press.

Murrell, Peter. 1992a. Conservative Political Philosophy and the Strategy of Economic Transition. *East European Politics and Societies* 6, no. 1: 3–16.

Murrell, Peter. 1992b. Evolutionary and Radical Approaches to Economic Reform. *Economics of Planning* 25, no. 1: 79–95.

Nemtsov, Boris. 2007. Putin Must Be the Luckiest Person on Earth. *Moscow Times*, July 19.

Nolan, Peter. 1995. *China's Rise, Russia's Fall: Politics, Economics and Planning in the Transition from Stalinism*. New York: St. Martin's Press.

Nordhaus, William D. 1990. Soviet Economic Reform: The Longest Road. *Brookings Papers on Economic Activity* 1990, no. 1: 287–318.

North, Douglass C. 1994. Economic Performance through Time. *American Economic Review* 84, no. 3: 359–68.

Nove, Alec. 1969. *An Economic History of the U.S.S.R.* Harmondsworth: Penguin.

Nove, Alec. 1977. *The Soviet Economic System*. London: George Allen & Unwin.

Nove, Alec. 1989. *Glasnost' in Action: Cultural Renaissance in Russia*. Boston: Unwin Hyman.

O korennoi perestroiki upravleniya ekonomikoi. Sbornik dokumentov (On Fundamental Reform of Economic Regulation. Collection of Documents). 1987. Moscow: Politizdat.

Odling-Smee, John. 2004. *The IMF and Russia in the 1990s*. IMF Working Paper 155. Washington: International Monetary Fund.

Odling-Smee, John, and Gonzalo Pastor. 2002. The IMF and the Ruble Area, 1991–93. *Comparative Economic Studies* 44, no. 4: 3–29.

O'Donnell, Guillermo, Philippe Schmitter, and Laurence Whitehead. 1986. *Transitions from Authoritarian Rule: Tentative Conclusions about Uncertain Democracy*. Baltimore, MD: Johns Hopkins University Press.

OECD (Organization for Economic Cooperation and Development). 1995. *OECD Economic Surveys: Russian Federation*. Paris.

OECD (Organization for Economic Cooperation and Development). 1997. *OECD Economic Surveys: Russian Federation*. Paris.

OECD (Organization for Economic Cooperation and Development). 2000. *OECD Economic Surveys: Russian Federation*. Paris.

OECD (Organization for Economic Cooperation and Development). 2002. *OECD Economic Surveys: Russian Federation*. Paris.

Ofer, Gur, and Aaron Vinokur. 1992. *The Soviet Household under the Old Regime: Economic Conditions and Behaviour in the 1970s*. Cambridge: Cambridge University Press.

Olcott, Martha Brill, Anders Åslund, and Sherman Garnett. 1999. *Getting It Wrong*. Washington: Carnegie Endowment for International Peace.

Olson, Mancur. 1971. *The Logic of Collective Action: Public Goods and the Theory of Groups*. Cambridge, MA: Harvard University Press.

Olson, Mancur. 2000. *Power and Prosperity. Outgrowing Communist and Capitalist Dictatorships*. New York: Basic Books.

Oomes, Nienke, and Katerina Kalcheva. 2007. *Diagnosing Dutch Disease: Does Russia Have the Symptoms?* IMF Working Paper 07/102. Washington: International Monetary Fund.

Orwell, George. 1949. *1984*. New York: Harcourt & Brace.

Owen, David, and David O. Robinson, eds. 2003. *Russia Rebounds*. Washington: International Monetary Fund.

Papernaya, Inessa. 2004. Regiony zagoniat v Federal'noie kaznacheistvo (The Regions Will Be Herded into the Federal Treasury). *Finans*, March 29–April 4. Available at www.finansmag.ru (accessed in August 2007).

Pappe, Yakov S. 2000. *"Oligarkhi:" Ekonomicheskaya khronika, 1992–2000 ("Oligarchs:" Economic Chronicle, 1992–2000)*. Moscow: Higher School of Economics.

Parthé, Kathleen F. 1992. *Russian Village Prose: The Radiant Past*. Princeton, NJ: Princeton University Press.

Pasvolsky, Leo. 1928. *Economic Nationalism of the Danubian States*. London: George Allen & Unwin.

Peck, Merton J., and Thomas Richardson, eds. 1991. *What Is To Be Done: Proposals for the Soviet Transition to the Markets*. New Haven, CT: Yale University Press.

Perekhod k rynku: kontseptsiya i programma (Transition to the Market: Concept and Program). 1990a. Moscow: Arkhangelskoe (August).

Perekhod k rynku: Proekty zakonodatel'nykh aktov (Transition to the Market: Draft Legal Acts). 1990b. Moscow: Arkhangelskoe (August).

Perotti, Enrico C., and Stanislav Gelfer. 2001. Red Barons or Robber Barons? Governance and Investment in Russian Financial-Industrial Groups. *European Economic Review* 45: 1601–17.

Petrakov, Nikolai, Vladlen Perlamutrov, Yuri Borozdin, and V. Manevich. 1992. Pravitel'stvo utratilo kontrol' nad eckonomicheskimi protsessami (The Government Has Lost Control over the Economic Processes). *Nezavisimaya gazeta*, March 6, 4.

Petrov, Nikolai. 2004. Federal'naia reforma i kadry (Federal Reform and Cadres). *Briefing moskovskogo tsentra Karnegi* 6, nos. 4-5.

Petrov, Nikolai. 2007. Open Season on Mayors. *Moscow Times*, April 4.

Pinto, Brian, Vladimir Drebentsov, and Alexander Morozov. 1999. *Dismantling Russia's Nonpayments System: Creating Conditions for Growth*. A Report by the World Bank. Moscow (September).

Pipes, Richard. 1984. Can the Soviet Union Reform? *Foreign Affairs* 63, no. 1: 47–61.

Pipes, Richard. 1990. *The Russian Revolution*. New York: Vintage Books.

Pipes, Richard. 2003. *Vixi: Memoirs of a Non-Belonger*. New Haven, CT: Yale University Press.

Pipes, Richard. 2005. *Russian Conservatism and Its Critics: A Study in Political Culture*. New Haven, CT: Yale University Press.

Politkovskaya, Anna. 2001. *A Dirty War: A Russian Reporter in Chechnya*. London: Harvill.

Popkova, L. 1987. You Cannot Be a Little Pregnant. *Novy mir* 63, no. 7: 239–41.

Pravitelstvennaya programma formirovania struktury i mekhanizma reguliruemoi rynochnoi ekonomiki (The Government Program for the Formation of Structures and Mechanism of a Regulated Market Economy). 1990. Moscow: Proekt.

Przeworski, Adam. 1991. *Democracy and the Market*. Cambridge: Cambridge University Press.

Putin, Vladimir V. 2000. *First Person*. New York: Public Affairs.

Putin, Vladimir V. 2002a. Annual Address of the President of the Russian Federation V. V. Putin to the Federal Assembly of the Russian Federation, April 18. Available at www.kremlin.ru (accessed in August 2007).

Putin, Vladimir V. 2002b. *Obrashchenie Prezidenta Rossii* (Statement by the President of Russia), October 26. Available at www.kremlin.ru.

Putin, Vladimir V. 2003a. Remarks by President Vladimir Putin on Yukos Affair at Government Meeting, RTR Vesti Program, October 27, Federal News Service.

Putin, Vladimir V. 2003b. Introductory Words and Answers to Questions from Journalists at Press Conference about the Results of the Russia-EU Summit. Rome, November 6. Available at www.kremlin.ru.

Putin, Vladimir V. 2003c. *Vstupitel'noe slovo na vstreche s predstavitelyami Rossiskogo soyuza promyshlennikov i predprinimatelei* (Introductory remarks at the meeting with representatives of the Russian Union of Industrialists and Entrepreneurs), February 19. Available at www.kremlin.ru.

Putin, Vladimir V. 2003d. Interview with the ANSA Italian news agency, *Corriere della sera* newspaper, and the RAI Television Company, November 3. Available at www.kremlin.ru.

Putin, Vladimir V. 2004a. Transcript of the Inauguration of Vladimir Putin as President of Russia, May 7. Available at www.kremlin.ru.

Putin, Vladimir V. 2004b. Remarks by President Vladimir Putin at a Meeting in the Ministry of Finance, RTR Vesti Program, March 19, Federal News Service.

Putin, Vladimir V. 2004c. Address by President Vladimir Putin, September 4. Available at www.kremlin.ru.

Putin, Vladimir V. 2004d. Speech to Campaign Supporters. February 12. Available at www.kremlin.ru.

Putin, Vladimir V. 2004e. Speech at the World Congress of News Agencies, September 24. Available at www.kremlin.ru.

Putin, Vladimir V. 2005. Annual Address to the Federal Assembly of the Russian Federation, April 25. Available at www.kremlin.ru.

Putin, Vladimir V. 2006a. Annual Address to the Federal Assembly of the Russian Federation, May 10. Available at www.kremlin.ru.

Putin, Vladimir V. 2006b. Transcript of the Hot Line with President of Russia Vladimir Putin, October 25. Available at www.kremlin.ru.

Putin, Vladimir V. 2006c. Transcript of the Press Conference for the Russian and Foreign Media, January 31. Available at www.kremlin.ru.

Putin, Vladimir V. 2006d. Joint Press Conference with Federal Chancellor of Germany Angela Merkel, October 10. Available at www.kremlin.ru.

Putin, Vladimir V. 2007a. Speech and the Following Discussion at the Munich Conference on Security Policy, February 10. Available at www.kremlin.ru.

Putin, Vladimir V. 2007b. Annual Address to the Federal Assembly of the Russian Federation, April 26. Available at www.kremlin.ru.

Putin, Vladimir V. 2007c. Transcript of Press Conference with the Russian and Foreign Media, February 1. Available at www.kremlin.ru.

Putin, Vladimir V. 2007d. Interview with Newspaper Journalists from G8 Member Countries, June 4. Available at www.kremlin.ru.

RECEP (Russian European Centre for Economic Policy). 1993. *Russian Economic Trends* 2, no. 4. Moscow.

RECEP (Russian European Centre for Economic Policy). 1999. *Russian Economic Trends* (February). Moscow.

Reddaway, Peter, and Dmitri Glinsky. 2001. *The Tragedy of Russia's Reforms: Market Bolshevism Against Democracy*. Washington: United States Institute of Peace Press.

Remington, Thomas F. 2002. Russia's Federal Assembly and the Land Code. *East European Constitutional Review* 11, no. 3: 99–105.

Remington, Thomas F. 2006. *Politics in Russia*. New York: Pearson Longman.

Remington, Thomas F., Steven S. Smith, and Moshe Haspel. 1998. Decrees, Laws, and Inter-Branch Relations in the Russian Federation. *Post-Soviet Affairs* 14, no. 4: 287–322.

Remnick, David. 1994. *Lenin's Tomb: The Last Days of the Soviet Empire.* New York: Vintage Press.

Rodrik, Dani. 2006. Goodbye Washington Consensus, Hello Washington Confusion? *Journal of Economic Literature* 44, no. 4: 973–87.

Rose-Ackerman, Susan. 1999. *Corruption and Government: Causes, Consequences, and Reform.* Cambridge: Cambridge University Press.

Rumyantsev, Fedor. 2003. *Prezidentu ne verili* (They Did Not Believe the President). Available at www.gazeta.ru (October 28).

Rustow, Dankwart. 1970. Transitions to Democracy: Toward a Dynamic Model. *Comparative Politics* 2, no. 3: 337–64.

Ryzhkov, Nikolai. 1992. *Perestroika: istoria predatel'stv (Perestroika: A History of Treasons).* Moscow: Novosti.

Sachs, Jeffrey D. 1994. Life in the Economic Emergency Room. In *The Political Economy of Policy Reform,* ed. John Williamson. Washington: Institute for International Economics.

Sachs, Jeffrey D. 1995. Why Russia Has Failed to Stabilize. In *Russian Economic Reform at Risk,* ed. Anders Åslund. New York: St. Martin's Press.

Sachs, Jeffrey D., and David A. Lipton. 1993. Remaining Steps to a Market-based Monetary System. In *Changing the Economic System in Russia,* eds. Anders Åslund and Richard Layard. New York: St. Martin's Press.

Sachs, Jeffrey D., and Katharina Pistor, eds. 1997. *The Rule of Law and Economic Reform in Russia.* Boulder, CO: Westview Press.

Sachs, Jeffrey D., and Andrew Warner. 1996. Natural Resource Abundance and Economic Growth. Harvard Institute for International Development, Cambridge, MA. Photocopy.

Sachs, Jeffrey D., and Wing Thye Woo. 1994. Reform in China and Russia. *Economic Policy,* no. 18: 101–45.

Sargent, Thomas J. 1986. The Ends of Four Big Inflations. In *Rational Expectations and Inflation,* ed. Thomas J. Sargent. New York: Harper and Row.

Satter, David. 2003. *Darkness at Dawn: The Rise of the Russian Criminal State.* New Haven, CT: Yale University Press.

Schumpeter, Joseph A. [1943] 1976. *Capitalism, Socialism and Democracy.* London: George Allen & Unwin.

Selyunin, Vasili, and Grigori I. Khanin. 1987. Lukovaya tsifra (Cunning Number). *Novy mir* 63, no. 2: 181–201.

Shapiro, Judith. 1995. The Rising Mortality Crisis and its Causes. In *Russian Economic Reform at Risk,* ed. Anders Åslund. New York: St. Martin's Press.

Sheinis, Viktor. 2004. The Constitution. In *Between Dictatorship and Democracy: Russian Post-Communist Political Reform,* eds. Michael McFaul, Nikolai Petrov, and Andrei Ryabov. Washington: Carnegie Endowment for International Peace.

Shevtsova, Lilia. 1999. *Yeltsin's Russia: Myths and Reality.* Washington: Carnegie Endowment for International Peace.

Shevtsova, Lilia. 2005. *Putin's Russia.* Washington: Carnegie Endowment for International Peace.

Shkolnikov, V. M., E. M. Andreev, and T. M. Maleva. 2000. *Neravenstvo pered litsom smerti v Rossii (Inequality Facing Death in Russia).* Moscow: Carnegie Moscow Center.

Shleifer, Andrei. 1997. Government in Transition. *European Economic Review* 41, nos. 3-5: 385–410.

Shleifer, Andrei. 2005. *A Normal Country: Russia after Communism.* Cambridge, MA: Harvard University Press.

Shleifer, Andrei, and Daniel Treisman. 1998. *The Economics and Politics of Transition to an Open Market Economy: Russia.* Paris: OECD.

Shleifer, Andrei, and Daniel Treisman. 2000. *Without a Map: Political Tactics and Economic Reform in Russia.* Cambridge, MA: MIT Press.

Shleifer, Andrei, and Daniel Treisman. 2004. A Normal Country. *Foreign Affairs* 83, no. 2: 20–38.

Shleifer, Andrei, and Robert W. Vishny. 1993. Corruption. *Quarterly Journal of Economics* 108, no. 3: 599–617.

Shleifer, Andrei, and Robert W. Vishny. 1998. *The Grabbing Hand: Government Pathologies and Their Cures.* Cambridge, MA: Harvard University Press.

Shmelev, Nikolai P. 1987. Avansy i dolgi (Advances and Debts). *Novy mir* 63, no. 6: 142–58.

Shmelev, Nikolai P. 1988. Novye Trevogi (New Troubles). *Novy mir* 64, no. 4 (April): 160-75.

Simis, Konstantin M. 1982. *USSR: Secrets of a Corrupt Society.* London: J. M. Dent & Sons.

Slay, Ben, and Vladimir Capelik. 1997. The Struggle for Natural Monopoly Reform in Russia. *Post-Soviet Geography and Economics* 38, no. 7: 396–429.

Slider, Darrell. 1997. Democratization in Georgia. In *Conflict, Cleavage, and Chance in Central Asia and the Caucasus,* eds. Karen Dawisha and Bruce Parrott. Cambridge: Cambridge University Press.

Solnick, Steven L. 1998. *Stealing the State: Control and Collapse in Soviet Institutions.* Cambridge, MA: Harvard University Press.

Solomon, Jr., Peter H. 2002. Putin's Judicial Reform: Making Judges Accountable as Well as Independent. *East European Constitutional Review* 11, no. 1/2: 117–24.

Soros, George. 1991. *Underwriting Democracy.* New York: Free Press.

Steele Gordon, John. 2004. *An Empire of Wealth: The Epic History of American Economic Power.* New York: HarperCollins.

Stern, Jonathan P. 2005. *The Future of Russian Gas and Gazprom.* Oxford: Oxford University Press.

Stiglitz, Joseph E. 1999a. Whither Reform? Ten Years of Transition. Paper presented at the Annual World Bank Conference on Development Economics, Washington, April 28–30.

Stiglitz, Joseph E. 1999b. Quis Custodiet Ipsos Custodes? Corporate Governance Failures in the Transition. Paper presented at the Annual World Bank Conference on Development Economics—Europe, Paris, June 21–23.

Stiglitz, Joseph E. 2002. *Globalization and Its Discontents.* New York: Norton.

Stiglitz, Joseph E. 2006. *Making Globalization Work.* New York: Norton.

Stoner-Weiss, Kathryn. 2006. *Resisting the State: Reform and Retrenchment in Post-Soviet Russia.* New York: Cambridge University Press.

Talbott, Strobe. 2002. *The Russia Hand.* New York: Random House.

Tanzi, Vito, and Ludger Schuknecht. 2000. *Public Spending in the 20th Century.* Cambridge: Cambridge University Press.

Taylor, Brian D. 2006. Law Enforcement and Civil Society in Russia. *Europe-Asia Studies* 58, no. 2: 193–213.

Tompson, William. 2005. The Political Implications of Russia's Resource-Based Economy. *Post-Soviet Affairs* 21, no. 4: 335–59.

Transparency International. 2007. Corruption Perceptions Index. Available at http://transparency.org (accessed in August 2007).

Tregubova, Yelena. 2003. *Baiki Kremlovskoga Diggera (Tales of a Kremlin Digger).* Moscow: Ad Marginem.

Treisman, Daniel S. 1998. Fighting Inflation in a Transitional Regime: Russia's Anomalous Stabilization. *World Politics* 50: 235–65.

Treisman, Daniel S. 1999–2000. After Yeltsin Comes . . .Yeltsin. *Foreign Policy,* no. 117: 74–86.

Treisman, Daniel S. 2000. The Causes of Corruption: A Cross-National Study. *Journal of Public Economics* 76: 399–457.

Trenin, Dmitri. 2005. *Reading Russia Right.* Special Edition Policy Brief 42. Washington: Carnegie Endowment for International Peace.

Trenin, Dmitri V., and Aleksei V. Malashenko, with Anatol Lieven. 2004. *Russia's Restless Frontier: The Chechnya Factor in Post-Soviet Russia.* Washington: Carnegie Endowment for International Peace.

United Nations. 2007. UN Comtrade Database. Available at http://comtrade.un.org (accessed on April 17, 2007).

UN Economic Commission for Europe. 1992. *Economic Survey of Europe, 1991–1992*. New York: United Nations.

UN Economic Commission for Europe. 1993. *Economic Survey of Europe, 1992–1993*. New York: United Nations.

UN Economic Commission for Europe. 2004. *Economic Survey of Europe*, no. 2. New York: United Nations.

UN Economic Commission for Europe. 2007. Statistical Database. Available at www. unece.org (accessed on various dates).

UNESCO Institute for Statistics. 2007. *Statistics in Brief: Russian Federation*. Available at www.uis.unesco.org (accessed on July 9, 2007).

US Census Bureau. 1999. *Statistical Abstract of the United States*. Washington. Available at www.census.gov (accessed in August 2007).

Vaksberg, Arkady. 1991. *The Soviet Mafia*. New York: St. Martin's Press.

Vasiliev, Sergei A. 1999. *Ten Years of Russian Economic Reform: A Collection of Papers*. London: Centre for Research into Post-Communist Economies.

VTsIOM. 2002. *Nationwide Surveys*. Available at www.russiavotes.org (accessed in August 2007).

Vishnevsky, Anatoli, and Vladimir Shkolnikov. 1997. *Smertnost' v Rossii: glavnye gruppy riska i prioritety deistviya (Mortality in Russia: The Main High-Risk Groups and Action Priorities)*. Moscow: Carnegie Endowment for International Peace.

Volkov, Vadim. 2002. *Violent Entrepreneurs: The Use of Force in the Making of Russian Capitalism*. Ithaca, NY: Cornell University Press.

Von Mises, Ludwig. [1920] 1972. Economic Calculation in the Socialist Commonwealth. In *Socialist Economics*, eds. Alec Nove and D. Mario Nuti. Harmondsworth: Penguin.

Wallich, Christine I., ed. 1994. *Russia and the Challenge of Fiscal Federalism*. Washington: World Bank.

Werning Rivera, Sharon, and David W. Rivera. 2006. The Russian Elite under Putin: Militocratic or Bourgeois? *Post-Soviet Affairs* 22, no. 2: 125–44.

Westin, Peter. 2005. *What If? Russia 2015 at $50/bbl and $100/bbl*. Moscow: Aton Capital (October 3).

White, Stephen. 1993. *After Gorbachev*. New York: Cambridge University Press.

White, Stephen. 1996. *Russia Goes Dry: Alcohol, State and Society*. New York: Cambridge University Press.

Williamson, John. 1990. *Latin American Adjustment: How Much Has Happened?* Washington: Institute for International Economics.

Williamson, John, ed. 1994. *The Political Economy of Policy Reform*. Washington: Institute for International Economics.

Williamson, Oliver E. 1975. *Markets and Hierarchies*. New York: Free Press.

Wilson, Andrew. 2006. *Ukraine's Orange Revolution*. New Haven, CT: Yale University Press.

Wilson, Dominic, and Roopa Purushothaman. 2003. *Dreaming with BRICs: The Path to 2050*. Goldman Sachs Global Economics Paper 99.

Winiecki, Jan. 1991. The Inevitability of a Fall in Output in the Early Stages of Transition to the Market: Theoretical Underpinnings. *Soviet Studies* 43, no. 4: 669–76.

World Bank. 1991. *World Development Report 1991: The Challenge of Development*. Oxford: Oxford University Press.

World Bank. 1994. *Averting the Old Age Crisis: Policies to Protect the Old and Promote Growth*. Oxford: Oxford University Press.

World Bank. 1996a. *World Development Report 1996: From Plan to Market*. Oxford: Oxford University Press.

World Bank. 1996b. *Fiscal Management in Russia*. Washington.

World Bank. 2002. *Transition—The First Ten Years: Analysis and Lessons for Eastern Europe and the Former Soviet Union*. Washington.

World Bank. 2004. *Russian Economic Report*, no. 7. Washington.

World Bank. 2005. *Economic Growth in the 1990s: Learning from a Decade of Reform*. Washington.

World Bank. 2007. *World Development Indicators* online database. Washington. Available at http://devdata.worldbank.org/dataonline (accessed on various dates).

World Bank and International Finance Corporation. 2006. *Doing Business in 2006: Creating Jobs*. Washington: World Bank. Available at www.doingbusiness.org (accessed in August 2007).

Yakovlev, Aleksandr N. 1991. *Muki prochteniya bytiya: perestroika: nadezhda i realnosti (Torments of Being: Perestroika: Hopes and Reality)*. Moscow: Novosti.

Yakovlev, Yevgeny, and Yekaterina Zhuravskaya. 2007. *Deregulation of Business*. CEFIR Working Paper no. 97 (February). Moscow: Center of Economic and Financial Research at New Economic School.

Yasin, Yevgeny. 2002. *Rossiskaya ekonomika: Istoki i panorama rynochnykh reform (Russian Economy: Origins and Overview of Market Reforms)*. Moscow: Higher School of Economics.

Yavlinsky, Grigori, and Serguey Braguinsky. 1994. The Inefficiency of *Laissez-Faire* in Russia: Hysteresis Effects and the Need for Policy-Led Transformation. *Journal of Comparative Economics* 19, no. 1: 88–116.

Yeltsin, Boris. 1990. *Against the Grain: An Autobiography*. London: Jonathan Cape.

Yeltsin, Boris N. 1991. B. N. Yeltsin's Speech. *Sovetskaya Rossiya*, October 29.

Yeltsin, Boris. 1994. *The Struggle for Russia*. New York: Crown.

Yeltsin, Boris. 1999a. Annual Address to the Federal Assembly. Federal News Service, March 30.

Yeltsin, Boris. 1999b. Yeltsin's Resignation Speech. BBC News, December 31. Available at http://news.bbc.co.uk (accessed in August 2007).

Yeltsin, Boris. 2000. *Midnight Diaries*. New York: Public Affairs.

Yergin, Daniel, and Thane Gustafson. 1993. *Russia 2010 and What It Means for the World*. New York: Random House.

Yudaeva, Ksenia V., Evgenia Bessonova, Konstantin Kozlov, Nadezhda Ivanova, Denis Sokolov, and Boris Belov. 2002. *Sektoral'ny i Regionalny Analiz Posledstvii Vstupleniya Rossii v VTO: Otsenka Izderzhek i Vygod (Sectoral and Regional Analysis of Russia's Accession into WTO: A Cost-Benefit Analysis)*. Moscow: Center of Economic and Financial Research at New Economic School (CEFIR). Available at www.cefir.ru.

Zakaria, Fareed. 2003. *The Future of Freedom: Illiberal Democracy at Home and Abroad*. New York: W. W. Norton & Co.

Zavarsky, Leonid. 1999. Imperiya Berezovskogo (Berezovsky's Empire). *Kommersant-Daily*, April 7.

Zelikow, Philip, and Condoleezza Rice. 1995. *Germany Unified and Europe Transformed: A Study in Statecraft*. Cambridge, MA: Harvard University Press.

Zemtsov, Ilja. 1976. *La corruption en Union sovietique (Corruption in the Soviet Union)*. Paris: Hachette.

Chronology

Date	Event
1985	
March 11	Mikhail Gorbachev is elected general secretary of the Central Committee of the Communist Party of the Soviet Union (CPSU)
April 23	Ligachev is appointed second secretary of the Central Committee of the CPSU
May 7	Gorbachev's antialcohol campaign starts
September 27	Ryzhkov is appointed prime minister
November 19–20	First summit between Gorbachev and Reagan in Geneva, Switzerland
December 24	Boris Yeltsin becomes first party secretary in Moscow
1986	
February 25– March 6	27th Congress of the CPSU adopts Gorbachev's "new thinking" on foreign policy
April 26	Meltdown at the Chernobyl nuclear power plant
May	Campaign against "unearned incomes" starts
October 11–12	Summit between Gorbachev and Reagan in Reykjavik, Iceland
November 19	Law on Individual Labor Activity adopted

(chronology continues next page)

Date	Event
1987	
January 27–28	Central Committee plenum on democratization
June 25–26	Central Committee plenum on economic reform
November 11	Yeltsin is ousted as first party secretary in Moscow
December 8	Intermediate-Range Nuclear Forces (INF) Treaty between the United States and the Soviet Union is signed
1988	
January 1	Law on State Enterprises comes into force
May 15	The Soviet Union starts withdrawing troops from Afghanistan
May	Law on Cooperatives is enacted
June 28–July 1	19th Party Conference reforms party and introduces elections
October 1	Gorbachev replaces Gromyko as chairman of the Supreme Soviet
December 7	Gorbachev's speech at UN declares freedom for Eastern Europe
1989	
March 26	First elections to the Congress of People's Deputies of the USSR
April 9	Soviet military attack peaceful demonstration in Tbilisi, Georgia
May–June	First session of the USSR Congress of People's Deputies brings freedom of speech
October	Abalkin reform program is presented
November 9	Fall of the Berlin Wall
November 10	Bulgarian communist dictator Todor Zhivkov is overthrown
November 17	Velvet Revolution starts in Czechoslovakia
December 21	Romanian dictator Nicolae Ceauşescu is ousted

Date	Event
1990	
March 4	First elections to the Russian Congress of People's Deputies
March 15	Gorbachev is elected president of the USSR by the USSR Congress of People's Deputies
March 16	Gorbachev creates the Presidential Council
May 29	Yeltsin is elected chairman of the new Russian Congress of People's Deputies
June 12	Russian Congress of People's Deputies declares Russia a sovereign state
July 2–13	28th Congress of the CPSU; Ligachev is ousted from the Central Committee
August	Shatalin 500-day program is written
October 15	Gorbachev is awarded the Nobel Peace Prize
October	Gorbachev dismisses the 500-day program
November 17	Gorbachev dissolves the Presidential Council
November 19	Multilateral Treaty on Conventional Armed Forces in Europe (CFE) is signed in Paris
1991	
January 13	KGB troops kill 14 peaceful Lithuanian protesters in Vilnius
January 14	Minister of Finance Valentin Pavlov replaces Ryzhkov as prime minister
March 17	Referendum on the future of the USSR
June 12	Yeltsin becomes Russia's first popularly elected president
July 31	Treaty on the Reduction and Limitation of Strategic Offensive Arms (START I) is signed
August 19–21	Abortive Communist coup against Gorbachev
August 24	Russia recognizes the independence of Estonia, Latvia, and Lithuania

(chronology continues next page)

Date	Event
October 28	Yeltsin's big reform speech
November 6–8	Formation of Gaidar's reform government
December 1	Ukrainian referendum on independence
December 8	Belovezhsky agreement between Belarus, Russia, and Ukraine on the dissolution of the USSR and the foundation of the Commonwealth of Independent States (CIS)
December 21	CIS broadens to 11 countries at meeting in Alma-Ata
December 25	Gorbachev resigns as president of the USSR; the USSR ceases to exist

1992

January 2	Comprehensive liberalization of prices and imports
April 3	Yeltsin dismisses Burbulis as first deputy prime minister
April 6	First severe confrontation of Russian Congress of People's Deputies with Yeltsin
May–June	Yeltsin appoints three industrialists as deputy ministers, including Viktor Chernomyrdin
June 11	Russian parliament adopts privatization program
June 15	Gaidar becomes acting prime minister
July 17	Viktor Gerashchenko is appointed chairman of the Central Bank of Russia
August 19	Yeltsin announces voucher privatization
December 12	Congress of People's Deputies sacks Gaidar as acting prime minister
December 14	Chernomyrdin is nominated prime minister

1993

March 10–12	Congress of People's Deputies tries to impeach Yeltsin
April 25	Yeltsin wins referendum

Date	Event
June 30	IMF agreement on Systemic Transformation Facility
July 24	Cancellation of Soviet ruble banknotes: end of ruble zone
September 21	Yeltsin dissolves parliament and orders new elections
October 3–4	Armed uprising in Moscow, storming of the White House
December 12	Elections to the State Duma and the Federation Council; national referendum backs Yeltsin's draft constitution

1994

January 5	Agreement on monetary union with Belarus is signed
March 22	IMF agreement on Systemic Transformation Facility
April 15	Formation of free trade area of all 12 CIS countries
October 11	"Black Tuesday": the exchange rate of the ruble collapses; Yeltsin sacks the economic policy team
December 11	First Chechen war starts

1995

January 20	Customs union between Russia, Belarus, and Kazakhstan is established
April 11	IMF standby agreement
June 14–19	Chechen militants seize 1,500 hostages in Budyonnovsk hospital
November–December	Loans-for-shares privatizations
December 17	Elections to the State Duma

1996

Spring	Oligarchs and reformers unite to support Yeltsin in presidential campaign

(chronology continues next page)

Date	Event
March 26	IMF Extended Fund Facility
June 16	First round of the presidential elections: Yeltsin wins
June 20	Yeltsin sacks the Party of War (Oleg Soskovets, Aleksandr Korzhakov, and Mikhail Barsukov)
July 3	Second round of the presidential elections: Yeltsin wins
August	Khasavyurt armistice between Russia and Chechnya
Fall	Yeltsin is absent for several months for heart surgery
1997	
June 22	Russia becomes a full member of the G-8
July 8	Poland, the Czech Republic, and Hungary join the North Atlantic Treaty Organization (NATO)
July 27	Privatization of one-quarter of Svyazinvest; "the bankers' war" erupts
1998	
March 23	Yeltsin sacks Prime Minister Chernomyrdin
April 24	Sergei Kirienko is confirmed as prime minister
July 13	IMF and World Bank emergency package is agreed
July 16	Duma refutes IMF conditions
August 17	Russian financial crisis; default on domestic debt and ruble devaluation
August 23	Yeltsin fires Prime Minister Kirienko
September 11	Duma confirms Yevgeny Primakov as Russia's new prime minister
1999	
January	First part of the Russian tax code comes into force
March 20	Kosovo crisis erupts

Date	Event
May 12	Yeltsin fires Primakov and nominates Sergei Stepashin as prime minister
May 15	Unsuccessful Duma attempt to impeach Yeltsin
August 7	Chechen incursion into Dagestan starts
August 9	Vladimir Putin is nominated as new prime minister
September 4–16	Four Russian apartment buildings bombed
September 24	Second Chechen war starts
December 19	Elections to the State Duma
December 31	Yeltsin resigns in surprise TV announcement and prime minister Putin becomes acting president

2000

Date	Event
February 7	Russian troops take the Chechen capital of Grozny and Putin declares direct rule from Moscow
March 26	Presidential election: Putin wins
May 7	Putin's presidential inauguration
May 13	Putin's decree changes Russia's federal order
May 17	Mikhail Kasyanov is confirmed as prime minister
June 13	Media magnate Vladimir Gusinsky is arrested
July	Gref program is adopted as the government's economic reform program
July 28	Putin meets with 21 oligarchs in the Kremlin
August 12	Russian nuclear submarine Kursk sinks in Barents Sea

2001

Date	Event
May 30	Putin sacks Rem Vyakhirev as CEO of Gazprom and appoints Dmitrii Medvedev and Aleksei Miller instead
July	Laws on deregulation of small and medium-sized enterprises are passed by the Duma
September 11	Terrorist attacks in the United States; Putin first to reach President George W. Bush by phone

(chronology continues next page)

Date	Event
December	Package of new laws on judicial reform is adopted
December 13	The United States abrogates the Anti-Ballistic Missile Treaty of 1972

2002

February	New labor code is adopted
July 24	Duma legalizes the sale of agricultural land
October 23–26	Moscow theater hostage crisis
October	New bankruptcy law is adopted
December 5	Slavneft is privatized

2003

February 23	Russia, Ukraine, Kazakhstan, and Belarus agree to form Common Economic Space
June	St. Petersburg tercentenary celebrations
October 25	Yukos owner Mikhail Khodorkovsky is arrested
November 2	Parliamentary elections in Georgia: Rose Revolution starts
December 7	Elections to the State Duma

2004

January	Customs code comes into force
February 24	Putin sacks Prime Minister Kasyanov
March 5	Mikhail Fradkov is nominated as prime minister
March 14	Presidential election: Putin wins
March 29	Bulgaria, Estonia, Latvia, Lithuania, Romania, Slovakia, and Slovenia join NATO
May 1	Poland, Hungary, the Czech Republic, Slovakia, Slovenia, and the three Baltic states become members of the European Union
May 21	Russia concludes WTO bilateral negotiations with the European Union
July 9	American editor of Russian *Forbes* Paul Klebnikov is murdered in Moscow

Date	Event
September 1–3	Beslan school hostage crisis
September 13	Putin proposes to eliminate the direct elections of regional governors
November–December	Ukrainian presidential elections: Orange Revolution
December 19	Yuganskneftegaz is sold in a fire sale

2005

Date	Event
January	Unsuccessful attempt to reform Russia's social benefit system
March 9	Former Chechen President Aslan Maskhadov is killed by the FSB
March 24	Kyrgyzstan's President Askar Akaev is overthrown
May 13	Uzbekistan's Andijan uprising is stopped by massacre
September 29	Gazprom buys Abramovich's oil company Sibneft
December	Restrictive law on nongovernmental organizations is adopted

2006

Date	Event
January	Gazprom's domestic stocks become freely tradable
January 1–4	Gazprom disrupts gas deliveries to Europe through Ukraine
March	Russia embargoes import of wine from Georgia and Moldova
July 15–17	G-8 summit is held in St. Petersburg
July 19	Rosneft carries out international initial public offering
October 7	Journalist Anna Politkovskaya is murdered in Moscow
November 19	Russia concludes WTO bilateral negotiations with the United States
November 25	FSB defector Aleksandr Litvinenko is poisoned to death in London

(chronology continues next page)

Date	Event
2007	
January 1	Bulgaria and Romania join the European Union
January 8	Russia cuts oil supply to Belarus
April 4	Putin appoints Ramzan Kadyrov Chechen president
April 27	Estonia removes Soviet war memorial; cyber war against Estonia
May 11	Vneshtorgbank's (VTB) initial public offering
June	Last pieces of Yukos are auctioned off

Index

Abalkin, Leonid I., 23, 52*n*, 56–57, 60
Abalkin Program, 60–62
Abkhazia, 267
ABM. *See* Anti-Ballistic Missile Treaty
  (ABM)
Abramovich, Roman
  elections, 205, 213–14
  oligarchy, 159, 162, 183, 184*n*
  and Putin, 200, 205, 226–27
  recentralization, 210, 238, 253
administrative reform
  postrevolutionary, 92–95, 284–85, 291
  by Putin, 245–46, 273–74
  Soviet, 18–21
Aeroflot, 252
Afghanistan, Soviet invasion of, 14, 34, 37,
  152, 286
Aganbegyan, Abel, 23, 39*n*, 52*n*, 62
Agrarian Party, 135, 135*t*, 138
agricultural sector
  collectivization of, 33
  omnibus decree on, 138
  privatization of, 110, 218–19
  reform, Soviet *versus* Chinese, 38
aircraft industry, 253–54
Akaev, Askar, 266
Aksenenko, Nikolai, 198, 226
alcoholism, 303–304
  disciplinary campaign against, 25–27
  Yeltsin, 94

Alekperov, Vagit, 142, 159–60, 163, 228,
  309
Alfa Bank, 162, 170, 179, 182–83, 219*n*
Allison, Graham, 309
Almaz-Antei, 252
Alrosa, 253
aluminum industry, 149, 183, 213, 280
Amalrik, Andrei, 18, 83, 309
Amsterdam, Robert, 309
The Anatomy of Revolution (Brinton), 282
Anderson, James H., 309
Andijan uprising, 266
Andreeva, Nina, 45–46
Andropov, Yuri, 13, 18–19, 81
Anti-Ballistic Missile Treaty (ABM),
  36, 231
anti-revolutionary movement, 284–85
apparatchiks, 93–94
Appel, Hilary, 294, 309
Arbatov, Georgi, 309
Armenia
  earthquake, 63–64
  independence, 82, 86
  national front, 50–51, 77
  arms control, 35, 67, 268, 286, 300
  arms race, 13–14, 16–17, 34–37, 67
  Soviet collapse and, 89, 118
Aron, Leon, 309
Arrow, Kenneth, 129*n*
Article 6, abolishment of, 48

budget surplus, 191, 192f, 194, 257, 301
Bulgakov, Mikhail, 233
Bulgaria, 64, 66
Burbulis, Gennady, 88, 92, 105–106
Bush, George H. W., 116–18, 297–98
Bush, George W., 167, 230–31, 269
business
    administrative categories of, 262
    development of, 227–28
    registration of, 217, 261

Camdessus, Michel, 179, 297–98
capital, primary accumulation of, 160, 185
capital flight, Soviet, 71
capital flows, financial crash and, 174
capitalism
    bandit, 170
    cooperatives and, 57
    models of, 52
    people's, 170
    reform program based on, 60
    state, 257–59
    US, condemnation of, 52
capitalist revolution, 1–2, 85–127
    development of, 281–84
    versus evolutionary reform, 290
    importance of leaders in, 2, 284–88
    outcome of, 123–27, 284–85
    policymaking during, 5–6
    reaction against, 284–85
capitalization, stock market, 279
Carrère d'Encausse, Hélène, 49
Carter, Jimmy, 35
Caucasus. See also specific state
    nationalism in, 50–51
Ceaușescu, Nicolae, 66
censorship, 211
Center for Strategic Problems (Gref
    Center), 214
Central Bank of Russia, 3, 58, 95, 98–99,
    112
central banks, 70, 196, 253
Central Committee, 53, 87
Central Committee Commissions, 47
Central Committee Secretariat, 47
Central Europe. See also specific country
    collapse of Soviet empire in, 63–67,
    82–83
Central Intelligence Agency (CIA), 16
central planning. See also recentralization
    abolishment of, 55
CFE. See Conventional Armed Forces in
    Europe (CFE)
Chechenization policy, 204, 249

Chechnya, ethnic population of, 90
Chechnya war
    first, 130, 151–53, 169, 287
    second, 202–205, 244, 246–49, 306
Chemezov, Sergei, 252
Chemicals Program, 24
Cheney, Dick, 116n
Chernenko, Konstantin, 13, 19, 36
Chernobyl accident, 31
Chernoi, Lev, 183
Chernoi, Mikhail, 183
Chernomyrdin, Viktor
    Chechnya war, 152–53
    elections, 135–36, 165–67
    financial stabilization, 143
    IMF agreement, 114, 298
    oligarchy, 140–42, 162, 172, 177
    political career, 106, 112, 120, 169–70,
    177, 229
    postrevolutionary stabilization, 189, 198
    rule by decree, 131–32
    social issues ignored by, 153–54
    state enterprise managers and, 137–39
Chernyayev, Anatoly, 63n
China
    economic reform in, 4–5, 38–41, 289–90
    military expenditures, 40
    WTO entry, 224
Chirac, Jacques, 230–31, 269
Chopin, Frederic, 13
Chubais, Anatoly
    anti-ideological stance, 285, 294
    currency crisis, 143–44
    economic reform programs, 92, 154–55,
    170
    elections, 166–68
    oligarchy, 169–71, 177
    political career, 92, 136, 165, 169,
    171–72, 177–78, 226
    postrevolutionary stabilization, 198, 200
    privatization, 107–11, 126, 161–62, 164,
    287
    renationalization, 252
    state enterprise managers and, 138
Chudo (miracle) scenario, 300
Churchill, Winston, 104, 126
CIA. See Central Intelligence Agency (CIA)
CIS. See Commonwealth of Independent
    States (CIS)
Civic Union, 120, 137–38
clientelism, 281
Clinton, Bill, 154, 297
collectivization, 258
    of agricultural sector, 33

colored revolutions, 264–68. *See also specific state*
Comecon. *See* Council for Mutual Economic Assistance (Comecon)
Committee on State Security. *See* KGB (Committee on State Security)
Committee to Investigate Privatization and Punish the Guilty, 162
commodity credits, 118
common currency zone
  end of, 113, 125, 289, 298
  financial crash and, 173
Common Economic Space, 265
"common European house" concept, 34, 63–64
Commonwealth of Independent States (CIS). *See also specific state*
  democracy building in, 124*n*
  formation of, 88–89
  free trade area, 154, 181, 224–25, 265
  Gazprom in, 142, 267–68
  Russian policy toward, 181, 264
communism
  economic ignorance and, 40, 52, 81, 104
  private enterprise and, 28
  reform, 14–15, 21, 80, 283
Communist Party of the Russian Federation, 104, 237
  1993 elections, 134, 135*t*
  1995 elections, 165, 165*t*
  2003 elections, 242, 242*t*
  formation of, 75
Communist Party of the Soviet Union (CPSU), 1
  divisions in, 18–21
  Gorbachev as head of, 12–13
  politically obsolete, 62, 76, 87, 285
  property confiscation, 87, 133–34
  reproduction of, 133
  suspension of, 86–87, 287
Community of Democracies, 296
comparative advantage, 223, 271, 280*n*
Congress of People's Deputies, 119
  conflict with reform government, 105–106
  dissolution of, 131, 140
  division of power, 101
  economic reform programs, 61, 90
  elections, 73–75, 101
  formation of, 33, 47–48
Consortium of Russian Commercial Banks, 161

constitution
  Brezhnev, 48, 86, 101, 133
  reform of, 121–22, 291
  and presidential third term, 306–307
  Yeltsin, 7, 86, 101, 120–21, 130–34
Constitutional Conference, 121
Constitutional Court, 120, 120*n*, 133–34, 306
Consumer Goods and Services Program, 24
consumer price index, 70
Conventional Armed Forces in Europe (CFE), multilateral treaty on, 66, 286
Cooper, Julian, 223
cooperatives, 3, 56–58
corporate governance, 184
corporate legislation, lack of, 186–87
corporate taxes, 98, 216
corruption. *See also* organized crime
  definition of, 259
  energy curse and, 272
  evolution of, 259–68
  legal system, 221
  limiting of, 192, 260–61
  oligarchy and, 171, 181, 184, 262
  prices of, 262, 263*t*
  Putin government, 200–201, 211, 230, 236–37, 261–64
  regional government, 134, 281
  renationalization and, 254, 281
  rise in, 199, 211, 261–68, 306
  state enterprise managers and, 130
  tax system and, 212, 215
  top-level, 261–62
  Yeltsin government, 200, 262
Corruption Perceptions Index, 259*n*, 263, 264*f*
Council for Mutual Economic Assistance (Comecon), 66, 96, 159–60
Council of Europe, 209, 242, 295
Council of Ministers, 62, 273
Council of National Strategy, 237
coup attempt (1991), 77–79, 85, 115, 283, 287
CPSU. *See* Communist Party of the Soviet Union (CPSU)
crime rate, 146, 151, 222, 249, 303. *See also* organized crime
criminal procedure code, 221
criminal syndicates, 148
cultural movements, Soviet, 14
Cultural Revolution (China), 38–39, 41

currency coefficients, 54
currency crisis, 143–44
currency reform, 96, 113, 125, 179
currency reserves, 301
  financial crash and, 176, 178–79, 194,
    195*f*
  postrevolutionary, 97
  Soviet, 71
currency union, 224–25
currency zone
  end of, 113, 125, 289, 298
  financial crash and, 173
current account balance, 194, 195*f*, 196, 257
customs code, 224
customs union, 154, 181, 224–25
Czechoslovakia
  economic reform, 92
  national currency, 113
  NATO membership, 180–81
  privatization, 109
  revolution, 64, 66
  Soviet invasion, 21, 63

Dagestan bombings, 202–203
debt
  Russian, 191, 194, 195*f*, 297–98
  Soviet, 70, 72*f*
debt-for-equity swap, 161
decentralization, 75, 272
deinstitutionalization, 247–50, 274, 288
democracy
  backlash against, 307
  definition of, 2–3
  degrees of, 278–79, 278*f*
  electoral, 295
  managed, 207
  sovereign, 275
democracy building
  advice on, 295
    lack of, 102, 123
  building blocks of, 291–92, 296–97
  success of, 124*n*
Democracy Derailed in Russia (Fish), 281
democratic centralism, 47
Democratic Russia movement, 74
democratization (*demokratizatsiya*), 46–48
  Eastern European, 65–66
  failure of, 1, 6–7, 277–307
    reasons for, 102, 277–307
  new wave of, 8
  under Putin, 272–73
  Soviet collapse and, 4, 82

support for, 6–7, 23, 29–30, 42–43
  under Yeltsin, 6–7, 124, 131, 286
demonetization, 95–96
demonstrations
  preceding Soviet collapse, 76
  prohibition of, 248, 305
Deng Xiaoping, 4–5, 38
depoliticization, privatization and, 108
Deripaska, Oleg, 183, 213–14, 227–28, 237,
  241, 253
de-statization (*razgosudarstvlenie*), 52
determinism, 284
dictatorship, 248, 282–84
dictatorship of law, 221–22
direct enterprise subsidies, 112
discrimination, 94, 258
division of power, 101, 291
Dmitriev, Mikhail, 219
Doing Business index, 279
dolgostroii, 31
dollarization, 72, 95–96
Dorenko, Sergei, 205
Dornbusch, Rudiger, 173
Dubynin, Sergei, 143
Dudaev, Dzhokhar, 151–52
Dyachenko, Leonid, 159
Dyachenko, Tatyana, 159, 166, 169, 198,
  200, 205, 227
Dynkin, Aleksandr, 184
Dzerzhinsky, Feliks, 87, 248

Eastern Europe. *See also specific country*
  collapse of Soviet empire in, 63–67, 76,
    82–83, 286
East Germany, 63–66, 82, 286
EBRD. *See* European Bank for
  Reconstruction and Development
  (EBRD)
economic diversification, 271
economic growth, 300–301
  financial stabilization and, 194, 196*f*,
    259, 274, 292–93
  technocratic attempts at, 23–24
economic reform
  early attempts at, 7, 27–28
    versus Chinese, 4–5, 38–41, 289–90
  energy curse and, 271–72
  failure of, 29–30, 38–41, 59, 67, 69, 282
  Gref program, 214–21
  ideological, 294
  international support for, 295
  pace of, 288–92

Glaziev, Sergei, 241–43, 244*n*
Goldman, Marshall, 129*n*
Goldman Sachs, economic growth study, 300
Gorbachev, Mikhail, 1–2
  administrative revitalization, 18–21
  antialcohol campaign, 25–27
  compared to Putin, 287–88
  compared to Yeltsin, 80–81, 83, 286–87
  conflicts with Yeltsin and Ligachev, 43–46, 79, 283
  coup against, 77–79, 85, 115, 283, 287
  democratization agenda, 29–30, 42–43, 46–48, 124
  Eastern European policy, 64, 82
  economic ignorance, 20, 81, 104
  economic reforms, 4–5, 17, 29–30
    failure of, 38–41, 59, 67, 69, 282
    programs, 61–62, 290
    rent seeking and, 3–4, 52–59, 81–82, 111
  elections, 48, 168
  foreign policy, 13, 33–34, 36–37, 41, 63, 286
  generational identity, 104
  German reunification, 63, 65–66, 286
  glasnost, 30–33, 42, 282–83, 286
  international agreements, 63, 67
  nationalism, 4, 49–52
  Nobel Peace Prize, 62, 66–67
  Outer Empire collapse, 63–64, 77, 82, 286
  perestroika, 12–13, 21–24, 282
  political career, 18
  political power, 38–39
  as reform communist, 80, 283
  resignation, 62, 86–87, 89
  revolutionary role, 85, 282–83, 286
  Soviet collapse, 43, 67–73, 76–80, 83, 88, 189, 200
  speeches
    1984 (December), 17
    1987 (January), 46
    1988 (December), 63–64
    1994 (December), 23
  trade liberalization, 54
  Western relations, 36–37, 119
"Gorbomania," 37
Gosbank, 58
Gosplan, 60, 93
gospriemka (quality control), 25
government
  parliamentary system of, 131–33
  regional (*See* regional government)

government institutions, location of, 105, 133
government licensing, 217, 261
government offices, selling of, 262, 263*t*
government reform, 92–95, 245–46, 273–74, 284–85, 291
Grachev, Pavel, 94, 136–37, 152, 168, 203
gradual market reform, *versus* radical reform, 288–92
Gray, Cheryl W., 309
great aluminum war, 149, 183
great awakening. *See* perestroika
great mob war, 150
Great Socialist Revolution (1917), 1, 282, 284–85
Great Terror (1937), 33, 49, 93, 104
Gref, German, 214–15, 224, 226, 244–45
Gref program, 214–21
Gromyko, Andrei, 48
Group of Eight (G-8), 181, 268–69
Group of Seven (G-7), 72–73, 154
  response to Soviet collapse, 115, 117, 297–98, 300
  Russian membership in, 119, 181
  support for Yeltsin, 174
growth Darwinism, 269
Grozny, 204
Gryzlov, Boris, 241
gubernatorial administrations, 132–33, 213–14
Gulag, 33
Gusinsky, Vladimir
  contract murder scandal, 168*n*
  oligarchy, 158, 170–72, 182
  and Putin, 205, 209, 226, 241
  television coverage, 153, 165, 167, 180, 205, 209
Gusinsky v. Russia, 209
Gustafson, Thane, 300

Halliburton, 164
health care sector, 304
Hellman, Joel, 125, 291
higher education, 301, 302*f*
Hitler, Adolf, 305
Hoagland, Jim, 117
homicide
  political, 249–50
  rate, 146, 147*f*, 151, 222, 222*f*, 249, 303
Honecker, Erich, 65
housing privatization, 110
human factor, in reform programs, 24–25
humanitarian aid, 112, 117
human rights violations, 203–204, 209

Hungary
  crime rate, 146
  democratization, 65
  NATO membership, 180–81
  popular uprising, 64
  privatization, 109
  Soviet invasion, 18
Huntington, Samuel, 230
Husák, Gustáv, 66
hyperinflation, 40–41, 62
  banking sector and, 58, 179
  budget deficit and, 121, 191
  postrevolutionary, 106, 111, 124, 189,
    289, 298
  ruble zone and, 113

Ickes, Barry W., 176
ideas, revolutionary, 294
Illarionov, Andrei, 136*n*, 225, 238
IMF. *See* International Monetary Fund
immigration, 303
imports, 257, 257*f*, 302
  Soviet, 70, 71*f*
  subsidized, 112
income taxes, 98, 216, 261
industrial ministries
  abolishment of, 89, 93
  corporatization of, 140, 140*n*
industrial sector
  Russian, 214, 227–28, 280
  Soviet, 39–41
infant mortality, 304, 304*f*
inflation. *See also* hyperinflation
  banking sector and, 58
  financial stabilization and, 143, 145*f*,
    179, 194, 196, 197*f*
  postrevolutionary, 95, 99, 100*f*, 111
  social costs of, 114, 125
inflationary rents, 144–45
inflation tax, 95, 98, 111, 114
information technology revolution, 17
infrastructure, renationalization of, 254
INF Treaty. *See* Intermediate-Range
  Nuclear Forces (INF) Treaty
Ingushetia, 151
initial public offerings (IPOs), 254, 280
Inkombank, 162
inspections law, 217–18, 261
Institute of Economic Policy, 92
institution building, and pace of reform,
  289–90
intellectual property rights, 224
interenterprise arrears, 111
interest rates, 114

Intermediate-Range Nuclear Forces (INF)
  Treaty, 37, 63, 286
International Finance Corporation, *Doing
  Business* index, 279
International Monetary Fund (IMF)
  economic policy, 113, 178, 190, 216, 290,
    296, 298
  Extended Fund Facility, 298
  loans, 118–19, 143–44, 154–55, 174–76,
    297–99
  Russian membership in, 118
  support for reforms, 295–97
  Systemic Information Facility, 114, 173,
    215, 298
  Yeltsin's interaction with, 95
international organizations. *See also
  specific organization*
  supporting democracy building, 295–97
  supporting reforms, 295
Inter-Regional Group, 74
investment policy. *See also* foreign
  investment
  technocratic improvements in, 24
Iraq War, 231
Itera, 142, 229–30
Ivanov, Igor, 265
Ivanov, Sergei, 225, 252, 275, 306
Ivanov, Viktor, 225, 229, 252

Jackson-Vanik amendment, 268
Japanese credit package, 178
Jaruzelski, Wojciech, 15, 35
jihad (holy war), 152
Johnson, Chalmers, 282*n*
journalists
  murders of, 249–50
  muzzling of, 210–11, 225–26
judicial reform, 190, 219, 221–22, 273
jury trials, 221–22
"A Just Russia" Party, 248

Kadyrov, Akhmad, 204, 249
Kadyrov, Ramzan, 249
Karimov, Islam, 266
Kasyanov, Mikhail, 198, 215, 226, 240, 244,
  260
Kazakhstan, 50, 154, 181, 224–25, 265
Keynes, John Maynard, 285, 294
KGB (Committee on State Security), 18
  corruption and, 262–63
  division of, 87, 94
  Putin in, 199–202, 225, 287
  strengthening of, 247–48, 252, 274, 306
Khakamada, Irina, 243

Khanin, Grigori, 15
Kharitonov, Nikolai, 243
Khasavyurt armistice, 202
Khasbulatov, Ruslan, 99, 102–103, 103n, 105, 119–22
Khattab, 202
Khloponin, Aleksandr, 214
Khodorkovsky, Mikhail
  arrest of, 233–41, 288
  oligarchy, 158, 163, 183, 228
Kholodov, Dmitri, 136–37
Khristenko, Viktor, 253
Khrushchev, Nikita, 104, 151
Kirienko, Sergei, 177–79, 189–90
Kiselev, Yevgeny, 205, 210
Klaus, Václav, 109, 294
Klebnikov, Paul, 167, 182, 199, 249
Klein, Lawrence, 129n
kleptocracy, 57–58, 112, 130, 150
Kogan, Vladimir, 228
Kohl, Helmut, 117
Kokh, Alfred, 171
Kołakowski, Leszek, 1
Kolbin, Gennady, 50
kolkhoz, 78, 136, 258
Kondopoga, 258
Kornai, János, 3
Korzhakov, Aleksandr, 94, 136, 152, 159, 166–68, 168n
Kosovo crisis, 198
Kostin, Andrei, 252
Kosygin, Alexei, 27, 52
Kovalchuk, Mikhail, 243
Kovalchuk, Yuri, 243
Kozak, Dmitri, 221, 225, 245
Kozhin, Vladimir, 225
Krasnoyarsk region, 213
Kravchuk, Leonid, 88
Kruchina, Nikolai, 71
krysha (private protection), 148–49
Kuchma, Leonid, 265
Kudrin, Aleksei, 200, 213, 215, 226, 245, 253, 260
Kulik, Gennady, 38, 190
Kulikov, Anatoly, 167, 177
Kursk explosion, 210
Kyrgyzstan, 154, 181
  crime rate, 147
  national currency, 113
  national front, 51, 266

labor market, 303
  reform of, 219–21
land privatization, 110, 218–19

Latin America, democratization in, 290
Latvia
  fish imports, 269
  independence, 86, 124
  national front, 50, 76, 82
  tax system, 216
law enforcement, 306
  Russian, 150–51, 154, 222
  Soviet, 148
Law on Cooperatives, 3, 56, 58, 185
Law on Individual Labor Activity, 29, 56
Law on State Enterprises, 3, 27, 30, 54–56, 107
  adoption of, 53
  Ryzhkov's support for, 22
  self-management allowed under, 57–58
  state enterprise managers and, 138
  wage hikes and, 68–69, 69f
LDPR. See Liberal Democratic Party of Russia (LDPR)
leasing, Soviet decree on, 107
Lebed, Aleksandr, 167–69, 202
Lebedev, Platon, 238, 240
legal anarchy, 148
legal system, 186–87
  corruption in, 221
  reform of, 190, 219, 221–22, 273
  regional government in, 213
  Soviet, 147
  WTO accession and, 224
Lenin, Vladimir, 248
  currency reform, 96
  New Economic Policy, 52, 258
  revolutionary situation as defined by, 16
  terror campaign, 33
Leninist ideology, abandonment of, 14, 39, 282
Leontief, Wassily, 129n
Leontiev, Mikhail, 248
Lermontov, Mikhail, 151
Levada, Yuri, 224
Lewis, Flora, 76
Liberal Democratic Party of Russia (LDPR), 134–35
  1995 elections, 165, 165t
  1999 elections, 206, 206t
  2003 elections, 241, 242t
licensing laws, 217, 261
Lieven, Dominic, 52
life expectancy, 303, 303f
Ligachev, Yegor
  conflicts with Gorbachev and Yeltsin, 43–46, 283

democratization, 47
economic ignorance, 20
on military spending, 34
perestroika programs, 22–23, 27
political career, 19–20
Soviet collapse and, 67, 76
on Yakovlev, 21
Linz, Juan, 2
Lipton, David, 119*n*
Lisin, Vladimir, 213
literary journals, 30–31
Lithuania
independence, 86
national front, 50, 76, 82, 286
oil pipeline in, 269
Litvinenko, Aleksandr, 250
Lloyd, John, 189
loan defaults, 96, 118, 179
loans, IMF, 118–19, 143–44, 154–55,
174–76, 297–99
loans-for-shares privatization, 161–64,
182, 292–93
Lobov, Oleg, 75, 90*n*
Logovaz, 158
Lopukhin, Vladimir, 106
Lukoil, 142, 160, 162–63, 210, 228
Luzhkov, Yuri, 186*n*, 260
elections, 205–206, 241–43
oligarchy, 209, 228
political career, 199
recentralization, 213
street trade prohibition, 97
Lvov, G. E. (Prince), 93

Machine-Building Program, 24
macroeconomic crisis
radical reform and, 91–92, 126, 291
Soviet, 68–69, 81
stabilization of (*See* financial
stabilization)
macroeconomic policy
assessment of, 301
ignorance of, 40, 52, 81, 104
introduction of, 59
Putin on, 250–51, 259
Soviet *versus* Chinese, 40
mafia, 148–49, 152. *See also* organized crime
Malkin, Vitaly, 159
managed democracy (*upravlyaemaya
demokratiya*), 207
Manevich, Mikhail, 171
market Bolsheviks, 285
market economy
definition of, 2–3

degree of, 278–79, 292
key features of, 278–79
socialist, 22, 52
transition to, 8, 278–80, 279*f* (*See also*
economic reform)
marketization, 52
Marxist ideology
abandonment of, 14, 39, 282
Putin and, 258, 264
Maskhadov, Aslan, 169, 202–203, 249
Masliukov, Yuri, 189, 191
mass media
election coverage, 167, 205, 209, 241
freedom of, 94, 165, 208–209, 286
muzzling of, 30, 208–11, 225–26, 246,
263, 272–73
oligarchy, 182, 210
mass privatization, 107–11, 124, 287,
292–93
Matiukhin, Georgy, 99, 106, 288
Matlock, Jack, 36–37
Mau, Vladimir, 282
McFaul, Michael, 233, 266, 291–92, 295*n*
McKinsey Global Institute, 214
MDM Bank, 182–83
means of production, nationalization of,
107, 259
Media-Most, 209
Medvedev, Dmitri, 225, 229, 245, 252, 267,
306
Melnichenko, Andrei, 183
Menatep, 161–62, 164, 183, 235
metallurgical industry, 138, 183–84, 213,
280, 293
middle class society, creation of, 301
Mikhailkov, Nikita, 234
Mikhailov, Aleksei, 60
military
acceptance of Soviet dissolution, 88,
123, 287
emphasis on, 12 (*See also* arms race)
joint command of, 89
renationalization of, 254
military expenditures
cutting of, 98, 124
foreign aid for, 299–300
Soviet, 15–16, 34, 63
versus Chinese, 40
Miller, Aleksei, 226, 229, 252
Milosevich, Slobodan, 198
Milyukov, Anatoly, 52*n*
Ministry of Economic Development and
Trade, 215–16, 223–24
Ministry of Economy, 93

Ministry of External Economic Relations,
223–24
Ministry of Finance, 93, 95
Mironov, Sergei, 243
Mogilevich, Semen, 230
Moldova, 77, 82, 86, 267
Molotov-Ribbentrop Pact, 4, 33, 50, 82
monetary overhang, 95–98, 103*n*, 111
monetary policy, financial crash and, 173
monetary stabilization, moderate, 288–89
money supply, 95–96, 98–99, 100*f*, 111
Morck, Randall, 184
Moscow Collegium of Lawyers, 239
Most Bank, 209
Motherland Party, 241, 242*t*
  murders
  political, 249–50
  rate of, 146, 147*f*, 151, 222, 222*f*, 249, 303
Murphy, Kevin A., 291
Murrell, Geoffrey, 120
Muslim population, 90

Nagorny Karabakh, 50–51
Napoleon Bonaparte, 282
Naryshkin, Sergei, 252
"*Nashi*" ("Ours") party, 248, 305
national champions, 254
nationalism, 4, 49–52, 74
  Baltic, 50, 76–77, 82
  Caucasus, 50–51
  Chechen, 151 (*See also* Chechnya war)
  political parties and, 134
  resurgence of, 248, 258, 267, 275, 305
nationalization. *See also* renationalization
  banking system, 196
  means of production, 107, 259
  ruble, 113
NATO. *See* North Atlantic Treaty
  Organization (NATO)
natural gas industry, 35. *See also* Gazprom
  CIS countries, 267
  production data, 236, 236*f*
  renationalization of, 254
  role in Russian economy, 270–72, 280
  role in Soviet development, 17–18, 40
Nazarbayev, Nursultan, 50
Nemtsov, Boris, 169–70, 198, 256
Nevzlin, Leonid, 235, 243
newspeak, 211, 239, 241, 251, 259, 269,
  273, 307
"new thinking" policy, 13, 33–37, 41, 63,
  286
Nicholas I (Tsar), 275
Nicholas II (Tsar), 275

NKVD, 200, 200*n*
Nobel Peace Prize, 62, 66–67, 129, 129*n*
nomenklatura, 44, 53, 93–94, 103, 137
  oligarchy, 159
  privatization, 107
nongovernmental organizations
  restriction of, 248, 268, 272–73
  supporting reform, 297
Nordhaus, William, 70
Norilsk Nickel, 162, 169, 182, 213, 228
North, Douglas, 129*n*
North Atlantic Treaty Organization
  (NATO), 14, 35, 65
  enlargement of, 180–81, 268
  Kosovo crisis, 198
North Stream, 270
Novolipetsk Metallurgical Corporation,
  213
NTV, 209
nuclear arms control, 35, 67, 268, 286, 300
nuclear arms race, 13–14, 16–17, 34–37, 67
  Soviet collapse and, 89, 118
nuclear submarine explosion, 210
nuisance taxes, 261

OECD. *See* Organization for Economic
  Cooperation and Development
  (OECD)
offset prices, 176–77
  elimination of, 192, 260–61
Ogarevo, Novoe, 77
oil industry
  exports, 70
  oligarchy in, 160, 164, 180, 183–84,
    235–36
  privatization, 219
  production data, 236, 236*f*
  renationalization of, 253–54, 293
  role in Russian economy, 193–94, 194*f*,
    249, 257, 259, 270–72, 280, 301–302, 304
  role in Soviet development, 17–18, 40
Okulov, Valery, 159
oligarchy, 157–87
  assessment of, 181–87
  banking sector, 158–59, 161–62, 169–73,
    179, 181–83, 187
  business strategy of, 183–84
  conflict with reformers, 170
  conflict with *siloviki*, 226–30, 244–45,
    257–58
  corruption and, 171, 181, 184, 262
  definition of, 158
  dominance of Russian economy, 280, 283
  elections and, 163–69

end of, 234–41, 273, 288
energy market, 160, 164, 180, 183–84, 235–36, 272
financial crash and, 173–80, 182–83, 187
mass media, 182, 210
opposition to, 170–72
security services, 150
social features of, 185–86
state enterprise managers and, 181–82
taxation and, 164, 170, 179, 192, 238
vote buying, 206, 237
Olson, Mancur, 137, 249
Olympic Games, 34
OMZ, 253
Oneximbank, 162, 170–71
openness. *See* glasnost
Open Russia Foundation, 236
Open Society Institute, 297
operative policy advice, importance of, 294
operative policymakers, importance of, 294
Orange Revolution (Ukraine), 234, 244, 248, 264–66, 268, 278
Organization for Economic Cooperation and Development (OECD), 70
Organization for Security and Cooperation in Europe (OSCE), 242, 295
organized crime
defeat of, 149–51
postrevolutionary reform and, 97, 112
rise of, 130, 146–51, 154–55
ORT, 210
OSCE. *See* Organization for Security and Cooperation in Europe (OSCE)
Ostankino television station, 122
Our Home is Russia party, 165, 165*t*
output
Russian, 99
Soviet, 72, 73*f*
ownership
economic effects of, 305
energy curse and, 271
of financial-industrial groups, 186–87, 280
voucher privatization and, 109

Pappe, Yakov, 172
Paris Club, 117
parliament
dissolution of, 7, 119–24, 284–85
revolt against Yeltsin, 99–107, 123
parliamentary elections, 86, 101
1993 (December), 122, 124, 131, 134–37, 135*t*
1995 (December), 165, 165*t*

1999 (December), 205–208, 206*t*
2003 (December), 234, 241–44, 242*t*
loss of democracy in, 273
referendum on, 121–23
parliamentary support, importance of, 295
parliamentary system, 131–33, 291
parochialism, of Soviet officials, 20
19th Party Conference (June-July 1988), 46–47
28th Party Conference (July 1990), 76
Party of War, 152, 166–67
Patrushev, Nikolai, 203, 225, 229, 248
Pavlov, Valentin, 69–70, 76, 78, 96, 113
Pavlovsky, Gleb, 233
payroll tax, 98, 193, 216
pension reform, 219–21
people's capitalism, 170
perestroika, 11–42, 282
beginning of, 12–13, 21–30
democratization and, 46
failure of, 41
reasons for, 13–18
Soviet collapse and, 4, 81
Peroff, Dean, 309
Petrakov, Nikolai, 60–61
pipeline embargo (US), 35
Pipes, Richard, 16, 274, 282
Piyasheva, Larisa, 32
Plehve, V. K., 152
Poland
crime rate, 146
democracy, 124
economic reform, 60, 92, 97, 119, 145
in European Union, 269
meat imports, 269–70
NATO membership, 180–81
privatization, 109
Solidarity, 14–15, 35, 64–65
policy declaration, importance of, 294
policy implementation, importance of, 295
policymaking, revolutionary processes and, 5–6, 294–97
Politburo, 47
political dissent, prohibition of, 248, 305
political freedom, degree of, 278, 278*f*
political leaders. *See also specific person*
importance of, 2, 284–88, 294
Politkovskaya, Anna, 250
Polozkov, Ivan, 75, 82
Popov, Gavriil, 260
Popov, Sergei, 183
population, 303
ethnic, 89–90

Other Publications from the Peterson Institute

* = out of print

Economic Sanctions Reconsidered (2 volumes)
Economic Sanctions Reconsidered:
Supplemental Case Histories
Gary Clyde Hufbauer, Jeffrey J. Schott, and
Kimberly Ann Elliott
1985, 2d ed. Dec. 1990 ISBN cloth 0-88132-115-X
ISBN paper 0-88132-105-2
Economic Sanctions Reconsidered: History
and Current Policy Gary Clyde Hufbauer,
Jeffrey J. Schott, and Kimberly Ann Elliott
December 1990 ISBN cloth 0-88132-140-0
ISBN paper 0-88132-136-2
Pacific Basin Developing Countries: Prospects
for Economic Sanctions Reconsidered: History
and Current Policy Gary Clyde Hufbauer,
Jeffrey J. Schott, and Kimberly Ann Elliott
December 1990 ISBN cloth 0-88132-140-0
ISBN paper 0-88132-136-2
Pacific Basin Developing Countries: Prospects
for the Future* Marcus Noland
January 1991 ISBN cloth 0-88132-141-9
ISBN paper 0-88132-081-1
Currency Convertibility in Eastern Europe*
John Williamson, editor
October 1991 ISBN 0-88132-128-1
International Adjustment and Financing: The
Lessons of 1985-1991* C. Fred Bergsten, editor
January 1992 ISBN 0-88132-112-5
North American Free Trade: Issues and
Recommendations*
Gary Clyde Hufbauer and Jeffrey J. Schott
April 1992 ISBN 0-88132-120-6
Narrowing the U.S. Current Account Deficit*
Alan J. Lenz/*June 1992* ISBN 0-88132-103-6
The Economics of Global Warming
William R. Cline/*June 1992* ISBN 0-88132-132-X
US Taxation of International Income:
Blueprint for Reform Gary Clyde Hufbauer,
assisted by Joanna M. van Rooij
October 1992 ISBN 0-88132-134-6
Who's Bashing Whom? Trade Conflict
in High-Technology Industries
Laura D'Andrea Tyson
November 1992 ISBN 0-88132-106-0
Korea in the World Economy*
Il SaKong
January 1993 ISBN 0-88132-183-4
Pacific Dynamism and the International
Economic System*
C. Fred Bergsten and Marcus Noland, editors
May 1993 ISBN 0-88132-196-6
Economic Consequences of Soviet
Disintegration* John Williamson, editor
May 1993 ISBN 0-88132-190-7
Reconcilable Differences? United States-Japan
Economic Conflict*
C. Fred Bergsten and Marcus Noland
June 1993 ISBN 0-88132-129-X
Does Foreign Exchange Intervention Work?
Kathryn M. Dominguez and Jeffrey A. Frankel
September 1993 ISBN 0-88132-104-4

Sizing Up U.S. Export Disincentives*
J. David Richardson
September 1993 ISBN 0-88132-107-9
NAFTA: An Assessment Gary Clyde
Hufbauer and Jeffrey J. Schott/*rev. ed.*
October 1993 ISBN 0-88132-199-0
Adjusting to Volatile Energy Prices
Philip K. Verleger, Jr.
November 1993 ISBN 0-88132-069-2
The Political Economy of Policy Reform
John Williamson, editor
January 1994 ISBN 0-88132-195-8
Measuring the Costs of Protection
in the United States Gary Clyde Hufbauer
and Kimberly Ann Elliott
January 1994 ISBN 0-88132-108-7
The Dynamics of Korean Economic
Development* Cho Soon
March 1994 ISBN 0-88132-162-1
Reviving the European Union*
C. Randall Henning, Eduard Hochreiter, and
Gary Clyde Hufbauer, editors
April 1994 ISBN 0-88132-208-3
China in the World Economy
Nicholas R. Lardy
April 1994 ISBN 0-88132-200-8
Greening the GATT: Trade, Environment,
and the Future Daniel C. Esty
July 1994 ISBN 0-88132-205-9
Western Hemisphere Economic Integration*
Gary Clyde Hufbauer and Jeffrey J. Schott
July 1994 ISBN 0-88132-159-1
Currencies and Politics in the United States,
Germany, and Japan C. Randall Henning
September 1994 ISBN 0-88132-127-3
Estimating Equilibrium Exchange Rates
John Williamson, editor
September 1994 ISBN 0-88132-076-5
Managing the World Economy: Fifty Years
after Bretton Woods Peter B. Kenen, editor
September 1994 ISBN 0-88132-212-1
Reciprocity and Retaliation in
U.S. Trade Policy
Thomas O. Bayard and Kimberly Ann Elliott
September 1994 ISBN 0-88132-084-6
The Uruguay Round: An Assessment*
Jeffrey J. Schott, assisted by
Johanna W. Buurman
November 1994 ISBN 0-88132-206-7
Measuring the Costs of Protection in Japan*
Yoko Sazanami, Shujiro Urata,
and Hiroki Kawai
January 1995 ISBN 0-88132-211-3
Foreign Direct Investment in the
United States, 3d ed.,
Edward M. Graham and Paul R. Krugman
January 1995 ISBN 0-88132-204-0
The Political Economy of Korea-United
States Cooperation*
C. Fred Bergsten and Il SaKong, editors
February 1995 ISBN 0-88132-213-X

International Debt Reexamined*
William R. Cline
February 1995   ISBN 0-88132-083-8
American Trade Politics, 3d ed.
I. M. Destler
April 1995   ISBN 0-88132-215-6
Managing Official Export Credits:
The Quest for a Global Regime*
John E. Ray
July 1995   ISBN 0-88132-207-5
Asia Pacific Fusion: Japan's Role in APEC*
Yoichi Funabashi
October 1995   ISBN 0-88132-224-5
Korea-United States Cooperation in the New
World Order* C. Fred Bergsten and Il SaKong, eds.
February 1996   ISBN 0-88132-226-1
Why Exports Really Matter!* ISBN 0-88132-221-0
Why Exports Matter More!* ISBN 0-88132-229-6
J. David Richardson and Karin Rindal
July 1995; February 1996
Global Corporations and National Governments
Edward M. Graham
May 1996   ISBN 0-88132-111-7
Global Economic Leadership and the Group of
Seven   C. Fred Bergsten and C. Randall Henning
May 1996   ISBN 0-88132-218-0
The Trading System after the Uruguay Round*
John Whalley and Colleen Hamilton
July 1996   ISBN 0-88132-131-1
Private Capital Flows to Emerging Markets
after the Mexican Crisis*
Guillermo A. Calvo, Morris Goldstein,
and Eduard Hochreiter
September 1996   ISBN 0-88132-232-6
The Crawling Band as an Exchange Rate Regime:
Lessons from Chile, Colombia, and Israel
John Williamson
September 1996   ISBN 0-88132-231-8
Flying High: Liberalizing Civil Aviation
in the Asia Pacific*
Gary Clyde Hufbauer and Christopher Findlay
November 1996   ISBN 0-88132-227-X
Measuring the Costs of Visible Protection
in Korea*   Namdoo Kim
November 1996   ISBN 0-88132-236-9
The World Trading System: Challenges Ahead
Jeffrey J. Schott
December 1996   ISBN 0-88132-235-0
Has Globalization Gone Too Far?
Dani Rodrik
March 1997   ISBN paper 0-88132-241-5
Korea-United States Economic Relationship*
C. Fred Bergsten and Il SaKong, editors
March 1997   ISBN 0-88132-240-7
Summitry in the Americas: A Progress Report
Richard E. Feinberg
April 1997   ISBN 0-88132-242-3
Corruption and the Global Economy
Kimberly Ann Elliott
June 1997   ISBN 0-88132-233-4

Regional Trading Blocs in the World
Economic System   Jeffrey A. Frankel
October 1997   ISBN 0-88132-202-4
Sustaining the Asia Pacific Miracle:
Environmental Protection and Economic
Integration   Andre Dua and Daniel C. Esty
October 1997   ISBN 0-88132-250-4
Trade and Income Distribution
William R. Cline
November 1997   ISBN 0-88132-216-4
Global Competition Policy
Edward M. Graham and J. David Richardson
December 1997   ISBN 0-88132-166-4
Unfinished Business: Telecommunications
after the Uruguay Round
Gary Clyde Hufbauer and Erika Wada
December 1997   ISBN 0-88132-257-1
Financial Services Liberalization in the WTO
Wendy Dobson and Pierre Jacquet
June 1998   ISBN 0-88132-254-7
Restoring Japan's Economic Growth
Adam S. Posen
September 1998   ISBN 0-88132-262-8
Measuring the Costs of Protection in China
Zhang Shuguang, Zhang Yansheng,
and Wan Zhongxin
November 1998   ISBN 0-88132-247-4
Foreign Direct Investment and Development:
The New Policy Agenda for Developing
Countries and Economies in Transition
Theodore H. Moran
December 1998   ISBN 0-88132-258-X
Behind the Open Door: Foreign Enterprises
in the Chinese Marketplace
Daniel H. Rosen
January 1999   ISBN 0-88132-263-6
Toward A New International Financial
Architecture: A Practical Post-Asia Agenda
Barry Eichengreen
February 1999   ISBN 0-88132-270-9
Is the U.S. Trade Deficit Sustainable?
Catherine L. Mann
September 1999   ISBN 0-88132-265-2
Safeguarding Prosperity in a Global Financial
System: The Future International Financial
Architecture, Independent Task Force Report
Sponsored by the Council on Foreign Relations
Morris Goldstein, Project Director
October 1999   ISBN 0-88132-287-3
Avoiding the Apocalypse: The Future
of the Two Koreas   Marcus Noland
June 2000   ISBN 0-88132-278-4
Assessing Financial Vulnerability: An Early
Warning System for Emerging Markets
Morris Goldstein, Graciela Kaminsky,
and Carmen Reinhart
June 2000   ISBN 0-88132-237-7
Global Electronic Commerce: A Policy Primer
Catherine L. Mann, Sue E. Eckert, and Sarah
Cleeland Knight
July 2000   ISBN 0-88132-274-1

WORKS IN PROGRESS

Australia, New Zealand,
and Papua New Guinea
D. A. Information Services
648 Whitehorse Road
Mitcham, Victoria 3132, Australia
Tel: 61-3-9210-7777
Fax: 61-3-9210-7788
Email: service@dadirect.com.au
www.dadirect.com.au

India, Bangladesh, Nepal, and Sri Lanka
Viva Books Private Limited
Mr. Vinod Vasishtha
4737/23 Ansari Road
Daryaganj, New Delhi 110002
India
Tel: 91-11-4224-2200
Fax: 91-11-4224-2240
Email: viva@vivagroupindia.net
www.vivagroupindia.com

Mexico, Central America, South America,
and Puerto Rico
US PubRep, Inc.
311 Dean Drive
Rockville, MD 20851
Tel: 301-838-9276
Fax: 301-838-9278
Email: c.falk@ieee.org

Asia (*Brunei, Burma, Cambodia, China,*
Hong Kong, Indonesia, Korea, Laos, Malaysia,
Philippines, Singapore, Taiwan, Thailand,
and Vietnam)
East-West Export Books (EWEB)
University of Hawaii Press
2840 Kolowalu Street
Honolulu, Hawaii 96822-1888
Tel: 808-956-8830
Fax: 808-988-6052
Email: eweb@hawaii.edu

Canada
Renouf Bookstore
5369 Canotek Road, Unit 1
Ottawa, Ontario KlJ 9J3, Canada
Tel: 613-745-2665
Fax: 613-745-7660
www.renoufbooks.com

Japan
United Publishers Services Ltd.
1-32-5, Higashi-shinagawa
Shinagawa-ku, Tokyo 140-0002
Japan
Tel: 81-3-5479-7251
Fax: 81-3-5479-7307
Email: purchasing@ups.co.jp
For trade accounts only. Individuals will find
Institute books in leading Tokyo bookstores.

Middle East
MERIC
2 Bahgat Ali Street, El Masry Towers
Tower D, Apt. 24
Zamalek, Cairo
Egypt
Tel. 20-2-7633824
Fax: 20-2-7369355
Email: mahmoud_fouda@mericonline.com
www.mericonline.com

United Kingdom, Europe
(*including Russia and Turkey*), **Africa,**
and Israel
The Eurospan Group
c/o Turpin Distribution
Pegasus Drive
Stratton Business Park
Biggleswade, Bedfordshire
SG18 8TQ
United Kingdom
Tel: 44 (0) 1767-604972
Fax: 44 (0) 1767-601640
Email: eurospan@turpin-distribution.com
www.eurospangroup.com/bookstore

Visit our Web site at:
www.petersoninstitute.org
E-mail orders to:
petersonmail@presswarehouse.com